Pentecostal Perspectives on Social Justice

Pentecostal Perspectives on Social Justice

Rationale, Form, and Practice.
A Dialogue with Jürgen Moltmann

Thomas U. Kurt

◆PICKWICK *Publications* · Eugene, Oregon

PENTECOSTAL PERSPECTIVES ON SOCIAL JUSTICE
Rationale, Form, and Practice. A Dialogue with Jürgen Moltmann

Copyright © 2025 Thomas U. Kurt. All rights reserved. Except for brief quotations in critical publications or reviews, no part of this book may be reproduced in any manner without prior written permission from the publisher. Write: Permissions, Wipf and Stock Publishers, 199 W. 8th Ave., Suite 3, Eugene, OR 97401.

Pickwick Publications
An Imprint of Wipf and Stock Publishers
199 W. 8th Ave., Suite 3
Eugene, OR 97401

www.wipfandstock.com

PAPERBACK ISBN: 979-8-3852-3033-4
HARDCOVER ISBN: 979-8-3852-3034-1
EBOOK ISBN: 979-8-3852-3035-8

Cataloguing-in-Publication data:

Names: Kurt, Thomas U. [author]. | Frestadius, Simo [foreword writer].

Title: Pentecostal perspectives on social justice : rationale, form, and practice. A dialogue with Jürgen Moltmann / by Thomas U. Kurt

Description: Eugene, OR: Pickwick Publications, 2025 | **Includes bibliographical references.**

Identifiers: ISBN 979-8-3852-3033-4 (paperback) | ISBN 979-8-3852-3034-1 (hardcover) | ISBN 979-8-3852-3035-8 (ebook)

Subjects: LCSH: Social justice—Religious aspects—Pentecostal churches. | Pentecostalism. | Holy Spirit—Pentecostal churches. | Poverty—Religious aspects—Pentecostal churches. | Church work with the poor—Pentecostal churches.

Classification: BX8762 K87 2025 (paperback) | BX8762 (ebook)

VERSION NUMBER 06/06/25

Democracy begins with language.
—Prof. Dr. Siegfried Zimmer

*The person about whom I speak
is the person about whom I have control over.*

*The person to whom I am speaking
is the person to whom I have submitted myself.*

This person will not comply.

In her face, I am myself at stake.

—Marianne Gronemeyer

Contents

Foreword by Simo Frestadius | ix
Acknowledgments | xi
Abbreviations | xiii

Introduction | 1

1   Social Justice and Pneumatology: An Unusual Partnership | 14
    Non-Pentecostal Voices | 15
    Social Justice in the Beginnings of the Pentecostal Movement | 54

2   Social Justice in Pentecostal Theology: A Selection | 86
    Matthias Wenk | 86
    Lisa Stephenson: A Feminist Approach | 109
    Samuel Solivan: An Approach with Latin American Roots | 142
    Amos Yong: An Approach with Asian Roots | 164
    Insights from the Inner-Pentecostal Discourse | 213

3   Social Justice According to Jürgen Moltmann | 220
    Introductory Thoughts | 220
    Mission, Hope, and Identity | 221
    The Spirit of God and Moltmann's Social Ethics | 225
    Sanctification | 241
    Unity in Diversity, Diversity in Unity | 245
    Eschatological Hope, Ethics, and Spirit | 249

4   Social Ethics in Dialogue: Convergences and Divergences
    Between Moltmann and the Pentecostal Voices | 254
        Collaborative Pneumatology | 254
        Encounter | 259
        Unity in Particularity and Particularity in Unity | 263
        Collaborative Eschatology | 265
        Eschatological Hope | 268

5   Findings in the Context of the Broader Theological Discussion | 274
        Theses | 274
        Social Justice: A Pneumatological/Eschatological Perspective | 279
        A Pentecostal Approach to Social Ethics and Social Justice in
            the Context of the Broader Academic Discourse | 287
        Further Questions | 294

Bibliography | 297

Foreword

PENTECOSTALS ARE ACTIVISTS BY temperament. Thus, they have always engaged with issues of social justice but have been slow to develop a social ethic to ground their practice. A lack of such ethic has meant that Pentecostal actions—even if well-intended—have been at times misguided, as they have confused the spirit of the age with the Spirit of God. For this reason, I welcome Thomas U. Kurt's important work that identifies Pentecostal ethical principles to help discern a Pentecostal approach to social justice.

This book is based on Kurt's PhD thesis at the Centre for Pentecostal and Charismatic Studies at Bangor University (UK) and informed by his experience as a Pentecostal believer and pastor in Switzerland. After setting the historical context, Kurt assesses some of the leading Pentecostal scholarly contributions on the question of social justice. He carefully categorizes main themes from this inter-Pentecostal discourse, before bringing them into a constructive dialogue with the work of Jürgen Moltmann. The resulting fruit is an articulation of the "cornerstones of Pentecostal social ethics," which according to Kurt are "pneumatology," "encounter," "unity in particularity and particularity in unity," "collaborative eschatology," and "eschatological hope." Kurt concludes the book by reflecting on what building on these "cornerstones" could look like in the context of broader ethical frameworks.

The merits of the present work are many. First, Kurt models a dialogical method that listens attentively to the Pentecostal discourse, as well as to the broader voices, not least that of Moltmann. This methodological approach is valuable for the future development of Pentecostal theology to guard it from becoming either a myopic Pentecostal monologue, or a generic discussion that privileges external voices at the expense of hearing the Pentecostal ones. Second, as a Swiss Pentecostal pastor-scholar, Kurt offers unique European perspectives and engages with sources in German commonly overlooked by (Pentecostal) scholarship in the English-speaking world. Third, the crowning contribution of the book is, of course, Kurt's pneumatologically and eschatologically infused Pentecostal vision for social ethics and justice. In the current cultural moment when the very idea of social justice has been weaponized by different parties, there is a need for Pentecostals and other Christians to theologically evaluate and envision the concept. Kurt's work is a fine guide in this task.

    Simo Frestadius, PhD, University of Birmingham, UK
        Vice Principal, Regents Theological College, UK
        PhD Supervisor, Bangor University, UK
        Chair, European Pentecostal Theological Association (EPTA)

Acknowledgments

THIS WORK IS A revised form of my PhD thesis which was submitted to Bangor University, Wales, in the School of Philosophy and Religion for the Centre for Pentecostal and Charismatic Studies. Without the help of a number of People it would not have been possible for me to complete it:

Special thanks go to my doctoral supervisor, Dr. Frank Maccia. His sheer inexhaustible knowledge, coupled with his inspiring way of imparting knowledge, has shaped me. The exchange with him was invariably encouraging and enriching for me and gave me the impression that I was making a contribution to the academic community with my work.

I am deeply indebted to Dr. John Chrisopher Thomas, Dr. Lee Roy Martin, and Dr. David Ray Johnson, the staff of the Centre for Pentecostal Studies, Cleveland. The regular exchange with them and my fellow students has broadened my horizons in other fields of research as well as my own.

Dr. Matthias Wenk was and is a key figure in my academic career. It was he who took me to the annual meeting of the Society for Pentecostal Studies, where I met Dr. Frank Maccia in person for the first time: in this sense, he were the midwife of my dissertation and opened up a new world for me. Thank you for your friendship!

Last but not least, I would like to thank my wife, Barbara, from the bottom of my heart. She sacrificed a lot to make my studies possible—which also had an impact on her professional career. Such sacrifices cannot be taken for granted. Furthermore, the work would hardly have been completed without Barbara's proofreading. I am deeply indebted to her. At this point I would also like to mention our children, Alec and Janna.

They have reminded me time and again that theology is not about theory but about concrete help for life.

Thomas Ulrich Kurt
Basel, Switzerland
September 2024

Abbreviations

EvTh	*Evangelische Theologie*
JPT	*Journal of Pentecostal Theology*
JPTSS	Journal of Pentecostal Theology Supplement Series
NIDPCM	*New International Dictionary of Pentecostal and Charismatic Movements*. Edited by Stanley M. Burgess and Eduard M. van der Maas. Grand Rapids: Zondervan, 2003.
RGG4	*Religion in Geschichte und Gegenwart: Handwörterbuch für Theologie und Religionswissenschaft*. Edited by Hans Dieter Betz, et al. 4th ed. 9 vols. Tübingen: Mohr Siebeck, 2008.

Introduction

KARL BARTH, PROBABLY THE most significant evangelical-reformed theologian of the first half of the twentieth century, in one of his last published articles takes stock with regard to his theological works. The arguably surprising assertion of this epilogue constitutes the following quotation at the end of his article:

> Everything which needs to be said, considered and believed about God the Father and God the Son in an understanding of the first and second articles, might be shown and illuminated in its foundations through God the Holy Spirit, the *vinculum pacis inter Patrem et Filium*. The entire work of God for His creatures, for, in and with human beings, might be made visible in terms of its one teleology in which all contingency is excluded.[1]

At the end of his working life, in 1968, Barth singled out pneumatology as fundamental for the understanding of God and Son. This statement is so astonishing precisely because he expressed this assertion at a time which in theology was recognized as a time of Holy Spirit obscurity.[2]

Barth never had a chance to write a pneumatology, but other theologians have begun to work on this neglected and overdue topic of reformed theology. A much-acclaimed study is presented in *God the Holy Spirit* (1991) by Michael Welker, which, as he himself would probably say, can be regarded as a "first comprehensive biblical theology of the Holy Spirit."[3] Welker is also of the opinion that the significance of pneumatology can hardly be overestimated. Indeed, he went as far as to claim, at the

---

1. Bolli, *Schleiermacher-Auswahl*, 311.
2. Dilschneider, "Geistvergessenheit," 261.
3. Welker, *Gottes Geist*, 13.

1993 conference of the *Society for Evangelical Theology* in Potsdam, that the skeptical state of the classical mainstream churches in Europe and North America can only be changed in the yet to be discovered and to be recognized creative, shaping power of God and of the Holy Spirit.[4]

Meanwhile, theology has enjoyed a renewed interest in pneumatology and its relation/influence on the various aspects of theology, including ethics. This study is intended to make a contribution toward a pneumatological and eschatological rationale of social justice because both of these aspects are vital for Pentecostal theology and spirituality.[5]

I received my personal approach on pneumatology within the framework of a Pentecostal church with a narrow eschatological and pneumatological understanding. Social-ethical questions in teaching and practice, however, were scarcely a theme. In the church, the power and presence of the Holy Spirit were certainly included, without, however, providing an actual pneumatology. Then, during my studies I came across, besides many other theologians, Jürgen Moltmann, who gave me a far broader pneumatological (and eschatological) understanding than I previously had. Since then, Moltmann has significantly shaped my theology and practice.

Within German-speaking regions, various magazines from different Pentecostal Movements are published in which current theological themes are discussed.[6] The theme of *social justice*, however, is more or less absent. Equally non-existent is an academic rationale for social ethics[7] which relates to the German-speaking Pentecostal context. As a result of current societal developments, we pastors are being confronted with the subject of social justice. Currently, we can raise questions about such responsibility based on our (German-speaking Pentecostal) theological foundation but can scarcely answer them. Within English-speaking regions, there is an intra-Pentecostal academic discourse on

---

4. Welker, "Gottes Geist, die Verheissung," 17–18.

5. Land, *Pentecostal Spirituality*, 49–116.

6. "Online," denominational magazine of BewegungPlus (Apostolic church, Wales, network), "Zoom" denominational magazine of the Swiss Pentecostal Mission (Assemblies of God), etc.

7. My major focus is on social "justice," but throughout the dissertation I will refer to social "ethics," knowing that social justice is both fundamental for and central to any understanding of social ethics. On the other side, any social ethics will raise numerous issues that are related to social justice. I will be using both terms interchangeably because, up to some degree, they are arguably overlapping and interrelated. I will discuss a more nuanced distinction between social "ethics" and social "justice," 279–83.

this theme which is hardly perceived in German-speaking regions.[8] I was greatly astonished when I realized that social justice is not merely a subject, but is also reflected within the intra-Pentecostal discussion, theologically, missiologically and sociologically, in the debate with academic Pentecostal theology. I discovered that very important developments and impetus from the global Pentecostal Movement had passed by the German-speaking Pentecostal church, more or less without any trace.[9]

In *Jürgen Moltmann*, we have a European theologian whose theology and ethics show an affinity to Pentecostal theology (Moltmann, like the Pentecostals, essentially establishes his theology pneumatologically and eschatologically). Moltmann has developed his theology independently and he does not shy away from critically questioning the prevailing political and theological system. Furthermore, Moltmann has already been chosen several times by Pentecostal theologians as a dialogue partner.[10]

By focusing on *pneumatology*, this study also concentrates on a neglected dimension of social justice: the Holy Spirit. In the past, liberation theology rather emphasized the role of God as a liberator of the oppressed (through election and exodus), as well as liberation in the life and ministry of Jesus. The pneumatological dimension, the significance of Pentecost for social justice and liberation, tended to be neglected. In this respect, research on pneumatology within the subject area of social justice is a (relatively) new field of theological reflection.

These observations have prompted me to select the subject of the present study: "Social justice in the Pentecostal Movement in dialogue with Jürgen Moltmann: rationale, form and practice."

---

8. In contrast to the intra-Pentecostal discourse, the examination of the Pentecostal church as a phenomenon has nowadays become relatively popular. E.g., the *Interdisziplinäre Arbeitskreis Pfingstbewegung* describes itself as "a forum for the networking of research work on Pentecostal and charismatic movements worldwide. It was founded on 11 June 2004 in Heidelberg. The working group networks people within the German-speaking regions who are interested in academic research on Pentecostal/ charismatic movements in the fields of theology, religious studies, sociology, ethnology and psychology, or those who are themselves conducting such research" (IAP, "Über uns"). Insofar as the working group is a forum for research of the Pentecostal *movement* and its *history*, it does not however participate in the *development* of its theology. The three most renowned intra-Pentecostal academic periodicals which academically deal with Pentecostal theology are the *Journal of Pentecostal Theology*, the *Journal of the European Pentecostal Theological Association*, and the *Asian Journal of Pentecostal Studies*.

9. See Haustein and Maltese, *Handbuch, pfingstliche*, 16.

10. See, e.g., Althouse, *Spirit of the Last Days*.

Research Aim and Research Questions

The aim of this research is to outline a pneumatologically justified Pentecostal social justice, as well as its form and significance in practice. This goal is to be reached by comparing the current academic intra-Pentecostal discourse with Jürgen Moltmann, and examining both positions for their rationale, form and practice. Specifically, the following questions shall be examined:

a. How do representative Pentecostal theologians justify pneumatological social justice?
b. What form would this take, and what practice would this lead to?
c. In what way do prominent Pentecostal positions differ from, complement or correspond with Jürgen Moltmann's approach?

Research Method

One of the most central matters of Western philosophy is the question "What is truth"? This question arises straight from the experience "that about one and the same matter there are various opinions."[11] The goal of science is, by using a suitable methodology, to bring the knowledge or thinking about one matter into harmony, as far as possible, with the actual object of thought. In order to answer the questions, set out in section above and to achieve the related research aim, I have chosen the methodology of constructive dialogue.[12]

Rationale of Methodology

Probably the most important contribution of a methodology for the dialogue has been made by Emil Brunner in his book *Truth as Encounter*. Just as the title implies, Brunner understands biblical truth not merely as a belief in "something true," but far more as a dialogical occurrence

---

11. Brunner, *Wahrheit als Begegnung*, 67.
12. The methodology of constructive dialogue theology employed in this work is repeatedly used within the framework of the Pentecostal academic discourse. See, e.g., Richie, "Approaching the Problem"; Macchia, *Spirituality and Social Liberation*. The reference to Emil Brunner by Macchia is, however, not to be found in a book publication but on page 2 in the original dissertation (University of Basel, 1989).

INTRODUCTION

which relates to God Himself "how He reveals Himself in His word, is present to us, addresses us and expects from us the response of trusting obedience."[13] Hence Brunner comes to the following conclusion:

> Therefore because He is the Word of God, all words have merely instrumental significance. Not only the linguistic expressions but even the conceptual content is not the thing itself, but just its framework, its receptacle and medium. Just as God in His word does not merely want to have our thoughts but we ourselves, in the same way He wants to give Himself in His Word—and that is Jesus Christ.[14]

Despite this fundamental recognition, Brunner is clear that this is only one side of the matter. "The other side is the fact that we cannot have this 'content,' this thing itself, other than simply within this vessel . . . without teaching the thing is not there."[15] This is already to be seen in the direct salutation of God, in its simplest form: "I am the Lord, your God." Right there "teaching inserts conceptual 'theology' intended to be grasped. . . . He [God] tells us forcefully who He is, what He wants for us and from us."[16] Encounter with God calls and leads people into action answerable to God. Thus, Brunner can say:

> The truth of which the Bible speaks is always happening, and indeed the happening of the meeting between God and man, an act of God which must be received by an act of man. The truth acting—this is the characteristic unphilosophical, non-Greek way in which the Bible speaks of truth.[17]

As already mentioned in the introductory quote from Brunner, there are different opinions about the same matter.[18] Despite there being one God, who encounters us with His truth, the worldwide church has

13. Brunner, *Wahrheit als Begegnung*, 130.
14. Brunner, *Wahrheit als Begegnung*, 132.
15. Brunner, *Wahrheit als Begegnung*, 132. At this point, I would like to mention the renowned individual psychologist and founder of logotherapy, Viktor Frankl, who emphasized the importance of this insight of Brunner's. Thus he wrote in his paper *Kritik der reinen Begegnung*: "I would now like to hazard the assertion that a real dialogue will not materialise so long as the dimension of the logos is not accessed. A dialogue without the logos amounts to a monologue à deux. The partners are then no longer involved with an intentional object, but are merely engaged in expressing themselves" (Frankl, *Frage nach dem Sinn*, 36). See also Buber, *Dialogische Prinzip*, 15.
16. Brunner, *Wahrheit als Begegnung*, 132–33.
17. Brunner, *Wahrheit als Begegnung*, 198.
18. Brunner, *Wahrheit als Begegnung*, 67.

developed the most diverse teachings and different practices.[19] In other words: God encounters us human beings in different contexts, and different contexts require different actions as a response to the same truth. In this respect, the human being is *always* shaped by his or her context, which is reflected in his thinking, action, and also in his theology and spirituality. Truth is, due to its context, primarily something that we, in our encounter with God, *are* and not so much something that we *possess*

Implications of a Truth-as-Encounter Methodology

Analogous to the God-person encounter, Brunner also sees "the encounter between people, from person to person."[20] Pentecostal spirituality can express itself very differently. Each of these forms of expression includes a part of the great truth of God, which takes place in the encounter between God and human being and takes shape differently in teaching and practice, in accordance with the context. The intention is that the dialogue between these different forms of expression will lead to a more holistic understanding of Pentecostal *social justice*. What, however, are the implications of a *truth-as-encounter m*ethodology in respect of this study?

a. Anyone who decides to use a *truth-as-encounter* methodology can in no way conduct the dialogue as an exclusively rational exercise, least of all when the researcher wishes to carry out the dialogue in the sense intended by Brunner. People do not *own* truth, but they *embody* it, so then the researcher must, in the present study, say farewell to the demands of objectivity (in the sense of an observer, who is in no way involved, so that his point of view is also in no way biased or blurred)—even the researcher will enter the dialogue from the background of his personal context and his life, the background of "his" truth.

b. Objectivity must, nevertheless, be compellingly sought. It is expressed, however, not in the supposed independence and impartiality of the researcher, but in that he endeavors to be true to the uniqueness of the contributions made by his dialogue partners, and to interpret according to the background of their context and environment.

---

19. The Pentecostal movement is a prime example of this. There is hardly a faith movement which could surpass the Pentecostals in their theology and practice with regard to heterogeneity. See Macchia, "Theology, Pentecostal," 1120.

20. Brunner, *Wahrheit als Begegnung*, 114.

Despite the striving for objectivity between researcher and dialogue partners, the dialogue remains a process which involves the researcher to a high degree: The researcher interprets the works of the dialogue partner according to the background of their life. In this process, the researcher is challenged to re-read and evaluate his life, his existence, against the background of the life and existence of his dialogue partner. I hope to describe this process in the closing thoughts.

The Methodology of the Dialogue

The structure of the dialogue presents a challenge from the point of view of theology: Although this methodology is continually used in theology (to advantage), until now no theological-scientific methodology has been known to me which provides specific approaches to the actual dialogue process. Viktor Frankl has already demonstrated that a dialogue will not automatically arise solely from the comparison of the different positions. If the present study is to be more than merely an expression of different positions, then the dialogue must be arranged in a manner in which the discourse is further developed in the sense set out by Brunner. That is to say that the dialogue must be constructed as a process[21] and in an exploratory fashion.[22] In my search for a suitable methodology, I came across the socio-scientific method of *qualitative heuristics*. It meets the criteria mentioned above as it works on the basis of heuristics, in that it is meant as an instruction "for meaningful searching and finding."[23] The aim is "the discovery of connections that were not recognizable to the research person."[24] Qualitative heuristics is not an exclusively socio-scientific method but is also used in the humanities and natural sciences,[25] as well as in textual studies.[26] In contrast to quantitative empirical research,

---

21. Because there is not "the one" Pentecostal social ethic, a Pentecostal position with representative character must be developed through the process of an intra-Pentecostal dialogue.

22. My research does not originate from a hypothesis but inquiries about a subject: Social ethics within the Pentecostal movement. At the beginning of the study, it remains to be discovered what this Pentecostal social ethic looks like, apart from its pneumatological justification.

23. Kleining, *Entdeckende Sozialforschung*, 225. All quotes by Kleining have been my translation.

24. Kleining, *Entdeckende Sozialforschung*, 230.

25. Kleining, *Entdeckende Sozialforschung*, 226.

26. Kleining, *Entdeckende Sozialforschung*, 227.

qualitative heuristics is not about collecting and evaluating as much data as possible, but rather are about the in-depth examination of a research subject from different perspectives. In this respect, I consider the application of this methodology to be suitable for the present work, and I hope that by using qualitative heuristics I will make a modest contribution to research into Pentecostal theology in the context of social ethics. This is with the reservation that this dissertation represents a beginning: It marks the start of the study of social justice in the Pentecostal church within the framework of the qualitative heuristic method.

Qualitative heuristics denotes the research process which is undertaken in the form of a dialogue between the research person and the research subject. According to Gerhard Kleining, the research subject of qualitative heuristics is never a theory about a theme, but is the theme in and of itself. Therefore, heuristic research does not begin with a theory or a hypothesis on possible findings, but always with the collection of data.[27] The research process is set in motion by questions about the subject. The "answers," are to lead to new questions and answers. The research process is dialectic and leads from the particular (the specific data) to the general (the structure determined by the analysis). According to Kleining, qualitative heuristics frames the dialogue between the research person and the research subject in accordance with the following four principles:

1. Openness of the research person.
2. Openness of the research subject.
3. Maximum structural variation of the perspectives with the data collection.
4. Analysis toward similarities.[28]

What is the significance of these four principles for the procedure in the present study?

Rule 1, Openness of the research person: The research person is never free from ideas or concepts in respect of the research theme. His or her own ideas and concepts do not always align with the assertions of the collected data. If this is the case, the research person is required to correct his or her ideas in respect of the research theme.[29]

---

27. Kleining, "Qualitative-Heuristic Approach," 225.
28. Kleining, "Qualitative-Heuristic Approach," 228.
29. Kleining, "Qualitative-Heuristic Approach," 232.

For my study, this means that even I already have my own understanding of a pneumatologically justified Pentecostal social ethic before beginning the research. Whatever my social ethic may look like—this is *not* the subject of the present study. My research study it is much rather concerned with how the four selected dialogue partners define their pneumatologically justified Pentecostal social ethic. If these definitions are in contradiction to my understanding, then further questions are raised toward me, such as why that is so, and what conclusions I have to draw in respect of my personal position.

Rule 2, Openness of the research subject: Heuristic research sees the research subject as provisional. The questions raised in the course of the research may completely change the research subject. This change is possible because (a) the observer is changing, (b) through the research process the subject shows itself as other than assumed, and (c) the subject itself can change in the course of time and then it no longer meets our expectations.[30]

What is the significance of the openness of the research subject for my study? Kleining says the following:

> Heuristic Rule 2 states that the research person may follow the development of his subject, not cling on to the first definition, not invest too much energy in his delimitation, but regard the selected subject as provisional, as that which shall be revealed only through the heuristic research process, for what it is.[31]

My research subject is pneumatologically justified Pentecostal social justice, with the aim of outlining its form and significance in practice. Which forms are part of this social ethic and what their conclusions look like in practice will continually change throughout the research process. Premature conclusions are to be avoided because they can cloud one's view of the research subject.[32] Which aspects of my research subject are changing in respect of the extent to which I have to adjust my research aim, shall be shown in the course of the research process. Accordingly, it is only at the end of the work that a Pentecostal contribution to the wider discussion of a Christian social ethic will be outlined.

Rule 3, Maximum structural variation of the perspectives with the collection of data: The best approach for comprehending a theme,

30. Kleining, "Qualitative-Heuristic Approach," 234.
31. Kleining, "Qualitative-Heuristic Approach," 236.
32. Kleining, "Qualitative-Heuristic Approach," 234.

according to heuristic understanding, is not only to select a single structural procedure, but to employ the most wide-ranging palette possible of procedures for data collection. The fundamental criterion of the heuristic collection of data is whether the new data is different from the existing data. The heuristic rule of data collection is the attempt to ensure a data pool with the most varied forms possible.[33] The variations occur in respect of the subject.[34]

For the present study, a maximum structural variation means the selection of dialogue partners from the most different possible contexts[35] of the Pentecostal Movement. The dialogue shall be conducted with five exponents from the different contexts of the Pentecostal church family. Then, in a further variation, the intra-Pentecostal dialogue shall be brought into conversation with a reformed-Lutheran outside voice (Moltmann).

Rule 4, Analysis toward similarities: The rationale of analysis toward similarities is "that with the maximum structural variation of the perspectives of the subjects, only those aspects which remain in the data of the variation as constant, that the respective diverse subjective perspectives were subjugated could also be considered as '*subject-closer*,' as Rule 3 has instructed us, the various images of the subjects are which to gather."[36]

Rule 4 has significance for the present study primarily for the intra-Pentecostal dialogue, which is concerned with defining a representative Pentecostal pneumatologically justified social ethic. However, this approach is also partly of significance for the dialogue between the Pentecostal position and the position of Moltmann. The Pentecostal-Moltmann discourse must, however, be extended by the discovery of the similarities and the discovery of the differences of both positions.

---

33. Kleining, *Entdeckende Sozialforschung*, 236.

34. Kleining, *Entdeckende Sozialforschung*, 242.

35. The variation of the context is a legitimate variation of qualitative heuristics (Kleining, *Entdeckende Sozialforschung*, 239).

36. Kleining, *Entdeckende Sozialforschung*, 242. According to Kleining, the discovery of consistencies or commonalities within the data represents the most difficult part of qualitative-heuristic research practice because "it contradicts the 'natural' everyday practice, which is the detection and evaluation of *differences*" (243).

Dialogue Partners and Sources

This study is made up of two dialogues: Firstly, an intra-Pentecostal discourse, and secondly, an inter-Pentecostal dialogue with Jürgen Moltmann.

The selection criteria for the dialogue partners of the *intra-Pentecostal dialogue* have been put together on the basis of the following principles:

- A fundamental prerequisite is the general acceptance of the dialogue partner within the Pentecostal academic discourse. This can be seen, on the one hand, by the fact that the dialogue partners participate regularly in making contributions to the current Pentecostal discourse, and on the other hand they are cited by other Pentecostal theologians.

- The second prerequisite is, in accordance with the third heuristic principle, that the Pentecostal theologians selected for the dialogue must, in aggregate, represent as great a variation as possible. We have created this variation by selecting dialogue partners from the most varied cultural contexts and with very different research emphases within the subject area of *social justice*.

On the basis of the aforementioned selection criteria, the dialogue partners of the intra-Pentecostal discourse for this present study comprise the following theologians:

- **Matthias Wenk,** in comparison with other dialogue partners, falls outside the framework: He is a New Testament scholar and not a systematic theologian. His place in the discussion is nevertheless more than merely justified because he currently belongs amongst the most significant German-speaking Pentecostal theologians and because he has published several articles on pneumatologically justified social ethics. Furthermore, as a New Testament scholar, he explains the socio-ethical dimension of the Lukan double work in his dissertation. Wenk enriches the discussion with a Swiss–European perspective.

- **Samuel Solivan**, although he completed his academic career primarily in the USA, he supplemented the discussion on social justice with the perspective of Latin-Americans. He originates from Puerto Rico and is one of the most prominent and well-known voices of the Hispanic community.

- **Lisa Stephenson** enriches the discussion in Pentecostal theology with an unusual approach, the feminist perspective. This approach is of interest because feminist theology is a continuation of liberation theology. Her cultural background is that of a white North American woman.

- **Amos Yong** has published extensive and comprehensive material on *social justice* and political theology and is presently one of the most prominent voices within Pentecostal theology. His cultural background is that of a Malaysian with Chinese roots. He will represent the perspective of the Asian Pentecostals in the discussion.

All of these are famous and recognized Pentecostal theologians who have made significant contributions within the framework of pneumatologically justified social ethics, and as such they cover a broad spectrum of different Pentecostal contexts.

The scope of this dissertation is limited by the specifications of Bangor University. Therefore, I have decided to limit myself to four dialogue partners. With this restriction, I will ensure that I can present and discuss their approaches with the required thoroughness and to the necessary extent. Thus, the list of Pentecostal dialogue partners mentioned here does not claim to be comprehensive, but rather a representative selection consisting of important personalities who have written distinctive Pentecostal contributions to pneumatological social ethics, and have done so in very different contexts.[37] In this sense, this dissertation marks

---

37. Other possibilities would be, e.g., Augustine, *Pentecost, Hospitality, and Transfiguration*; *Spirit and the Common Good*; Johns, *Pentecostal Formation*; Wariboko, *Pentecostal Principle*, to present just a few prominent names. For the reasons mentioned above, I have limited the number of dialogue partners to four voices. What motivated me not to examine Daniela Augustine is her close proximity to Amos Yong's "many tongues" approaches. However, her work focuses even more on topics that also affect economic ethics. Further, with Lisa Stephenson, we have already had a female voice and with Matthias Wenk a European one. Regarding Cheryl Bridges Johns, she has contributed important approaches to Pentecostal social ethics, but with a focus on the *Christian Formation*. Stephenson also repeatedly draws on Bridges Johns in her work. Like Stephenson, Cheryl Bridges Johns would be a white North American female voice. I therefore limited myself to one North American female voice, Stephenson, and one Hispanic voice, Solivan. Because of his Nigerian roots, Nimi Wariboko would have made a significant contribution to the diversity of the dialogue partners. In the discussion of James Cone and his Black Liberation Theology, it is probably not a Pentecostal voice but an African American voice that is given a prominent place in chapter 2. For reasons of diversity, I chose Yong (as an Asian voice) and therefore decided against Wariboko. However, since Wariboko is undoubtedly an important African Pentecostal voice, some of his thoughts will be included in the discussion. There would have been

a beginning: It marks the start of the study of social justice in the Pentecostal church within the framework of the qualitative heuristic method. The Pentecostal voices mentioned here which have not found their way into the present dialogue may—indeed, must—be brought into extended dialogue in further examinations of the results developed here.

I have chosen **Jürgen Moltmann** as a non-Pentecostal dialogue partner. There are several reasons which attest to him and his works:

- Moltmann is probably the most influential contemporary systematic theologian. His works having shaped theology for decades and worldwide.
- Pentecostal theologians are in regular dialogue with Moltmann's theology. This occurs in dissertations as well as in periodicals. His influence on the Pentecostal theologians, their theology and practices is a fact.[38]
- Moltmann sees himself as a dialogue partner with the Pentecostal Movement.[39]
- Contributions composed by Moltmann regularly appear in Pentecostal periodicals.[40]

The literature shall include relevant primary and secondary literature of academic Pentecostal theology, as well as the works of Jürgen Moltmann.

Limitations

With the presentation of Pentecostal social ethics, this study shall use intra-Pentecostal and relevant non-Pentecostal publications. With the presentation of the positions of Moltmann, first and foremost his primary literature shall be used. In this study, the theology of the 'oneness wing' of the Pentecostals will not be taken into consideration.

---

reason to discuss Wariboko in chapter 6, when placing the findings of this thesis in the broader theological discussion of social ethics, because Wariboko's use of the term "Pentecostal" goes beyond a distinct Christian movement (cf. no. 290) See Wariboko, *Pentecostal Principle*, viii. However, because of his association with the Society of Pentecostal Studies, I have decided to consider him as a Pentecostal voice.

38. Moltmann, *Broad Pace*, 352.

39. Moltmann, *Broad Pace*, 351–52.

40. See, e.g., Moltmann, "Blessing of Hope"; "On the Abundance of the Holy Spirit."

1

Social Justice and Pneumatology
An Unusual Partnership

THIS CHAPTER SETS THE stage for the dialogue between Pentecostal theology and Jürgen Moltmann by exploring the larger question of pneumatology and social justice. The aim of this chapter is to demonstrate the significance of Jürgen Moltmann as a dialogue partner for Pentecostal social justice.

In dialogue with liberation theologies, Moltmann emerged as someone who implicitly pointed to the need for a greater emphasis on pneumatology (and eschatology) when discussing social justice.[1] Pentecostal praxis prior to our recent situation also seemed to call for greater attention to social justice when discussing pneumatology.[2] Just as Moltmann points liberation theologians to a greater emphasis on the Holy Spirit, he could also point Pentecostals to a greater emphasis on social justice. The aim of this chapter is, therefore, to demonstrate the significance of Jürgen Moltmann as a dialogue partner for a theological rational of a pentecostal understanding of social justice that is rooted both in pneumatology as well as in eschatology.

In a first step, I will show Moltmann's influence on the development of present theological social ethics. We begin with Leonhard Ragaz, whom Moltmann significantly influenced with the development of his

---

1. Moltmann, *Broad Place*, 332.
2. Macchia, *Spirituality and Social Liberation*, 162–63.

strategic focus on Theology of Hope.³ Furthermore, we shall consider James H. Cone and Gustavo Gutiérrez, two of the most influential liberation theologians, who were both significantly influenced by Moltmann.⁴ At a later point, the dialogue with Cone and Gutiérrez became a major source of Moltmann's reflection, which in turn influenced the further development of his theology.⁵ Ragaz, Cone and Gutiérrez are theologians who, in their totally different respective contexts, dared to question the preservation of the status quo. In these three theologians, we have both the European heritage as well as North American and Latin American cultural contexts, which by example show the diversity of Moltmann's dialogue partners. Last but not least, it can be stated that Ragaz, Cone and Gutiérrez are significant for this present work because they emphasize the socio-ethical significance of the Holy Spirit, even though they themselves have not developed a pneumatology of social ethics. In a second step we shall consider the beginnings of the Pentecostal Movement and analyze its dealings with the subject of social justice. We shall also discuss here the differences and similarities which exist between the early Pentecostal Movement, and Moltmann and his influences.

Non-Pentecostal Voices

Time and again, individual people and minor movements have pointed out the significance of social justice for theology and practice. Despite this, it can be said that traditionally *social justice* (and in this connection often also the term *liberation*) in the first half of the twentieth century has not been a primary topic of the European and North American theological mainstream.⁶

In this context, two important theological streams stand out which have raised social justice to a central issue and thus have also made this

---

3. Moltmann, *Broad Place*, 154.
4. Moltmann, *Broad Place*, 228.
5. Moltmann, *Broad Place*, 29–30.
6. This assertion is already supported with the thematic field social justice, and it is even true to say regarding this assertion in respect to pneumatology, it is not without good reason that Emil Brunner calls pneumatology a "stepchild" of reformed theology (Senn, *Geist*, 26). Theodor Schneider, in his analysis of Catholic theology (at least from the time before the Second Vatican Council), speaks of a "spiritual void" and "spiritual oblivion" (Schneider, *Zeichen der Nähe Gottes*, 323–29).

once again a theme for the wider church context. These are *liberation theologians* and the so-called *Radical Evangelicals*.[7]

Liberation theology, as a rule, is considered as having four significant subgroups: *Black Liberation Theology, Latin American Liberation Theology, Korean Minjung Theology* and *Feminist Theology*.[8] Both Black and the Latin American liberation theology have in the past rather emphasized the role of God as the liberator of the oppressed (through the election and the exodus), as well as the element of liberation in the life and ministry of Jesus. Feminist theology has, in turn, chosen other distinctive aspects of liberation. The pneumatological dimension, i.e., the significance of Pentecost for social justice and liberation, is overall neglected in all the characteristics of liberation theology.[9]

In the following sections we shall consider three non-Pentecostal voices: Leonhard Ragaz, James H. Cone and Gustavo Gutiérrez. As he himself recounts in his autobiography, Moltmann concedes to all three voices a formative role in his theological development and work.[10] We shall begin with Ragaz, who in a number of ways can be identified as the grandfather of liberation theology[11] and was (as already mentioned above) thereby also influential for Moltmann's *Theology of Hope*.

---

7. The Radical Evangelicals, who sprung up from the impetus of Evangelicals who, within the framework of the Lausanne Movement, came into contact with Black Liberation Theology and Latin American Liberation Theology (Hardmeier, "Ganze Evangelium," 64). The concern of social justice within this evangelical submovement can hardly be overemphasized. However, according to Hardmeier (PhD, University of South Africa, forerunning authorities in respect of radical evangelicals in German-speaking areas), also within this evangelical phenomenon, a pneumatologically substantiated social ethic is inexistent. Hardmeier can imagine that within the movement of Radical Evangelicals there is a selective pneumatological rationale; however, there is no pneumatologically substantiated overall outline of a social ethic known to him.

8. Moltmann, *Experiences in Theology*, 183.

9. Arguably, feminist theologians have highlighted "Spirit" as a category for God in place of a one-sided Christocentric emphasis and understanding of God that is clearly male-centered. But they have not generally considered the Pentecost event of Acts 2 as a narrative resource for understanding the role of the Holy Spirit in regard to social justice.

10. See Moltmann, *Broad Place*, for Ragaz (65, 154), Cone (145), and Gutiérrez (108, 157, 211, 228).

11. See also Stähli, *Reich Gottes und Revolution*; Moltmann, *Broad Place*, esp. 232.

Leonhard Ragaz[12]

It is impossible to discuss the relation between Holy Spirit, eschatology and social justice in the theology of Jürgen Moltmann, without first considering one of his major influences on his theological thinking thereof: Leonhard Ragaz, about whom Moltmann writes: "At that time I wanted to follow Leonhard Ragaz: 'From religion to the Kingdom of God, from the church to the world, from concern from my own self to hope for the whole.'"[13] It also seems that Ragaz was one of the major influences that led Moltmann to emphasize the Holy Spirit in his later dialogue with liberation theologians.[14] But who is this Ragaz, what does he have to say that prompted Moltmann to follow him?

We shall start right at the beginning: Leonhard Ragaz was born on July 28, 1868, in Tamins, Switzerland, with a peasant farming background.[15] After he left school, Ragaz studied theology in Basel, Jena, and Berlin. He was a pastor at Heinzenberg (Graubünden) (1890–1893), a religion and language teacher at the Cantonal School in Chur (Gymanisum) (1893–1895), and subsequently a pastor in Chur (1895–1902) and at Basel Minster (1902–1908). From 1908, he worked as Professor of Systematic and Practical Theology at the University of Zürich.[16] In 1921, he withdrew from his professorship and devoted himself to educational work in the Zürich working class district of Aussersihl and invested himself in the religio-social movement. On December 6, 1945, Ragaz died in Zürich. Besides his active engagement in social struggles of his time, he focused on women's rights, the struggle against war and the protection of the environment.[17]

---

12. All quotes from Ragaz have been my translation.

13. Moltmann, *Broad Place*, 154.

14. Even though Moltmann makes no explicit reference to this, he does make statements that reflect almost word-for-word the arguments of Ragaz in this regard. Some of Moltmann's statements in "Presence of the Kingdom of God in the Holy Spirit" (*Experiences in Theology*, 248) seem to be inspired by Ragaz, *Kampf*, 132, 139. Another hint in this direction is found in Moltmann, *Power of the Spirit*, 283, in which Moltmann implies Ragaz influenced his turn to the "poor and the oppressed" as a theological focal point (which is the focal point of liberation theology). The implied reference to Ragaz is found in part 5, "The Church in the Presence of the Holy Spirit" and "The Messianic Way of Life." So, Ragaz seems to have influenced Moltmann's view on the "Messianic" (Spirit-anointed) way of life, which has become a major impetus of his emphasis on the liberation of the poor and the oppressed.

15. Mattmüller, *Leonhard Ragaz*, 51.

16. Flückiger, "Ragaz Leonhard," 1665.

17. See also, e.g., Schmid-Ammann, *Natur im religiösen Denken*.

Ragaz is an important voice, not only for religious socialism, but also for liberation theology in general, the significance of which can hardly be overestimated.[18] Within the German-speaking regions, even today, there is no theologian who has undertaken anything like his extensive research on the theme of the Kingdom of God. It is primarily due to him (together with Hermann Kutter) that the social question came back on the horizon of salvation history in the evangelical church of Switzerland and could no longer be ignored.[19] In this connection, Ragaz's essay presented on September 5, 1906, within the framework of the *Evangelist Gathering*[20] in Basel played a key role. His message was published under the title *The Gospel and the Social Struggle of the Present Day* in several editions, and it also attracted much attention outside church circles. The essay is remarkable in so far as it began with a detailed analysis of the social and economic state of the nation and thereby chose a hermeneutic which, approximately fifty years later, became a hallmark of liberation theology.[21] Ragaz established his essay in three steps, beginning with the social analysis of society. In addition, he asked the four central questions of modern politics:

a. The worker question (capitalist employers versus workers) . . .

b. The middle-class question (merchants and master craftsmen versus socialist labor force, capitalist large businesses, commodity buyers and co-operative societies) . . .

c. The agrarian question (agriculture versus industry) . . .

d. The women's rights question (status of women versus status of men).[22]

All four questions are seen by Ragaz as ultimately founded on the collision of three economic orders: "The declining pre-capitalists, the dominating capitalists, and against both these, the emerging anti-capitalists, which we call socialist (or even communist, collectivist)."[23] The

---

18. Theologians such as Harvey Cox and Jürgen Moltmann cite Ragaz as an important influence for their theology. See Cox, "Cox on His Critics"; Moltmann, *Broad Place*, 154.

19. Buess and Mattmüller, *Prophetischer Sozialismus*, 76–77.

20. Annually held assembly of preachers from the Swiss Reformed National church.

21. See also the dissertation by Stähli, *Reich Gottes und Revolution*.

22. Ragaz, *Evangelium*, 2–3.

23. Ragaz, *Evangelium*, 3–4.

pre-capitalist economic order structured society according to manual labor.[24] By manual labor, Ragaz means manufacture which is organized semi-privately (the manual laborer is still in ownership of his means of production) and semi-societally (guilds).[25] As a result of the limited options, trading and the accumulation of capital were set within tight limits. No dichotomy of work and capital existed yet. Even in the pre-capitalist time, there were also abusive conditions, although the telos of this system was "not that through trade and industry money would be acquired for its own sake, if possible in unmeasurable quantities, but so that everyone might have his food."[26] In contrast to this, capitalism does not have the fulfillment of the human (basic) needs as its goal, but "money acquisition, increase of money, profit."[27] Instead of people, "the thing (in this case, capital)"[28] is now the focal point. The consequence of this is the optimization of the production process. Division of labor, rationalization and mechanization in order to produce more and more in the shortest time possible, are further resulting consequences. Ragaz ascertains "that man does not master capital, but capital masters man."[29] Mechanization and the related increase in production were breaking up the old craft and trading systems, commerce and economic latitude were stepping into their place. Through overproduction, a system of competitiveness arose which, through modern means of transport, increasingly developed into a global market. In order to be able to reach this global market, high capital was required, which the mid-sized business sector did not have. Thereby, work and capital was becoming separated:

> An industrial proletariat has arisen and with that, the labor question. The laborer is, to use the terms of Marxist literature, separated from his work equipment and also from his work product. He has become a wages slave. . . . The living conditions of the masses are especially wretched in the first stages of capitalism beyond measure. Because the craftsmen streaming out of their desolate workshops, and even more numerous multitudes streaming out of the countryside, make the supply of labor

---

24. Ragaz also regards the trade and agriculture of the pre-industrial era as manual labour, Ragaz, *Evangelium*, 4.

25. Ragaz, *Evangelium*, 5.
26. Ragaz, *Evangelium*, 4–5.
27. Ragaz, *Evangelium*, 6.
28. Ragaz, *Evangelium*, 7.
29. Ragaz, *Evangelium*, 8.

cheap, which was discussed in socialist literature a long time before any robust wages law that strove to keep the working wage on the bottom rung. Because the machine itself is skilled and has strong arms at its command, this meant that untrained workers, physically as well as intellectually weak or immature, could also operate it. Therefore, the first bloom of capitalism is associated with the most shameful exploitation of women and child labor.[30]

The exploitation of the industrial proletariat stands in stark contrast to the groundswell of individual fortunes, as well as national wealth.[31] The outward symbol of the expansion of industry is the expansion of the city. The demand for building land in turn led to huge profits from land speculation, which drew its profits from the intermediate trade. Conversely, one of the consequences of the rising land prices was the housing shortage which, because of demand, caused a rise in the price of housing rental, once again to the burden of the laborer. The high rental costs had an impact on families: "The blessing of children was turned to a curse, the family disintegrated, the former status of the wife was forfeited, and then arose the question of women's rights. Lingering illness and vice flourished in this appropriately well-prepared ground."[32] In the cities, the increasing demand for foodstuff also forced agriculture into mechanization. Products which the farmers occasionally produced themselves were produced much more cheaply industrially—from now on even the farmer was compelled to think capitalistically:

> He needs money, he must learn to work in a capitalistic way and the farmer's union is already there, and the agricultural cooperative system is there, and this means that milk and meat are becoming rarer for the working-class child. The agricultural machine drives the agricultural worker into the city, where he adds his number to the industrial reserve army—the loop is closed, capitalism is the winner right down the line.[33]

Capitalism has now, however, come up against a new system: socialism. In contrast to capitalism, which fosters a private monetary economy with the welfare of people and society only being respected when legally required, socialism emanated from the rights and obligations of society.

30. Ragaz, *Evangelium*, 9.
31. Ragaz, *Evangelium*, 10, 11.
32. Ragaz, *Evangelium*, 11.
33. Ragaz, *Evangelium*, 12.

Socialism is a system which "turns the production and consumption of goods from an issue of the individual to an issue of the community, and so the point of exploitation is displaced by one of cooperation. . . . The economic order should no longer serve the acquisition of money, but to surmount the material hardships of people."[34]

In a second step, Ragaz now considers Christianity, the church and its contribution to the response to current social questions. Ragaz identifies two streams within the church: One he calls the "dormant," the other, the "forward-surging," form of religion. The dormant religion is an aesthetic-ritualistic piety.[35] It strongly relates to Johannine and Pauline theology; it looks for a place to rest. Rest from guilt and the cares of the world and from the self. It finds this rest in the salvation of Christ, "founded primarily through His atoning death."[36] In this respect, this piety is an individualistic piety: "Their own rest in salvation is so much the essential that everything else recedes by contrast."[37] Because the central element of this piety lies in the past, it is backward oriented. The world of the present is, in the respect of significance, regarded as a place of probation. In order to be able to survive it, the process of salvation must be present within the dogma, within the teaching. Mere teaching moves to the center place of piety, and the church to the guardian of teaching. The negative dynamic of such a piety can reveal the fact that the teaching is overrated, and this leads to orthodoxy and it thus comes into conflict with the human search for truth, even extending as far as the persecution of heretics.

> Individualism turns into religious egotism, which appears to be very concerned for one's own salvation, but to one's fellow man, if he is not a comrade of the "believing" circle, at best handouts are given, but in fact part of one's own heart is not accorded, that kind of loveless Christianity which is worse than paganism. This kind of piety has caused Christianity to become a conservative power.[38]

The forward-surging form of religion is, on the other hand, an ethical-prophetic piety.[39] It emphasizes less the *belief* in Christ and more the

34. Ragaz, Evangelium, 12.
35. Ragaz, Evangelium, 21.
36. Ragaz, Evangelium, 21.
37. Ragaz, Evangelium, 21.
38. Ragaz, Evangelium, 22.
39. Ragaz, Evangelium, 21.

following of Christ. "It does not look up to the righteous exalted Son of God, but to the Son of Man, who walked on earth 'unrecognized and very lowly' in order to help His fellows."[40] A characteristic of this piety is the act of redeeming one's fellow man from his distress. "The wellbeing of a brother is more important to you than your own wellbeing."[41] The promises of the Sermon on the Mount view this piety as a message of hope. In this respect, the earthly conditions are not an unchangeable system for you. This is a piety such as was seen as early as with St. Francis and the Anabaptists. Most significantly, however, you see this with Christ. In particular seeing "the Kingdom of God message of Jesus as the broad form of His gospel, then the soul as unique and of infinite value (adoption as a child of God), as is also the common bond of people before God (brotherhood)."[42] Ragaz considered the prayer of Jesus "Thy Kingdom come," as a key to understanding ethical-prophetical piety—"The Gospel is essentially hope," because:

> In the Kingdom of God all evil is abolished, all creatures are liberated and beatified. Guilt, the sufferings of the world, death are annulled, the Father rules. The world must however once more belong to Him. We immediately see here that salvation does not lie in the past, but in the future. The Kingdom of God is not dormant, but rather emergent, coming. God is at work and Jesus works with Him.[43]

An eschatological expectation is, according to Ragaz, the prominent hallmark of forward-surging piety. Whether or not Jesus in the process saw the coming Kingdom of God as very close, does not affect the core of the gospel. On the contrary,

> This question of time is secondary. In Jesus' sermon on the Kingdom of God it is about the relationship of God toward people, and that of people toward God, and his fellow man. The truth of this revelation has nothing to do with the expectation of the imminent end of the present world, although arguably it directly shows with what tremendous force the original gospel surged forward, with what trembling eagerness and blissful joy

---

40. Ragaz, *Evangelium*, 23.
41. Ragaz, *Evangelium*, 23.
42. Ragaz, *Evangelium*, 24.
43. Ragaz, *Evangelium*, 24.

Jesus was waiting for this, that this miserable world would pass away and God would step into His promised reign.[44]

From this central aspect of Jesus' sermon, the ethic of the gospel has been derived. One of the poles is the "incomparable value of the soul."[45] Christ has come to make the human soul free. "Mammon is, in the eyes of Jesus, the greatest of all God's enemies"[46]—because it binds the human soul, enslaves us and thereby separates us from God. "The soul, however, belongs to God, Him alone should we serve and through this restriction, we should be free from all earthly bondage":[47]

> The soul is the person. Thereby Jesus has lifted human beings to the sign, the human being as such, completely detached from status, education, possessions, nationality and other paraphernalia, the human being as a child of God. He alone counts; he should serve God and his fellow man, anything but himself.... It was this individualism of the gospel, this royal freedom and glory of the child of God, that Paul and Luther understood best, and have most wonderfully portrayed.[48]

The second pole is the common bond of human beings before God. Ragaz calls this the "socialism of the gospel." Ragaz himself summarizes this socialism in one single sentence: "Everything that the Father wants to give us, He gives to us only in communion with our fellow man."[49] He attaches this pole to the double commandment of love (Matt 22:34–40) and further texts from Matthew's gospel. Solidarity, the practice of compassion or, more simply expressed, serving one's neighbor, is the social characteristic of the gospel.[50] For Ragaz it is clear that the social characteristic of the Kingdom of God goes much further than the economic: "It does not occur to us to identify Jesus' Kingdom of God with the 'welfare

---

44. Ragaz, *Evangelium*, 24. Whether this section likewise is directly based on Albert Schweizer's paper "Von Reimarus zu Werde" (1906), better known under its title in later editions, "Geschichte der Leben-Jesu-Forschung," with the thesis "the error of the Christian" is not apparent. However, it is interesting that, even when he (whether deliberately or not) qualified the question on the expectation that Christ will return soon, Ragaz together with Schweizer, ascribed crucial significance to eschatology.

45. Ragaz, *Evangelium*, 25.
46. Ragaz, *Evangelium*, 25.
47. Ragaz, *Evangelium*, 25.
48. Ragaz, *Evangelium*, 26.
49. Ragaz, *Evangelium*, 27.
50. Ragaz, *Evangelium*, 28.

state.' But may we therefore say it relates only to the intellectual and spiritual, and not also to material things?"[51] Whoever reduces the Kingdom of God to merely intellectual and spiritual things, according to Ragaz, strikes the gospel in the face.

In his analysis, in a third step, Ragaz brings together the two factors into one question: "How does the gospel of Jesus react to the economic struggle of the present day?"[52] The answer to this question is not solely a national economic evaluation. It is not about weighing up economic advantages and disadvantages, and considering whether the present economic system can be replaced with another. It is, in the first instance, merely to clarify whether the capitalist economic system complies with the basic requirements of the gospel. Ragaz answers this question with an emphatic no.[53] He appreciates the increase in foodstuff production, the research and the newly evolving opportunities of the modern as a benefit of capitalism, but he also clearly points out its darker side. What Ragaz now demands is "a better economic system, not mode of operation":

> It has much more to do with employing the wonderful skilful machine technology and modes of operation, hence the large enterprise, derived from capitalism, as different and better ways in the service of people. It is not the tools that should be changed, but the spirit in which they are used.[54]

The new economic system should serve human beings, not subjugate them.[55] Human beings should serve their fellow humans with the new system.[56] It should become a mutual support for surmounting material hardship. By so doing, the new economic system becomes a "form of exercising brotherhood."[57] Finally, the economic system should, "like everything earthly, serve God and glorify Him . . . so that our life becomes a service to God."[58] This new system, this new spirit Ragaz occasionally calls socialism.[59] It is not the case that Ragaz sees socialism as the "new

---

51. Ragaz, *Evangelium*, 28.
52. Ragaz, *Evangelium*, 30.
53. Ragaz, *Evangelium*, 31.
54. Ragaz, *Evangelium*, 33.
55. Ragaz, *Evangelium*, 34.
56. Ragaz, *Evangelium*, 35.
57. Ragaz, *Evangelium*, 36.
58. Ragaz, *Evangelium*, 37–38.
59. Ragaz, *Evangelium*, 33. Despite all that, Ragaz was also absolutely critical of socialism. Thus, he wrote in 1929: "There must be more than socialism in order that

gospel." He is not of the opinion that a new program, in the face of all the injustice described above, would bring the long-desired change. On the contrary: Ragaz is of the opinion that the country does not need new programs, but far more, it needs a new ethos. In his eyes, however, the economic model of socialism, in many areas, comes significantly closer to the ethos of the Kingdom of God than capitalism.[60] Ragaz realized that the church did not have the monopoly on the Kingdom of God.[61] On the contrary, in his opinion, socialism served God (with all its weaknesses) as a prophetic voice to shake the church awake: "This was the reality: there, with the Christians was the Kingdom of God, but it has become religion; here, with the social democrats was the Kingdom of God, but without religion."[62] The fact that socialism is critical of the church and religion did not prevent Ragaz from seeing in it God's intervention in contemporary affairs: "God has not been named, but could He therefore not still be there just as, conversely, He is often enough not there where He has been named? In short: behind the ideals of social democracy everywhere there stand the basic truths of the Kingdom of God."[63] Precisely this is the conclusion of Ragaz's social analysis:

> Jesus' hope of the Kingdom of God must again be at the heart of our piety. We must come to the place that belongs to Jesus: at the forefront—ahead of the lethargic, unbelieving world. This is where God certainly wants to place us. Why has He given us

---

socialism can exist. If socialism involved the restructuring of social circumstances, to be feasible, this means certain spiritual powers must be defeated, other spiritual powers come into play, otherwise we get, at best, the old capitalist world with a socialist varnish. In the mind there must be a breakout from the power of egoism, from mammon, from the spirit of anxiety, from faith in power, and there must be an outbreak of desire to serve, of joy in God and brother, of reverence for the sacred rights of human beings, of courage to live for God instead of for self, mammon and power" (Ragaz, *Marx zu Christus*, 196).

60. Ragaz, *Das Evangelium*, 40. In *Weltreich, Religion und Gottesherrschaft* he later explained his turning to socialism: "We have gone for social democracy because we believed we would find something of the Kingdom of God within it, that is to say of the Kingdom of God as opposed to religion" (Ragaz, *Weltreich*, 2:10).

61. Hints of this can already be found in the Reformers Huldrich Zwingli and John Calvin. Both were not prepared to reduce the work of the Holy Spirit to Christology and recognized His work outside the churches and outside the gospel. See Calvin, *Insitutio* 1.13–14; Krusche, *Wirken des Heiligen Geistes*, esp. chapter 2. On Zwingli, we recommend the literature and discussions in Hollenweger, *Erfahrungen der Leibhaftigkeit*, 327–29; *Geist und Materie*, 157–59.

62. Ragaz, *Kampf*, 12.

63. Ragaz, *Kampf*, 13.

His pledges and promises? We are immeasurably rich, without making use of our treasures. What a wonderful task, instead of being afraid of decadence, foolishness and ungodliness in all new developments, to embolden people to stride forward and upward, even on steep and unknown paths. Then the world would recognize what a great and wonderful thing it is to believe in an almighty God.[64]

For Ragaz it is clear: The dominating economic system of his time, in all its key points, does *not* comply with the rules of life in the gospel. For a Christian, it is therefore impossible to defend the present system, or to have an interest in its continuation.[65] What should the Christian do in view of this knowledge? The first task is to understand. Understanding comes from an objective clarification of the facts, through encountering and acknowledging the poverty of the working class.[66] The second task is to work on the ethical and religious foundations of the new system. The aim is "to play a mediation role, as a bridge builder between the old and the new times."[67] For this purpose, prophetic preaching is necessary, "the preaching of justice and truth, which love must underlie."[68] Ragaz anticipates that this message will introduce abuse and persecution of the church—which, in this case, is a good sign because, were there no persecution "God would not be with us."[69] The solidarity of the privileged with the underprivileged cannot happen without a religious rebirth.[70] It is endowed by the Heavenly Father, the Bible speaks of this when it tells of the unity in Christ of "master and slave, man and woman, Jew and Greek and barbarian," in Gal 3:21:

> We must be like that again. The Holy Spirit must blow upon the surging chaos of the present day world. Then the spirits of the abyss, which have unleashed terrible turmoil, will be subdued and the high and godly, for which we have hoped, will be brought to light. A new creation must take place; people must be made new through the breath of God and thereby also a new community. Our generation must be baptised with fire and

---

64. Ragaz, *Evangelium*, 52.
65. Ragaz, *Evangelium*, 52.
66. Ragaz, *Evangelium*, 61.
67. Ragaz, *Evangelium*, 63.
68. Ragaz, *Evangelium*, 63.
69. Ragaz, *Evangelium*, 63.
70. Ragaz, *Evangelium*, 64.

Spirit; strong, divine power must be released, power of trust, of love, of enthusiasm and of overcoming the world. Mere worldly power could not be sufficient for us.[71]

Ragaz, in *Das Evangelium und der Soziale Kampf der Gegenwart* [*The Gospel and the Social Struggle of the Present Day*] does not discuss the connection between the Holy Spirit and social justice further. The quote cited above already shows, however, the direction of impact of this collaboration, which he expands further in the altercation with Blumhardt. In *Der Kampf um das Reich Gottes* [*The Struggle for the Kingdom of God*], Ragaz points out that the Holy Spirit first makes human beings truly human: He qualifies human beings to become sons and co-workers of God.[72] The power of the Holy Spirit means the "victory of the new over the old human being, which is at the same time the new glimmerings of that which through the divine creation has been placed in the human being, but through the infiltration of evil has become corrupted. It means overcoming vice in all its various forms."[73] For Ragaz, vice by no means merely comprises aspects of moral nature, but much more comprises mammon, propensity for violence, lust for power, hatred, etc.[74] Only through (or, in) the Holy Spirit can the human being grasp the new world of God, "recognize it as the true reality and build on it alone."[75] Only through the Holy Spirit can human beings hope, serve in love, yes, and even love their enemies:

> That is the power which qualified those weak human beings, the first disciples and the communities of Christ, one so totally tremendous as to confront in every respect the unassailable world and to overcome it, to conquer fate, guilt, adversity and injustice, sickness and death—to perform these incredible miracles.[76]

Through this same Spirit, human beings attain true knowledge of God, about their fellow humans, indeed about the world in general. Nevertheless, the Holy Spirit does not merely want to give revelation but wants to change the present world:

---

71. Ragaz, *Evangelium*, 65.
72. Ragaz, *Kampf*, 129.
73. Ragaz, *Kampf*, 139.
74. Ragaz, *Kampf*, 131.
75. Ragaz, *Kampf*, 131.
76. Ragaz, *Apostel*, 11.

The Kingdom of God is supposed to complete itself under the leading and the creative impetus of the Holy Spirit. It should truly be the creator spirit. The feast of Pentecost as the last, is also the greatest of the feasts. It is the feast of the living God, the feast of hope, the feast of the completion of the Kingdom of God in the ongoing creation.[77]

Only according to the measure that the Holy Spirit is given can the Kingdom of God be newly proclaimed and extended. For Ragaz, it is clear that a hitherto unforeseeable powerful work of the Holy Spirit still lies ahead, as Christ Himself promised His disciples that the Paraclete would reveal the truth to them and give them power (John 14–16), which would surpass what came before.[78] "This is why the primary objective of the church of Christ must be the plea: . . . Come Holy Spirit, return to us."[79]

Appreciation and criticism: The scope of Ragaz's work and his exemplary lifestyle as a consequence of his theology make it difficult to honor this exceptional theologian in a couple of short sentences. We can start with Moltmann discovering the vision of "forward hope in eschatology for the Kingdom of God," for the first time through Ragaz (and Christoph Blumhardt), which significantly influenced the development of the Theology of Hope.[80] Along with Ragaz, for Moltmann, the Kingdom of God moved to the central place of theology.[81] Doubtless, Ragaz's extensive research on the Kingdom of God and his tireless struggle in favor of the underprivileged contemporaries are amongst his most remarkable achievements. It is precisely these achievements which have especially inspired theologians such as Cox, Moltmann and many others. Not to mention his prophetic intuition in respect of ecology, the equality of men and women, etc. which enabled him to be far ahead of his time. In regard to the subject of this present work, I would like to set my focus on the following aspects of his work: the recognition of socialism as a prophetic voice of God, and the emphasis of eschatology and pneumatology.

As already mentioned, Ragaz saw in the socialist movement a prophetic discourse of God, which was also directly addressed to the church. In this sense, Ragaz viewed the work of God as something much bigger than the church. The church is for him very certainly an important

77. Ragaz, *Kampf*, 132.
78. Ragaz, *Kampf*, 132.
79. Ragaz, *Kampf*, 133.
80. Moltmann, *Broad Place*, 65.
81. Moltmann, *Broad Place*, 164.

instrument of God for the realization of the eschatological Kingdom of God. He also sees, however, how the church, similarly to the Old Testament people of God, needs God's prophetic guidance in order to be the Kingdom of God in the midst of the kingdom of the world. The recognition that God thereby also employs people and movements which are not classically attributed to be the people of God has, for Ragaz, released God from the limitations of the church.[82] Perhaps it was precisely this recognition which also released Ragaz to apply the instrument of social analysis within the framework of theology, which also made him a forerunner of liberation theology. The significance of this recognition, that God and His Spirit also work through secular vessels and movements, robbed the church of its exclusivity of being able to speak in the name of God.[83] The question of how Moltmann deals with this knowledge and what this signifies, in particular for the Pentecostal church, is to be examined in the further development of this study.

The fact that pneumatology plays a central role for Ragaz in the implementation of the eschatological Kingdom of God is also remarkable. Once again, the church has a thoroughly exclusive role in Ragaz's theology: It is the community of the spirit-filled children of God. Church can only be church in the sense of the Kingdom of God when its members are filled with the power of the Holy Spirit of God and their everyday life is shaped by this power. The fact that this work of the Holy Spirit cannot be understood as merely individualistic, Ragaz repeatedly makes very clear, in that he points out that the church cannot define itself according to class affiliation, social status, etc., but must even confront socio-political and economic topics, and has a responsibility to help shape these. To this effect, the Pentecostal church undoubtedly can and must learn a great deal from Ragaz. I could, as a Pentecostal, direct a critical question at Ragaz if I were to follow on right there: Socialism, as a mass movement, was a formidable power factor in Ragaz's lifetime: Socialists had so much power that they significantly influenced, and continue to influence, the political landscape of Switzerland. But what does a life in the power of the Holy Spirit look like, which seeks change from a position of weakness?

---

82. Moltmann also comes to a similar conclusion in his work *God in Creation*. There is a positive recession to this work by Kay, review of *God in Creation*.

83. Whether this circumstance actually constitutes a theft, or possibly even a liberation, for the church, must arguably be considered differently, depending on the viewpoint of the observer. From Ragaz's perspective, it was a necessary means which God *had to* employ for the welfare of a blinded church.

What does a life in the power of the Holy Spirit look like, which has experienced no social changes over decades? What does the struggle for social justice in the context of the so-called "global village" look like, where economic trade is increasingly shifting from the domestic to the world market? How does Ragaz understand life within the church in the power of the Holy Spirit in such a context? How shall the unity of Christians, in all their diversity, be lived out in the long term?

A life derived from the power of the Holy Spirit will shape all areas of life—and thereby Ragaz rightly includes the sociological, economic and environmental dimensions of our existence. Whether his ideas are also helpful to give direction for a spirit-filled life in other areas of life, we shall (hopefully) be able to discover in the further progression of this paper.

James H. Cone

James Hal Cone is a long-standing friend, dialogue partner, and fellow pathfinder of Moltmann's. Their relationship goes back to the year 1969.[84] Right from the early beginnings of Black Liberation Theology, there was a dialogue with Moltmann, which from 1971 also found expression in written form.[85] Amongst other things, the dialogue with Cone at the *Encounter of Theologies* conference 1977 in Mexico contributed to the emergence of the noteworthy article "Die Befreiung der Unterdrücker."[86] However, it is not only the dialogue with Moltmann that makes Cone interesting for this present work. Cone's essay "Sanctification and Liberation in the Black religious Tradition," and the book *The Spirituals and the Blues* make important contributions on the relationship between spirituality and social justice (both publications are discussed in this section). Cone underlines the significance of spirituality in the African American struggle for social justice in a unique way.

Cone is an ordained pastor of the African Methodist Episcopal church and Professor of systematic theology at the Union Theological Seminary, New York. He is known for his foundational contributions to Black liberation theology.[87]

---

84. Moltmann, *Experiences in Theology*, 190.

85. Moltmann, *Broad Place*, 157, 167, 169. Moltmann was also actively involved in making some of Cone's books and papers (e.g., *Black Theology and Black Power*; *Spirituals and the Blues*) accessible to German-speaking readers.

86. Moltmann, "Befreiung der Unterdrücker," 229–30.

87. The early Black Liberation Theology generally indicates a European-Protestant

Furthermore, he is one of the few liberation theologians who link social justice with a pneumatological point of view. In this regard, of particular importance is the essay "The Holy Spirit and Black Worship."[88] As the title of the article implies, Cone expands on the significance and impact of the Holy Spirit in respect of the African American experience of social (in-)justice and illustrates this on the basis of Black worship, such as worship in the African American church service.

The context of the Afro-American reality is, according to Cone, only understood with difficulty from the outside.[89] One defining element is the Afro-American experience of humiliation and oppression through the structures of *white society*. Cone experienced both at first hand from his earliest childhood on:

> I was born in Arkansas, a lynching state. During my childhood, white supremacy ruled supreme. White people were virtually free to do anything to blacks with impunity. The violent crosses of the Ku Klux Klan were a familiar reality, and white racists preached a dehumanizing segregated gospel in the name of Jesus' cross every Sunday.[90]

In his book *The Cross and the Lynching Tree*, Cone describes the atrocities of the so-called lynching era, which began during the *Reconstruction*[91] after the Civil War. In the time of the lynching era (1880–1940), approximately five thousand Afro-Americans were lynched by white North Americans.[92] These lynchings, as a rule, included indignities and torture which found their terrifying climax in the form of executions, be

---

influence (according to Cone, these are primarily Karl Barth and Paul Tillich). Although Cone's African American approach has substantial similarities to the Roman Catholic phenomenon of Latin American Liberation Theology—e.g., contextualization plays a central role in the methodology of both theological streams (see Grenz and Olson, *Twentieth-Century Theology*, 214)—there are also essential differences: Cone, within the framework of racism, deals primarily with the cultural question, whilst the Latin American Theology of Liberation deals primarily with the economic question. Cone's influence on the development of Black Liberation Theology has endured from the first appearance of his book *Black Theology and Black Power* in the year 1969 until the present day.

88. Cone, "Holy Spirit and Black Worship," 174–92.

89. Cone, "Sanctification and Liberation," 179.

90. Cone, *Cross*, xv.

91. The Reconstruction Act of 1867 was adopted by Congress subsequent to the Civil War in order to guarantee Afro-Americans citizenship and civil rights. Cone, *Cross*, 4.

92. Cone, *Cross*, 31.

that through hanging, shooting, burning alive or bludgeoning to death. All of this was, in the truest sense of the word, "celebrated," generally speaking in public, in the presence of up to a thousand sightseers, which included women and children.[93] The public character was even further compounded in that the executioners and spectators would pose next to the bodies for photos, which were then sent to relatives as postcards.[94] The goal of the systematic oppression in the southern states, which is summarized under the collective term Jim Crow Law,[95] was to deny the living former slaves any social, political or economic freedom.[96] What it means to spend one's childhood in such an environment, as one can only agree with Cone, is difficult for outsiders to comprehend. The open practice of brutality had an even more terrifying effect in view of the fact that the wider public, and thus also the justice system and the church, in the best case, silently tolerated the injustice committed, and in the worst case, supported or even actively participated in the atrocities.[97]

How is it possible that human beings (in particular Christians) could not discern the injustice being practiced in their midst? Cone tries to answer this question by means of the example of Reinhold Niebuhr.[98] As already mentioned, Cone points out that for those not affected it is difficult to put themselves in the shoes of a black Afro-American who lives under the system of segregation.[99] It is difficult, but not impossible. However, for this end it takes "eyes to see," and "a heart to feel."[100] As easy as that is to say, it seems as difficult to actually do. Cone combines the "eyes to see," with the ability to recognize injustice as such. To see injustice, let alone to recognize it is, however, difficult when the encounters are clouded by prejudice and stereotypes.[101] However, even if, as Cone demonstrates with the example of Niebuhr, injustice is recognized as such and is unmasked, this is still not enough to create justice. It is merely a first step, even though an important one, which of itself alone is insufficient for creating justice.[102]

93. Cone, *Cross*, 46.
94. Cone, *Cross*, 9.
95. Cone, *Cross*, xvi.
96. Cone, *Cross*, 4–5.
97. Cone, *Cross*, 9.
98. Cone, *Cross*, 30–64.
99. Cone, *Cross*, 40.
100. Cone, *Cross*, 41.
101. Cone, *Cross*, 43.
102. Cone, *Cross*, 41.

Besides the "eyes to see," there is also need for a "heart to feel," or in other words, the ability to identify with the oppressed—only then will there be a chance that those not personally affected become people who are affected, and actively do something against the injustice.[103] The question arises why the great majority of whites cannot comprehend the perpetrated injustice and why there is no identification with the victims. Cone finds an explanation for this in the lack of dialogue, the barely existent meeting between black and white. "Eyes and hearts," or otherwise expressed, the ability to recognize injustice and to show solidarity with the oppressed, is only possible through meeting, in dialogue: "No true reconciliation can come about between blacks and whites without relating the painful and redeeming truth about their common life."[104] And yet the accomplishment of such a dialogue seems to be precisely *the* challenge, because segregation has the opposite goal, i.e., the strict separation of black and white Americans. Afro-Americans try to overcome this separation in a variety of ways in which they give expression to their concerns. Thereby Cone particularly emphasizes the creative arts such as painting, photography and sculpture,[105] poetry,[106] and music in the form of spirituals and blues,[107] which the has thematized the Afro-American reality in an artistic manner. Nonetheless, the road to justice is a long and stark undertaking. With sustained oppression, the question arises for the Afro-American of how injustice can be endured over a long period if it cannot be resolved in the foreseeable future. In this connection, Cone ascribes a central meaning to the church service. However, just as the Afro-American everyday life within the Jim Crow Laws is difficult for outsiders to understand, the same hold true for the Afro-American church service. Even the church service can only be understood in light of the background of the Afro-American experience, i.e., the reality of segregation:

> It is difficult for an outsider to understand what is going on in a Black worship service. To know what is happening in this eschatological event, one cannot approach it as a detached observer in the role of a sociologist of religion or a psychologist, looking for an explanation not found in the live-experience of the people.

103. Cone, *Cross*, 44.
104. Cone, *Cross*, 113 (see also 165).
105. Cone, *Cross*, 100.
106. Cone, *Cross*, 95.
107. Cone, *Cross*, 12.

> One must come as a participant in black reality, willing to be transformed by one's encounter with the Holy Spirit.[108]

In the context of the Afro-American, the seventh day of the week, the Sunday, gains an eschatological meaning: Not only a change in the day of the week takes place, but far more, on this day the congregation experiences a *rupture in time*—the future, eschatological Kingdom of God becomes present through the power of the Holy Spirit in the here and now of the church service.[109] During the worship of the church service, the power of the Holy Spirit, which transforms all things, is manifested, which, although it does not bring about the cosmic eschaton, does transform the identity of people and thereby also the whole assembled community:

> The Janitor becomes the Chairperson of the deacon board; the maid becomes the president of Stewardess Board Number 1. Everybody becomes Mr or Mrs and Brother and Sister. The last becomes first, making a radical change in the perception of self and one's calling in society.[110]

In the worship, liberation is transformed from an occurrence expected in the future to an event in the present.[111] This is also expressed in the texts of the spirituals. Thus, Cone writes in The Spirituals and the Blues:

> Even where there is no overt or hidden reference to specific historical events, the spirituals employ eschatological language to express transcendence in the slaves' present existence. "I've started to make heaven my home," "Marching up the heavenly road, I'm bound to fight till I die,"—such lines make clear that black slaves were not passively waiting for the future; they were actively living as if the future were already present in their community.[112]

According to Cone, the Holy Spirit is not perceived as some metaphysical being, but experienced as the power of Jesus, "which breaks into the life of the person, gives him a new song as a confirmation of God's presence/support in his historical struggle."[113] The presence of the Holy Spirit thereby becomes a liberating experience which is expressed in his self-perception, in his interaction one with another, in his enthusiastically

---

108. Cone, "Sanctification and Liberation," 179.
109. Cone, "Sanctification and Liberation," 175.
110. Cone, "Sanctification and Liberation," 176.
111. Cone, "Sanctification and Liberation," 177.
112. Cone, *Spirituals*, 92.
113. Cone, "Sanctification and Liberation," 175.

celebrated church service.[114] Physical manifestations, such as running, clapping, beating on the legs, waving of hands or simply just sitting still, can likewise be reactions to the presence of the Holy Spirit.[115] The forms of expression in the church service are integral elements of its content: Both point to the same theme, liberation.[116] It is this power of the Holy Spirit which has prevented the victims of segregation from losing their minds.[117] It is this power of the Holy Spirit which helps them maintain their dignity.[118] It is this power which again and again keeps giving the Afro-Americans new strength to battle on. The vision of freedom which is revealed and experienced in the church service becomes an important factor, a significant force in the mobilization of people for the transformation of society:[119]

> If the oppressed, while living in history, can see beyond it, if they can visualize an eschatological future beyond this world, then the "sight of the oppressed creature," to use Marx's phrase, can become a revolutionary cry of rebellion against the established order.[120]

Appreciation and criticism: As a white European who has never experienced the African American reality himself, I can appreciate the integrity of Cone's theology with nothing other than deep respect. Nevertheless, in addition to this appreciation, I would also like to express two critical observations from a Pentecostal theological perspective: Cone demonstrates in a convincing way that social justice is an encounter event—justice is to be understood as an answer which is defined in the encounter with injustice. In the realization of this response, the work of the Holy Spirit plays a central role—He enables the Black church members to receive their dignity, He gives them the power to endure, not to give up despite opposition and in their gathering together, even allows them to experience a partial anticipation of their longed-for final justice. This justice is not only a hope for a distant eschatological future, but a hope that believes that even the present can be changed. Hope and the ability to

---

114. Cone, "Sanctification and Liberation," 177.
115. Cone, "Sanctification and Liberation," 178.
116. Cone, "Sanctification and Liberation," 179.
117. Cone, *Cross*, xviii.
118. Cone, *Cross*, 74.
119. Cone, "Sanctification and Liberation," 189.
120. Cone, "Sanctification and Liberation," 190–91.

"persevere," are undoubtedly important works of the Holy Spirit, which are essential in protracted and difficult processes. Nevertheless, when the Holy Spirit, as Cone says, works an eschatological anticipation, does He then not have to do much more than "merely," cause empowerment for the struggle for more justice? Is the anticipation of the eschatological future primarily the (re-)establishment of justice, or is it not even more so what Matthias Wenk stated at the EPCRA Conference[121] in August 2009 in Oxford, UK,[122] namely reconciliation? Miroslav Volf[123] points in the same direction, even if in his rationale he place a less strong emphasis on pneumatology than Wenk. Volf advocates, in a similar way to Cone, the view that justice is an indispensable element in interpersonal relationships: Community without justice is not possible.[124] Yet at the same time Volf also demonstrates that restorative justice has boundaries, indeed ultimately it is even a thing of impossibility.[125] Nevertheless justice should be fought for (as says Cone). For this purpose injustice must be called by name.[126] But when restorative justice cannot be established, what then? According to Volf just one single way remains open: The waiver of rights, or otherwise expressed, reconciliation.[127] This way of reconciliation is the ultimate, eschatological goal of God for all creation.[128] If we agree with Volf, then this also has an effect on pneumatology. To this end there is yet another critical question: Cone interprets the working of the Holy Spirit as an event which is experienced in the life and the community of the victim.[129] It is an event exclusively within the church: God's Spirit empowers the people effected so they can raise their voice until such time as social injustice is overcome. If striving for justice is merely an intermediate

---

121. European Pentecostal Charismatic Research Association.

122. This presentation was published as Wenk, "Reconciliation and Renunciation."

123. Miroslav Volf, born September 25, 1956, in Osijek, Yugoslavia, is a theologian with Pentecostal roots, recognized for his work on systematic theology. Because of his experiences in the Yugoslavian Civil War, he has developed a theology of forgiveness which he essentially developed in Volf, *From Exclusion to Embrace*, 10–30.

124. Volf, *From Exclusion to Embrace*, 156–57.

125. Volf, *From Exclusion to Embrace*, 157.

126. Volf, *From Exclusion to Embrace*, 144, 209.

127. Volf, *From Exclusion to Embrace*, 157.

128. Wenk also says this in "Reconciliation and Renunciation," 58.

129. The same observation is also made by Moltmann. He points out that Cone has developed "a *Theology for the Victim*, but has not, or only indirectly, developed a theology for the perpetrator" (Moltmann, *Experiences in Theology*, 213). Also from the same ranks, Cone was confronted with the same accusation, e.g., Roberts, *Liberation and Reconciliation*.

step, and the final goal is reconciliation, then the work of the Holy Spirit cannot only be an event narrowed down to the victim. His work must be extended to the sphere of the perpetrator—reconciliation is an event which involves the willingness of both sides, victim and perpetrator, and furthermore, it will determine their common future.[130]

According to Pentecostal understanding, the eschatological event already begins before justice and reconciliation have been overcome: As already mentioned, the eschatological future has already become a present reality where the oppressed, despite all feelings of inferiority, appropriate their identity of equal value (Gal 3:28). This is a pneumatological occurrence, as it is a manifestation of the Kingdom of God.[131] However, the Spirit of God already works before the pneumatologically operated endowing of identity is enacted: The Holy Spirit groans together with and comes before God for the suffering creation (Wenk on Romans 8:18–30). It is remarkable that Cone, although he dedicated an entire book, *The Spirituals and the Blues*, to the theology in African American music, does not discuss the pneumatological dimension of protest.

Even in his work *The Cross and the Lynching Tree*, Cone draws no connection between social justice and pneumatology—and yet his approach does contain implications in respect of the relationship between the Holy Spirit and justice. Cone's focus is set on the cross as a sign of hope for oppressed African Americans. If the cross is to be more than merely a sign of hope, then to engage with pneumatology is indispensable. Only through the work of the Holy Spirit can the oppressed have a part in the present and the future of the crucified and resurrected Christ and thereby create hope for their own present and future.

Moltmann has identified Cone as one of his theological influences, which is expressed in the fact that Cone's insights find mention in Moltmann's works over and over again. With regard to this present work, it is interesting that even Moltmann expresses criticism of Cone's one-sided theology of sacrifice[132] and pursues his understanding of social justice. In chapter 3, Moltmann's more comprehensive understanding of social justice is explored further, as well as the significance that pneumatology has assumed as a result.

---

130. Volf calls this reconciled future peace: "Peace is the fellowship of former enemies, not merely just the absence of hostilities because there is no contact" (Volf, *From Exclusion to Embrace*, 161).

131. Ragaz, *Kampf*, 172.

132. Moltmann, *Experiences in Theology*, 213–14.

Gustavo Gutiérrez

Generally, the emergence of liberation theology is associated with the Roman Catholic Bishop's Conference (CELAM) in Medellín, Colombia in 1968.[133] In 1971, the Peruvian Dominican and Priest Gustavo Gutiérrez was the first to propound a liberation theological outline with his book *Teología de la Liberación*. This outline became the basis for Latin American liberation theology. As with all other theological traditions, also within Latin American liberation theology, there is a multiplicity of approaches and rationales to be found. The relationship between Moltmann and liberation theology is anything but tension free, and it is also partly associated with misunderstandings.[134] In the following section, we shall concentrate on Gustavo Gutiérrez, who is an important, albeit moderate, voice of liberation theology, with whom Moltmann remained in a constructive and appreciative dialogue from very early on and over decades.[135] Similarly to Cone, Moltmann, with his Theology of Hope, also became an important influence on Gutiérrez, which later flowed back again from the Latin American liberation theology, in turn enriching Moltmann's theology.[136]

Gustavo Gutiérrez was born in 1928, studied medicine, philosophy, psychology and Catholic theology in Latin America and Europe, acquiring the respective diplomas. After his return to Peru, he was appointed as a Professor at the Pontifical Catholic University in Lima. For Gutiérrez, Moltmann (Theology of Hope) and Metz (Political Theology) as well as the Second Vatican Council (1962–1965)[137] are important influences.

As in the case of Ragaz and Cone, also with Gutiérrez, it was the context (in this case the realities of life of the Latin American-Caribbean population) that became the starting point of liberation theology. Gutiérrez wrote of the background of increasing impoverishment of the majority of the population in Latin American. His analysis is set in the early 1950s, a time in which, as a result of industrial development, one hoped for a reduction of widespread poverty and a certain economic independence: "Latin America in the 1950s was characterized by great

---

133. Gutiérrez, *Theology of Liberation*, 63.

134. See also, amongst others, Bonino, "Reading Jürgen Moltmann," 105–14; Moltmann, *Broad Space*, 215, 224.

135. Moltmann, *Experiences in Theology*, 213–14.

136. Moltmann, *Broad Place*, 157.

137. Grez and Olson, *Twentieth-Century Theology*, 211.

optimism regarding the possibility of achieving self-sustained economic development."[138] Domestic economic development should be stimulated with the "instruments of imports, enhancements of the internal market and awakening in industrialization." The goal was an independent society. This goal could, however, only be reached if the domestic economic market was supported by non-economic growth, which in turn was pursued through the export of raw materials and the import of manufactured goods. In order to realize this development model in Latin America, social, political and cultural obstacles would first need to be overcome, so that these so-called "underdeveloped nations," could develop into so-called "societies in transition."[139] In this development ideology, Western industrial nations were seen as a model. Accordingly, it was accepted that the societies in transition into industrial nations, by and large, should gain the same experience as the industrial nations did in their time: "Underdevelopment and development constituted a continuum. Dysfunctional groups would arise within the social system of traditional societies, leading to the creation of social forces opposed to the existing order."[140]

It transpired that with the industrial development model for the impoverished Latin American masses, no change was brought about; on the contrary, the precarious conditions were even consolidated. Between 1960 and 1970, the industrialized nations had increased their wealth by about 50 percent, whilst the situation of the developing nations, two-thirds of the global population, had hardly changed.[141] At the end of the 1960s, Gutiérrez observed that there was an acceleration of the "internationalization of the domestic market." This was reflected increased foreign investments in the emerging local industry. However, the traditional "imperialistic," presence in the form of control over mining and plantations remained firmly established exactly as before. Instead of strengthening economic independence, the dependency on the leading economic nations increased. The result was that the local industry was bound "ever more closely to international capitalism." A new variety of dependency emerged, "less apparent, but no less real."[142]

138. Gutiérrez, *Theology of Liberation*, 49.
139. Gutiérrez, *Theology of Liberation*, 50.
140. Gutiérrez, *Theology of Liberation*, 50.
141. Gutiérrez, *Theology of Liberation*, 51.
142. Gutiérrez, *Theology of Liberation*, 52.

The differential based on the dependent relationship between developed and underdeveloped nations becomes even more serious when one also considers the cultural side.[143] The economic pressure fell particularly heavily on the shoulders of the poorest classes of the population, which led to protests by these very people. The resistance against the establishment, however, contributed to an intensification of the needy situation of the people, in which a radicalization took place on both sides, the people and the holders of power.[144] Groups of guerrillas organized themselves, mobilized and radicalized the masses, but without actually offering a long-term political program.[145] The establishment reacted to the revolutionary grassroots movements with reprisals, partly through government institutions, partly through para-military institutions—the spiral of violence started to turn and the "process of revolutionary fermentation" began. Besides the structural poverty, institutionalized violence exacerbated the situation of the people.

Gutiérrez concludes: "The development oriented model has proven to be ineffective and inadequate to enable to interpretation of the economic, social and political evolution of the Latin American continent."[146] What could provide an alternative for this defective interpretative model? Increasingly, in Latin America, the point of view is prevailing that the situation in Latin America is the outcome of a process described as follows:

> Therefore, it must be studied from a historical perspective, that is, in relationship to the development and expansion of the great capitalist countries. The underdevelopment of the poor countries, as an overall social fact, appears in its true light: as the historical by-product of the development of other countries. The dynamics of the capitalist economy lead to the establishment of a center and a periphery, simultaneously generating progress and growing wealth for the few and social imbalances, political tensions, and poverty for the many. Latin America was born and developed in this context.[147]

143. Gutiérrez, *Theology of Liberation*, 53.

144. From 1930, in the Latin American nations within the framework of industrialization and urbanization, the oppressed groups gradually became "conscious of their interests as classes" (Gutiérrez, *Theology of Liberation*, 55). Through the above-mentioned failure of development policy, the emergence of international companies and the consequent relating growing dependency, a general deterioration of conditions has brought about a process of political radicalization.

145. Gutiérrez, *Theology of Liberation*, 56.

146. Gutiérrez, *Theology of Liberation*, 77.

147. Gutiérrez, *Theology of Liberation*, 51.

Gutiérrez comes to the conclusion that the only right starting point for an appropriate understanding of the underdevelopment in Latin America is the situation of dependency because the Latin American nations have been dependent for their origin and for their constitution.[148] "The notion of dependence emerges therefore as a key element in the interpretation of the Latin America reality."[149] Gutiérrez sees this fact borne out by history: Right from the start of the Iberian colonization, Latin America was in a dependent relationship. This dependency found expression in various forms, differing to a certain degree from region to region, but up to the present day has not been overcome as such. What is actually at stake with the opposition between oppressed nations and dominant nations has been recognized only with the dependency theory within an analysis of the class level itself, i.e., within the framework of class struggle.[150]

The analysis shows that an autonomous development of Latin America within the framework of the international capitalistic system is impossible.[151] For Gutiérrez, there is only one single possible way forward: The split with the development ideology and the political system, at home and abroad, which have an interest in the preservation of the current situation. This split takes place in a social revolution in which people are freed from the dependency and are led to freedom.[152] Freedom is a process, but ultimately a historical conquest.[153] With this terminology, Gutiérrez understands history as "the conquest of new, qualitatively different ways of being a human person in order to achieve an ever more total and complete fulfillment of the individual in solidarity with all

---

148. Gutiérrez, *Theology of Liberation*, 52.

149. Gutiérrez, *Theology of Liberation*, 52. Gutiérrez refers to the definition of the term dependency by Cardoso: "Dependency is the position of a specific group of nations whose economy is limited by the development and expansion of another economy. The relationship of inter-dependance between two or more economic systems becomes dependent when some nations (i.e., dominant ones) are able to expand and, on their own, to gain momentum, whilst others (i.e., dependent ones) into the bargain are able only by virtue of the reaction to this expansion, which can have a direct positive or negative influence on their development. In any case, the basic state of dependency leads to a global situation in which the dependent nations become ever more behind the game and eventually are merely the objects of exploitation from the side of the dominant nations" (Cardoso in Gutiérrez *Theology of Liberation*, 79n16).

150. Gutiérrez, *Theology of Liberation*, 54.

151. Gutiérrez, *Theology of Liberation*, 54.

152. Gutiérrez, *Theology of Liberation*, 16–17.

153. Gutiérrez, *Theology of Liberation*, 18.

humankind."[154] This life should be free "of all alienation and servitude"[155] and the individual is enabled to live an authentic human life.[156] This cannot happen merely through outward liberation. Besides the collective and historical levels, there is also the necessity for individual, personal liberation, which includes the psychological realm.[157] Nothing less than *a permanent cultural revolution* is aspired to, the conquest of new, qualitatively different forms, of being human, in which the individual is constantly oriented toward a fuller realization of itself in solidarity with the whole of mankind.[158] The highest goal of liberation is the "creation of a new humanity."[159]

Liberation also demands answers from the church. The church which sees itself as the primary option for the poor[160] can only answer the challenge of oppression in the form of practice. The practice of lived love is the central point of the Christian life.[161] Faith becomes effective through love: "Love is the nourishment and the fullness of faith, the gift of one's self to the Other, and invariably to others. This is the foundation of the praxis of Christians, of their active presence in history."[162] This direction of impact was approved by the Catholic church: "Vatican Council II has strongly reaffirmed the idea of a church of service and not of power. This is a church which is not centered upon itself and which does not 'find itself' except when it 'loses itself,' when it lives 'the joys and the hopes, the griefs and the anxieties of persons of this age.'"[163] In concrete terms, the Catholic church explains the related practice of liberation as follows:

- Among *lay people*, the practice of liberation is often expressed by engagement in revolutionary political groups. The political activities are suppressed with legal violence from the side of the state, which drives many activists underground. Current church structures and

---

154. Gutiérrez, *Theology of Liberation*, 22.
155. Gutiérrez, *Theology of Liberation*, 19.
156. Gutiérrez, *Theology of Liberation*, 30.
157. Gutiérrez, *Theology of Liberation*, 20.
158. Gutiérrez, *Theology of Liberation*, 21.
159. Gutiérrez, *Theology of Liberation*, 81.
160. Moltmann, *Experiences in Theology*, 230–37.
161. Gutiérrez, *Theology of Liberation*, 6.
162. Gutiérrez, *Theology of Liberation*, 6.
163. Gutiérrez, *Theology of Liberation*, 7.

- *Priests and holy orders* are one of "the most dynamic and restless groups in the Latin American church," in terms of shaping the future.[164] Groups of priests have arisen which "want to channel and reinforce their growing concern."[165] The driving force of this group of priests is the will to "commit themselves to the obligation for the liberation process," and the desire to change the church structures as well as the form of its activities and make them fit the Latin American reality. Also amongst the priests and people in holy orders, there are those who very openly collaborate with revolutionary political groups.[166]

- Even *bishops* engage in the struggle for liberation. In particular, bishops from regions which suffer most heavily from poverty and exploitation are active in pointing out the causes of abuse. Public statements are the expression of the bishops' engagement; sometimes, however, they are also involved in interventions such as workers strikes or participation in demonstrations.[167]

All three groups, laymen, people in holy orders and priests, as well as bishops, experience similar challenges in their struggle for liberation. All experience this resistance and hostilities from two sides: On one hand, from the side of the establishment,[168] and on the other, from elements of the church which fraternize with the establishment.[169] There are however also further elements which these three groups have in common. All are involved with producing pamphlets and publications in an attempt to clarify the situation of the people and the role of the church and its duty to reflect on the process of liberation.[170] The publications present the following core thoughts:

a. The church should recognize its responsibility within the current situation and "fulfill a role of prophetic denunciation of these grave

---

164. Gutiérrez, *Theology of Liberation*, 61.
165. Gutiérrez, *Theology of Liberation*, 61.
166. Gutiérrez, *Theology of Liberation*, 61.
167. Gutiérrez, *Theology of Liberation*, 62.
168. Gutiérrez, *Theology of Liberation*, 60, 61, 62.
169. Gutiérrez, *Theology of Liberation*, 59, 61, 62.
170. Gutiérrez, *Theology of Liberation*, 62.

injustices rampant in Latin America, which have already been characterized as 'sinful situations.'... They are moved to make this denunciation by the duty of solidarity with the poor, to which charity leads us. This solidarity means that we make ours their problems and their struggles, that we know how to speak with them."[171] Solidarity is thus understood in the sense that the church would make these problems and struggles their own. This is expressed in the denunciation and in the struggle against injustice. The denunciation contains the refusal to continuously defend the existing order with Christendom—this does not work without the strict division of church and state.[172] The prophetic function of the church is critical in the designation of prevailing conditions as injustice, it is but also constructive in that it points out the humanizing processes, too.[173]

b. The second principle of the publications is *awareness-raising evangelization*. In this respect, the function of the church is meant to mold the conscience and to stimulate, encourage and help orientate all initiatives which contribute to the formation of people.[174] The goal of awareness-raising evangelization is to promote the liberation of the people, humanized and integrated. It has to ensure that faith becomes completely new and vibrant and knows it is committed to the human community.[175] For this reason, the bishops decided to consider the social and community-related dimensions of Christianity in preaching, catechesis and liturgy. By doing so, the oppressed should be helped to envision their mission and co-responsibility in the process of liberation.

c. Related to this, the call for the *poverty of the church* becomes a central aspect of liberation theology. This is the reason why the bishops in Medellín claim that the church, instead of being a *church for the poor* must become a *poor church*—otherwise the church is not truly in solidarity with the oppressed.[176] The focal areas of the practice of a church of the poor are thus "evangelization of the poor, the

---

171. Gutiérrez, *Theology of Liberation*, 68.
172. Gutiérrez, *Theology of Liberation*, 69.
173. Gutiérrez, *Theology of Liberation*, 69.
174. Gutiérrez, *Theology of Liberation*, 69.
175. Gutiérrez, *Theology of Liberation*, 69.
176. Gutiérrez, *Theology of Liberation*, 70.

denunciation of injustice, a simple lifestyle, a spirit of service, and freedom from temporal ties, intrigue, or ambiguous prestige."[177]

d. The structures that the church maintains often hinder its functions in the process of liberation; hence, a renewal is needed. The same also pertains to the priestly lifestyle, which requires a revision, since it has a duty to side with the development of a new society. In addition, the question of the purchase of the means of subsistence is raised. How can priests finance themselves if their mission is not viewed as within the framework of the ministry at the altar and religious education? Furthermore: "Changes are also urged regarding greater participation of lay people, believers, and priests in the pastoral decisions of the church."[178]

The above depicted practice is reflected upon theologically by Gutiérrez. In the light of the gospel, he poses the question: What is the significance of the struggle against an unjust society?[179] This question led Gutiérrez to central theological themes, e.g., how to freshly explain *salvation, Christ* and relationships such as *God and history, eschatology and politics*. In the following, we shall concentrate on the terms *salvation, eschatology* and *pneumatology*.

Salvation: Gutiérrez questions the present church understanding and practice of salvation, which considers the term from a quantitative perspective, by which it is solely a matter of the *salvation of unbelievers*. This approach involves the question of the number of the redeemed, the conditions for salvation and the function of the church in the salvation process.[180] Usually, the question is answered to the effect that one considers life as a test:

> One's actions are judged and assessed in relation to the transcendent end. The perspective here is moralistic, and the spirituality is one of flight from this world. Normally, only contact with the channels of grace instituted by God can eliminate sin, the obstacle which stands in the way of reaching that life beyond.[181]

---

177. Gutiérrez, *Theology of Liberation*, 70.
178. Gutiérrez, *Theology of Liberation*, 71.
179. Gutiérrez, *Theology of Liberation*, 83.
180. Gutiérrez, *Theology of Liberation*, 83.
181. Gutiérrez, *Theology of Liberation*, 84.

In search of a comprehensive understanding of salvation, the internalized ability to experience redemption gains significance.[182] If salvation can be experienced not only transcendently but also immanently, then the question arises not only of the quantity but again also of the quality. Not merely the question of the number of converts, of the redeemed, is put forward, but again also the question of which levels of human existence experience redemption. So Gutiérrez quoted the Documento de trabajo, in Signos 210b:

> Thus the center of God's salvific design is Jesus Christ, who by his death and resurrection transforms the universe and makes it possible for the person to reach fulfillment as a human being. This fulfillment embraces every aspect of humanity: body and spirit, individual and society, person and cosmos, time and eternity. Christ, the image of the Father and the perfect God-Man, takes on all the dimensions of human existence.[183]

Gutiérrez hence concludes:

> Therefore, sin is not only an impediment to salvation in the afterlife. Insofar as it constitutes a break with God, sin is a historical reality, it is a breach of the communion of persons with each other, it is a turning in of individuals on themselves which manifests itself in a multifaceted withdrawal from others. And because sin is a personal and social intrahistorical reality, a part of the daily events of human life, it is also, and above all, an obstacle to life's reaching the fullness we call salvation.[184]

Sin cannot be reduced by a legal process between God and man but involves the inner-worldly reality. Therefore, salvation, which Christ fully accomplished in the conquest of sin, can also be experienced already, in this world, and must become tangible: "Salvation is also an innerhistorical reality. Even more: Salvation as a community of people with God, and a community of people amongst themselves, orientates history, changes it and brings it to its completion."[185] In this respect, there is no separation between world history and the history of salvation: "there is only one history—a 'Christo-finalized' history."[186] Creation and salvation

---

182. Gutiérrez, *Theology of Liberation*, 224.
183. Gutiérrez, *Theology of Liberation*, 85.
184. Gutiérrez, *Theology of Liberation*, 85.
185. Gutiérrez, *Theology of Liberation*, 140.
186. Gutiérrez, *Theology of Liberation*, 140.

are seen as an integral part of the same single history. Both are revelations of God in historical events).[187] The Exodus story is interpreted under the same auspices: "The Creator of the world is the Creator and Liberator of Israel, to whom is entrusted the mission of establishing justice. . . . And this fact is a political liberation through which Yahweh expresses love for the people and the gift of total liberation is received."[188] It relates to more than merely leaving the land of Egypt:

> The Exodus is the long march toward the promised land in which Israel can establish a society free from misery and alienation. Throughout the whole process, the religious event is not set apart. It is placed in the context of the entire narrative, or more precisely, it is its deepest meaning. It is the root of the situation. In the last instance, it is in this event that the dislocation introduced by sin is resolved and justice and injustice, oppression and liberation, are determined. Yahweh liberates the Jewish people politically in order to make them a holy nation.[189]

Gutiérrez therefore also sees the covenant of God with Israel and the preceding liberation of Israel as different aspects of one and the same movement, which led to the encounter with God. For the eschatological horizon is anchored at the center of the Exodus concepts.[190] Creation, liberation and the new creation are to be understood as cohesive, inseparable, saving acts of God. It is also under these auspices that the salvation act of Jesus is understood:

> The work of Christ forms a part of this movement and brings it to complete fulfillment. The redemptive action of Christ, the foundation of all that exists, is also conceived as a re-creation and presented in a context of creation (cf. Col 1:15–20; 1 Cor 8:6; Heb 1:2; Eph 1:1–22). . . . But the work of Christ is presented simultaneously as a liberation from sin and from all its consequences: despoliation, injustice, hatred.[191]

In the liberation through Christ, we are made a new people of God, which again includes all of humanity. Thereby creation and redemption gain a profoundly Christological character: "Creation and salvation

---

187. Gutiérrez, *Theology of Liberation*, 87.
188. Gutiérrez, *Theology of Liberation*, 88–89.
189. Gutiérrez, *Theology of Liberation*, 89.
190. Gutiérrez, *Theology of Liberation*, 146.
191. Gutiérrez, *Theology of Liberation*, 90.

therefore have, in the first place, a Christological sense: all things have been created in Christ, all things have been saved in him (cf. Col 1:15–20)."[192] This now also gives work a fundamental new meaning: This work, which Gutiérrez understands as a continuation of God's act of creation according to Genesis 2, he views as a human contribution to the comprehensive salvation process.

> To work, to transform this world, is to become a man and to build the human community; it is also to save. Likewise, to struggle against misery and exploitation and to build a just society is already to be part of the saving action, which is moving toward its complete fulfillment.[193]

This recognition is so central for Gutiérrez that he comes to the conclusion that a theology of human work and social practice must emanate from these fundamental observations. The human contribution to redemption/liberation therefore takes on central importance in the theology of liberation.

Eschatology: Just as for Gutiérrez creation and redemption were inseparably linked with one another from the beginning on, he also sees the promise of eschatology as a theme which pervades the Bible from the beginning. However, it is not just ever present, rather it is the "promise, which is at the same time revelation and good news" that constitutes the central thought of the Bible.[194] The eschatological promise is not something that fulfils the end of history but that repeatedly freshly determines the present:

> The Promise is gradually revealed in all its universality and concrete expression: it is already fulfilled in historical events, but not yet completely; it incessantly projects itself into the future, creating a permanent historical mobility. . . . But by the same token, the Promise illuminates and fructifies the future of humanity and leads it through incipient realizations toward its fullness.[195]

Eschatological promise has therefore also been understood as a historical promise.[196] The same is true also for the historical word of God, which also is to be understood as an eschatological promise. The Old

---

192. Gutiérrez, *Theology of Liberation*, 90.
193. Gutiérrez, *Theology of Liberation*, 91.
194. Gutiérrez, *Theology of Liberation*, 91.
195. Gutiérrez, *Theology of Liberation*, 92.
196. Gutiérrez, *Theology of Liberation*, 95.

Testament discourse of God through the Exodus story, the prophets and the Law have not "only a historical,"[197] sense for us today:

> The hidden sense is not the "Spiritual" one, which devalues and even eliminates temporal and earthly realities as obstacles; rather it is the sense of a fullness which takes on and transforms historical reality. Moreover, it is only in the temporal, earthly, historical event that we can open up to the future of complete fulfillment.[198]

If we understand the message of the Old Testament as a historicalization of eschatological promise, then it gains a timeless significance. Thus, for Gutiérrez the prophetic word becomes the mission of the present day:

> The prophets announce a kingdom of peace. But peace presupposes the establishment of justice: "Righteousness shall yield peace and its fruit [shall] be quietness and confidence forever," (Isa 32:17; cf. Ps 85). It presupposes the defense of the rights of the poor, punishment of the oppressors, a life free from the fear of being enslaved by others, the liberation of the oppressed. Peace, justice, love, and freedom are not private realities; they are not only internal attitudes. They are social realities, implying a historical liberation. A poorly understood spiritualization has often made us forget the human consequences of the eschatological promises and the power to transform unjust social structures which they imply. The elimination of misery and exploitation is a sign of the coming of the Kingdom. It will become a reality, according to the Book of Isaiah, when there is happiness and rejoicing among the people because "men shall build houses and live to inhabit them, plant vineyards and eat their fruit; they shall not build for others to inhabit nor plant for others to eat. . . . My chosen shall enjoy the fruit of their labor" (65:21–22) because the fruit of their labor will not be taken from them. The struggle for a just world in which there is no oppression, servitude, or alienated work will signify the coming of the Kingdom. The Kingdom and social injustice are incompatible (cf. Isa 29:18–19 and Matt 11:5; Lev 25:10ff and Luke 4:16–21).[199]

The eschatological promise is meeting with the Lord, which becomes a constant reminder of the awakening of the creation. Impossible to plan or predict, it impels humanity forward: As an "unknown

---

197. Gutiérrez, *Theology of Liberation*, 95.
198. Gutiérrez, *Theology of Liberation*, 96.
199. Gutiérrez, *Theology of Liberation*, 97.

quantity," it turns the hope of the Kingdom into an active, and not an engagement-avoiding, power.[200]

Pneumatology: With Gutiérrez's theology of liberation, pneumatology has no central role. Only in three sections of text is the Holy Spirit mentioned. Gutiérrez sees the Holy Spirit as "the Holy Spirit of promise," which fertilizes the historical nurturer of human beings and brings them from the beginning through still incomplete realization to completion.[201] However, promising eschatological revelation, which gives orientation, is not enough. This clearly becomes evident in the second section:

> We need a vital attitude, all-embracing and synthesizing, informing the totality as well as every detail of our lives; we need a "spirituality." Spirituality, in the strict and profound sense of the word is the dominion of the Holy Spirit. If "the truth will set you free" (John 8:32), the Holy Spirit "will guide you into all the truth" (John 16:13) and will lead us to complete freedom, the freedom from everything that hinders us from fulfilling ourselves as human beings and offspring of God and the freedom to love and to enter into communion with God and with others. It will lead us along the path of liberation because "where the Holy Spirit of the Lord is, there is liberty" (2 Cor 3:17). A spirituality is a concrete manner, inspired by the Holy Spirit, of living the Gospel; it is a definite way of living "before the Lord," in solidarity with all human beings, "with the Lord, and before human beings. It arises from an intense spiritual experience, which is later explicated and witnessed to."[202]

Spirit-filled life orientates itself toward the historical and eschatological promises of God. It is the same Spirit through whom people are liberated and empowered to be in solidarity with their fellows. Then they can lead the poor and exploited to liberation.[203]

In the third section of text, Gutiérrez presents the Spirit of God as the Spirit of joy—joy which is given despite the oppression by "the mighty ones of this world," and nevertheless is not frivolous and cheap but is reconciled with the tensions of an unjust world. It is an Easter joy which attains life through the cross.[204]

---

200. Gutiérrez, *Theology of Liberation*, 97.
201. Gutiérrez, *Theology of Liberation*, 92.
202. Gutiérrez, *Theology of Liberation*, 113.
203. Gutiérrez, *Theology of Liberation*, 118.
204. Gutiérrez, *Theology of Liberation*, 120.

In the later paper *Aus der eigenen Quelle trinken*, Gutiérrez explains the significance of the Holy Spirit more comprehensively. The direction of impact and content correspond with the pneumatology of *The Theologie of Liberation*, except that the Holy Spirit is now also connected with the Kingdom of God: "Life according to the Holy Spirit therefore signifies neither an existence according to the soul, nor against or without the body, rather *against death* and in harmony *with life*, love, peace and justice, that is to say, with the greatest values of the Kingdom of God."[205]

In summary, it can be said that the Spirit-filled life expresses itself in liberated living: liberated to be a child of God, liberated to have solidarity with the oppressed and liberated to have joy. Life in the Holy Spirit is living in harmony with the values of the Kingdom of God.

Appreciation and criticism: Gutiérrez's work and influence on Latin American theology can hardly be overestimated. The strength and sacrifice which the pioneers of the theology of liberation required to withstand all political and ecclesiastical opposition are enormous. With good reason, Gutiérrez recognizes that sin and redemption are not merely a purely legal matter between God and people which opens up the door of heaven for the forgiven sinner. If the Kingdom of God is near, already breaking out in the midst of the disciples, then it is also an imminent occurrence. Gutiérrez's emphasis of this immanent dimension compels people in the here and now to assume responsibility.[206] The central issue, to liberate the Latin American masses from poverty and to free them from their dependency, is the driving element of Gutiérrez's theology. The concentration on the economic question of society is a strength and, at the same time, a weakness of the Latin American liberation theology: Concentrating on the liberation of the poor draws together and

---

205. Gutiérrez, *Eigenen Quelle trinken*, 82, my translation.

206. One of the most commonly mentioned points of criticism in respect of the Latin American liberation theology is the allegation that Gutiérrez pursued an immanent eschatology at the cost of a transcendent eschatology (see, e.g., CDF, "Instructio De Quibusdam Rationibus"). Initially, Moltmann also commented critically in this respect. In the course of time, the liberation theology developed further and thereby Moltmann's criticism also changed. Actually, Gutiérrez hardly commented on the apocalyptic (transcendent) dimension of the Kingdom of God; his focus is directed completely toward the immanent future. However, as much as the immanent dimension in Gutiérrez's theology is present, he established it nevertheless as present and future without linking it together further and without them being dissolved within one another (Moltmann, *Experiences in Theology*, 237–38). Later, Moltmann defended Gutiérrez's liberation theology explicitly against the reproach of the contemporization of God's Kingdom (Moltmann, *Experiences in Theology*, 149f). For Moltmann's initial critique of Latin American liberation theology, see Moltmann, "Open Letter."

consolidates the forces of the movement, but it also lets them become one-sided. This one-sidedness has also been responded to critically by Moltmann. He recognizes fighting against structural poverty as an important issue; however, even though the liberation of the poor is important, human life cannot be reduced to the economic question. A society cannot be liberated in the comprehensive biblical sense only through prosperity and economic self-determination, since it is too multi-layered: "'The poor' in Latin America are also Indios and mestizos with their own culture, blacks and mulattos, women and men. . . . The analysis of 'the poor' in comparison with 'the wealthy' must therefore give way to a more differentiated, multi-perspective analysis of the richer and more complex reality."[207] Furthermore, Moltmann's criticism applies to Gutiérrez's understanding of freedom (freedom as dominion), which corresponds in its essence with that of the oppressor. Unfortunately, at the same time, Gutiérrez also defines freedom in this way:

> It is "historical conquest" (conquista). But whoever understands freedom as conquest and lordship can only be free at the cost of others. Even when we say: One is free who can do and allow what he wants, we understand freedom as lordship and align it with the ideal of the Lord. Even when we say: One is free who is no longer defined by others but defines himself, we understand freedom as lordship: Each should be his own lord.[208]

A theology of liberation can and must not simply be a theology of the oppressed, even though the oppressed need liberation: "In this dimension freedom is liberation from poverty, suffering and death; it is liberation from historical guilt and its consequences, which are the urge for justification and the compulsion toward repetition."[209]

A further question is posed: Even though Gutiérrez attaches the liberation of disenfranchised and oppressed people to Christ, it seems that it is not Christ who liberates but the oppressed who must liberate themselves. He writes: "The actual liberation shall become the work of the oppressed themselves. In the disenfranchised the Lord rescues history."[210]

---

207. Moltmann, *Experiences in Theology*, 229. In the second generation of liberation theologians, subjects such as women's rights, racism, ecology, and the dialogue with other cultures were also thematized.

208. Gutiérrez, *Theology of Liberation*, 289, my translation.

209. How Moltmann alternatively explains the concept of freedom is the subject of chapter 3.

210. Moltmann, *Experiences in Theology*, 241.

From the object of liberation, they suddenly become the subject of the liberation,[211] which overcomes injustice in the social revolution. This leads Pöhlmann to the following criticism:

> Here it is no longer clear that Christ alone saves us and that the disenfranchised are saved, but he does not save himself, that Christ alone rescues history, not the human being together with Him. And His work of redemption is never carried out with violence. The Crucified One, who exercises His power in the powerless, is an annulation of any spirituality of violence. Unjust structures are not broken with violence, but are overcome from within—through the Holy Spirit of God, who is the Holy Spirit of love (Gal 5:22).[212]

Thereby, Pöhlmann alludes to a crucial aspect of Gutiérrez's pneumatology. As already mentioned above, for Gutiérrez, the Spirit-filled life is liberated to be a child of God, liberated for solidarity with the oppressed and liberated for joy. Life in the Holy Spirit means living in harmony with the values of the Kingdom of God. The Spirit points out the final outcome, i.e., the goal and, along with that, He points out the way, giving orientation. It seems that for Gutiérrez, the Holy Spirit is only a position, a function by which *to* get liberation; the actual liberation, however, in his view, occurs through the people without the influence of the Holy Spirit. The function of the Holy Spirit is reduced to the role of the giver of orientation. Pentecost as the empowerment for liberation is not a theme with Gutiérrez. This is astonishing, given that the text in Luke 4:18–19 explicitly establishes the connection between the presence of the Holy Spirit and empowerment for the liberation of the poor, the sick and the captive. This is where Pentecostal criticism would come in. Thus says L. Lovett, an African American theologian:

> The Black Pentecostal Movement adheres to the biblical dogma that liberation is always a consequence of the workings of the Holy Spirit. Authentic liberation can absolutely not happen outside of a genuine Pentecost experience. Similarly, no genuine Pentecost experience can occur without liberation following as a consequence.[213]

---

211. Pölmann, *Heiliger Geist*, 85.
212. Pölmann, *Heiliger Geist*, 85, my translation.
213. Hollenweger, *Charismatisch-pfingsltiches Christentum*, 44.

It is the Holy Spirit who in the first place enables the church to be the body of Christ and to act in the spirit of Christ. Pentecost completes Easter in that it lets us know why Christ has liberated us: To be a Spirit-filled community which already in the here and now experiences and lives the coming reign of God. Only through Pentecost can the church be the primary option for the poor (and all other marginalized people). From these ideas, a subsequent question is posed: What does a theology of liberation which significantly references Pentecost look like? Moltmann gives us a pointer as he writes:

> The Latin American Pentecostal Movement could become the true criticism and continuation of liberation theology. For there are points of contact, for example, the healing of the exploited and sick bodies of men and woman. Services of healing have a liberating force. Without them sociological situation analyses merely paralyse.[214]

Social Justice in the Beginnings of the Pentecostal Movement

Moltmann's significance in possibly turning liberation theology toward a more pneumatological understanding of social justice is worth noting. At the same time, Pentecostal theology and spirituality also seem to be ripe for Moltmann's emphasis on relating the work of the Holy Spirit more systematically to social ethics and issues of social justice. The critical inter-Pentecostal debate of the last decades has brought forth various contributions doing so, but all of them have focused either on one specific aspect of social justice or have been written from one specific perspective. Hence, Pentecostalism is indeed ripe for Moltmann's influence[215] and makes him a crucial dialogue partner for the development of a Pentecostal approach to social ethics. Hollenweger already noted in his work *Enthusiastisches Christentum* in 1969 that this dialogue partly exists and goes back to the early beginnings of Moltmann's *Theology of Hope*. Hollenweger refers to and indicates the significance of Moltmann's eschatology for the Pentecostal Movement and the implications associated with it for a Pentecostal social ethics:

---

214. Moltmann, *Broad Place*, 222, my translation.

215. This is also Moltmann's assessment, in which he refers in particular to the work of Frank Macchia and Peter Althous. Moltmann, *Broad Place*, 351.

> The Pentecostal preachers saw everything as appearing complicated and difficult. However, I asked for their forbearance. It is worthwhile for them to grapple with this [Moltmann's] view of the last things, because here a view of the last things is presented which believes in heaven, without telling the earth which is hoping for the return of the Lord, without giving up participation in society, actually on the contrary, which gets inspiration and strength from the expectation of the coming One, to change the present in light of the coming One.[216]

Since then, Moltmann has repeatedly emerged as a reference point in the discussions of Pentecostal theologians and is referred to by the Pentecostals.[217]

Yet, even reversed, the dialogue becomes an asset. Moltmann's previous dialogue partners have barely demonstrated pneumatology with its appropriate significance. In Pentecostal thinking about the church's outreach to the world, pneumatology takes a prominent role. The theology and practice of the Pentecostal Movement can make a contribution here. Even though we are looking at a dialogue which stretches back over two decades: In 1991, Moltmann took part in the Pentecostal-charismatic conference in Brighton. In the same year, he published *The Spirit of Life*, in which he describes *The Charismatic Powers of Life* in chapter 9, where he discusses topics such as spontaneous healing and speaking in tongues. In general, Brighton seems to be a milestone in the relationship between Moltmann and Pentecostal spirituality. Thus, Moltmann writes, "The Brighton Conference and this dialogue have awakened in me the wish to learn more about the experience of the Holy Spirit in the Pentecostal tradition. For this I am very grateful to the Journal of Pentecostal Theology."[218] In 1995 he came to meet with the well-known Pentecostal preacher Yonggi Cho in Korea.[219] Further conferences followed in 2002 in Bangor, and 2004 at the Yong San International Theological Symposium.[220] Moltmann also

---

216. Hollenweger, *Enthusiastisches Christentum*, 476–78, my translation.
217. E.g., Kay, review of *God in Creation*; Moltmann, "Response"; Althouse, *Last Days*.
218. Moltmann, "Response," 66.
219. Moltmann, *Broad Place*, 350.
220. In June 2004, Moltmann was one of the main speakers at the Yong San International Theological Symposium. The theme of the symposium was "Dr. Yongi Cho's Theology of Hope." Moltmann presented a seminar paper, which appeared in *JPT* as Moltmann, "Blessing of Hope."

wrote responses to Pentecostal literature[221] and indicated their potential and significance.[222]

In order to understand the significance of pneumatology in the Pentecostal social ethic, a glance at the beginnings of the Pentecostal Movement is indispensable. We shall address this task in the following section before we apply ourselves to contemporary Pentecostal theology in chapter 2.

Introductory Thoughts

Three introductory thoughts for the examination of the beginnings of social justice in the Pentecostal Movement: First, the Pentecostal Movement is a movement primarily guided by mission and not by theological concepts. Thus, for example, the authors of *Called & Empowered: Global Mission in Pentecostal Perspective* maintain in their introduction to the first part of their collected volumes:

> The modern-day Pentecostal Missionary movement was not birthed as a theological movement. From the inception of the movement Pentecostals have been "doers," rather than "reflective thinkers." . . . The Baptism of the Holy Spirit, as Russell Spittler has emphasized, created missionaries, not theologians. This "on fire," missionary activity, in Grant McClung's view, produced "a theology on the move . . . its character has been more experimental than cognitive, more activist than reflecting."[223]

This observation also has validity for the beginnings of the Pentecostal social ethic: Social justice is inexistent as a systematic-theological factor in the early Pentecostal Movement. Hence, the analysis must be oriented toward socio-ethical practice and its interpretation by the persons affected. Secondly, it should be considered that as early as within the first months of the Azusa Street Mission, this had developed into an international movement: Up to the end of 1906, that is, within the first three quarters of the year, sympathizers and members of the Street Mission had

---

221. See, e.g., Moltmann's response to Macchia's "Baptized in the Holy Spirit" in Moltmann, "On the Abundance of the Holy Spirit."

222. See also, e.g., Moltmann, *Broad Place*, 224.

223. Demster, *Called & Empowered*, 3. C. Peter Wagner also comes to a similar conclusion. He also is of the opinion that in the Pentecostal Movement, practice has a fundamentally higher importance than doctrine. Thus, he writes: "You can tell Pentecostals more by what they do than by what they teach" (Wagner, *Look out*, 35).

established nine churches in Los Angeles and the surrounding area.²²⁴ Evangelists from the church had spread the message along the entire West Coast and right across the continent to New York, as well as sending at least thirteen missionaries to Africa.²²⁵ By the beginning of 1907, missionaries had already arrived in Canada, Mexico, Western Europe, the north of Russia, the Middle East, West Africa and various countries in Asia.²²⁶ It can rightly be said that the Pentecostal Movement, right from the beginning, has been an international movement.²²⁷ If we wish to draw a picture of the beginnings of the Pentecostal social ethic, it is imperative to look at Los Angeles and to point to the international context. Thirdly: The powerful working of the Holy Spirit in the beginnings of the Pentecostal Movement was often interpreted as within the framework of the Latter Rain.²²⁸ In dependence upon the promise of Joel 2:23 the powerful outpouring of the Holy Spirit in the Azusa Street Mission became as the *Latter Rain*, understood as a second outpouring of the Holy Spirit for the restoration of the church, which was to immediately precede the second coming of Christ.²²⁹ On the basis of this combination of the working of the Holy Spirit and imminent expectation, Pentecostal pneumatology is also always to be understood as eschatological.

History and Context

To elaborate on the Pentecostal Movement, we shall begin right at the beginning, in Los Angeles, in Azusa Street, or even earlier, with Pastor William J. Seymour. His story is representative of the realities of life for many African Americans at the turn of the last century.²³⁰ Seymour was born in May 1870 in Centerville, Louisiana, as a child of a former slave.

---

224. Hollenweger, *Enthusiastisches Christentum*, 25.

225. Robeck, *Azusa Street*, 7.

226. Robeck, *Azusa Street*, 8.

227. Robeck went as far as to say that the 1908 Awakening was in many ways a global phenomenon. Robeck, *Azusa Street*, 281.

228. See also "The Pentecostal Baptism Restored," the main article in Seymour, *Azusa Street Papers*, 23.

229. Robeck, *Azusa Street*, 235–36.

230. Thus Hollenweger wrote: "Seymour and his black brothers and sisters suffered bitterly. During Seymour's adult life, 3,436 blacks were known to be lynched. This means two per week. Enormous brutality was perpetrated against them, much of which caused by Christians" (Hollenweger, *Charismatisch-pfingstliches Christentum*, 32).

He grew up in poor conditions and received a simple school education.[231] In 1895, Seymour moved to Indianapolis and worked there in catering. It is also there that Seymour experienced conversion and became a member of a *colored Methodist episcopal church*.[232] His interest in John Wesley's theology was awakened. However, later Seymour changed to the church of the *Evening Light Saints*—one of the very few churches which made no differentiation in their community service between race and gender. Thus, Robeck writes: "In the late 1890s the Evening Light Saints was one of the few groups in which blacks and whites were treated equally and gifted woman were encouraged to preach."[233]

At a later point in time Seymour visited two different Bible schools, although with an interruption of several years between them. In 1900, he joined in Martin Wells Knapp's *God's Bible School and Missionary Training Home* in Cincinnati, Ohio,[234] where black and white people learned together in mixed classes. The school advocated a premillennialist eschatology and gave dreams and visions high importance.[235] At the beginning of 1906, Seymour then travelled to the Bible school of Charles Fox Parham in Topeka, Kansas, where he came into contact with the teaching of praying in tongues as a sign of the baptism in the Holy Spirit.[236] Since participation in the classroom was prohibited for the African American, he followed the lessons in the corridor, through the half-open door—which for Parham, a Ku-Klux-Klan sympathizer, was already a great concession.[237] Against Parham's will, Seymour accepted the invitation from Julia Hutchins to lead a small Holiness Assembly in Los Angeles. Following some challenges, the awakening then began in April 1906, in the Azusa Street Mission, Los Angeles. It celebrated its zenith in the years 1906 to 1909 and marked the beginnings of the Pentecostal Movement.[238]

231. Robeck, *Azusa Street*, 25.
232. Robeck, *Azusa Street*, 28.
233. Robeck, *Azusa Street*, 30.
234. Robeck, *Azusa Street*, 31.
235. Robeck, *Azusa Street*, 33.
236. Robeck, *Azusa Street*, 50–51.

237. Hollenweger, *Charismatisch-pfingstliches Christentum*, 32. Hollenweger takes a prominent place with his analysis in the following pages. This has several reasons: On the one hand, Hollenweger is recognized as the father of academic Pentecostal research. This role is attested to him not only by Pentecostals but also by non-Pentecostals. On the other hand, with his contributions, he has introduced a specifically Swiss viewpoint into this current work, which is of significance for the context of the author.

238. For the discussion, see Hollenweger, *Charismatisch-pfingstliches Christentum*, 31–36.

In order to understand the extraordinary dynamic of the early Pentecostal Movement, the events must be located in the historical context of Los Angeles: In just six years, the population of the city doubled, and in the year 1906, it reached the staggering number of 238,000 inhabitants, swelling by a further 3,000 each month. The city was well linked to its suburbs through a tram network, but also nationally and internationally Los Angeles was easily accessible. Several trans-continental railroad companies served the city and, with a seaport, access to the entire Pacific was assured.[239] Demographically, the majority of the city was composed of whites with European roots. Many had German, Swedish, Danish, Russian, Polish or Spanish origins. The largest minority was composed of African Americans (approximately one-fifth of the city's population), followed by Mexicans and Hispanics. In addition, further smaller groups of Moluccans, Armenians and Chinese formed organized communities within the city. Considering the times, African Americans were amazingly well integrated into the city life of Los Angeles, "many of them well-educated, professional, middle-class homeowners." Thus, Robeck writes:

> African Americans were generally integrated into the life of the city. By 1907 some held positions in the city's police and fire departments. Others served as doctors, dentists, pharmacists, veterinarians, lawyers, teachers, and building contractors. Children from the community attended fully integrated public schools . . . at least 90 percent of black Angelenos belonged to a Christian church of some sort.[240]

Even though there was segregation in Los Angeles, in many respects it was more moderate than in other cities and regions;[241] nevertheless, the various ethnic groups lived their everyday lives predominantly divided and within homogenous groups. This also expressed itself in religious life. Thus, the different races, as well as the various language groups, generally met within their own cultural circles even at church meetings.[242]

In this context, there arose a new church under the leadership of Seymour, an African American. However, even though the church began amongst African Americans, Seymour carried within him the vision of a multi-ethnic and multi-racial community.[243] It is well possible that at the

239. Robeck, *Azusa Street*, 53–54.
240. Robeck, *Azusa Street*, 56–57.
241. Robeck, *Azusa Street*, 14.
242. Robeck, *Azusa Street*, 56–57.
243. Robeck, *Azusa Street*, 88.

beginning of the awakening, he had no clear idea of how such a church service should be celebrated. Seymour was not a dominant leader personality.[244] However, he had the gift of making space for many: "Seymour provided the 'space,' for ordinary people to make their contributions."[245] He discovered, together with the constantly growing diversity amongst the church service attendees, a new multi-ethic and multi-cultural spirituality step by step. Seymour succeeded in integrating the most diverse forms of expression of faith into the church service, and so the church services developed collectively over time.[246] There were, for example, African American influences in the form of spirituals, clapping and tapping the feet, the significance of dreams and visions and the form of "call and response," preaching.[247] There were unique influences from the side of the Moluccans: From their church services, they were familiar with ecstatic elements such as jumping, dancing, falling down under the power of the Holy Spirit and a kind of singing which is similar to *singing in tongues*.[248] These and further influences mingled together and created a new and unparalleled inclusive spirituality.[249] The church service was strongly characterized by an oral liturgy. The church service attendees participated "at the level of reflection, prayer in public areas, and in decision making, from this there resulted a reconciliatory form of spirituality."[250] Central significance was attributed to the working of the Holy Spirit in the form of dreams and visions, praying in tongues, and praying for the sick.

However, in the Azusa Street Mission, there was more than a multi-ethnic integration of believers. It was witnessed that men, women, educated and uneducated were integrated with one another: "Blacks, whites, and Hispanics worshiped together. Men and women shared leadership responsibilities. The barrier between clergy and laity vanished, since participants believed that the endowment with spiritual power for ministry

244. Robeck, *Azusa Street*, 90–93.

245. Robeck, *Azusa Street*, 128. Thus also Hollenweger's assessment. Hollenweger, *Charismatisch-pfingstliches Christentum*, 35–36.

246. Robeck, *Azusa Street*, 177.

247. Robeck, *Azusa Street*, 23.

248. Robeck, *Azusa Street*, 57. Robeck explains *this singing in tongues* as "a multi-layered, harmony-rich singing in tongues that are unknown to the singers and are believed to be inspired by the Holy Spirit."

249. An eyewitness who critically opposed the movement described it as follows: "They rant and dance and roll in a disgusting amalgamation of African voodoo superstition and Caucasian insanity" (Robeck, *Azusa Street*, 88).

250. Hollenweger, *Charismatisch-pfingstliches Christentum*, 31.

was intended to be received by all."²⁵¹ This fact also found expression in that, within the leadership team of the Azusa Street Mission, blacks, whites, men, women, old and young took leadership roles.²⁵²

The unprecedented freedom of all to be integrated into the church service was linked with Seymour's understanding of the baptism in the Holy Spirit: "This meeting has been a melting time. The people are all melted together by the power of the blood and the Holy Ghost. They are made one lump, one bread, all one body in Christ Jesus. There is no Jew or Gentile, bond or free, in the Azusa Street Mission."²⁵³ It is no longer the social status, education, race, age or gender which authorizes anyone to speak and to give testimony.²⁵⁴ It is much more that the Holy Spirit who has been poured out on "all flesh," who empowers: "But, praise our God, He is now given and being poured out upon all flesh. All races, nations and tongues are receiving the baptism with the Holy Ghost and fire, according to the Prophecy of Joel."²⁵⁵ Whoever was filled with the Holy Spirit, and through Him reckoned as worthy, shall also be reckoned by the church as worthy to serve.²⁵⁶ However, at first, the empowerment for ministry was not understood as the work of the Holy Spirit. Already the fact that people recognized and respected each other as equal brothers and sisters, independent of the prevailing conventions of society, was interpreted as the work of God's Spirit. Thus Bartleman, an eyewitness, writes:

> We wanted to hear from God, through whomever He might speak. We had no respect of persons. The rich and educated were the same as the poor and ignorant, although the former found it much harder to die to self. We only recognized God. All were equal. No flesh might glory in His presence (1 Cor 1:29). He could not use the self-opinionated. These were Holy Spirit meetings, led by the Lord.²⁵⁷

251. Hollenweger and Anderson, "Introduction," xvii–xxiii. Hollenweger writes: "In the awakening of Los Angeles there were wise bishops and black workers, men and women, Asians and Mexicans, white professors and black washerwomen equal to one another (1906!)" (Hollenweger, *Charismatisch pfingstliches Christentum*, 32). Robeck also mentioned American indigenous people. He went so far as to say that the Azusa Street Mission "became one of the most racially inclusive, culturally diverse groups to gather in the city of Los Angeles at that time" (Robeck, *Azusa Street*, 88).

252. Robeck, *Azusa Street*, 99–100.

253. Seymour, *Azusa Street Papers*, 68.

254. Robeck, *Azusa Street*, 138.

255. Seymour, *Azusa Street Papers*, 54.

256. See Seymour, *Azusa Street Papers*, 14; Powers, "Pentecostalism 101," 133–51.

257. Bartlemann, *Azusa Street*, 56–57.

Brotherly love toward people who had become excluded from society was not only practiced in the church service. Marginalized people categorically had a high priority in the Azusa Street Mission:

> The poor, those incarcerated in the city's jail, those without physical sight or with other physical needs, and the oppressed, whether through addictions or prejudice were all high on the mission's agenda. Seymour's commitment to the poor can be seen in his statement, "The Apostolic Faith Movement stands for 'missions' and for 'street . . . work.'" His commitment to prisoners is present in his declaration that "The Apostolic Faith Movement stands for . . . 'prison work.'" His commitment to the blind and to all who needed physical healing came in his claim that "God is able to heal," and his desire to lay his hands upon the sick and pray the prayer of faith. But his commitment to the oppressed, whether they were former slaves, or women, or members of any other race or class, was always uppermost in his mind.[258]

Seymour understood, on the basis of Luke 4:18–19, that the ministry to the weak is founded in the empowerment of the Holy Spirit.[259] This empowerment found expression in the concrete ministry to those who had been excluded from society.[260] For Seymour, the baptism in the Holy Spirit was proven ultimately by the fruit of love and not, as with Parham, primarily in the gift of tongues. Thus, Seymour wrote in the Azusa Street Papers:

> Tongues are one of the signs that go with every baptized person, but it is not the real evidence of the baptism in everyday life. Your life must measure with the fruits of the Holy Spirit. If you get angry, or speak evil, or backbite, I care not how many tongues you may have, you have not the baptism with the Holy Spirit.[261]

Robeck also writes:

> The leaders at the mission agreed that baptism in the Holy Spirit would be recognized when someone spoke in tongues, and not a moment before. As a result, at first they embraced all who spoke in tongues. As time passed and Pastor Seymour reflected further

---

258. Robeck, *Azusa Street*, 14.

259. Seymour, *Azusa Street Papers*, 286.

260. Robeck, *Azusa Street*, 14. The Azusa Street Mission wanted to connect with others in social issues, despite all the animosities. So, for example, Florence Louise Crawford, a member of the leadership team, maintained contact with social clubs that engaged with voluntary work, the Sheriff of Los Angeles, and a number of policemen. Furthermore, she regularly visited the slums and the local prison. Robeck, *Azusa Street*, 102.

261. Seymour, *Azusa Street Papers*, 205.

upon the subject, he decided that speaking in tongues could be accepted as the Bible evidence of a person's baptism in the Holy Spirit only if it were also accompanied by divinely given love. Without evidence of this "fruit," of the Holy Spirit in the claimant's live, Seymour was not convinced that the tongue had been divinely given.[262]

Traces of this cornerstone of spirituality in the Azusa Street Mission can be seen in the further development of the Pentecostal church. In the following lines, we shall consider which social ethical aspects of their path have gone beyond Los Angeles. The following statements have no claim of completeness, but are rather an attempt to broadly sketch out the influence of the Azusa Street Mission on the social ethic of the early Pentecostal Movement:

Equality of the Sexes

It is striking how many women were mentioned in relation to their ministry and functions in the early movement and what formative roles they occupied. As mentioned above, in the Azusa Street Mission, the equality of the ministry of women is justified by the empowerment of the Holy Spirit. The emergence of this theology is ascribed to theologian Janet Everett Powers by Phoebe Palmer, a representative of the Holiness Movement, who first published her ideas in 1859.[263] Her theology is based on the Pentecostal incident described in the Book of Acts:

> She bases it on the account of Pentecost in Acts 2 and maintains that because women as well as men received the mighty baptism of the Holy Spirit, women as well as men are empowered to preach and prophesy in the Christian Dispensation.[264]

Palmer's approach found wide proliferation within the Holiness Movement and was very influential. Half a century later, her teaching made its way into the Pentecostal Movement via Parham, as it supplemented Palmer's approach with the gift of tongues as evidence of the baptism in the Holy Spirit.[265] The theology of empowerment through

262. Robeck, *Azusa Street*, 182.
263. Palmer, *Promise of the Father*.
264. Powers, "Pentecostalism 101," 136.

265. Unfortunately, Powers provided no references which support her statement that Parham had taken over the teaching of empowerment by the Holy Spirit from Palmers. Only the fact that Parham's and Palmer's teachings are very similar makes her thesis very believable.

the Holy Spirit shaped and formed the church service practice of the Azusa Street Mission in Los Angeles and beyond. The significance of Palmer's theology for the ministry of women, according to Powers, can hardly be overestimated:

> This understanding of woman in ministry led to an unprecedented number of women being licensed or ordained in Pentecostal churches. In the early days of Pentecostalism, women assisted in every aspect of the ministry of this rapidly growing movement. Even today, over 50 percent of all women who have ever been ordained come from the Holiness-Pentecostal tradition.[266]

As wonderful as this may sound, Lisa P. Stephenson warned about overly glorifying the role of women in the beginning of the Pentecostal Movement. With good reason, she points out that women participated in the church service and on the governing bodies of the church as well as being treated as equals, but eventually they had to subordinate to male leadership. Thus, Stephenson refers to the article "Who May Prophesy" in second volume of *The Apostolic Faith* (1908), which thematized the role of women:

> Before Pentecost the woman could only go into the "court of women" and not onto the inner court. The anointing oil was never poured on a womans [sic] head but only on the heads of kings, prophets and priests. But when our Lord poured out Pentecost, He brought all those faithful women with the other disciples into the upper room, and God baptized them all in the same room and made no difference. All the women received the anointed oil of the Holy Ghost and were able to preach the same as men.
>
> The woman is the weaker vessel and represents the tenderness of Christ, while the man represents the firmness of Christ. . . . No woman that has the Holy Spirit of Jesus wants to usurp authority over men. The more God uses you in the Holy Spirit, the more humble and tender you are and [t]he more filled with the blessed Holy Spirit.
>
> It is contrary to the Scriptures that woman should not have her part in the salvation work to which God has called her. We have no right to lay a straw in her way. . . . It is the same Holy Spirit in the woman as in the man.[267]

---

266. Powers, "Pentecostalism 101," 134.
267. Seymour, *Azusa Street Papers*, 265.

Seymour underlines the fact that the same Spirit which empowers the men also works through women and simply nothing should be done to hinder this ministry. However, at the same time, he subordinates women to men and thus again sets boundaries on equality. Stephenson finds similar tendencies in the beginnings of the various Pentecostal denominations.[268] Even in *The International Church of the Foursquare Gospel*, which was founded by a woman, Aimee Semple McPherson, there were limits to the ministry of women.[269] However, women made vital contributions in the beginning of the Pentecostal Movement. Hollenweger even comes to the conclusion that "in almost all nations women were significant in the foundation phase, for example in France, in Scandinavia, in Great Britain, in the black British churches, in Chile,[270] in Holland, and in other places."[271]

At the same time, he sees this practice in contradiction to the above-described theology: Not brought into agreement "is the theory of the Pentecostal Movement about women and the actual role which women played in the Pentecostal Movement."[272] Hollenweger concludes, "In the Pentecostal Movement there was an informal but effective values system, which stood in contrast to the official, preached teaching."[273] For Hollenweger, women such as Aimee Semple McPherson, Lillian Trasher, Anna Larsen Bjørner, Mara Fraser and Florence Louise Crawford are the evidence that "an obvious gifting in the Pentecostal Movement is stronger than strict fundamentalism."[274]

---

268. Stephenson, *Dismantling the Dualisms*, 22.

269. Stephenson, *Dismantling the Dualisms*, 53.

270. See also Frei, *Pädagogik der Bekehrung*, 87, 107.

271. Hollenweger, *Charismatisch-pfingstliches Christentum*, 296, my translation. In the beginning of BewegungPlus (Apostolic church in Switzerland, not to be confused with the Apostolic church in the USA), the initial situation was comparable with that of the Pentecostal churches in America. The initial large influence of prophetesses within the framework of the national movement leadership was starkly reduced after a conflict. Rossel, *Erinnerungen*, 36. The Swiss Pentecostal Mission (Assemblies of God) pointed out, in the book published to mark its eightieth anniversary year, that the mission had many women in deployment and that the deployment of women in the mission field was often undervalued. Plüss, *Vom Geist bewegt*, 153n47. The position of women within the movement in Switzerland is not thematized in the book.

272. Hollenweger, *Enthusiastisches Christentum*, 558.

273. Hollenweger, *Enthusiastisches Christentum*, 561.

274. Hollenweger, *Enthusiastisches Christentum*, 563.

Equality of the Races

The equality of races is justified with the work of Christ and the empowerment through the Holy Spirit. In the *Azusa Street Papers* 1.7, published in April 1907, it was noted:

> It is the Blood of Jesus that brings fellowship among the Christian family. The Blood of Jesus Christ is the strongest in the world. It makes all races and nations into one common family in the Lord and makes them all satisfied to be one. The Holy Ghost is the leader and He makes all one as Jesus prayed, "that they all may be one."[275]

Despite the Jim Crow segregation laws, the multi-racial beginnings of the Azusa Street Mission occurred in an environment which was not entirely unprepared. Thus David D. Daniels writes:

> Black Pentecostalism emerged out of three nineteenth-century renewal movements within the black church: the black Holiness Movement, the black Restorationist Movement, and the Healing Movement—and all three had from the beginning a desire to bring blacks and whites together.[276]

The beginnings of the Apostolic Street Mission were along the lines of white and black sanctification churches, which proclaimed a multi-racial ideal but did not put it into practice until Seymour came about. Relevant effects followed, as Davis points out:

> So impressive was this model that by 1910, prominent black and white Pentecostal leaders were campaigning to make the interracial vision of the Azusa Street Revival a keystone of Pentecostalism. Black Holiness congregations in Los Angeles, Portland, Memphis, Indianapolis, and New York City introduced Pentecostalism to these cities, conspicuously modelling the interracial worship brought from Los Angeles.[277]

The practice of the ethnically embracing church service was implemented by missionaries in nations with similar demographic and cultural realities. Thus Allan H. Anderson described the beginnings of the

---

275. Seymour, *Azusa Street Papers*, 172.
276. Daniels, "They Had a Dream," 19.
277. Daniels, "They Had a Dream," 20.

Pentecostal church in South Africa as follows: "Pentecostalism in South Africa thus began in a black church with fully integrated services."[278]

What happened in the Azusa Street Mission cannot be reduced to multi-racial, multi-ethic communal singing, praying and giving testimony. Many fundamental things happened: For instance, a number of attendees overcame their racism and let go of their prejudices against others. A prominent testimony to this is the report of Frank Bartleman, in which he recounts "The 'color line' was washed away in the blood of Christ."[279] Unfortunately, Parham did not share this experience with the others:

> Sadly, Parham's bigoted tendencies were not among these. He caricatured Seymour's "disgusting," Azusa Street revivals as "Southern darkey camp meetings." The short-lived relationship between Seymour and Parham foreshadowed the inability of Pentecostalism to maintain the racial harmony for very long.[280]

Already the beginnings show that the struggle for equality of the races within an awakening church is itself a challenge.[281] Seymour was repeatedly subjected to takeover attempts, his role as a leader was disputed several times:

> The bold attempts by Charles F. Parham in 1906, by Florence L. Crawford in 1908, and by William H. Durham in 1911 to take control of the Apostolic Faith movement, and the doctrinal challenge raised by the "apostolic," revelation that arose during the 1913 meeting, hurt William J. Seymour deeply. Parham, Crawford, Durham, and those who promoted baptism in "Jesus' Name," at the 1913 camp meeting were all white folks. When many of the white ministers in the predominantly black church

---

278. Anderson and Hollenweger, *After a Century*, 91.
279. Bartlemann, *Azusa Street*, 51.
280. Daniels, "They Had a Dream," 19.
281. This was true not only for the USA. Hollenweger reported about South Africa: "Although the South African Pentecostal movement was initiated by blacks, the first church service took place in a black church in Doornfontein. John G. Lake (1870–1935) and Thomas Hazmalhach (1845–1934), the first Pentecostal missionaries in South Africa, had taken part in Seymour's church services and were therefore familiar with the non-racist practice of the early Pentecostal movement. There was, however, a theory that states that Lake approved of racial segregation in society. Despite this, it is certain that he tolerated no racism in the church. After Lake was moved from the black church in Doornfontein to a white Zionist church in the center of Johannesburg, he often publicly resisted those whites who wanted to expel from the church the later well-known Pentecostal leader, Elias Letaba, and kissed him before the eyes of the whole congregation" (Hollenweger, *Charismatisch-pfingstliches Christentum*, 57).

of God in Christ left that denomination in April 1914 and formed the Assemblies of God, not even the racially progressive Seymour was willing to trust many of his white Pentecostal brother and sisters. It is easy to understand why.[282]

There were consequences for Seymour from this experience: In 1915, he decided that until further notice, no more whites would take on responsibility within the church leadership—not until the climate in respect of the racial question had changed. He justified this step in *The Doctrines and Discipline of the Azusa Street Apostolic Faith Mission*:

> We find according to God's word to be one in the Holy Spirit, not in the flesh; but in the Holy Spirit, for we are one body. 1 Cor 12:12–14. If some of our white brethren have prejudices and discrimination (Gal 2:11–20), we can't do it, because God calls us to follow the Bible. Matt 17:8; Matt 24. We must love all men as Christ commands. (Heb 12:14). Now because we don't take them for directors it is not for discrimination, but for peace. To keep down race war in the churches and friction, so they can have greater liberty and freedom in the Holy Spirit. We are sorry for this, but it is the best now, and in later years, for the work. We hope everyone that reads these lines may realise it is for the best; not for the worse. Some of our white brethren and sisters have never left us in all the division; they have stuck to us. We love our white brethrens [sic] and sisters and welcome them. Jesus Christ takes in all people in his Salvation. Christ is all and for all. He is neither a black nor white man, nor Chinaman, nor Hindu, nor Japanese but God. God is Spirit because without his Spirit we cannot be saved. St. John 3:3–5; Rom 8:9.[283]

Robeck's interpretation of the events is as follows: "Clearly, Seymour may be credited with providing the vision of a truly color-blind congregation. His was a radical experiment that ultimately failed because of the inability of whites to allow for a sustained role of black leadership."[284] What was proclaimed in the Azusa Street Mission finds its continuation in the very early Pentecostal Movement: in North America, the movement divided into white and black organizations.[285] In South Africa, the Pentecostal church buckled under the pressure of society and within a

---

282. Robeck, *Azusa Street*, 318.
283. Seymour quoted in Robeck, *Azusa Street*, 319.
284. Anderson and Hollenweger, *After a Century*, 349.
285. Hollenweger, *Charismatisch-pfingstliches Christentum*, 32.

few months developed into a segregated movement.[286] The overcoming of racial discrimination, one of the loveliest flowers on the rosebush of the Pentecostal Movement, started to wither almost as soon as it had begun to bloom. Some denominations struggled for about twenty-five years (1909–1937) against the spreading segregation in the Pentecostal churches. The church *of God in Christ* and the *Pentecostal Assemblies of the World* are probably the two denominations which were most actively engaged in integrating black and white Christians in common churches.[287] In this sense, the equality of races can by no means be reduced to the awakening in the Azusa Street Mission but must be recognized as an important integral part of the early Pentecostal Movement.[288]

Underprivileged

With the term "underprivileged," we are describing those people who in terms of education, prosperity and social class (irrespective of gender of race) suffer disadvantages. In this section, we want to turn our attention toward these people.

William J. Seymour sees the mission to the marginalized pneumatologically justified in Luke 4:18.[289] This finds its expression in the confession of faith of the Azusa Street Papers: "The Apostolic Faith movement stands for . . . street and prison work."[290]

Empowerment through the Holy Spirit is obligated to the service of one's neighbor, in particular toward the underprivileged of society. The Azusa Street Mission was very active in its prison work, in service to people with physical limitations and addictions, people who were under oppression or suffered from prejudice, etc.[291] This obligation is part of the early Pentecostal DNA.[292] Besides the lived-out solidarity and the practical support for people in need, within the framework of the church service, the marginalized were able to have further important experiences:

286. Anderson and Hollenweger, *After a Century*, 94.
287. Daniels, "Transcending the Exclusionary," 143.
288. See also Daniels, "Everybody Bids You Welcome," 223–52.
289. Seymour, *Azusa Street Papers*, 286.
290. Seymour, *Azusa Street Papers*, 8.
291. Robeck, *Azusa Street*, 14.
292. As further literature, it is recommended to read Hollenweger, *Charismatisch-pfingstliches Christentum*, 209–11.

- The giving of honor[293]
- The awareness of belonging[294]
- A function/mission[295]
- Empowerment for service
- Strategies for the empowerment in everyday life[296]

Against the background of these experiences, it is not surprising that in 1936 the majority of Pentecostals in America lived in the poorly industrialized Southern States, were predominantly female, and the proportion of blacks in the church services was higher than their percentage in the population.[297] Moreover, "the average income of the members per Pentecostal church was below that of all American church communities, even below that of all American Negro churches."[298] In Latin America, the Pentecostal Movement likewise spread strongly amongst the underprivileged. Thus, Wilson writes about the Pentecostal beginnings in Chile:

> The practical consequences of Pentecostal doctrines and practices were the replacement of foreign control with national leadership and the formation of communities whose legitimacy was based on a radical interpretation of the nature of the church. In addition, the groups provided their adherents with a distinctive cause whose success rewarded them with an affirmation of their personal worth, an identity and corporate strength in a world hostile to the socially detached individual.[299]

293. Seymour, *Azusa Street Papers*, 116. Thus also the Swiss Pentecostal Widmer, *Gegen Satans Reich*, 46–50.

294. Seymour, *Azusa Street Papers*, 7.

295. Seymour, *Azusa Street Papers*, 8.

296. Seymour, *Azusa Street Papers*, 12. Thus Bryan R. Roberts writes: "I argue that Protestant sects . . . recruit such individuals because the sects alone provide accessible sets of social relationships that enable such individuals to cope with the practical problems of living in Guatemala City" (Roberts, "Protestant Groups," 759).

297. Hollenweger, *Enthusiastisches Christentum*, 27.

298. Hollenweger, *Enthusiastisches Christentum*, 27.

299. Wilson, "Passion and Power," 72. Even Kessler located the Pentecostal growth primarily amongst the poor of Chile: "Pentecostal growth has taken place chiefly among the hundreds of thousands of poor people who . . . have migrated from the countryside to the larger cities in search of a better living. These people needed new communities to replace those that they had left behind in their villages. The warmth of the meetings satisfied the religious longings of these simple people [and] participation of the congregation in several aspects of the service gave them the feeling that once again they belonged to a group" (Kessler in Wilson, "Passion and Power," 71–72).

According to Wilson, the development in Central America[300] and Brazil are comparable.[301] However, also in Europe the Pentecostal Movement found above-average acceptance amongst the underprivileged, as Hollenweger shows in an example from Italy, in the following passage:

> In the Pentecostal Movement the despised and exploited Italian discovered his human worth. He was taken seriously as a child of God amongst other children of God. He received a function (missionary work in his village) which he could carry out, if he had the courage to revitalise the centuries old hierarchical structure of his village. Thus a social-psychological process of far-reaching significance took place. With a diversity of songs learned by heart and a guitar he would go to the next village in the neighborhood and sing: "Dimmi la storia di Gesù [Bring me the message of Jesus]!" And now will the contempt of Jesus, his mockery, the "years of sorrow," "the suffering that He bore," His fear and aloneness was so described that the listeners recognized their fears in the sufferings of Jesus. In the glorification, resurrection and lordship of Christ he can relate to his own incarnation and resurrection to a new life. One fact necessary for this: The door to the human heart is only to be opened from within. From outside there is no door handle. "If you wish that Jesus comes to you then open the door from inside!" This decision is of great biographical and social-psychological significance for the Pentecostals. Thereby it is the first step toward the overcoming of a centuries old hierarchical society and church structure.[302]

In Switzerland, the ministry of Johann Widmer is denoted as one of the founding fathers of BewegungPlus. The ministry of Widmer does not so much appear to be "proof," for the validity of the biblical evidence for miracles but rather a struggle against poverty: Many could not afford the expensive medications, and prayer for healing was the only option against sickness. Accordingly, Widmer protested that the pharmaceutical companies were not interested in alleviating the hardships of the sick but were far more controlled by greed for profits and dividend-earning policy.[303] In its beginnings, the Swiss Pentecostal Mission, too, recruited the majority of its rank and file from the social background of the underprivileged. It is characteristic that Hollenweger termed the emergence

---

300. Wilson, "Passion and Power," 73–77.
301. Wilson, "Passion and Power," 77–80.
302. Hollenweger, *Enthusiastisches Christentum*, 300.
303. Widmer, *Gegen Satans Reich*, 71.

of the Zurich Pentecostal Church as a protest—"a group of people who found no home in the largest Swiss industrial city."[304]

These promising beginnings have also transformed over the course of time. Many Pentecostal churches in North America and Europe have evolved into middle-class churches. Cecilia Loreto Mariz says: "The Catholic church has decided for the poor, precisely because it is not a church of the poor. The Pentecostals do not have to decide for the poor, because they are already a church of the poor. And therefore the poor have decided for them."[305] The Pentecostals must now level this criticism of the Catholic church at themselves.

Pacifism

How have I come to deal with pacifism within the framework of social justice? This question appears to be justified for the reason that in den Azusa Street Papers the term pacifism is not mentioned. Now, the justification is to be found with Arthur Sydney Booth-Clibborn,[306] one of the earliest and most prominent voices in the service of pacifism, who labeled war as "organized sin":

> The Scriptures show us that organized sin or apostasy is much worse in the sight of God than are the sins of individuals, committed perhaps in sudden passion or a moral blindness induced by a laxity of principles in the religious, social or governmental strata above them, and the almost incredible want of respect for the Word of God which exists in a day when the word of man in every possible kind of publication is so passionately sought after.[307]

Hollenweger translated the somewhat curious term *organized sin* with the now familiar expression *structural injustice*.[308] The book *Blood against Blood,* in which Booth-Clibborn sets out his thoughts, was

---

304. Hollenweger, *Enthusiastisches Christentum*, 264.

305. Mariz quoted in Hollenweger, *Charismatisch-pfingstliches Christentum*, 234.

306. Arthur Sydney Booth-Clibborn (1855–1939) was a member of the Salvation Army and the son-in-law of William Booth, the founder of the Salvation Army. Even though Booth-Clibborn was not a Pentecostal, his influence on the early Pentecostal Movement was profound (Pipkin and Beaman, *Early Pentecostals*, xix).

307. Booth-Clibborn quoted in Hollenweger, *Charismatisch-pfingstliches Christentum*, 211.

308. Hollenweger, *Charismatisch-pfingstliches Christentum*, 211.

repeatedly extolled in the periodicals of the American Pentecostal Church (e.g., *Word and Witness*, church of God in Christ or *Weekly Evangel*, Assemblies of God) and was warmly received by the readership.[309] However, Booth-Clibborn is not the only one to point out the connection between war and structural injustice. Bartleman also shows in his article "War and the Christian" in the magazine *Word and Work* that war constitutes a profitable undertaking in which "Wall Street interests, Pork Barrel administration, Brewer's Corporation, Syndicate and Monopoly, Steel Trust and Armor Plate, Powder Trust, etc. without end," make great profits at the cost of the common man.[310] Bartleman argued that war makes the rich richer and the poor poorer. Profit is generated at the cost of the poor, in that the suffering of others is exploited: "Monopolists are increasing prices in food stuffs, etc., against the common people. Fattening on their blood, taking advantage of their distress. They are human leeches. The rich man's dog gets more meat than the poor man's family."[311]

For Beaman, it is unequivocal that pacifism was not a marginal issue within the early Pentecostal Movement and was intimately linked with the Pentecostal worldview: "Early Pentecostal leaders used a rhetoric which represented pretty much the whole movement as pacifist."[312] Many influential Pentecostals express themselves as pacifists, for example, in 1905, such as Charles Fox Parham in his article "Imminent Events in the United States"[313] and Aimee Semple McPherson in her paper "The Way to Disarm is to DISARM."[314]

We can make the assumption that the beginning of the Pentecostal Movement fostered a clearly pacifist ethos.[315] In 1917, the official politics of the Assemblies of God[316] were made clear in a letter to President Woodrow Wilson, in which the denomination, as a church of peace, declared: "Every branch of the movement, whether in the United States as well as in Canada, Great Britain and Germany" is pacifist.[317]

---

309. Hollenweger, *Charismatisch-pfingstliches Christentum*, 215.
310. Bartleman quoted in Pipkin and Beaman, *Early Pentecostals*, 112–25.
311. Bartleman quoted in Pipkin and Beaman, *Early Pentecostals*, 60–63.
312. Beaman, *Pentecostal Pacifism*, 2.
313. Pipkin and Beaman, *Early Pentecostals*, 2–5.
314. Pipkin and Beaman, *Early Pentecostals*, 144–46.
315. Hollenweger, *Charismatisch-pfingstliches Christentum*, 211.
316. See also the article by Robins, "Chronology of Peace."
317. Hollenweger, *Charismatisch-pfingstliches Christentum*, 212.

Beaman sees Pentecostal pacifism as eschatologically and missiologically motivated:

> Chief among the elements of that worldview were intense millennial expectations coupled with anti-nationalistic allegiances. Millennial expectations placed hope for a just society outside of the present configuration of power in this world. This fuelled an anti-nationalistic sentiment as did their missionary zeal and redemptive identification with other peoples around the world. They found war repulsive because of its obvious incongruence with the missionary impulse. . . . These elements of their world view, coupled with a restorationist view of the church, provided a matrix of which pacifism was an integral part.[318]

This is also evident for example with Bartlemann. He writes in *Christian Citizenship*:

> One of the greatest crimes of the late war was that of robbing the church of her sacred calling to a "pilgrim" role, turning her aside from the saving of souls, to plunge her into the vortex of world politics and patriotism, with all its fallen prejudices and preferences, avarice, cruelties, hate and murder . . . the church has no place to flaunt flags of national preference. God's grace and gospel are international. Christ died for all men.[319]

Likewise, the Swiss Pentecostal Mission was pacifist in its beginnings. Jean Daniel Plüss quotes Richard Ruff, who wrote in 1935 that war

> is in every case a work of Satan. . . . Nationalism and patriotism are deep forces in the human soul and emotional life which then become most dangerous when they combine with religious ideas of calling and mission. . . . However would a child of God follow me without more ado these days if I also presented the war of liberation as an expression of force, which is soulish and not godly . . . and as a defensive war? . . . That he also merely fill the land with dead bodies.[320]

For Ruff, it is important not to be thrown into the same pot as secular pacifists:

> We are not pacifists in the sense of this world; also not anti-militarists, such as are making trouble for the rulers in this present

---

318. Beaman quoted in Beaman, *Pentecostal Pacifism*, 37–38.
319. Bartlemann quoted in Beaman, *Pentecostal Pacifism*, 55.
320. Plüss, *Vom Geist bewegt*, 72.

time as conscientious objectors.... But we hate war and cannot uphold it as a valid means for the establishment of justice and peace in the world.[321]

Ruff is aware that pacifism does not prevent suffering and bloodshed. However, "We nevertheless cry out in view of the final victory of light over the darkness: 'Curse the murder of brothers, curse war! Hail our King and Prince of Peace, Jesus Christ, who is to come!'"[322] Even when war is condemned: Military service for the defense of the fatherland was observed by many Pentecostals, and in 1940 was even denoted as biblical by the movement leaders of the Pentecostal mission: "We are in principle not conscious objectors. Military service is biblical, especially in our nation, where one is not forced to carry a weapon."[323]

In Germany, the situation was more complex. The Pentecostal churches in Germany in the pre-war period were, in the majority, pro Hitler because they saw in him an ally against the threat of atheistic communism. Pentecostals participated in the German army during the Second World War, and at the same time others suffered for their faith in concentration camps.[324]

The pacifist attitude of the majority of the Pentecostal Movement changed over the decades. One expression of this is that, for example, the Assemblies of God, as well as other Pentecostal denominations, provided military chaplains.[325]

Criticism and Appreciation

In the various sections on the equality of women, the equality of race, the mandate in favor of the underprivileged and pacifism, I have already included appreciative and critical thoughts. To complement these, we shall now consider the beginnings of the Pentecostal Movement through the eyes of Ragaz, Gutiérrez, Cone, and Moltmann:

Fully aligned with the values of Ragaz, Cone, Gutiérrez and Moltmann, the early Pentecostal Movement was (primarily) a church of the

---

321. Plüss, *Vom Geist bewegt*, 72.

322. Plüss, *Vom Geist bewegt*, 72.

323. Plüss, *Vom Geist bewegt*, 81.

324. Plüss, *Vom Geist bewegt*, 87–92. See also, for example, the history of the Mülheim association in Junghardt and Vetter, *Ruhrfeuer*, 144–50.

325. Hollenweger, *Charismatisch-pfingstliches Christentum*, 212.

marginalized, which was recruited from an African American congregation. It *was*, to use the words of Gutiérrez, the "primary option for the poor." The Azusa Street Mission managed to create a community with which those excluded from society could identify.[326] It was a community which was not defined by the usual criteria such as race, language or nationality. Rather, it saw itself, as Ragaz would say, as a community of Spirit-filled children of God. The culture of this community indicated unmistakable traces of the various influences, although it was significantly characterised by a pneumatological-eschatological identity: the Kingdom of God identity.[327] Ragaz would probably say it is precisely this identity that brings the authentic supernatural and prophetic power to the Pentecostal Movement. The movement was also very close to the vision of Cone, who in enthusiastically celebrated church services saw, through the working of the Holy Spirit, a realization of the future eschatological Kingdom of God. During the church service worship, the power of the Holy Spirit, which changes everything, was manifested; it did not bring about the cosmic eschaton but the identity of the people and thus also transformed the entire gathered community. The presence of the Holy Spirit thereby became a liberating experience, which expressed itself in self-perception, in the interaction between people and in the enthusiastically celebrated church service. The approach formulated by Cone, the "eyes to see" and "heart to feel," was not only a living experience in the Azusa Street Mission but it also bore fruit with guests and visitors. The liberty brought about by the Holy Spirit is not merely an inversion of the power relationships but, as Moltmann claims, a liberation for reconciled fellowship: Under the leadership of Seymour, we find a community of blacks, Asians, Hispanics, whites, women, men, children, educated, uneducated, poor and rich, etc., who celebrated the reign of God as equals. In this sense, at the beginnings of the Pentecostal Movement, we find an unprecedented concentration of the most diverse elements of different theologically justified social ethics.

There are, however, also significant differences between the non-Pentecostal voices and the Azusa Street Mission: The Pentecostal

326. This approach followed the confirmation by Catholic Julio de Santa Ana: "The theology of liberation provided one option for the poor, however the poor opted for the Pentecostal churches" (Wenk, "Pfingstliche Pneumatologie," 301). See also, for example, the commentary by Kliewer: "The Pentecostal church is the 'church of the poor,' in contrast to the Catholic church, the 'church of rich people,' and the traditional protestant denominations committed to the middle class" (*Neue Volk der Pfingstler*, 92).

327. See, for example, Pipkin and Beaman, *Early Pentecostals*, 6–16.

response to social justice was, as already mentioned, an alternative society, hence primarily an inner-church event. This event was taken to the world through mission work in society, by which the people were invited to become part of the community, part of the church. Structural injustice (e.g., segregation, warmongering) was well thematized, but the causes were not tackled on an economic, political or legal level. With regard to the economic question, the engagement was restricted to combatting the effects of poverty. Segregation was condemned but not fought legally. Besides Ragaz, also Cone and Gutiérrez have expressed criticism of this Pentecostal practice. The fact is that despite the direct encounter between blacks and whites, and all the powerful working of the Holy Spirit, not all eyes were opened and not all hearts had feeling. This was true not only for people outside the Pentecostal community—but racism also remained present within the Pentecostal Movement.[328] Here I shall pose the following question to the Pentecostal church: Can the struggle for social justice be reduced to inner-church events, or does the church not perhaps also have the task of fighting for justice outside the church, as for example Ragaz preached? The Catholic-charismatic periodical *New Covenant* is of the opinion: "An authentic move of the Holy Spirit would not be content with giving only to the family or to the church community. It would inevitably partake in the establishment of justice and liberty in national and international relationships."[329]

How to Go Forward

The beginnings of the Pentecostal Movement in the Azusa Street Mission are fascinating and challenging in a number of respects. What continuing impetus can be gained from this chapter for the remaining work? In order to discover this, we shall follow the development of the Pentecostal Movement beyond its beginnings and attempt to sharpen the image in order to draw further conclusions.

The Further Development

The Pentecostal Movement was, in its beginnings, an extremely heterogeneous movement whose social practice was strongly influenced and

---

328. Hollenweger, *Charismatisch-pfingstliches Christentum*, 34, 59.
329. "Leaders of Latin American Renewal."

formed by the needs and questions of the respective local circumstances. The practice of social justice in the Pentecostal setting shines strongly against the areas of conflict in societal conditions and the overwhelming experience of the Holy Spirit "breaking out." The existential experience of God and the integration of various spiritual forms of expression are of central importance for the Azusa Street Mission. This unique fusion of different cultures occurred through the participants who came from a diversity of ethnic and national backgrounds. It is also exactly these characteristics which triggered opposition.

The church culture of the Azusa Street Mission was experienced as offensive by the secular society because they violated the conventional rules of society. Therefore, it is not surprising that the inclusion practised in the Pentecostal church service partly led to violent reactions:

> While Los Angeles was not yet the hotbed of "Jim Crow," activity that many other parts of the nation were at the time, the racial sensitivities of many Angelinos were deeply challenged by the mingling of races, classes, and genders at the mission. . . . From the perspective of many Angelinos,[330] it was a scandal that carried far reaching implications for the status quo of the larger social order in the United States.[331]

The consequence of this was that members of the mission were regularly publicly ridiculed for their zeal. And not only that: "Viewed as fanatics, many of its members were arrested, fined, and jailed on grounds that they were insane."[332] The Los Angeles Police Department even went so far as to send police officers into the revival meetings.[333]

The working of the Holy Spirit also did not automatically lead to an overcoming of social conventions and boundaries within the movement. Thus, there were also racist statements and segregative efforts within the Pentecostal Movement. Prominent examples of this in the USA are Charles Fox Parham, Warren Faye Carothers, and Kathryn Kuhlmann.[334]

---

330. Inhabitants of Los Angeles.
331. Robeck, *Azusa Street*, 14.
332. Robeck, *Azusa Street*, 12.
333. Robeck, *Azusa Street*, 12.
334. Hollenweger handles this fact as though he interprets racism as a loss of the Holy Spirit (Hollenweger, *Charismatisch-pfingstliches Christentum*, 34). Such an interpretation is questionable, in my opinion. However, it is also certain that the claim to be a Spirit-filled Christian in combination with racism should rightly raise questions. See also Hollenweger, *Charismatisch-pfingstliches Christentum*, 43–44.

These phenomena did not only occur in the USA; for example, in Europe, Levi Petrus can be named.[335] The early movement soon developed into a segregated movement, which until today—except for a couple of exceptions—has a majority of racially separated congregations.[336]

> The racial harmony of Azusa Street waned within a few months, and as a result, Pentecostalism remains racially divided with very limited progress toward reconciliation. While in the early years women enjoyed considerable freedom in ministry, often surpassing that of women in the established Protestant denominations, their prominence has declined with but few exceptions.[337]

It has already been stated that the equality of women underwent a similar development to that of racial equality.[338] Certainly, in comparison with their usual position in society, or in comparison with other churches, women played a major role in the beginnings of the Pentecostal Movement despite all the restrictions.[339] At the same time, it is certain

---

335. Levi Petrus has been sympathizing with the German *Naitonalsozialismus*. He was familiar with Hitler's *Mein Kampf*, wore a *Führer*-style Mustache, etc. But there is also to mention that Levi was one of the first to protest against antisemitism after the Nazi started to persecute Jews in Norway.

336. That the Pentecostal Movement is very well aware of this abuse is reflected in that, for example, the Assemblies of God has taken steps toward integration, such as the so-called Memphis Miracle of 1994. With this incident, the exclusively white Pentecostal Fellowship of North America was dissolved and a new organization named Pentecostal/Charismatic Churches of North America was founded, which was composed of white and black Pentecostal churches. Whether the miracle of Memphis is more than merely a symbolic act remains to be seen. A critical view of the significance of the Memphis Miracle is found in *Pneuma* 18.1 (1996) with articles by Frank Macchia, Samuel Solivan, Barbara A. Amos, Cecil M. Robeck, Leonard Lovett, Ithiel E. Clemmons, and Manuel J. Gaxiola-Gaxiola.

337. Anderson and Hollenweger, "Introduction," xviii.

338. The handling of the ordination of women in Switzerland is symptomatic for the whole of Europe. In Switzerland, in BewegungPlus, it was not until 2004 that the first woman was ordained (Russel, *Erinnerungen*, 128–29). In the Swiss Pentecostal Mission, the ordination of women is not recognized even today (https://www.pfingstmission.ch/bereiche/ausbildung/pastor/#c166).

339. Besides the Azusa Street Mission, there are only very few exceptions known which practice equality against current societal norms. I would like to mention three noteworthy examples here. The Salvation Army, whose first corps was founded in 1880 in the USA, already practiced equality of the sexes at an institutional level (Heimowski, *Heilsarmee*, 22). Furthermore, there are individual people whose ministries are recognized as equal, such as Elizabeth Mix, the first African American with a full-time evangelistic healing ministry, who leads a group of the African American Healing Movement (Daniels, "They Had a Dream," 20).

that the outpouring of the Holy Spirit did not remove all the boundaries in this connection. It is with good reason that Stephenson writes:

> What becomes evident is that while Pentecostals' belief in the outpouring of the Holy Spirit removed some barriers for women in Pentecostal churches, it certainly did not remove all of them. In the beginning of the movement, Pentecostals merely superimposed an ideology of empowerment over a dualistic anthropology. The outpouring of the Holy Spirit did not affect Pentecostals' anthropological dualism. It only complemented the ideas that were already present. Consequently, Pentecostal women's experience has been that of perpetual ecclesial restrictions in one way or another.[340]

From a church of the marginalized arose (at least in the industrialized nations) a predominantly middle-class church, which through social advancement has disconnected from the issues of the underprivileged. Harvey Cox, a theologian who identifies himself as one of the Pentecostal Movement's associates, in *Personal Reflections on Pentecostalism* summarizes the development of the Pentecostal Movement as follows:

> There is cause for genuine concern. In America, most white Pentecostals have become terribly comfortable with "this world." They started out as a faith that brought hope to the rejects and the losers. Today, some of their most visible representatives have become ostentatiously rich. They started out as a rebellion against creeds. Today many of their preachers cling doggedly to such recently invented dogmas as the verbal inerrancy of the Bible. They started out teaching that the signs and wonders that took place in their congregations were not some kind of spectral fireworks but harbingers of God's new day. Today some Pentecostals have become so obsessed with the techniques of rapture that they have forgotten the original message. They started out as radical antagonists of the status quo, refusing to fight the bloody wars of this fallen age. Many have now turned into flag-waving super-patriots, easy marks for the demagogues of the new religious right. They started out as a radically inclusive spiritual fellowship in which race and gender discrimination virtually disappeared. That is hardly the case, at least in most white Pentecostals churches today.[341]

---

340. Stephenson, *Dismantling the Dualisms*, 57.
341. Cox, "Personal Reflexions," 34.

Cox's criticism is at least also applicable to the Pentecostal churches in Switzerland, if not also for the majority of the Pentecostal churches native to the industrialized nations. However, we also wish to hear the optimistic side of Cox's analysis:

> But I have not given up hope. In fact what impressed me most about the people I met at the SPS was not just their openness to dialogue but also their commitment to rescue their own movement from the distortions it has suffered, especially in recent years. What I found there was an expanding company of young Pentecostal leaders who are determined not to barter the power of their remarkable movement for a questionable batch of currently popular religious and political slogans. They are determined not to lose touch with the poor and disinherited with whom they started out. And they are determined that the Holy City, seen of John, which has been so central to their vision for so long, will not remain forever a dream.[342]

Further Questions and Ideas

Must the Pentecostal Movement be rescued, as Cox says? If so, where and how? How did it happen that the Pentecostal Movement betrayed its social values, which were so important for the original Pentecostal DNA? Why did white preachers from the Southern States come and allow Seymour to lay hands on them so that they would be filled with the Holy Spirit—and then found their own segregated white churches and movement? Did the white Pentecostals only cooperate with Seymour until they got what they wanted? As they were "touched," by the Holy Spirit, did they have the feeling that the blacks were no longer needed? Was the temporary inclusion of the races merely a means to an end and the racial prejudice ultimately stronger? It is not seen as totally absurd that there were repeated attempts by white brothers to take over the leadership of the Azusa Street Mission, at least with regard to these ideas.[343] However, as Michael Palmer rightly observes: The reasons that the Pentecostal Movement has moved so far away from its roots are complex and

---

342. Cox, "Personal Reflexions," 34.
343. See above Underprivileged in "Social Justice and Pnematology," 69–72.

multi-layered.³⁴⁴ Nevertheless, we wish to consider a couple of attempts at explanation:

Hollenweger he sees the cause of the problem in social ascent. The Pentecostal Movement developed from a church of the poor and marginalized into a middle-class church. This middle-class church may well have a Pentecostal concept theology, but in its practice, it adopted an evangelical theology.³⁴⁵ He considers the evangelical theology of dispensationalism as particularly problematic, which links salvation unilaterally to the conversion of sinners.³⁴⁶ Thus, socio-ethical engagement, if there is any, is only deemed justified if souls are saved as a result. Social engagement is reduced to a means to an end, and no longer has intrinsic value. Women are at once defined by the evangelical understanding of Scripture and are relegated to the second row.

Robeck pulls in a similar direction with his explanatory approach. He also sees evangelicalization as the main reason for the theological development of the Pentecostal Movement. In this respect, Robeck recognizes the change from postmillennialism to premillennialism (dispensationalism), and the identification of social justice as a tool of liberal theology, as concrete consequences of evangelicalization.³⁴⁷

L. Lovett, an African American Pentecostal, provides a further approach. He says,

> The black Pentecostal Movement adheres to the biblical dogma that liberation is always a consequence of the working of the Holy Spirit. Authentic liberation can absolutely not happen outside of a genuine Pentecostal experience. Similarly, there can be no genuine Pentecostal experience without liberation following as a consequence. In other words, nobody can experience the fullness of the Holy Spirit and remain a racist with a good conscience.³⁴⁸

Lovett's statement leads us into the middle of the inter-Pentecostal debate about the significance of Pentecost and the characteristics of a Spirit-filled life. We shall present this debate in chapter 3. What can already be said with certainty at this point is that the powerful effects of the Holy

---

344. Palmer, "Ethics and the Classical Pentecostal Tradition," 608.
345. Hollenweger, *Charismatisch-pfingstliches Christentum*, 31–32.
346. Hollenweger, *Charismatisch-pfingstliches Christentum*, 229–30.
347. See also Althouse, *Last Days*, 193.
348. Lovett in Hollenweger, *Charismatisch-pfingstliches Christentum*, 44.

Spirit are clearly not linked to a "right," or "false," theology, just as good theology is not necessarily produced by the powerful effects of the Holy Spirit. The working of the Holy Spirit can therefore not be used as proof for a "right," "good," or "biblical," theology. And yet it is the Holy Spirit who, in the beginnings of the Azusa Street Mission, first caused integration to become very real and tangible.[349]

What conclusion can we draw from these attempts at justification for our further approach?

a. The doctrine for racially integrated church services and for the ministry of women being recognized as equal already existed a long time before the Azusa Street Mission. This was likewise true for theologically justified pacifism. These approaches are not spontaneous fruits of the Pentecostal fire but the result of longer processes of ecclesial and spiritual formation into which the experiences of women, men, blacks, whites, etc. have been incorporated.[350] As long as there is a mixing of the privileged, the oppressed and the disadvantaged and their voices are heard as equal, then social justice is a theme within the congregations.

b. The process set out in (a) is closely related to Gutiérrez's and Segundo's hermeneutic. It starts with the status quo of society and the churches' practice in response to this. A critical theological reflection on this church practice is undertaken, from which new, further-reaching approaches of action are formulated for practice which find their expression in the everyday life of attendees of the Azusa Street Mission.[351] This observation shows how important it is

---

349. A less plausible explanation attempt is the argument of a change of generations. After twenty years, the majority of the founding generation had died off. With the disappearance of the founding generation the first fire went out, and the central concerns of the first Pentecostals disappeared. An argument against this explanation is the fact that the Assemblies of God, for the most part, presented a segregated structure right from the beginning. On the contrary, other movements, such as the Salvation Army, have managed to maintain their social concern for the poor over a time period of more than 160 years. The devaluation of social concern in the Pentecostal movement, in my opinion, can only be poorly justified by generational change.

350. Donald Dayton points out that the Pentecostal holiness movement inherited a Lukan focus on the Pentecostal narrative and the role of the Holy Spirit in holiness (Dayton, *Theological Roots*, 87–92). As we shall see with Wenk, for example, Pentecostals utilize Acts as a narrative context in which they can speak about social justice.

351. This approach is also suggested by Peterson, "Kingdom," 44–56.

to have a serious theological confrontation between the realities of society and church practice.

c. If the critical-theological reflection wants to be true to the Holy Spirit of the Azusa Street-Mission, it has to be eschatological-pneumatological by nature. On the way to such a theology, there are no shortcuts via theological "import systems," which are borrowed from other church traditions and "Pentecostalized" with the baptism in the Holy Spirit. Rather, this theology must be developed against the background of the Pentecostal experience, the teaching of Jesus about the emerging Kingdom of God and the working of the Holy Spirit.

d. Parham and Seymour knew the teachings of the healing movement, had the same experience of the Holy Spirit, drank from the same well—and yet, in the racial question, they arrived at completely different applications of practice. Does this have to do with the fact that one pointed to the Pentecostal experience from the position of the privileged and the other from the position of the oppressed? One thing is certain: For the privileged equality meant (whether this now referred to the racial or the gender question) surrendering privileges, whilst for the oppressed equality meant a new freedom.

e. The Azusa Street Mission experience makes its contribution to the formation of theology when it includes the voices of all participating groups, cultures and backgrounds. Only when the voices of the oppressed and the marginalized, with their everyday experiences, are heard and understood, can their criticism of the societal reality and the practice of the church be brought together, and a constructive contribution be developed.

f. In the context of this theology, the Holy Spirit can be experienced as comforting, identity-giving, overcoming, healing, and reconciliatory power. It is this context that prevents the Pentecostal Movement from reducing the work of the Spirit to signs and wonders. However, it is also the context of this theology which shows that the Kingdom of God is not possible without the working of the Holy Spirit. What was previously only possible in individual cases became "normal," through the working of the Holy Spirit in the church and allowed this to become a prophetic counter-society.

Whatever the reasons may be for the later development of the Pentecostal Movement, its beginnings show that it provided an alternative to the contemporary societal interaction with 'otherness.' In this sense I shall conclude chapter 2 with a quote from Robeck:

> The Azusa Street Mission provides a glimpse of what is possible if we allow space for the Holy Spirit to change hearts and minds. It may also provide a model for congregations in our own day to embrace this same kind of diversity, to demonstrate before the world the power of the gospel to break down the artificial racial and ethnic walls that otherwise divide us, as the apostle so eloquently noted in Ephesians 2:11–22.[352]

---

352. Robeck, *Azusa Street*, 14–15.

2

Social Justice in Pentecostal Theology

A Selection

THE EMPHASIS ON SOCIAL justice could not be more different within the current global Pentecostal Movement. While questions of social justice arise in the majority of the world due to the prevailing political, economic and environmental circumstances, this topic was neglected in the European and North American Pentecostal churches for a long time.[1] The fact that this is changing for the better is shown by the publications that explicitly address the issue of social justice. Many communities and movements are rediscovering the importance of social issues and are making this part of their social engagement,[2] be this of a political nature, in the fight against poverty and disease, in education or in efforts toward peace and reconciliation.[3]

Matthias Wenk

Born 1960 in Switzerland, Matthias Wenk grew up with his mother as the youngest of three brothers. Following banking studies (equivalent to a

---

1. Hollenweger, "Social Justice"; Wenk, "Holy Spirit as Transforming Power"; Warrington, *Pentecostal Theology*, 226–29.
2. Warrington, *Pentecostal Theology*, 229.
3. Warrington, *Pentecostal Theology*, 236; Volf, *Exclusion and Embrace*.

bachelor's degree in business administration), he decided to study theology. He graduated with a Bachelor of Arts in Theology at the *Europäisches Theologisches Seminar* (ETS)[4] in Rudersberg, Germany, in 1989, and with a Master of Divinity at the Pentecostal Theological Seminary in Cleveland, Tennessee, in 1990. In the following, Wenk returned to the ETS in Rudersberg, this time as a lecturer. In parallel to his lecturing activities, he worked on a dissertation with the title *Community-Forming Power: The Socio-Ethical Role of the Holy Spirit in Luke-Acts*. In 1998, the dissertation was submitted, accepted, and in 2000 it was published by Brunel University London under the supervision of the London Bible College (Dr. Max Turner).

In 1999, Wenk returned to Switzerland and took up his duties as a pastor in a small Pentecostal church in the village of Hindelbank. In parallel to his pastoral activities, Wenk took on a part-time position as a lecturer at the Theologisch-Diakonische Seminar in Aarau (1999–2017). Furthermore, he held guest lectures at the Ecumenical Institute in Bossey and with IGW (Institut für Gemeinde Weiterbildung). Meanwhile, Wenk became co-pastor of the BewegungPlus church at Burgdorf, a member of the national committee of *BewegungPlus*[5] and, in addition to leading the theological training course *Professional*,[6] he continued to teach as a guest lecturer. Together with Jean Daniel-Plüss, Matthias Wenk is one of the most renowned active Pentecostal theologians in German-speaking regions. His works are well known throughout the German-speaking world. Wenk is married to Elisabeth, is the father of three grown-up sons, and grandfather to three grandchildren.

The theses developed by Wenk in his dissertation are fundamental for his further theological works. His dissertation shall therefore provide the main focus in the analysis of his theology in the following section, and further publications shall likewise be considered in a second part.

---

4. Formerly the Europäisches Bibelseminar (EBS).

5. BewegungPlus (formerly Gemeinde für Urchristentum) is a Pentecostal church. It is a member of the international Pentecostal church association of the Apostolic church, which traces its roots back to the revival of 1904–1905 in Wales, UK, and was later significantly influenced by the Azusa Street Revival.

6. The Professional is a church-based theological training course of BewegungPlus.

The Socio-Ethical Role of the Holy Spirit in the Lukan Double Work

Wenk approached the subject of social ethics from the perspective of the New Testament scholars.[7] This is also the starting point of his dissertation: He poses the question of whether the Lukan pneumatology exhibits an ethical dimension, a thesis which was then rejected by the majority of New Testament research.[8] In his investigations Wenk used the method of speech-act theory from Austin and Searle.[9] In simple terms, using the speech-act theory, Wenk has divided the speech of God into (1) the content of the Spirit-inspired message, (2) the divine purpose behind the Spirit-inspired message, and (3) the transformative effects of the Spirit-inspired message on the listeners. With the methodology of the speech-act theory, Wenk manages to demonstrate that in the Lukan double work, the Spirit-inspired spoken word is more than simply prophetic/Spirit-inspired information. Rather, whenever God speaks (be it through angels, dreams, prophets or circumstances), it is a complex, interactive process between God, the mediator, the inspired message and the audience to whom the message is addressed. The intention of this process is, as already mentioned, not a simple exchange of information, but the transformation of the speaker and the listeners.

In order to illustrate Wenk's working method, we shall look at the beginning of his analysis, which he positions in the intertestamental period. For the time between the prophet Malachi and the birth of Jesus (a period of approximately four centuries), no biblical evidence is found for God speaking *amongst* His people. One widely held theory assumes that God actually remained silent for various reasons during that time.[10] Wenk demonstrates in a plausible way that the intertestamental period is not characterized by the silence of God,[11] but by the lack of willingness to recognize God's messengers and message as such, and to get involved with God's purpose:

---

7. Wenk, "Holy Spirit as Transforming Power," is a good example of how the New Testament shaped Wenk's social ethics work.

8. See also Gunkel, *Influence of the Holy Spirit*; Schweizer, *Heiliger Geist*; Menzies, *Development of Early Christian Pneumatology*.

9. Wenk, *Community-Forming Power*, 133. For notes on the use of the speech-act theory within theology, see Wenk, *Community-Forming Power*, 133n33, 134n37.

10. See also Sommer's arguments in Wenk, *Community-Forming Power*, 124.

11. Wenk, *Community-Forming Power*, 125.

> Whenever the target audience no longer acknowledges the prophet as such, the audience is neither cooperative nor adversarial but distant and thereby does not engage in the transformative process that is usually anticipated by the prophetic utterance. *In this sense* prophecy has ceased—at least from the perspective of the audience that does not recognize the prophetic word. From the perspective of the prophet, the message proclaimed does not engage the audience in a process leading to the intended transformation, but prophecy as such has not ceased.[12]

This understanding led Wenk further, to a working hypothesis:

> Prophetic speech was recognized as the initiation of a process by which the people of God were engaged in covenantal interaction with the divine. Often the aim of inspired speech was to restore or enhance covenant loyalty among God's people. In other cases, it was to provide special insight which in turn became the avenue by which Yahweh realised his salvific intentions for God's people (his covenant faithfulness). . . . This in turn suggests that often the transformation of the audience, either in their deeds or hope, was the ultimate aim of prophecy and of the Spirit's activity. It seems thus that the Spirit's role cannot be limited to the content of the speech, stripping it artificially from God's intention through speech.[13]

This conclusion further led to the question of what kind of transformation is intended through the Spirit-inspired speech. Wenk's analysis of the childhood narrative of Jesus indicates that it amounts to nothing less than the enunciation of a new worldview, which in turn will shape the ethos of an entire population group.[14] As an example of Wenk's line of argument within the childhood account, we shall take a look at Luke 1:13–17. On the one hand, Wenk addresses the promise which is related to the reconciliation ministry of John the Baptist, and on the other hand the Jewish expectations in connection with the coming Elijah. In conclusion, he says regarding the work of John: "The covenant with God will be restored and so will Torah obedience; what and who is clean or unclean will be newly defined, and peace will return to this world. The primary

---

12. Wenk, *Community-Forming Power*, 127.
13. Wenk, *Community-Forming Power*, 132.
14. Wenk, *Community-Forming Power*, 147.

result is not described as a renewal of prophecy, but as a renewal of the covenant, including a redefinition of the community."[15]

In Luke 1:39–80 it can be seen how the divine promise transformed relationships through the power of the Holy Spirit. Wenk describes the events as follows:

> John's relationships as established above exemplify his ministry. He is to reconcile what is separated. He is placed in relationship to the various parties involved in the narrative that are alienated from each other. Filled with the Holy Spirit while still in his mother's womb he stands between God and humanity and between "fathers and sons" as a mediator, expected to fulfil the role of the eschatological Elijah. His ministry is defined as "to make a people prepared for the Lord," specified with a double ἐπιστρέφω. John will "turn" the sons of Israel to the Lord their God, and the hearts of the fathers to their sons. His ministry is expected to lead the people to a renewed Torah obedience and an interpersonal reconciliation. Thus, in Luke 1:13–17 expectations of renewed obedience, reconciliation and restoration of the covenant and community are correlated with the Spirit's work in and through John. . . . John is not simply introduced as one who will speak Spirit-inspired words, but as one who due to the infilling of the Spirit will be great before the Lord and who under the influence of the Spirit will "make ready a people prepared for the Lord." Hence, the Spirit is expected to have an ethical influence on John and on the community's life.[16]

Wenk sees the first two chapters of Luke's gospel as an introduction to the Lukan double work, which sets the scene for "God's final intervention in human history."[17] The filling with the Holy Spirit of John is not primarily portrayed in connection with Spirit-inspired speech, but with empowerment for a ministry of reconciliation which manifests itself at two levels: The people are to be reconciled with God and also with each other. Furthermore, it is also to be attributed to the work of the Holy Spirit that John will become "great" in the sight of the Lord (Luke 1:15). In relation to Jesus, Wenk sees the Holy Spirit as the power which creates new life, produces divine Sonship as well as the holiness of Christ. Thereby the working of the Holy Spirit in the Lukan childhood narrative cannot be reduced to inspired speech, but even here it is seen as the power at work

15. Wenk, *Community-Forming Power*, 159.
16. Wenk, *Community-Forming Power*, 160–61.
17. Wenk, *Community-Forming Power*, 171.

which will affect the regeneration of the people of God, and thereby also signals an ethical influence, on and through John and Jesus.[18]

Then, in the later ministry of John, the working of the Holy Spirit announced in the childhood narrative also became real. Through John, a redefinition took place, which changed radically the requirement for membership to God's covenant people and led his listeners into a transformative experience (reconciliation between the generations and between God and His people).[19] The transformative experience which John initiated finds its continuation and completion in the ministry of Christ, who baptizes not with water but with "Spirit and fire."

In the following section, we shall not discuss the biblical-theological argumentation of Wenk's dissertation, but concentrate on the socio-ethical issues which are significant for this present study.

The New Exodus

In his argumentation, Wenk refers to Strauss and Turner, who emphasize a "new Exodus motif" in Jesus' anointing and mission. According to Turner and Wenk, Luke builds

> upon this Isaianic New Exodus to characterise Jesus' mission: his "ministry of proclamation and action, undertaken in the full power of God's Spirit, was thus to lead her [Israel] to her 'salvation,' making her a light to the Gentiles." For Turner this becomes evident in Luke's account of Jesus' baptism as well as the programmatic sermon in Nazareth. In both instances the Isaianic Servant of the Lord, who is to liberate Israel along a New Exodus typology, plays a central role in defining Jesus' mission.[20]

Wenk further develops Turner's motif with respect to the new Exodus, by demonstrating the ethical significance of the Lukan pneumatology: For Judaism in general, and for Luke in particular, it holds true that the liberating action of God is normative for the ethos of fellowship. In the Old Testament, the connection between salvation and ethics in the decalogue is evident. Thus, it says in Exodus: "I am the LORD your God! I have brought you out of Egypt, I have freed you from slavery. You

---

18. Wenk, *Community-Forming Power*, 172.

19. Wenk, *Community-Forming Power*, 188.

20. Wenk, *Community-Forming Power*, 191–92, quoting Turner. See also Turner, *Power from on High*, 204–8, 244–53.

should . . ." (Exod 20:2, Gute Nachricht Bibel). Also in Deuteronomy, several Laws were put in place in respect of God's liberating action. In this respect, Wenk stresses that this connection with social laws is made remarkably often (for example the treatment of widows, orphans and strangers). Conversely, the connection to the Exodus experience is also to be found with the prophets whenever the people sinned against the Law and were called to turn back to God. It is therefore not surprising that the prophets, in their repentance call to the people, also directly refer to the Sabbath year and the Jubilee year—both motifs which were established in connection with the Exodus and intended to ensure justice.[21]

Luke follows this Old Testament pattern and uses God's saving intervention as a paradigm for the ethos of the new people of God. He ties this ethos to the ministry of Jesus in the form of the new Exodus.[22] As an example, in Luke 6:36 Jesus establishes the commandment to love one's enemy based on God's compassion, which the disciples had experienced in their own lives.

The motif of the "new Exodus" stands out most clearly in the text of Luke 4:16–30. The quoted text from Isaiah 58:6 and 61:1–2, found in Luke 4:16–30, is a prophetic call for the restoration of the Exodus people.[23] It is God's Spirit who rests upon the messianic messengers, and the same Spirit restores righteousness, mercy and the knowledge of God through the Messiah. The emphasis of Isaiah 58:6 and 61:1–2 is focussed almost exclusively on renewed interpersonal relationships. In summary Wenk writes:

> The realisation of the good news for the poor, accomplished by the anointed messiah, is expected to be expressed in a restoration of relationships and is expressed in a renewed order—which is to become God's new people. This can be summarized as the "year of the Lord's favour."[24]

In order to understand the significance of the liberation proclaimed in Luke 4:16–30, it is important to identify those who are denoted as the "poor." This is even more important for recognizing the intended transformation of the inspired word. If we consider the recipients of the good news between Luke 4:16–30 (the prolepsis) and 7:22 (the analepsis), the "poor" can be identified:

21. Wenk, *Community-Forming Power*, 204.
22. Wenk, *Community-Forming Power*, 205.
23. Wenk, *Community-Forming Power*, 209.
24. Wenk, *Community-Forming Power*, 210.

They are the various persons that have been healed and delivered from demonic bondage (Luke 4:31–44); a man with leprosy (Luke 5:13–16); a paralytic (Luke 5:17–26); the tax-collector Levi (Luke 5:27–32); a centurion's son (Luke 7:1–9); a widow whose son has been raised from the dead (Luke 7:11–17), and many more. They embody all levels of society, including the economically poor, the sick, the dishonoured, those excluded from God's people by their fellow Jews, those held in satanic bondage and those in need of forgiveness of their sins. With the inclusion of the centurion, a Gentile, the poor represent all of humanity in its need of God's eschatological salvation. Any attempt to restrict the "poor" to any of the above categories falls short of Luke's wide-ranging portrayal of the recipients of good news.[25]

Thus, in Luke 4:18, besides the materially disadvantaged, the socially and ethnically disadvantaged are also included within the term "poor." Now, if "poverty" is best understood holistically, then this must likewise apply to the saving ministry of εὐαγγελίζω, as Wenk argued: "The soteriological significance of Luke 4:16–30 is that, for Luke, salvation is not a purely other-worldly reality but has a this-worldly beginning within the Christian community, expressed with 'today this Scripture has been fulfilled in your hearing' (4:2; cf. Luke 6:20–26)."[26] This experience, according to Wenk, has an impact on the ethos of the liberated community: "It is to be expected that the experience of such salvation will become normative for the community's ethos: The anointed community in Acts will continue the ministry of their anointed liberator; the community's ethics are inspired by their (own) experience (and reading) of salvation (Luke 6:40, cf. chapter 12)."[27]

The liberating message of Jesus in Luke 4:16–30 becomes real and experiential through the power of the Holy Spirit in the ministry and works of Jesus: "The Spirit is related to the life of the people of God in its entirety: daily provision of food, forgiveness of sins by God and by each other, protection *from* apostasy and deliverance from demonic enslavement."[28] People of every kind experience liberation in that they are accepted by Jesus, and are recognized and taken seriously in their affliction and need. This common experience connects people:

25. Wenk, *Community-Forming Power*, 214.
26. Wenk, *Community-Forming Power*, 218.
27. Wenk, *Community-Forming Power*, 218.
28. Wenk, *Community-Forming Power*, 231.

In a community in which sickness was not purely a physical thing, but also a question of guilt, shame and social isolation, each healing was a radical shift in the social structure of a healed person (cf. Matt 9:20). Along with him belong those whom nobody wants, with him they receive dignity, whose dignity has been destroyed by others and who have been treated with contempt. God's good news applies to those who are not able to attain a joyful life. Thus there emerges, as with the Exodus, a contrast society (Acts 2:42–47), in which there is neither male nor female, neither Jew nor Greek, neither slave nor free (Gal 3:28).

The salvation which Jesus brought is, in the most radical manner, community transforming—it could not be otherwise.[29]

Pentecost as a Continuation of the New Exodus

The second Lukan work is the continuation, but also the fulfillment, of that which Jesus began to do and teach.[30] Thus, the anticipated baptism in Spirit and fire first became a reality in Acts 2:33. Also the fulfillment of the promise to Abraham (Gen 12:2–3), which Mary again took up in the Magnificat (Luke 1:54–55), finds its fulfillment in the Book of Acts, when the gospel was preached to the Gentiles.[31] In the Book of Acts, the global Kingdom of God finds its advent.[32] And also here, elements of the new Exodus can be heard. As the first Exodus led the nation of the Israelites to Mount Sinai, so with the new Exodus at Pentecost a comparable experience can be seen.[33]

However, the new Exodus leads further. Thus God's liberating action is not limited to the Israelites, but includes all who hope for liberation. Also, liberation does not occur, as with the first Exodus, in the sense that distance is created between oppressor and oppressed, but by reconciliation between them. "So it leads to reconciliation between Jews and Gentiles (Acts 10), between a Jew and an unclean eunuch (Acts 8), between Jews and Samaritans (Acts 8)," and further groups, from which

---

29. Wenk, *Community-Forming Power*, 32.

30. Wenk, *Community-Forming Power*, 242. For a comprehensive exposition of the Book of Acts as a continuation, see Wenk, "Book of Acts," 116–28.

31. Wenk, *Community-Forming Power*, 243–44.

32. Wenk, *Community-Forming Power*, 244.

33. Wenk, *Community-Forming Power*, 246–57.

Jews are ordinarily separated.[34] Through the work of the Holy Spirit, social boundaries and discrimination are overcome: "What the spirit-spoken word has included (the realization of salvation), the community cannot exclude. The way in which the renewed community previously experienced God's restoration of justice and mercy among the marginalized must determine its own relation to them (Luke 6:40)."[35] The liberating work of the Holy Spirit creates a place in the community for the marginalized. Wenk describes this place as "This-Worldly Dimension of Salvation."[36] Wenk points out that the terms "to be saved," and "to be in community," are in essence identical.[37]

The new Exodus community consists of people who all experience their own Pentecost: There is the Samaritan Pentecost (Acts 8:14–17), the Gentile Pentecost (10–11) and the Pentecost of the disciples of John (19:1–8).[38] Through Pentecost, all become part of the Messianic people of God—which does not come without background noise: "Each influx of new individuals and groups of people into the community was at the same time a crisis moment, characterized by the struggle between continuity and discontinuity with the community's previous character."[39] The new people of God are constantly required to review their life and practice. This struggle is particularly apparent in the four conversion narratives of the Samaritans, the eunuch, Paul and Cornelius.[40] In this regard, Wenk speaks of a "prophetic process." This process is only successfully completed when the dialogue between the parties involved finds an adequate conclusion, that is to say, that the marginalized become part of the new Exodus community.[41] In this process, the Holy Spirit plays a central role, as the example of the Samaritans illustrates:

> It is only after the Spirit-manifestation and the implicit bonding between Jerusalem and Samaria that Peter and John preached the gospel in many Samaritan villages (8:25; πολλάς τε κώμας τῶν Σαμαριτῶν). This may in turn suggest that Spirit-manifestation was not simply for the 'empowerment' of the mission of

---

34. Wenk, *Community-Forming Power*, 32.
35. Wenk, *Community-Forming Power*, 220.
36. Wenk, *Community-Forming Power*, 278.
37. Wenk, *Community-Forming Power*, 280.
38. Wenk, *Community-Forming Power*, 274.
39. Wenk, *Community-Forming Power*, 281.
40. Wenk, *Community-Forming Power*, 289.
41. Wenk, *Community-Forming Power*, 286.

the church (we read of no missionary activity by the Samaritan believers; the mission at Samaria was accomplished by Peter and John) but the identity marker for a community that had *ipso facto* come to comprise both Jews and Samaritans.[42]

It is the Holy Spirit who through the baptism in Himself, gives the indication that the "unclean," Samaritans now also belong. Also, in the conversion narrative of the eunuch, the Holy Spirit does not work primarily in missional empowerment but rather specifies the direction of Philip's missional activity.[43]

> The church represents God's new people in the messianic age which includes foreigners and eunuchs and, although perhaps only unconsciously, becomes the fulfillment of Isaiah 56:3–5. . . . The Spirit is initiating a communication process that would otherwise never have begun. The Spirit induces the restored Israel in Acts to be inclusive and thereby represents the warrant that God's *telos* is achieved. Eunuchs were thus included, even though the story is told in a way that might indicate the reluctance of the church in this process, which enforces the crucial role of the Spirit in it.[44]

The consequence of this encounter compels the community (at least, the readers) to redefine their self-perception. The story of the pagan centurion Cornelius points in the same direction. Wenk emphasizes in various places that even when the Holy Spirit is the initiator of the liberation process, the people involved are of importance. In this process, the parties concerned (the community and the marginalized) are dependent upon one another in order to recognize God's purpose:

> A similar pattern is found in the narratives of the Ethiopian eunuch (Acts 8:26–40) and Cornelius (Acts 10:1–11, 18). In neither case did the respective apostles know God's will absolutely, in contrast to their audience, rather they knew just in part. In both cases the initiated a communication process that otherwise would not have begun and both times the story is told in a way to reflect the initial reluctance on part of the "missionary."[45]

---

42. Wenk, *Community-Forming Power*, 294.
43. Wenk, *Community-Forming Power*, 296–97.
44. Wenk, *Community-Forming Power*, 297–303.
45. Wenk, *Community-Forming Power*, 314.

The Objective of Liberation in Wenk's Publications

As mentioned above, Wenk points out that with the integration of the marginalized, the messianic Exodus community stands in a constant state of tension between continuity and discontinuity of its identity. With the acceptance of "the other," into the new Exodus community, the tension is certainly not ending; rather, the church has to face new challenges: How can they shape communal life which, with every integration of new "others," becomes even more diverse and thereby even more full of tension?[46] One answer to this question can be found in Wenk's lecture "Den Gefangenen zu verkünden, dass sie frei sein sollen [Proclaiming Release to the Captives]."[47] In it, Wenk examines what is the aim of the liberating action of God in the New Testament. Because, even as significant and fundamental the liberation from bondage, exclusion and isolation is, liberation *from* cannot be enough if the messianic Exodus community is to have a chance as a community:

> Freedom is however not only fundamental to the Christian faith, it is also its fulfillment: *Even the creation is to be freed from its slavery and futility into the freedom and glory of the children of God* (Rom 8:21). Thus, freedom serves as a comprehensive term for the coming salvation, and thereby for the Kingdom of God. Hence, freedom is for the Christian faith as much a foundation as a fulfillment, and it is not individual, but includes the entire creation.[48]

Here, Wenk differs from both the liberation theologians Gutierréz and Cone. Gutiérrez understands liberation as *conquista*,[49] and Cone as the restoration of justice, whereas Wenk sees liberation as freedom for a shared life:

> In the bible freedom is always a relational term; it concerns the realization of relationships and not a "personal condition," which one can experience for himself alone. This is also true for "inner freedom," such as, for example, freedom from fear. Even

---

46. The overcoming of tensions within the messianic Exodus community is certainly introduced, but not extensively discussed by Wenk in his dissertation. We find a detailed analysis on this in Wenk, "Reconciliation and Renunciation," 44–58.

47. The lecture was given by Wenk at the 2015 theological conference of Bewegung-Plus in Gunten. The lecture was published two years later in Wenk, *Erneuerung durch Begegnung*.

48. Wenk, *Community-Forming Power*, 246–57.

49. Moltmann, "Befreiung der Unterdrücker," 537.

this form of freedom is always relational because an unfree person, who for example is trapped in his alcohol addiction, never suffers for himself alone. There is also always an environment that is affected by it. The same also applies to all other forms of "inner bondage": They always have an external impact and touch other human beings. Therefore freedom can only ever be experienced together with other people, or it is not real freedom. Freedom is thus not only liberation for life, but it is liberation for community life and it confirms the diversity of life.[50]

Liberation for community life is repeatedly threatened by oppression, isolation, and loneliness. In oppression through "the dominance of the one," which "signifies the end of the freedom of the other,"[51] in isolation and loneliness by the "instability," of the "uncommitted people."[52] In contrast to this, trusting in God and one's fellow human beings constitutes the foundation of freedom.[53] When trust is the foundation, then love shapes the living environment for freedom, which simultaneously preserves the diversity of freedom (Rom 14). Since "only love gives the freedom of a free world in which all have space to live, and only love leads to solidarity with the world."[54] Love releases hope, which constitutes the "landscape," of freedom:

> Freedom is . . . always hopeful. It is not naive, neither is it overoptimistic, but it is hopeful, because the freedom from the power of death which Christ has effected through the resurrection, does away with death and thereby, all endings. And when the power of death and all endings is put to an end, then the future is free and full of hope.[55]

According to Wenk, the route to freedom is not through revolution—such a route can only lead to a new domination and thereby a new oppression.[56] But if not through a revolution, then how else should liberation happen? Wenk sees, particularly in the New Testament, that *God* brings freedom. Most commonly, the Holy Spirit is spoken of in this

---

50. Wenk, "What Is Prophetic," 101–2.
51. Wenk, "What Is Prophetic," 102.
52. Wenk, "What Is Prophetic," 103.
53. Wenk, "What Is Prophetic," 104.
54. Wenk, "What Is Prophetic," 105.
55. Wenk, "What Is Prophetic," 105–6.
56. Wenk, "What Is Prophetic," 103.

connection.⁵⁷ Even the Old Testament sees the Holy Spirit as the primary instrument of freedom. However, there are also differences: There, freedom is often also defined as political. Thus, the Judges delivered Israel from political and economic oppression by military means. Because in the New Testament the people of God are no longer understood as the political/ethnic majority, this aspect ceases to apply in the new Exodus. But: "Liberation from economic hardship, however, is still experienced (Acts 2:42–47), just like the new freedom in respect of social status, gender or ethnic grouping (Gal 3:28)."⁵⁸

In summary, it can be said that freedom for the Judaeo-Christian faith is of such central and crucial significance that it is often effective as a paraphrase for the Kingdom of God. "This freedom comes from God, in that God liberates us human beings, and ultimately the entire creation, into a life with each other. . . . This liberation includes the political, economic, military, social, spiritual and psychological dimension."⁵⁹ It is a liberation which ends every form "of domination and power of people over people, and people over the creation." It is a freedom which leads "out from isolation and into a common life of freedom." This common life of freedom is put into effect "on the basis of mutual trust, of solidarity," and "it opens the entire creation to a future full of hope."⁶⁰

A life of freedom has to be learnt. As in the decalogue God taught the liberated slaves to preserve their newly won freedom, thus He guides the messianic people of God in their life of freedom. Wenk, in his lecture, points out relevant parallels between the Torah and the gospel of Matthew:

> With His five discourses, which serve as a means of structure, this gospel consciously makes reference to the Torah and wishes to be understood as the new law, which replaces the old, the five books of the Torah. The gospel of Matthew is therefore also a major guide for a life of freedom and ends with the invitation by Jesus to make disciples of people. The means to this is baptism, and the instruction to teach them to observe everything that Jesus commanded.⁶¹

---

57. Wenk points out that in Romans 6, Paul surprisingly also speaks of baptism in conjunction with liberation from sin. This is also the case in Galatians 3:27; Matthew 28:18 (Wenk, "What Is Prophetic," 106–7).

58. Wenk, "What Is Prophetic," 106.

59. Wenk, "What Is Prophetic," 108.

60. Wenk, "What Is Prophetic," 108.

61. Wenk, "What Is Prophetic," 107.

In this sense, Wenk sees the task of the church as instructing other people to live a life of freedom, by becoming bound to Jesus. This life must be learnt, and hence the church takes up its promise: "Positive discipleship therefore means to help others on the basis of trust, in love, and to act and to live full of hope, so that the freedom effected by God can be fully realized."[62] Through action and speaking, the church should bear witness to its gained freedom and "let itself be visible to the whole world." At the same time, it is also the task of the church "to train each other to live in this freedom. For us therefore, obedience to the words of Jesus and freedom are not contradictory."[63] Rather, the instructions of Jesus are to be understood as a "directive for a life of freedom."[64]

For Wenk, the Holy Spirit plays a central role in this process. It is God's Spirit who helps believers by being a support to bridge the time up to the ultimate (eschatological) liberation. It is the Spirit who leads the church into solidarity with the world.[65] Without the Holy Spirit, discipleship declines into a legalistic and strict experience, "just as the charismatic experience of the Holy Spirit without personal and political discipleship becomes spiritistic and illusionary."[66] God's Spirit is plainly the agent that integrates people into the community and allows them to participate in the worldly dimension of redemption.[67]

Yet how can we, in our Western European Pentecostal context of the charismatic Holy Spirit experience, pursue personal and (in particular) political discipleship? Because "despite the fact that Pentecostals constantly experience how the Holy Spirit topples the social rules instituted by the successful, the beautiful and the powerful ones, such manifestations of the Holy Spirit do not always give birth to a contrasting society."[68] In "The Holy Spirit as Transforming Power within a Society: Pneumatological Spirituality and its Political/Social Relevance for Western Europe," Wenk lists a number of reasons which, in his opinion, are the cause why Pentecostals from the Western hemisphere are not associating their faith with the political and social questions of their time. One cause, according to Wenk, is that among Western Pentecostals, the desire for

62. Wenk, "What Is Prophetic," 107.
63. Wenk, "What Is Prophetic," 108.
64. Wenk, "What Is Prophetic," 108.
65. See also the detailed explanations in Wenk, "Heilige Geist."
66. Wenk, "What Is Prophetic," 107.
67. Wenk, *Community-Forming Power*, 288.
68. Wenk, "Transforming Power," 138.

spiritual *experience* is greater than the desire to interpret this experience theologically and systematically. Through lack of reflection, their spiritual experiences have also had correspondingly less corrective effect on ethics.[69] Furthermore, he sees the interpretation of God's Kingdom from the perspective of Western European Pentecostals as a challenge. God's Kingdom is mostly interpreted from this perspective through the lens of personal happiness and bourgeois individualistic values. Wenk sees this perspective as analogous to Pentecostal theology which has shifted from "a more oral, testimony-based theology to an evangelical, if not fundamentalist, approach to theology."[70] On the basis of these observations, Wenk suggests the following concepts of action: He sees a great urgency for the rediscovery of the Pentecostal legacy and emphasis of the social and political relevance of an experience with God which was prevalent in the first church.[71] A reappraisal of the current individualistic, and other-worldly, eternity-related interpretation of God's Kingdom is needed, as well as overcoming the fear of a more temporal, inner-worldly Kingdom of God spirituality. Ways must be found to rediscover and live the early community-based Pentecostal spirituality within an individualistic society. In particular, Western European Pentecostals are facing the challenge of how they can live in community and solidarity with the poor, oppressed and lonely of society. Also, if they want to take seriously the role of the Holy Spirit in the emergence of creation, Pentecostals must campaign against the exploitation of this creation and develop an economic theory, "which does not grieve the Holy Spirit." The campaign for disarmament is, in Wenk's view, also a compelling expression of Pentecostal spirituality, precisely because the visible Kingdom of God must reflect the qualities and values of the coming Kingdom of God. For Pentecostals, the rejection of social injustice cannot merely be justified in "political correctness," and certainly not in church trends that "go with the flow," but it must be understood as obedience to the Holy Spirit.[72] So Wenk concludes the article with the following words:

> Thus, a pneumatological criticism of our Western society's values and norms, along with its capitalism, is nurtured by a passion for the Spirit-anointed messiah and the kingdom of God. It

---

69. Wenk, "Transforming Power," 139.
70. Wenk, "Transforming Power," 140.
71. Wenk, "Transforming Power," 140.
72. Wenk, "Transforming Power," 142. See also Vilafane, *Liberating Spirt*, 169–81.

will create a contrast society that no longer sustains such typical Western European values as wealth, strength, success, beauty, self-sufficiency and individual freedom.[73]

Romans 8:18–30 as a Basis for Social Ethics

One interesting aspect in Wenk's theology is the central role which Romans 8:18–30 occupies in his social ethics.[74] Wenk summarizes Paul's argument from Romans 8 as follows:

> Without reference to law, God through His Spirit creates a new people, comprising Jews and gentiles. And the reconciling power which becomes visible to the whole world in the new people of God is of eschatological significance because its ultimate consummation will be the salvation of the entire creation.[75]

For Wenk, Paul's statement in v. 17, that Christians are co-workers with Christ, only has a transitory character. For him, the actual culmination of the argument happens in the statement of v. 21: "Even the creation is to be liberated from slavery and futility into the freedom and glory of the children of God" (EÜ). Therefore, for Wenk, not an "individualistic understanding of salvation, but the eschatological renewal of creation" stands at the center:

> [The] present salvation experience of the children of God—even here not individualistically defined—becomes the proleptic experience of the eschatological state of salvation for the whole creation: in and through the salvation experience of the children of God it is already seen, here and now, what shall be true for the entire creation in the future.[76]

A further particularity in Romans 8 is that the eschatological salvation is not tied to the parousia of Christ, but to the Holy Spirit. Therefore, the

---

73. Wenk, "Transforming Power," 142.

74. The lecture was delivered at the M&D study day on March 1, 2013, with IGW in Olten. Whilst a number of Pentecostal theologians have grappled with Romans 8, Wenk's approach as a basis for socio-ethical considerations is unique, at least up to the development point of the lecture. Wenk himself wrote to me about the significance of this lecture for his theology and that this lecture should have particular mention.

75. Wenk, *Erneuerung durch Begegnung*, 58. Wenk, in his exposition of Romans 8, refers to Fee, and at the same time points out that, in this case, the eschatological dimension does not take the place which it actually deserves.

76. Wenk, *Erneuerung durch Begegnung*, 59.

soteriology in this text is not developed christologically but pneumatologically: "The Spirit, which has been given to the children of God as, or even for, a first fruit, guarantees the eschatological fulfillment and implementation of salvation." Hence, there is "for those who, through the Holy Spirit, cry 'Abba, Father' and are glorified with Christ (Rom 8:17) no ultimate liberation without the co-liberation of the entire creation (Rom 8:21)."[77]

In the redemption of creation, Wenk sees the Holy Spirit in a threefold role:

- As a support for believers in their present suffering, which helps them bridge the time leading up to the ultimate liberation.
- As a guarantee in respect of those whose hope is in the liberation of the entire creation becoming the ultimate reality for all life.
- As the one who draws believers into solidarity with creation.

Wenk points out that, in Romans 8:18–30, also other themes, which are elsewhere christologically explained, are linked to the Holy Spirit; for example, even the topic of the solidarity of God: "Whilst in Christology it is usual to speak of the crucified Christ as the expression of the solidarity of God with a suffering creation, Paul connects the solidarity of God with the suffering and oppressed life to the Spirit."[78] This is all the more surprising because the theology of the Holy Spirit primarily speaks of the categories of authority and power. Yet for Wenk, this observation alone is reason enough to rethink and redefine the theme of power and authority through the Holy Spirit in connection with solidarity.[79]

Wenk expresses the sum of the above gained insights within the category of the Missio Spiritu, thus: "The mission of the Spirit brings the Holy Spirit directly into the inconsistency and fragility of creation to take up its cry in solidarity, and to bring it before God until the ultimate liberation. And that leads us now to socio-ethical considerations."[80] The question arises of how the church must live in order to participate in the mission of the Holy Spirit. There is also the question as to the shape of such a pneumatological (and eschatological) ethic, because the text itself does not give clear instructions to the reader.[81] For Wenk, the above-

77. Wenk, *Erneuerung durch Begegnung*, 59.
78. Wenk, *Erneuerung durch Begegnung*, 60.
79. Wenk, *Erneuerung durch Begegnung*, 60.
80. Wenk, *Erneuerung durch Begegnung*, 61.
81. Wenk, *Erneuerung durch Begegnung*, 62. Thus Wenk writes: "White Western

mentioned trio of solidarity, hope and responsibility on behalf of the oppressed, is trailblazing:

> A church which is allows itself to engage in this mission through the Spirit, will always allow itself to enter into solidarity with endangered, vulnerable and defenceless lives, or it does not partake in the mission and liberation through the Spirit. This means that in evangelisation, not only the legal or moral aspects of redemption are to be emphasized, but also always the socio-ethical and the cosmic.[82]

As a prime example of this, Wenk refers to the actions of the Truth and Reconciliation Commission after the end of the Apartheid regime.[83] The reduction of redemption to legal/moral categories means that mission is "no longer Trinitarian, and therefore no longer Missio Dei in the real sense."[84] For Wenk, the task of the church consists, on the one hand, of the embodiment of the reconciling, healing and restoring dimension of the power of the Holy Spirit, and on the other hand, of "working toward reconciling reunification."[85] Wenk sees the "unreconciled division," of people not only in family conflicts, but also in unjust structures, power relationships and the unfair distribution of resources, ethnic groups and geographic regions. In the face of these defilements, Missio Dei for the church means "solidarity with the marginalised, to join with them in their situation, to endure and suffer their injustice with them, because even the Spirit of God does precisely that."[86] One consequence of solidarity with the life of oppression is, amongst other things, the acceptance of

---

European Pentecostals also have to be aware that their emphasis on a pneumatological spirituality might differ significantly from, for example, a Black British or Hispanic American one. Whereas Black British Pentecostals and/or Hispanic American ones may experience the Holy Spirit's liberating power as those who are normally marginalized and/or experience themselves as oppressed by the dominant culture, Western European Pentecostals are part of the 'oppressing element' within the same larger society. While it may be true that a number of Western European Pentecostals are part of the lower working class, they are—globally speaking—still part of the 10 percent of this world's population that earn at least 80 percent of the world's income. Thus, Western European Pentecostals need to develop their pneumatological social ethic 'from the other end of the game'" (Wenk, "Transforming Power," 132).

82. Wenk, *Erneuerung durch Begegnung*, 63.
83. Wenk, *Erneuerung durch Begegnung*, 63.
84. Wenk, *Erneuerung durch Begegnung*, 63.
85. Wenk, *Erneuerung durch Begegnung*, 63.
86. Wenk, *Erneuerung durch Begegnung*, 63.

the tangible disadvantages and inconveniences in the lives of those who are in solidarity with oppressed creation (1 Thess 2:8–9).

Wenk highlights the mission of the Holy Spirit as a mission of life on the basis of the following example:

> A church in the power of the Spirit is, for example, prepared to support addicts [sic]. However, they do this not primarily because their addictive behavior is immoral and, legally seen, is reprehensible before God, but because addiction destroys the lives of those people. The same can also be said with regard to the sexual ethic. A church, which by the Spirit of God allows itself to engage in solidarity with the life of oppression, also campaigns for a healthy sexual ethic—not because everything else is simply immoral or indecent, but because it represents the degradation of the healthy togetherness of husband and wife. Parallel to this they should work to achieve the protection of women who are forced into prostitution, and campaign against the trafficking of girls and discrimination against the female sex in general. The equivalent is true for the handling of money. Also here a church cannot simply insist that its members pay a tithe or must not be controlled by materialism. Because it is called to fight specifically against covetousness, against greed (always having to get the latest thing at the cheapest price) and ultimately against the exploitation of people and creation. The maxim of a pneumatological social ethic therefore does not conform to the criteria: What is immoral and what, by contrast, is spiritual—in other words, moral? Rather it asks: what thwarts life and what promotes life? And because where life is thwarted, the church shows solidarity with the vulnerable and the oppressed.[87]

Critical Appraisal

As already mentioned at the beginning, Matthias Wenk is not a systematic theologian, but he developed his theology of liberation from the perspective of a New Testament scholar. This perspective, which differs from previously analyzed theologians in its methodology, brings new insights into the discussion. His starting point is not the specific experience of a group of underprivileged, but he begins with God's aim of salvation: The creation, liberated into community life, effected through the Holy Spirit. This deductive approach sets the discussion on liberation and freedom in

---

87. Wenk, "Pneumatologie als Solidarität," 107.

a broad arena because it begins with the universal (the destiny of every creature) and not with the specific (the actual experience of individuals). The role of Romans 8 as a starting point for a pneumatological soteriology sets Wenk's understanding of salvation in a cosmic context, in which the entire creation is to share in redemption.[88] From this broad arena, Wenk then passes on to the specific and thinks about what is specifically depicted as injustice, as oppressive and life threatening, and how this can be overcome. The strength of this approach is its adaptability. It can be used in the most varied of contexts, for the liberation of the oppressed, as well as for the liberation of the oppressor.

A further strength of Wenk's approach is that it does not merely concern liberation *from* something. For him, it is not about the liberation of a group of people who, for example, must be set free from the poverty trap. For him it is also not about the liberation of people who suffer oppression and discrimination because of their race or their gender. Instead, it is about liberation *for* community life. This eschatological context not only provides orientation with regard to what injustice is and how to overcome it, but also how the newly won freedom can be lived and what must be done to prevent it from being lost. In this regard, clear parallels to Moltmann's Theology of Hope are apparent, even though this does not emanate from a pneumatologically motivated soteriology.[89]

Wenk consistently conceptualizes liberation for community life pneumatologically. In addition, he challenges the reduction of the Lukan pneumatology to an almost exclusively missiological or prophetic focus, as do Menzies and Stronstad.[90] Similar to Wenk, Turner already conceptualizes the Lukan pneumatology more broadly; however, Wenk is more fundamental in his approach.[91] For Wenk, the Holy Spirit shows solidarity with the oppressed and marginalized life in that He helps them to bridge the time up to the eschatological liberation.[92] It is God's Spirit who brings people together; in and through these encounters He overcomes

---

88. Wenk, "Pneumatologie als Solidarität," 111. Although other Pentecostal theologians use Romans 8, Wenk's approach is unique in using just this text as a systematic theological starting point for a pneumatological soteriology.

89. See Moltmann, *Ethics of Hope*, 253.

90. See Menzies, *Empowered for Witness*; Stronstad, *Charismatic Theology*.

91. See Turner, *Power from on High*. Kuecker writes in *Spirit and the "Other"* about Wenk's thesis in reference to other Pentecostal theologians. "His project is by far the most sensitive to the role of the Holy Spirit both within the early community and for group reconciliation" (Wenk, "Pfingstliche Pneumatologie," 11).

92. Here also there are parallels to Moltmann. See Moltmann, *Crucified God*, 27–28.

the social rifts and reconciles with each other that which is divided. It is God's Spirit who forms the ethos of the new community and ensures that they do not have to break apart in their full diversity. And it is God's Spirit who always repeatedly revitalizes hope in the community by reminding them of the eschatological context of God's Kingdom.

However, Wenk also sees a weakness which lies, not so much in his approach but originates more in the Swiss context:

> Our strengths lie definitively in the area of personal discipleship, but in the area of political, social or economic liberty we certainly still need to catch up. We have neither a theology nor an appreciation of discipleship which takes account of our globalised world and our life in a globalised world. To some extent, we are in the process of transcending an individualistic spirituality, but we have still hardly considered the implications of a globalised world. My guess is that we shall gain a lot of freedom when we do this.[93]

Because of the purchasing power and consumerism of us Swiss people, the whole world has actually become our neighbor—although as consumers we do not come into contact with the consequences brought about in the countries of origin. The fragmentation caused by world trade has a similar effect to segregation: The person oppressed by consumerism is never going to encounter the exploited person.

If the encounter is one of the key elements through which the Holy Spirit gives *eyes to see and heart to feel*, which in turn will lead to a liberating transformation, then the oppressor has no inducement to strive for change. How can the privileged recognize that they are not free but trapped in guilt if they are not confronted with the devastating consequences which their conduct is having upon the oppressed? How can the encounter lead to the formation of a contrast society? How can acts and measures of solidarity succeed?[94] Wenk himself points out that this does not happen automatically, not even with Pentecostal churches.[95] Wenk also thematized this shortcoming in the above-mentioned article, "The Holy Spirit as Transforming Power within a Society: Pneumatological Spirituality and its Political/Social Relevance for Western Europe." Here he provides further approaches on how the Western European Pentecostal

---

93. Wenk, "Pneumatologie als Solidarität," 107.
94. See also Cone, *Cross*, 41–44.
95. Wenk, "Transforming Power," 138.

church can develop more strongly into a contrast society. People of color, the poor and the marginalized have a weight of suffering which urges them forward, toward change. The oppressor and the privileged do not know the pressing weight of suffering. How the willingness for transformation within the Western European Pentecostal church could occur in concrete terms, ultimately remains a mystery, even for Wenk.[96]

As mentioned in the introduction, Wenk's very approach as a New Testament theologian introduces new insights into the discussion on a Pentecostal social ethic. However, the approach of the New Testament theologians also sets boundaries which, in part, are narrower than those of a systematic theologian. In this way, Wenk, for example, deals with the story of the Ethiopian eunuch in Acts 8:26–40 within the questioning of his dissertation.[97] An interpretation of the same text, from a socio-ethical and liberation theological perspective, can provide approaches which lead beyond Wenk's analysis: The eunuch identified himself with God's suffering servant from the background of his own suffering. The text that he was reading from Isaiah 53 points to the fact that the servant has no offspring. Also he, as a eunuch, will never have offspring. Just like God's suffering servant, he is also excluded from the community, because as a eunuch, he is excluded from temple worship services; at best, he is allowed to enter the temple courtyard. He again recognizes himself in the unfairness suffered in the text from Isaiah 53, which connects him with God's suffering servant. From the background of his experience of unfairness, the eunuch is brought into the new Exodus community

---

96. Shane Claiborne and Chris Haw describe one way in which such an encounter can come about: "Years ago, some folks from our communities attended a rally against overseas sweatshops. They had not invited the typical rally speakers—lawyers, activists, and academics. Instead, they brought the kids themselves from the sweatshops to speak. We listened as a child from Indonesia pointed to the giant scar on his face. 'I got this scar when my master lashed me for not working hard enough. When it began to bleed, he did not want me to stop working or to ruin the cloth in front of me, so he took a lighter and burned it shut. I got this making stuff for you.' We were suddenly consumed by the overwhelming reality of the suffering body of Christ. Jesus now bore not just the marks from the nails and scars from the thorns but a gash down his face, for when we have done it to the 'least of these,' we have done it to Christ himself. How could we possibly follow Jesus and buy anything from that master? The statistics had a face. Poverty became personal. And that messes with you'" (Claiborne, *Jesus for President*, 189). Claiborne's story shows that the church can certainly make a contribution so that a transformative dynamic can occur—in the above case, the invitation of a sweatshop worker. But that the encounter also actually has a transforming effect on consumers, however, is again beyond human capability.

97. Wenk, *Community-Forming Power*, 294–98.

through baptism. The powerless (he cannot undo the effect of castration) and excluded are given dignity and inclusion. Here it is recorded that the initiative for his baptism originates from the eunuch, thus he is in no way passive in his powerlessness. In this way, the story of the Ethiopian becomes a story full of hope, in which the powerlessness experienced becomes the starting point for God's saving intervention.[98] In the conflict illustrated in Acts 6:1–7,[99] the whole church, members of Hebrew origin and Greek origin, contributed to the conflict resolution process through the selection of deacons. However, it was the oppressed who took the initiative and pointed out the injustice toward the Greek widows. Being filled with the Holy Spirit is deemed by the church as the central criterion for the fulfillment of the diaconal ministry for sustaining the unity of the congregation. Even though the Holy Spirit has been present in the ministry of the apostle and in the church since the events of Pentecost, the protest of the Hellenistic church members is *the* prophetic element which ultimately initiates the modification of church structures and the change of church practice.

These observations are significant for a Pentecostal social ethic because they make reference to our reality of life and our context. They challenge us to ask the following questions: To which of the marginalized in the community and the church is the Holy Spirit leading us? What does God's Spirit want to say to us, in and through the encounter with the marginalized? How and what will God speaking through the marginalized change in the church so that nobody becomes neglected or marginalized?

Lisa Stephenson: A Feminist Approach

Lisa P. Stephenson completed her PhD in the subject *Religious Studies* at the Marquette University in 2009. She is Assistant Professor of Systematic Theology at the Lee University (Cleveland, Tennessee), where she is, amongst other things, Director for the MA Program for Biblical and Theological Studies. Stephenson has produced various publications for which she has been honored with awards.[100] She is an ordained pastor of the Church of God (Cleveland, Tennessee) and is married with

---

98. See also Solivan's thoughts on powerlessness as a starting point for orthopathos in Solivan, *Spirit, Pathos and Liberation*, 86–92.

99. Wenk, *Community-Forming Power*, 290–91.

100. https://webpages.leeu.edu/lstephenson/.

children.[101] In her research, her main interests are in the subject areas of anthropology, ecclesiology and political theology. Stephenson has become particularly known for her contribution to a Pentecostal feminist theology, to which consideration will be given in this paper.

Stephenson's starting point is the proposition that the *Magna Carta* of Acts 2 has never resulted in completely releasing praxis for women in clerical functions. She attests that within the academic circles of Pentecostal theology, the problem has probably been acknowledged in recent decades but so far to an insufficient extent. Stephenson's criticism is that the role of women is neither investigated against the background of a pneumatological perspective, nor has the subject been associated with the findings of feminist theology. But precisely these two perspectives Stephenson considers as key for the development of a Pentecostal-theological position on the question of women's rights: The pneumatological perspective is important because it forms a central element of Pentecostal methodology and because it helps to avoid one-sided anthropological concepts for feminist theology.[102] Stephenson's monograph, *Dismantling the Dualism for American Pentecostal Women in Ministry: A Feminist-Pneumatological Approach* intends precisely to satisfy this concept. In a first step, she examines which historical and theological factors have led to the marginalization of women in the present-day Pentecostal church. In a second step, Stephenson suggests a concept which picks up the anthropological as well as the ecclesiological aspects, whilst using pneumatology as her methodological starting point. In the following, Stephenson has chosen to use the terminology, "Women in Ministry," instead of the term "Women's Ordination."

Historical Context

Stephenson begins her task by first analyzing the historical context of her tradition as well as the role of women within it. The question of whether women are allowed to participate as equals in a formal Christian ministry (in the form of a pastorate, administering the sacraments, etc.), was already a subject of discussion in the USA in the early seventeenth century. Even though development in the direction of equal rights has proceeded slowly, nevertheless in the last two centuries (particularly in the twentieth

---

101. https://webpages.leeu.edu/lstephenson/.
102. Stephenson, *Dismantling the Dualisms*, 2.

century), there have been significant changes. Still, there are Christian traditions, which struggle with enabling women to have a ministry in the church—one of these is *classical Pentecostalism*,[103] which believes that the outpouring of the Holy Spirit described in Acts 2 is not only historical, but also a present phenomenon, through which God equips and empowers the church.[104] This belief is a central aspect of Pentecostal identity. Although it is recognized that the Holy Spirit empowers people regardless of their gender, the outpouring of the Holy Spirit amongst Pentecostals has seldom led to an equal ministry praxis of men and women. This has primarily to do with the fact that the opportunities of ministry for women are repeatedly restricted. This limitation is justified by a hierarchical anthropology which subjugates women to men, even though it is universally acknowledged that God operates His works through men as well as women. This stance has existed from the beginnings in the Azusa Street Mission up to the present day.[105] Stephenson has researched the historical context of the Pentecostal Movement in order to draw a valid picture of these restrictions.

The earliest of Stephenson's research evidence concerning the understanding of roles is to be found in the origins of the Pentecostal Movement, with Charles Fox Parham's *Bethel Bible School* in Topeka, Kansas, and with William Joseph Seymour's *Azusa Street Mission*. We are provided with one piece of evidence by Frank Bartleman, an eyewitness to the awakening beginnings of the movement. He describes the church services as meetings in which there was no hierarchy. All participated in the church services, regardless of status, race or gender. All that mattered was the empowerment of the Holy Spirit.[106] Simultaneously, Bartleman disassociated himself from equality between men and women:

> A female Ministry is naturally a weak ministry. . . . Effeminate men follow a female ministry too, largely through a spirit of fleshly attraction to the opposite sex. How can such ministry

---

103. Stephenson defines classical Pentecostalism according to the following criteria: "The term 'classical Pentecostalism' is used to denote those Pentecostals who trace their origins back to either the events at Charles Parham's Bethel Bible School on January 1, 1901, or the revival at the Azusa Street Mission led by William J. Seymour in Los Angeles, California, from 1906 to 1909. . . . Throughout the remainder of the book, any references to Pentecostalism are references specifically to classical Pentecostalism within the United States" (Stephenson, *Dismantling the Dualisms*, 8).

104. Stephenson, *Dismantling the Dualisms*, 17.

105. Stephenson, *Dismantling the Dualisms*, 18.

106. Stephenson, *Dismantling the Dualisms*, 21.

work real righteousness? It cannot. It is abnormal, unscriptural. Because men will not obey God is the real reason for the general acceptance and popularity of flapper evangelism. God is not changing His order, raising woman to equality with man in the ministry. The Apostles were men. The early church is our example. God made Adam first. Then the woman for his helper.[107]

Even though Bartleman accepted that women could be in the service of the Kingdom of God, he was of the opinion that their role should be reduced to that of a helper. This stance was also reflected in the periodicals of the Azusa Street Mission, the *Apostolic Faith* in the year 1908. In an article with the title "Who May Prophesy?," for which no authorship is recorded, initially the prophetic ministry of women is affirmed, but immediately afterwards the subordination of women is postulated:

> Before Pentecost, the woman could only go into the "court of women" and not into the inner court. The anointing oil was never poured on a womans [sic] head but only on the heads of kings, prophets and priests. But when our Lord poured out Pentecost, He brought all those faithful women with the other disciples into the upper room, and God baptized them all in the same room and made no difference. All the women received the anointed oil of the Holy Ghost and were able to preach the same as men. The woman is the weaker vessel and represents the tenderness of Christ, while the man represents the firmness of Christ.... No woman that has the Spirit of Jesus wants to usurp authority over man. The more God uses you in the Spirit, the more humble and tender you are and [t]he more filled with the blessed Holy Spirit. It is contrary to the Scriptures that woman should not have her part in the salvation work to which God has called her. We have no right to lay a straw in her way.... It is the same Holy Spirit in the woman as in the man.[108]

In the awakening gatherings of the Azusa Street Mission, women could function in a ministry as long as they did not seize authority over men through their ministry. This restricted freedom of women, according to Stephenson, is also symptomatic of the wider Pentecostal Movement.[109]

Next, Stephenson investigated the role of women in a historical analysis of four classic Pentecostal denominations: The church *of God*

---

107. Bartleman quoted in Stephenson, *Dismantling the Dualisms*, 21.
108. Stephenson, *Dismantling the Dualisms*, 22.
109. Stephenson, *Dismantling the Dualisms*, 22.

(Cleveland, Tennessee), *Church of God in Christ*, *Assemblies of God* and the *International Church of the Foursquare Gospel*.[110] All have in common, to greater or lesser extent, that women were subject to restrictions in respect of their ministries and functions. Women could function in various ministries even to the point that they de facto occasionally led congregations and preached.[111] Nevertheless, even these very ministries undertaken by women are a witness to their restrictions:

- They were only permitted to practice a leading function in the absence of a male pastor.[112]
- As a matter of principle, even in Amee McPherson's church, the Foursquare Gospel Church,[113] the ultimate responsibility (governmental functions) of women over men was rejected.[114]

Stephenson's conclusion on the beginnings of the Pentecostal Movement:

> What becomes evident is that while Pentecostals' belief in the outpouring of the Spirit removed some barriers for women in Pentecostal churches, it clearly did not remove all of them. In the beginning of the movement, Pentecostals merely superimposed an ideology of empowerment over a dualistic anthropology. The outpouring of the Spirit did not affect Pentecostals' anthropological dualism. It only complemented the ideas that were already present. Consequently, Pentecostal women's experience has been that of perpetual ecclesial restrictions in one way or another.[115]

Current Concepts

In a further step, Stephenson gives an overview of the Pentecostal discourse of the present day. In so doing, she differentiates between descriptive and constructive investigation. The descriptive investigations describe the development of the role of women within the Pentecostal

110. Stephenson, *Dismantling the Dualisms*, 8.
111. Stephenson, *Dismantling the Dualisms*, 31.
112. Stephenson, *Dismantling the Dualisms*, 31.
113. Stephenson, *Dismantling the Dualisms*, 55.
114. Stephenson, *Dismantling the Dualisms*, 26.
115. Stephenson, *Dismantling the Dualisms*, 57.

Movement but make no suggestions as to how this could be changed. Stephenson divides the descriptive analysis into four subgroups, each with different concepts. Firstly, there is the concept of *Routinization and Regimentation,* which is guided by the methodology of Max Weber's *The Sociology of Religion.*[116] Then, there is the concept of *Primitivism and Pragmatism,* which relates tensions within the Pentecostal Movement as a restorative movement to pragmatism, expressed by Pentecostals becoming aware of the social and cultural expectations of society.[117] A third concept is that of the church *Mothers,* which is found in Pentecostal Afro-American research. It covers the influence of West African family structures, which until today is evident in the form of church Mothers in Afro-American church structures.[118] The fourth and last concept which Stephenson lists is *Biographical Studies,* which examines the history of women within the American Pentecostal Movement.[119]

In the constructive studies she identifies three concepts. There is the *biblical* concept, which examines biblical texts which restrict women in the practice of ministry and the analysis of the texts used for traditional exegesis and hermeneutical approaches.[120] Another constructive approach is what Stephenson identifies as a *theological* concept, which can be termed most simply as a systematic theological approach.[121] The last constructive approach Stephenson categorizes as a *pastoral* concept. This concept is primarily characterized by the fact that its target audience does not consist of theologians but laypeople who should be made aware of the issue of women in ministry. The pastoral concept works strongly

---

116. Stephenson, *Dismantling the Dualisms,* 60. Mentioned are Barfoot and Sheppard, "Prophetic vs. Priestly Religion"; Poloma, *Assemblies of God*; Roebuck, "Limiting Liberty."

117. Stephenson, *Dismantling the Dualisms,* 64. Mentioned are Blumhofer, *Assemblies of God* and *Restoring Faith*; Wacker, *Heaven Below*; Stanley, "Wesleyan/Holiness and Pentecostal Women Preachers"; Ware, "Spiritual Egalitarianism."

118. Stephenson, *Dismantling the Dualisms,* 67. Mentioned are Gilkes, *Black Women's Experience*; Butler, *Women in the Church of God.*

119. Stephenson, *Dismantling the Dualisms,* 67. Mentioned are: Alexander, *Women of Azusa Street* and *Limited Liberty*; Lawless, *Handmaidens of the Lord.*

120. Stephenson, *Dismantling the Dualisms,* 71. Mentioned are: Thomas, "Women in the Church"; Powers, "'Your Daughters Shall Prophesy'" and "Recovering a Woman's Head."

121. Stephenson, *Dismantling the Dualisms,* 76. Mentioned are: Johns (see her essay "Pentecostal Spirituality and the Conscientization of Women") this would be an eschatological-pneumatological approach.

with biblical texts and theological argumentation, from which it derives inferences for church praxis.[122]

Even though Stephenson recognizes the above-mentioned approaches and concepts, all of which contribute their part to raising awareness and promoting the role of women in spiritual ministry, she also sees shortcomings. Thus, she concludes that although the descriptive studies may well show historical and sociological aspects, they deliver no theological solutions. Theological solutions are found to some extent with constructive studies but are not satisfactory in Stephenson's view. Likewise, she ascertains that the pneumatology is seldom taken into account in the respective concepts. When pneumatology is discussed in relation to women, then this is exclusively in done so reference to their ministry and not to their humanity. Additionally, apart from one exception,[123] ecclesiology is never addressed, and feminist theology generally is in no respect taken into account. On the basis of these observations, Stephenson poses three questions: Why does pneumatology not play a greater role in Pentecostal anthropology? Why is ecclesiology mostly overlooked, and why are feminist-theological contributions ignored?[124]

Unmasking a Dualistic Theological Anthropology

Stephenson writes that Pentecostals interpret Acts 2 in regard to the role of women only as justification for the extension of their ministry. She ascribes this one-sided approach to the fact that in Pentecostal theology, Lukan pneumatology is understood exclusively as empowerment for ministry and for mission.[125] Whilst the woman was excluded from ritual life in the Old Testament, she was empowered after Pentecost by the Holy Spirit, for example for the prophetic ministry. Such an interpretation of Acts 2 had (and still has) considerable influence on the Pentecostal understanding of the ministry of women.[126] However, as already mentioned, such an approach only addresses the *function* of women. With good reason Stephenson comments, "A theology of empowerment does

122. Stephenson, *Dismantling the Dualisms*, 79. Mentioned are: Gill and Cavaness, book: *God's Women Then and Now*; Alexander and Gause, *Women in Leadership*.

123. See Gill and Cavaness, *God's Woman Then and Now*.

124. Stephenson, *Dismantling the Dualisms*, 85.

125. For rationale, see Stephenson's remarks on Stronstad, Menzies, and Shelten in Stephenson, *Dismantling the Dualisms*, 92–97.

126. Stephenson, *Dismantling the Dualisms*, 91.

not necessarily eliminate a hierarchy between male and female. As the history of Pentecostalism has illustrated, the two can coexist."[127] What is required, in order to take the discussion on the role of women in the Pentecostal Movement one step further, is a theology which focusses attention on the *humanity* of women. However, whilst the Holy Spirit in Acts 2 is separated from any soteriological dimension, Pentecostals must draw upon other resources. Thus, they have made use of popular theological and christological methodologies in order to focus attention on the theological identity of women, rather than turning toward pneumatology.[128]

The above-described charismatic interpretation of Acts 2 Stephenson now contrasts with a concept which, in addition to the empowerment for ministry in the Pentecost event, also sees a soteriological dimension. Thus, she draws upon James Dunn and Max Turner, who in their interpretation of the Lukan double work, similarly to Wenk, are led by the paradigm of the *New Exodus*. In contrast to Wenk, Stephenson does not interpret the Lukan double work against the background of the original Exodus, but through the paradigm of the new Exodus of Isa 40–55.[129] The Isaiah paradigm of Isa 40:1–11 presents the following aspects, structured into four focal points: The first focal point is found in Isa 40:1–2 and deals with the restoration of God's people. This subject likewise resonates in Isa 49:13; 51:3; 52:9; 55:3. The second focal point is found in Isa 40:3–5 and address the issue of the universal revelation of God's glory, and likewise appears in Isa 42:4; 49:6; 51:4–6; 52:10; 55:5. The third focal point emphasizes the power of God's word in Isa 40:6–8 and is repeatedly mentioned in 45:23; 55:10–11.[130] In Isa 40:6–8, as a fourth focus point, the sovereignty of God is highlighted, as God's word is associated with the fragility of humankind. This last theme is also addressed in Isa 40:12–31; 44:9–20; 46:5–7. The prologue concludes with the verses from Isa 40:9–11, in which it again addresses the restoration of God's people. The Lukan double work is also structured in correspondence to the four focus points in Isa 40–45, whereby Luke specifically emphasizes Isaiah's focus points one (the restoration of Israel), and two (the status of the

---

127. Stephenson, *Dismantling the Dualisms*, 89.

128. Stephenson, *Dismantling the Dualisms*, 90.

129. Stephenson, *Dismantling the Dualisms*, 99. Stephenson essentially follows the theologians in her explanation.

130. Gill and Cavaness, *God's Woman Then and Now*. Stephenson, *Dismantling the Dualisms*, 101.

gentiles and the nations).[131] Against the background of the new Isaian Exodus paradigm, the soteriological dimension of Lukan pneumatology also becomes apparent.[132]

In the Book of Acts, it becomes evident how Isaiah's focus points fulfil the new Exodus. Luke recounts how salvation begins in Jerusalem, how Israel is reunited, a process that also includes the Samaritans, and how finally also the gentiles are added to God's people. This restoration of Israel constitutes the content the first chapter of the Book of Acts. But even broader topics emerge, which are connected with the hope of restoration. Amongst other things, the full number of the Apostles is restored (Acts 1:12–26), the early church becomes an eschatological community of the Holy Spirit (Acts 2), the Davidic kingdom is restored (Acts 15:16–18), repentance and conversion are recurring themes (Acts 2:41; 3:19; 4:4) and outcasts are re-integrated into the community (Acts 8:26–40).[133] After Israel is restored, the focus is turned from inward to outward, i.e., the mission to the gentiles.[134] Here, Stephenson assesses the soteriological aspect of Lukan pneumatology and, in doing so, references Turner. Every form of salvation, according to Luke, is to be understood against the background of the Isaianic New Exodus:

> A Christocentric version of the Isaianic New Exodus hopes for Israel's restoration, based largely (but not exclusively) on Isaiah 40–55. Within this, salvation begins with that forgiveness of Israel's sins which terminates God's historical chastisement of the nation . . . and allows Yahweh's "return" to Zion as peace-bringing restorer king, liberating forlorn Israel from her national and spiritual doldrums, and restoring her as a light to the nations.[135]

According to Stephenson, this insight leads Turner to the following conclusions:[136]

> First, contra Dunn, Turner maintains that the disciples did experience salvation to a limited degree before Pentecost. Turner understands Jesus' reception of the Holy Spirit in Luke 4 to be an endowment for the purpose of initiating Israel's liberation and

131. See Stephenson, *Dismantling the Dualisms*, 102–7.
132. See also Turner, "Spirit and Salvation in Acts," 107.
133. See also Pao, *Acts and the Isaianic New Exodus*, 111–46, 217–48.
134. Stephenson, *Dismantling the Dualisms*, 107.
135. Turner in Stephenson, *Dismantling the Dualisms*, 107.
136. Stephenson, *Dismantling the Dualisms*, 108.

restoration. Jesus receives the Holy Spirit as the power to effect the kingdom of God among Israel, not for his own experience of the kingdom. Throughout the remainder of the Gospel of Luke at least some of Jesus' disciples and followers have experienced the manifestation of this salvation (e.g., acts of deliverance healing, the constitution of the Twelve), even if in limited ways. Nonetheless, though this salvation is made present in the ministry of Jesus-empowered-by-the-Spirit, the question arises as to how this salvation will continue once Jesus has ascended.

This issue leads to Turner's second conclusion that, *contra* classical Pentecostals, the outpouring of the Holy Spirit in Acts is soteriologically related in that the Holy Spirit is the power by which Israel's salvation/transformation can be continued and deepened after Christ's ascension. At the end of the Gospel of Luke and the beginning of Acts, Luke mentions only one means that will be given to accomplish this act: the outpouring of the Holy Spirit (Luke 24:47–49; Acts 1:1–8). Turner says:

> Luke's reader will surely not be taken by surprise at this point, and ask what the "Spirit of prophecy" has to do with salvation, for she will have seen that it was the Holy Spirit's work in and through Jesus which made 'salvation' powerfully present in the period of the ministry in the first place. The outpouring of the Holy Spirit upon the full circle of Jesus' disciples could then only be expected to deepen and further it, as well as extending it to others.... The transitional passages (especially Acts 1:1–8) would strongly suggest to the reader that it is the gift of the Sprit to Israel that provides the ongoing self-manifesting and transforming presence of God in strength, and so the gift of the Holy Spirit which lies at the heart of the hope for Israel's ongoing salvation/transformation and her mission as the Isaianic servant and light to the nations.[137]

Stephenson concludes that the outpouring of the Holy Spirit is necessary for soteriological reasons.

The Pentecostal event in Acts 2 heralds the eschatological era, and various indications in the text point toward this: The modification of the introductory words of the Joel citation (from "after these things" [LXX] to "in the last days") point toward an eschatological interpretation of the

---

137. Turner, *Power from on High*, 346–47, quoted in Stephenson, *Dismantling the Dualisms*, 108.

outpouring of the Holy Spirit. Thus, also the implied parallels between the giving of the Law at Sinai, and the Pentecost event, the refreshing in Acts 3:20, which was promised after the repentance and conversion of Israel, or even the juxtaposition of the outpouring of the Holy Spirit and the immediately ensuing heavenly community in Acts 2:42–47. All these indicating signs of the restoration of Israel are ultimately linked with the working of the Holy Spirit.[138]

Beside the motif of the restoration of Israel, the working of the Holy Spirit is also connected with the process of conversion and initiation, as established in Acts 1:8.[139] In a first phase, an outpouring of the Holy Spirit comes upon the Jews in Jerusalem (Acts 2:38–39). In a second phase, the gospel goes out to the Samaritans (Acts 8:1), thus it also alludes to a further aspect of the restoration of Israel, in which Judah and Samaria are reunited within the New Exodus community. In a third phase, the gospel and the working of the Holy Spirit reach the gentiles (Acts 10:34–48; 11:11–18; 15:7–11). In all three phases, the Holy Spirit plays a significant role, in which, through the baptism in the Holy Spirit, the Jerusalemites, Samaritans and gentiles are confirmed, by God Himself, as part of the new people of God.[140] It is the Holy Spirit who ultimately creates a soteriological equality between the Jews and the gentiles: "The spirit is received as the soteriological Spirit and not as an empowerment for mission, altogether removed from soteriology."[141] This has the following consequences:

> In receiving the Holy Spirit of prophecy, one also receives the transformational soteriological Spirit that removes all previous distinctions from which dualistic paradigms emerge. The import of the Holy Spirit baptism is that reception of the Holy Spirit is not just a *donum superadditum* that is tacked on to a dualistic anthropology, but a transformative experience that eradicates this dualistic ideology altogether. The outpouring of the Holy Spirit removed the dualisms of old/Yong, male/female, master/servant, Jews/Samaritans, and Jews/Gentiles. The outpouring of the Holy Spirit necessitated a new way of living that transformed the anthropological assumptions that had been operating.[142]

---

138. Stephenson, *Dismantling the Dualisms*, 109.
139. Stephenson, *Dismantling the Dualisms*, 110.
140. Stephenson, *Dismantling the Dualisms*, 111.
141. Stephenson, *Dismantling the Dualisms*, 112.
142. One argument, which, according to Stephenson, is repeatedly used in support of the subordination of women, is the concept that men and women are equal in their being but are called to different functions—a common explanation within evangelical

Feminist-Pneumatological Anthropology in the Creation Account

The starting point of Stephenson's feminist-pneumatological anthropology is the *Imago Dei* concept, derived from Genesis 1:26–27: the act of creation begins with the Holy Spirit, who broods over the chaos.[143] Through the Holy Spirit, the spoken word becomes reality, and the creation takes on form. It is also the immanence of God's living Spirit that gives life to humankind and reveals their attachment to the Creator. Through the Holy Spirit, the human being is created, as man and woman, as the image of God. It is important to note that, in contrast to other early cultures, within the creation narrative of Genesis 1:26–27, not only the king is denoted as the image of God, or as a child of God, but mankind per se: "The Old Testament has democratized the understanding of 'image' and all persons are God's representatives within creation."[144]

The image of God carried by humankind is expressed not least in his calling to rule over creation and to administrate it in alignment with the Creator.[145] Because the image of God carried by humankind also retained its legal validity after the fall (Gen 5:1–3), mankind still carries, even now, the commission to administrate creation in alignment with God.[146] With regard to the *Imago Dei* of humanity, both men and women are equally called for the purpose of ruling over creation. Especially with regard to the democratization of the image of God (Gen 1:26–27), it becomes apparent that in the calling of humanity to rulership, there is inherent equality of all people:

> The fact that the Genesis narrative democratizes the understanding of the *imago Dei* and pronounces that all persons are capable of maintaining this function implies a vocational equality and mutuality that addresses one's very being. Because male and female are made in the image of God, there is an egalitarianism present that situates both of them on level ground.[147]

---

circles used to justify imposing restrictions on women—a justification which even Pentecostals have adopted. Stephenson sets this concept against a feminist-pneumatological anthropology: "While it is true that different functions do not necessarily entail personal inferiority or superiority, this is not the case when this claim is applied to the situation of women's subordination to men. That is, functional subordination is not the same as female subordination" (Stephenson, *Dismantling the Dualisms*, 115).

143. Stephenson, *Dismantling the Dualisms*, 120.
144. Stephenson, *Dismantling the Dualisms*, 119.
145. Stephenson, *Dismantling the Dualisms*, 118.
146. Stephenson, *Dismantling the Dualisms*, 119.
147. Stephenson, *Dismantling the Dualisms*, 121–22.

As a result of the fall, human beings no longer rule merely over the animals and the earth but also over their fellow humans. Nowhere in the creation account is there a mandate by which God gives people rulership over other human beings. In Genesis 3, this changes as a consequence of the fall:

> Instead of understanding the consequence of the Fall to imply prescriptives for the way in which male and female *should* live together, it functions descriptively portraying how the male and female will live together as a result of sin (Gen 3:16). That is, the woman desiring her husband and his rule over her is not God's desire, but a perversion of creation. In the Genesis primal history, sin is depicted in terms of violence, as persons exercise their power against one another in destructive ways. This is certainly no less true with respect to the male and female.[148]

In this regard, the *imago Dei* gives new perspectives:

> The *imago Dei* points to what God originally intended for male and female, in which there was no dualism present. Any dualism that emerges is brought by sin and thus mars the imago Dei. Whereas humans were fashioned to serve as God's royal representatives and be creatures of equality and mutuality, sin frustrates this divine calling and results in persons becoming creatures of oppression. Subordination and supremacy, especially against one another, are perversions of creation. It is only with the advent of *new* creation that the *imago Dei* can be renewed and restored. This renewal and restoration will rectify humankind's vocation as God's representatives and promote a renewed theological anthropology.[149]

The ultimate image of God is found in Christ, hence the concept of *imago Christi*. Galatians 3:26–28 serves as a foundational text for this purpose. In this text Paul, states that whoever believes in Christ and has been baptized in Christ's name, has put on Christ and has become equal to all other believers:

> The implication behind this language is to suggest that when one puts on Christ, one takes on the characteristics, virtues, and intentions of Christ so that one actually becomes like Christ (cf. Rom 13:14; Eph 4:24; Col 3:10).

---

148. Stephenson, *Dismantling the Dualisms*, 122.
149. Stephenson, *Dismantling the Dualisms*, 122.

> In v. 28 the significance of the implication of all believers becoming sons of God and putting on Christ (vv. 26–27) is explicitly offered: old divisions and inequalities have come to an end and new relationships emerge. Specifically, three couplets are listed: Jew/Greek (ethic), slave/free (social), and male/female (sexual).[150]

It seems appropriate to the early church, especially in the light of Jewish and Greek culture, to point out that they acknowledged that ethical, social and gender fractures within society were healed in their community through baptism: "In particular, by taking on the image and likeness of Christ through water baptism, one also takes Christ's sonship, so that all who are *imago Christi* are sons of God (Gal 3:26). In Christ, the prodigal sons have come home to reclaim their sonship."[151] Nevertheless, in order to be able to embrace Christ's intentions, virtues and characteristics, the working of the Holy Spirit is needed. And Stephenson leads this, in respect of the *imago Dei*, to a Trinitarian reflection: Just as Christ's life and work is inextricably connected with God's Spirit, equally the *imago Christi* will be formed in our life in as much as we are inseparably connected with the Holy Spirit:

> From beginning to end, the missions of the Holy Spirit and of Jesus are intertwined. Thus, an imago Christi approach cannot be devoid of pneumatology because the life of Christ was not devoid of the spirit. It is only possible to "image" Christ—live a life that is consistent with Jesus' compassionate and liberating life in the world—thorough the power and presence of the Holy Spirit.[152]

Thereby she poses the question of the *imago Spiritus*. Stephenson guides this question to the assertion that a pneumatological concept which is oriented toward the Lukan double work must begin with the baptism in the Holy Spirit, though not simply as empowerment for ministry according to traditional Pentecostal understanding, but as described by Turner. Thereby, interesting parallels with Pauline Christology arise. Paul describes both water baptism and Spirit baptism with the same imagery: "In Galatians 3:26–28, Paul depicts the act of water baptism as a 'putting on,' or a 'being clothed with,' (*enduo*) Christ."[153] Whoever has

---

150. Stephenson, *Dismantling the Dualisms*, 124.
151. Stephenson, *Dismantling the Dualisms*, 128.
152. Stephenson, *Dismantling the Dualisms*, 126.
153. Stephenson, *Dismantling the Dualisms*, 129.

been baptized with water has "put on" Christ and is therefore the *imago Christi*. Luke uses this same imagery of "attiring oneself in" (*enduo*): "However, instead of orientating this christologically, with water baptism, Luke orientates it pneumatologically, with Spirit baptism.... The Spirit, like Christ, is a garment that envelops the believer. In a sense, those who have been baptized in the Holy Spirit are *imago Spiritus* because they have 'put on,' the Holy Spirit."[154] A further similarity between Paul and Luke is that both water baptism and Spirit baptism function as a means of participation in the new creation:

> Just like Paul, Luke is working with the concept of new creation. In contradistinction though, Luke highlights Spirit baptism as the means by which persons come to participate in the new creation, which within the Isaianic new Exodus motif is presented as the restoration of Israel. For Luke, this new creation is not being affected because of water baptism per se, but because of Spirit baptism.... Moreover, participation in this new creation through the Holy Spirit is not limited. Israel is receiving its restoration, but the boundaries of that restoration are being expanded to include those who had heretofore been on the margins.[155]

Yet a further aspect is that, for Paul and Luke, the participation in the new creation has ethical implications. Paul primarily argues christologically, but the rationale with Luke is of a pneumatological nature: "For Luke, however, the substance of the theological argument for the ethical imperative is not that Christ nullifies the dualisms that have served to exclude others, but that the Holy Spirit abolishes these dualisms as the believer is baptized in the Holy Spirit."[156] In this aspect, Stephenson follows the exposition of Wenk.[157] Through the outpouring of the Holy Spirit and ethical implications related with it, a community arises which anticipates aspects of the future salvation whilst practicing a new social order which is free from dualism. For Stephenson, it is particularly significant that the restoration of Israel through the Holy Spirit is newly defined as an inclusive community: "The symbolic act of the Samaritans receiving the Holy Spirit at the hands of Peter and John probably was meant to signify the reunification of the two kingdoms of Samaria and

---

154. Stephenson, *Dismantling the Dualisms*, 129.
155. Stephenson, *Dismantling the Dualisms*, 130–31.
156. Stephenson, *Dismantling the Dualisms*, 131.
157. Wenk, *Community forming Power*, 43, 236, 294–307.

Judea and the acceptance of the Samaritans as the restored people of God."[158] Further on in the course of the Book of Acts, a eunuch, and ultimately Gentiles, became part of the community: "The reception of the Holy Spirit becomes the significant event within the narrative indicating that they are to be considered equal members of the restored Israel."[159] This leads to the following conclusion: "These unclean and uncircumcised people are no longer to be marginalized. Being baptized in the Holy Spirit removes the significance of these distinctions and becomes the very principle by which this inclusion is accepted by the community."[160] Through baptism in the Holy Spirit, people are now able to participate in activities from which they were originally excluded (e.g., women are now allowed to prophesy). Besides the new functional perspective, there is also the addition of a soteriological perspective: "Spirit baptism does not just transform what one can do, but who one is. Reception of the Holy Spirit is not just a sign of the new creation but also the causative agent of the new creation. That is, it offers a new dignity to persons who formerly were not recognized as equals."[161] This assertion is at the same time also a requirement: "Through the Holy Spirit, persons have the ability, as well as the responsibility, to actualize their potential to exist as full and equal human beings and realize the present dimension of salvation, which will ultimately be fulfilled on the other side of the eschaton."[162] This does not mean, however, that there is no difference between men and women:

> An imago Spiritus approach to theological anthropology suggests a common anthropology in that both male and female are affirmed in their full and equal humanity, but it also suggests a distinctive anthropology in that the biological differences among persons are not obliterated. The effect of Spirit baptism is not that persons are transformed into androgynous beings, of course, but that who they are is preserved and taken up into the life-giving and life-affirming presence and power of the Holy Spirit. In this way, the Holy Spirit enlivens and accentuates one's humanity.[163]

---

158. Stephenson, *Dismantling the Dualisms*, 132.
159. Stephenson, *Dismantling the Dualisms*, 133.
160. Stephenson, *Dismantling the Dualisms*, 133.
161. Stephenson, *Dismantling the Dualisms*, 133.
162. Stephenson, *Dismantling the Dualisms*, 134.
163. Stephenson, *Dismantling the Dualisms*, 134–35.

Unmasking a Dualistic Ecclesiology

Even though the limitation of women has its roots in a dualistic anthropology, it is not sufficient to unmask this without demonstrating the necessary consequences for ecclesiology. Stephenson rises to this challenge in her sixth chapter. She introduces three feminist concepts which she combines and enhances further on. Since the confrontation with feminist ecclesiology is relevant to the constructive part of Stephenson's monograph, I will go more deeply into the three models.

The first concept is Schüssler Fiorenza's *The Ekklesia As a Discipleship of Equals*. Her starting point is the theory that the church is called to be a community of equals, which is justified by the historical beginnings of Christianity.[164] Accordingly, a feminist-theological reconstruction of Christian roots is one of Schüssler Fiorenza's central concerns. Thus Stephenson writes:

> [Schüssler Fiorenza] claims that from the very beginning, Christianity did not conform to the patriarchal ethos and structures that surrounded it. Rather, it was committed to a vision and practice of a radical democracy that was inclusive of all and, as such, was a discipleship of equals. She maintains that one can catch a glimpse of this way of life in certain biblical texts, but that these texts only represent the tip of the iceberg that breaks the surface. Her efforts to reconstruct the Christian origins are thus an attempt to uncover the remainder of the iceberg that is submerged.[165]

In this connection, for Schüssler Fiorenza, Galatians 3:27–29 plays a groundbreaking role. In her view, that text expresses the theological self-image of a "church of equals": "Within this movement, baptism into Christ was the rite of initiation. In Christ, Christians became new creations, entered into a new family of believers, and were filled with and lived by the Holy Spirit."[166] From this resulted the formation of a community in which the previous societal differences became meaningless:[167]

> All privileges possessed before baptism are relinquished. All have equal access to the gifts of the Holy Spirit because God's

---

164. Stephenson, *Dismantling the Dualisms*, 143.
165. Stephenson, *Dismantling the Dualisms*, 144.
166. Stephenson, *Dismantling the Dualisms*, 146.
167. Stephenson, *Dismantling the Dualisms*, 146.

Spirit has been poured out on everyone. Describing this reality, Schüssler Fiorenza says,

> In baptism Christians enter the force field of the Holy Spirit, share in ecstatic experiences, and are "sent" to proclaim the gospel in the power of the Holy Spirit, attested to by miraculous sings and persuasive eloquence. They have become "a new creation," the Holy Spirit-filled people, those who have been purified, sanctified, and justified. They all are equal, because they all share in the Holy Spirit, God's power; they are all called elect and holy because they are adopted by God, all without exception.... The household of God concretized in the house church constitutes the new family of God, where all without exception are "sisters and brothers." Galatians 3:28 belongs to this theological setting and missionary environment.... Galatians 3:28 is a key expression, not of Pauline theology but of the theological self-understanding of the Christian missionary movement which had far-reaching historical impact.[168]

Fiorenza Schüssler points out that with the transition of the original Jewish-Christian church into a Greek-Roman church, it underwent a cultural adaptation to the culture of the community. As Stephenson writes: "This gradual concession became more concretized in the second century as the church leadership changed from a charismatic and communal authority open to all the baptized into an authority vested in local officers accessible only to male heads of households,"[169] with corresponding ramifications: "Consequently, an understanding and embodiment of the church as the discipleship of equals was obscured further and women became increasingly marginalized."[170]

For Schüssler Fiorenza, the above-described beginnings of the church provide a permanent vision for a church of equals. This vision is, however, only implemented once women are fully and completely integrated into the church in every respect. At the same time, she argues that this will not take place merely through the facilitation of women's ordination:

---

168. Schüssler Fiorenza, *In Memory of Her*, 160–84, quoted in Stephenson, *Dismantling the Dualisms*, 146.

169. Stephenson, *Dismantling the Dualisms*, 147.

170. Stephenson, *Dismantling the Dualisms*, 147.

Because the historical church has largely been characterized by a kyriarchal[171] infrastructure, merely opening up the upper echelons of this hierarchy to women does not remedy the situation. To juxtapose "feminist" with "priesthood" is to construct an oxymoron. These two realities are not compatible because they both subscribe to fundamentally conflicting spiritual realities. The radical democratic equality of the discipleship of equals is mutually opposed to the hierarchical office that perpetuates an essential religious status difference through ordination.[172]

In order to effect fundamental changes, new theological and ecclesiological structures are needed which expose every dualism. Schüssler Fiorenza sees a way to achieve this through the concept Women-Church. Such a church should evolve its function hermeneutically, re/constructively and politically. Hermeneutically, because she has verbally signalled that even women are church and, for that reason, the church will never become a historical reality without the full integration of women.[173] When women are church, then there is also a narrative of women as church— a narrative which must be reconstructed again. In this sense, the term Women-Church constructs a theoretical and practical space in which women have the freedom to discover their own voice and to establish a different vision of church.[174] However, Schüssler Fiorenza is not suggesting a separatist concept or an inversion of hierarchy with women reigning over men: "Therefore, the constructive aim of the *ekklesia* of women is not to gather over and against men, but to provide a space in which women can regain their spiritual and ecclesial authority so that true mutuality can

---

171. Schüssler Fiorenza has created the term *kyriarchal* to replace the widespread term *patriarchal*. She justifies this step as follows: "In contrast to gender feminism, which understands 'patriarchal' in terms of gender dualism as global male domination of all women equally, I theorize it as a complex pyramidal system of domination and subordination, profit and exploitation. Such a conceptualization of patriarchy simply in terms of gender however, is not able adequately to theorize interstructured racial, class, and colonial oppression. Hence I have suggested replacing the terminology of patriarchy with that of kyriarchy, defined in classical socio-political terms. In antiquity, kyriarchy connoted the rule of the lord/master/father/husband over those subordinated to and dependent on him. Kyriarchy is a socio-political and cultural system of domination that has produced dualistic asymmetric justifications of systemic exclusions and forms of exploitation" (Schüssler Fiorenza quoted in Stephenson, *Dismantling the Dualisms*, 141, from Segovia, "Looking Back, Looking Around, Looking Ahead," 19–20).

172. Stephenson, *Dismantling the Dualisms*, 148.
173. Stephenson, *Dismantling the Dualisms*, 149.
174. Stephenson, *Dismantling the Dualisms*, 150.

become a reality."[175] Ultimately, Women-Church also has a political dimension because it points to a specific political reality: "A democratic assembly of free citizens, also referred to as the discipleship of equals. The *ekklesia* of women seeks to embody this political reality, not so that this becomes an end in itself, but so that the ekklesia of women might ultimately transform the kyriarchal church into the discipleship of equals."[176]

The second feminist-ecclesiological concept is Rosemary Radford Ruether's *The Church as a Community of Liberation from Patriarchy*. As Schüssler Fiorenza has already reasoned, so also does Ruether on the basis that two competing church models are in conflict with one another: that of the Holy Spirit-filled community and that of the historical institution: "Whereas Christianity began as a Spirit-filled messianic community whose model of ministry was charismatic, it gradually changed into a hierarchical, historic institution."[177] According to Ruether, these two models should not be in opposition but much more interrelate in a "creative dialectic." In order to maintain the dialectic tension between the two models,

> it must find a way to transmit itself historically, but in a way that is open for the continual renewing of the Holy Spirit and reformation of Spirit-filled community in its midst. Consequently, the historic institution should understand itself to be the occasion and context for the experience of the Holy Spirit, but not the source of the Holy Spirit. Likewise, the Holy Spirit-filled community must understand that institutionalization per se is not illegitimate because inevitably it must adopt some historic forms if it is to transmit its culture to succeeding generations. What must be rejected is not institutionalisation, but the myth that there is a particular form of historical institution that is *the* correct form for all times and places.[178]

It is within this dialectic tension that Radford Ruether seeks to place her understanding of Women-Church. She sees the historical institution as a dialogue partner with which one can enter into conversation without limiting the community of Women-Church. Conversely, the historical institutions provide a springboard whose resources can be used for creative advancement. Through this dialogue, Ruether sees the possibility

---

175. Stephenson, *Dismantling the Dualisms*, 150.
176. Stephenson, *Dismantling the Dualisms*, 150.
177. Stephenson, *Dismantling the Dualisms*, 153.
178. Stephenson, *Dismantling the Dualisms*, 154.

that even the historical institutions become more flexible and can serve as "vehicles of further creativity."[179] Within the biblical traditions, Ruether relates the Women-Church to the prophetic tradition. For her, this tradition has a twofold function: publicly convicting and proclaiming. Prophecy convicts publicly where judgment is proclaimed on the rich and powerful who practice social oppression. Prophetic proclamations occur wherever people, in particular leaders, are called back to God's vision of a righteous life, which results in a transformation of heart and concrete changes. For Ruether, it is the task of Women-Church, in consideration of patriarchal churches and structures, as a feminist Exodus community, to raise the prophetic voice: "As a feminist Exodus community, Ruether envisions Women-Church to be one stage in an ultimate process of the church becoming a redemptive community of both woman and men, who are liberated from patriarchy."[180] Notwithstanding, Ruether sees Women-Church as a community which at its inception should be independent and exclusively reserved for women. Only in this way can Women-Church avoid patriarchal control and limitation. This independence is important in order for women to share their experiences and analyze them. They must find their own cultural form through which they can define and resist patriarchal marginalization: "Women-Church nurtures women through their death to the old order of patriarchy and rebirth into a new redemptive community of liberated women."[181] However, in the eyes of Ruther, Women-Church being an exclusively feminine community of believers must be a transitional phase.[182] The moment must come in which no more is spoken of Women-Church, but only of church in which "men begin to critique their own dehumanization by patriarchy and form their critical culture of liberation from it in a way that truly complements the feminist Exodus and allows the formation of real dialogue."[183]

One of the most central impediments for Women-Church is any form of clericalism. For Ruether, clericalism is

> the separation of ministry from mutual interaction with community and its transformation into hierarchically ordered casts

179. Stephenson, *Dismantling the Dualisms*, 155.
180. Stephenson, *Dismantling the Dualisms*, 157.
181. Stephenson, *Dismantling the Dualisms*, 157.
182. For criticism of Ruether's concept, see Stephenson, *Dismantling the Dualisms*, 75.
183. Ruether quoted in Stephenson, *Dismantling the Dualisms*, 157.

of clergy and laity. The clergy monopolize teaching, sacramental action, and administration and turning [sic] the community into passive dependents who are to receive these services from the clergy but cannot participate in shaping and defining themselves. An understanding of ministry as originating from the community and continually based in it is suppressed in favour of ministry as "the ordained" who possess a heteronomous power beyond the capacity of the community.[184]

Clericalism constructs relationships in polarity, comprising dominating and dependent parties, and correspondingly always works to restrict and diminish people. In the eyes of Ruether, this happens for example with the administration of the sacraments, with the stewardship of appropriate teaching and with the administrative management of the church, where individual people or a group of selected people decide on the fate of the church as a whole.[185] Instead of a select caste of a few, leadership should be established, according to Ruether, on the basis of function and gifting. The goal of such a leadership would then not be the exercise of power over others but rather the empowerment of others.[186]

The third feminist-ecclesiological concept is Letty Russell's *The Church as a Sign of God's Household of Freedom*. Russell understands the gospel, as other liberation theologians, as a message of liberation from internal and external oppression: "Salvation is a journey toward freedom, in which one travels with others and for others toward God's promised future: the new creation."[187] From this concept, Russell has developed her understanding of church: the church as a household of freedom. At the same time, *household,* as a metaphorical term does not merely stand for the church but for much more: *Household,* in combination with the term freedom, for Russel describes God's intention for the entire world, namely that it functions as a *Household of Freedom*. The church thereby has a symbolic role for God's intentions within creation. Through the work of Christ, God as caretaker intends to liberate the *entire* creation. Russell understands this liberation as both present and future.[188] One key

---

184. Ruether quoted in Stephenson, *Dismantling the Dualisms*, 158.
185. Stephenson, *Dismantling the Dualisms*, 158.
186. Stephenson, *Dismantling the Dualisms*, 158.
187. Stephenson, *Dismantling the Dualisms*, 160.
188. Stephenson, *Dismantling the Dualisms*, 161.

role in the establishment of a *Household of Freedom* poses the question: How are power and authority are to be experienced?[189]

> Power and authority are usually associated with domination, competition, and control. But do they need to be understood this way? From the perspective of the Christian gospel and from the perspective of feminist theory the answer is no. Power and authority can be exercised through domination and they most frequently are, in a world patterned by patriarchal paradigms of reality. But they can also be exercised through empowerment and authorizing, as they sometimes are where people are seeking to live out the gospel vision of shared community of service. This form of relationship has some very clear precedent in the biblical theology, both as a lived reality and as a hoped-for promise of a new house of freedom (Gal 5:1).[190]

In order to develop new, creative paradigms of power and authority Russell sets the contrasting patriarchal dynamic and the dynamic of the *Household of Freedom* face to face against one another. Thereby using the description of the two counter dynamics, the labels "authority of domination" and "authority of partnership" emerge. The authority of domination is expressed in a posture which understands itself not as part of the community but as standing above it. Often, this form of authority is expressed in paternalism or even as autonomy. Russell identifies paternalism as a form of false love. Paternalism cultivates an atmosphere of benevolence and covers needs, which however fosters dependence and consequently cumulates power at the cost of others. In this way, authority in the form of power is practised over a community. Autonomy, conversely, is authority without love. Autonomy suggests strength which is needed by third parties, without however needing others. It is a paradigm which operates not over but outside the community.[191] If authority is understood as a partnership, then it must be lived out within the setting of mutual dependence within the community.

---

189. Because the terms *authority* and *power* are often confused, Russell clarifies how she uses them: She understands power as something with which desired results are made to happen, which is not per se obtained in consensus with other parties. In contrast to this, authority through consensus is legitimized power. See also Stephenson, *Dismantling the Dualisms*, 161.

190. Stephenson, *Dismantling the Dualisms*, 161.

191. Stephenson, *Dismantling the Dualisms*, 162.

> This perspective encourages cooperation rather than competition, and is open to and desirous of contributions from a diversity of persons. . . . Unlike paternalism and autonomy, authority exercised as partnership realizes that persons need to learn to care for themselves and others, and that self-dependence is not an end in itself but a part of a process that leads to full interdependence. In this new paradigm, "authority is understood as authorizing the inclusion of all persons as partners, and power is understood as empowerment for self-actualization together with others."[192]
>
> Power is not hoarded at the top but shared with others, especially those on the margins, in ways that empower them.[193]

Russell emphasizes that the concept she has formulated does not have its origins in feminist liberation theology. Instead, she sees her concept much more justified by the Exodus experience, as well as by the birth, life, crucifixion and resurrection of Christ, in God Himself. Even though Russell's concept has the entire creation in focus, for her the church/community as a sign of God's *Household of Freedom* is a particular focal point. In order for the community to actually become this sign, however, it must, according to Russell, be a *church in the round*. For her, the round table symbolizes the embodiment of a household in which all are welcome to take part and to break bread with one another: "Participating in this life at the table is important because through table fellowship people become contributors to their own journey of faith and active participants in the struggle for the healing and liberation of creation."[194] Part of this *church in the round* is a renewed understanding of ministry and leadership which fundamentally integrates all baptized members within a shared responsibility and is oriented toward the gifting of individuals. Leadership as described above understands itself as a partnership-based ministry to the community, which refuses any dominance.[195]

A Feminist-Pneumatological Anthropology and Ecclesiology

For Stephenson, the three above-described feminist concepts facilitate fundamentally new ways to conceptualize the church free from dualisms:

192. Russell, *Household of Freedom*, 61, 91–93.
193. Stephenson, *Dismantling the Dualisms*, 163.
194. Stephenson, *Dismantling the Dualisms*, 164.
195. Stephenson, *Dismantling the Dualisms*, 165.

> Grounded in biblical and historical narratives, feminists' proposals have aimed at recapturing an egalitarian vision of the church. This objective has been described as transforming the church into a discipleship of equals (Schüssler Fiorenza), or a community of liberation from patriarchy (Ruether), or even a household of freedom (Russell). All of these ways of depicting the church portray it as inclusive, non-hierarchical, and functioning in a manner that relies upon peoples' varied giftings.
>
> Schüssler Fiorenza's, Ruether's, and Russell's ideas are essential for constructing an ecclesiology that does not just tolerate women in ministry, but nurtures them. Only in a church characterised by these features can women in ministry truly not be oppressed or become oppressor themselves.[196]

In chapter 7, Stephenson brings feminist ecclesiology into a dialogue with the Pentecostal church and thereby gains further action strategies:

In observing the Pentecostal church through the lens of Schüssler-Fiorenza's *Discipleship of Equals,* Stephenson sees great development potential in the democratization of the congregations. In contrast to Schüssler-Fiorenza, Stephenson does not justify the need for the democratization process according to Pauline theology, but pneumatologically on the basis of Acts 2:17–21: "Here Spirit baptism becomes the rite of initiation, and new creation centres on the believer being 'in the Spirit,' in addition to being 'in Christ.' The resulting community that is defined by such distinctives will be characterized as a discipleship of equals as the outpouring of the Spirit constitutes a radical democratizing of the people."[197] The Christian discipleship presented in Luke's gospel finds its continuance and fulfillment in a pneumatological manner. After the ascension of Christ, it is the Holy Spirit who speaks *to* and *through* the community,[198] which brings Stephenson to the following conclusion:

> The Spirit's presence in others means that one is not just a disciple based on the ability to listen and respond to the unmediated voice of the Spirit in one's own life, but also based on the ability to listen and respond to the mediated voice of the Spirit through others. This pneumatological perspective expands the idea of discipleship within a community of equals beyond a

---

196. Stephenson, *Dismantling the Dualisms,* 165.
197. Stephenson, *Dismantling the Dualisms,* 168.
198. Stephenson, *Dismantling the Dualisms,* 169.

christological and individualistic approach to a more pneumatological and communal one.[199]

For Stephenson, one problem area which is depicted as obstructive for the democratization process is the use of terminology. Traditionally *service* (thereby also the term *servant*) is associated with disenfranchised or underprivileged people.[200] This circumstance is not least fed by the fact that, to this day, it is primarily people with a low educational background and/or immigration background who work in the services sector.[201] With reference to Jacqueline Grant,[202] Stephenson advocates that the term 'service' be replaced with *follower/discipleship* because this corresponds more with an egalitarian community understanding. As Stephenson says:

> This language is especially empowering for women who have not been considered disciples in the full sense. While women respond to the call to discipleship, the truth of the matter is that frequently when they join churches they are not allowed to become full members with equal privileges and rights. Their discipleship is circumcised, but, of course, they are permitted to become servants. The switch to language of discipleship is not just semantics. It is about liberating women to be full members of the church.[203]

In this connection, Stephenson even criticizes an often one-sidedly understood sacrifice concept. Self-sacrifice and self-abandonment are not bad things in and of themselves. On the contrary: In Christ, we find the ultimate self-sacrifice for the benefit of others. It would however be wrong to reduce the life of Jesus merely to His self-sacrifice, just as it is also wrong to reduce anyone else to this role. Likewise, it is problematic when self-sacrifice amongst people is generally expected from women—something that can often be the case by virtue of societal models. One-sided self-sacrifice incapacitates and jeopardizes women in their development as equal disciples of Christ.[204]

In considering the Pentecostal church through the lens of Rosemary Radford Ruether's *Exodus Community from Patriarchy*, Stephenson

---

199. Stephenson, *Dismantling the Dualisms*, 169.

200. Stephenson, *Dismantling the Dualisms*, 169.

201. Even though there may be parallels to the European context, Stephenson is describing the context and community of the North American Pentecostal churches.

202. Here Stephenson is referring to Grant, "Sin of Servanthood."

203. Stephenson, *Dismantling the Dualisms*, 170.

204. Stephenson, *Dismantling the Dualisms*, 172.

sees two aspects as significant. Firstly, she sees in Ruether's approach a church understanding of the congregation as a community which is moving away from captivity into the direction of freedom. Stephenson, in contrast to Ruether, does not see the goal of this move in the direction of freedom in Women-Church: "Although there are merits to Women-Church as conceived by Ruether . . . Pentecostal churches are ultimately not Women-Church.[205] Nonetheless, this does not restrict Pentecostalism from embracing her other useful ecclesial concepts."[206]

Secondly, Stephenson sees in the church as an Exodus community the continuation of the prophetic tradition, which, in turn, is significant for the self-conception of the church as a contrasting society. "Both of these notions resonate with Pentecostalism, thought this may not clearly be obvious until pneumatology is explicitly connected. However, this pneumatological connection is quite natural once the Exodus is identified as the *Isaianic New* Exodus."[207] Thus, Stephenson regards even Ruether's dynamic, which points away from captivity toward a liberated community, as groundbreaking in connection with overcoming the patriarchs. For too long the prophetic tradition has kept silent about oppression through sexism and patriarchalism. Yet, how should this path to freedom be pursued?

> The prophetic tradition should not just be reclaimed for women, but by women. That is, the prophetic tradition should not only move to incorporate the concerns of women, but also incorporate the voice of women as well. One of the ways in which women's voices can be incorporated into this prophetic tradition is to acknowledge what bell hooks calls "talking back." This talking back is not just about speaking, but the repositioning of voices in the direction of change by unrecognized people refusing to be only "talked at." Talking back provides a strategy for moving in the direction of mutual recognition. She says,
>
>> Moving from silence into speech is for the oppressed, the colonised, the exploited, and those who stand and struggle side by side a gesture of defiance that heals, that makes new life and new growth possible. It is that act

---

205. Stephenson adds: "The main difference is that, according to Ruether, Women-Church is an autonomous base comprised solely of women, while Pentecostal churches are not autonomous and are not comprised solely of women" (Stephenson, *Dismantling the Dualisms*, 175).

206. Stephenson, *Dismantling the Dualisms*, 175.

207. Stephenson, *Dismantling the Dualisms*, 174.

of speech, of "talking back," that is no mere gesture of empty words, that is the expression of our movement from object to subject—the liberated voice.[208]

The fact that these voices express themselves quite angrily, is not deemed problematic by Stephenson. On the contrary: "To deny women the right to talk back and be angry promotes a false sense of unity and wellbeing. The fact that women are angry means they have not given up on the Pentecostal community."[209] Their protest shows that women still understand themselves as part of the Pentecostal church, and their relationship to the community is so important to them that they are prepared to invest in changes. Conversely, Stephenson sees far more ground for concern when the voices of women fall silent: "Because when their voices no longer resound within the Pentecostal church it may very well be a sign that the prophetic women of the Holy Spirit have given up and have moved on to other life-sustaining communities."[210]

In Letty Russell's *Household of Freedom* concept Stephenson sees various similarities with Schüssler's and Ruether's concepts. Stephenson sees Russell's understanding that God aims to liberate the world from internal and external oppression as a significant addition to previous feminist concepts. Russell designates this world as a *Household of Freedom*, whereby she understands the church as a visible sign of this new order. "As such, the church must become a church in the round, thereby employing a leadership that is characterized by its use of authority as partnership, and reorienting its concept of ministry."[211] The way power and authority are handled is, according to Russell's concept, characteristic of whether the church is actually a sign of God's eschatological intentions or not. What Stephenson criticizes about Russell's concept is that it certainly considers the Exodus and the life of Jesus as keys but that it mentions the working of God's Spirit in no way: "Russell fails to recognize that it is only with the outpouring of the Spirit that authority as partnership can continue to manifest itself as it creates a New Exodus community that fulfils the mission of Christ."[212] It is the Holy Spirit which through Pen-

---

208. Stephenson, *Dismantling the Dualisms*, 176. See also bell hooks, *Talking Back*, 5–9.
209. Stephenson, *Dismantling the Dualisms*, 180.
210. Stephenson, *Dismantling the Dualisms*, 180.
211. Stephenson, *Dismantling the Dualisms*, 181.
212. Stephenson, *Dismantling the Dualisms*, 182.

tecost empowers the whole church and not just individual people. Here, Stephenson applies her criticism to the Pentecostal church:

> However, whereas Pentecostals have tended to understand this as an empowerment for ministry, Russell's paradigm of authority as partnership also challenges one to understand this empowerment as ministry. That is, the reception of the Holy Spirit enables one to empower others to engage in their own callings.[213]

Yet, not only the understanding of leadership must change, but also the understanding of service so that church *in the round* becomes reality. The term *service* must not be reduced to the functions of ordained leaders but should inherently describe all the functions of church members. Otherwise, a rift is created between clergy and laity, which stands in contradiction to the church *in the round*.[214] For Stephenson, it is clear that the empowerment, equipping and thereby the equality of all church members (in all their diversity) is essential for a pneumatologically oriented service concept. Precisely this concept is lacking in the praxis of the Pentecostal churches, even though she mentions that there are exceptions.[215]

To come back once again to the *Ekklesia of Women*: Even if Stephenson understands the Pentecostal church as "ultimately not Women-Church,"[216] she asks herself whether this concept could be of significance for Pentecostals. For Schüssler Fiorenza, the Women-Church is significant in connection with the church as the Body of Christ: Also the female body is an image of the Body of Christ. Stephenson now goes one step further and interprets the church also as the *Body of the Spirit*: "Although there is no particular body that the Spirit adopts, if individual persons are bodies of the Spirit, it stands to reason that collectively they can also be considered the Body of the Spirit."[217] If the terminology Women-Church is now interpreted in the sense of Fiorenza Schüssler, as hermeneutical, re/constructive and political against a pneumatological background,[218] this imposes implications on Pentecostal churches: Hermeneutically, the *Ekklesia* of Women implies that the Pentecostal church will not become a historical reality until women are fully and equally incorporated into

---

213. Stephenson, *Dismantling the Dualisms*, 182.
214. Stephenson, *Dismantling the Dualisms*, 183.
215. Stephenson, *Dismantling the Dualisms*, 185.
216. Stephenson, *Dismantling the Dualisms*, 175.
217. Stephenson, *Dismantling the Dualisms*, 187.
218. Stephenson, *Dismantling the Dualisms*, 149.

the church: "The body of the Spirit suffers when all of the Spirit are not being utilized to their fullest potential."[219] As a re/constructive statement, Women-Church implies that there is a history and a legacy of women who have served the church and have sacrificed themselves for it: "Instead of focusing exclusively on the faith of the fathers of the church, the faith of the mothers should come to the fore."[220] As a political statement, Women-Church furthermore implies that the Pentecostal church should embody a reality which is characterized by the outpouring of the Holy Spirit:

> The Pentecostal church should look to women as the Body of the Holy Spirit to assist in helping transform Pentecostals churches into a discipleship of equals. Perhaps if women's ministries begin to re-conceive themselves as spaces in which women are the church, then whatever their praxis of being the Body of the Spirit is can be transmitted and enacted within the rest of Pentecostal churches.[221]

In conclusion, Stephenson brings the insights she has gained from feminist theology to the following points:

> In order for genuine change to occur with respect to the issue of women in ministry, Pentecostal churches need to be characterized as a discipleship of equals, an Isaianic new exodus community from patriarchy, and a household of freedom. . . . The people of God must reorient themselves to a new way of being the church. The outpouring of the Spirit calls Pentecostal churches to be a transformed communities, representative of the new creation of God.[222]

For her, it is clear that only this direction of impetus is logical for Pentecostal churches. If the Holy Spirit, as at the beginning of the Pentecostal Movement, is also to play a fundamental role in our churches today, then the church must again become aware of its identity in the Holy Spirit: "The way forward for Pentecostals is to own their identity and allow pneumatology to shape their theology and praxis."[223] And this means change:

---

219. Stephenson, *Dismantling the Dualisms*, 189.
220. Stephenson, *Dismantling the Dualisms*, 189.
221. Stephenson, *Dismantling the Dualisms*, 189.
222. Stephenson, *Dismantling the Dualisms*, 190.
223. Stephenson, *Dismantling the Dualisms*, 194.

Just as the outpouring of the Spirit at Pentecost necessitated a new future for Israel, the continual outpouring of the Spirit among Pentecostals today necessitates a new future for women. In order to be authentically "Pentecostal," Pentecostals must allow for the manifestation of the Spirit in their midst. While this manifestation implies *supernatural* gifts, it also implies a *natural* ordering of reality that exhibits the new creation effected by the Spirit.[224]

Critical Appraisal

Lisa Stephenson examines the role and understanding of women within the Pentecostal Movement. She does this against the background of a feminist-pneumatological anthropology and ecclesiology. Stephenson weaves very diverse methods and concepts into her discourse and wants this to further evolve in its own right in a fruitful way. Therein also lies a certain tension: Stephenson works largely biblical-theologically on the one hand and systematically on the other one hand.[225] One central element in Stephenson's line of reasoning for anthropology incorporates the motif of the new Exodus, which we also find with Wenk. We shall briefly consider the similarities and differences in the reasoning of the two authors. As already emphasized above, in his reasoning, Wenk starts with the original Exodus and works in this connection with the speech-act theory. In his dissertation, he develops the ethical significance of the community-shaping demands of Lukan pneumatology. Stephenson includes the new Exodus motif from Isaiah 40:1–11 and derives soteriological implications from this, which in turn have ethical and ecclesiological implications. Wenk basically deals with the community-forming significance of the work of God's Spirit, whilst Stephenson focusses on the role of women within the Pentecostal church. With Wenk, as also with Stephenson, within their respective lines of reasoning, eschatological, pneumatological, anthropological, soteriological and thereby also ecclesiological elements are discovered and discussed. For both authors, the formation of the new people of God, according to pneumatological

---

224. Stephenson, *Dismantling the Dualisms*, 195.

225. In all fairness, it must also be said that the synthesis of both methodologies makes sense for Stephenson's implicit readership. Her target audience consists of Pentecostals, to whom she wants to bring closer the analyses and ideas of her book (Stephenson, *Dismantling the Dualisms*, 8) and "to provide Pentecostals with a sound theological argument for Women in Ministry" (6).

criteria, constitutes a central concept.[226] Equally, Stephenson and Wenk come to the conclusion, and this seems to me a decisive observation, that the Lucan double work delivers an inclusive form of the people of God and the understanding of the Kingdom of God, in which all ethical, social and gender barriers are overcome. Thereby, they show the way that the church can repeatedly engage with constantly changing surroundings, so that God's liberating acts become manifest. A second element which occupies a central place in Stephenson's argumentation is her confrontation with feminist theology. The acceptance of Schüssler Fiorenza's analysis is significant, i.e., that a feminist concept cannot "only" involve the attainment of equal church functions because the causes and forms of oppression are manifold in nature—namely racial, class-related, and colonial.[227] This observation demonstrates the complexity of the problem, whilst at the same time it is also shown that the solution of the problem cannot be assured through individual measures. The solutions of Schüssler Fiorenza, Ruether and Russell, expanded by Stephenson, point in the same direction. Her summarized conclusion is actually not new: Fundamental and sustainable change is only possible when the church evolves into a community of equal disciples of Christ and as such is an Exodus community on its way to *the household of freedom*. Although her contribution is significant for the present work, at the same time it points out possible action approaches which are not "merely" fruitful for American Pentecostal women in ministry. Stephenson's concepts provide effective fundament conclusions for a Pentecostal social ethic.

However, I regard as problematic Stephenson's unreserved joining in with the feminist criticism of self-sacrifice.[228] I agree with her that one-sided self-sacrifice, according to the expectations and conditions demanded by the oppressor, can in no way be justified; no person has the right to demand something of this kind from others. However, this does not mean that self-sacrifice within the service of women per se is not permitted as a topic. To dismiss self-sacrifice with the argument that it would be dangerous for women would ultimately imply, at least partially, submitting to the oppressor, specifically at least as far that her definition

---

226. In this connection it is worth mentioning that both Stephenson and Wenk (as with Frank Macchia, e.g., *Justified by the Holy Spirit*) do not have a "classical" individualistic understanding of the baptism in the Holy Spirit, but one incorporating soteriology and ethics.

227. Stephenson, *Dismantling the Dualisms*, 145.

228. Stephenson, *Dismantling the Dualisms*, 170–72.

of this concept is accepted. Although the rejection of self-sacrifice constitutes one form of resistance, it results in hardly any transforming effect being achieved.[229] Rather, self-sacrifice must again become a subject for discussion for the lives of men and women. Self-sacrifice exploited by oppressors must be liberated through the self-sacrifice of Christ. Thus, Christ offered His life in resistance *against* the expectations and demands of the powers of this world. He resisted the Jewish nationalistic hopes, even the expectations of His disciples. He ultimately sacrificed His life for them all, but in resistance to their exploitative expectations. His self-sacrifice happened entirely in compliance with the will of the Heavenly Father. Christ's understanding of self-sacrifice is a self-sacrifice in the name of resistance *and* of restoration. In this sense, Jesus' self-sacrifice is a criticism of the establishment and of societal expectations. So, also women (and basically all people) are called to sacrifice in resistance to exploitative expectations for the Kingdom of God. In this sense, Jesus, in His self-giving, represents the resistance but also the hope of all mankind, in all its diversity and multiplicity. On the cross, Christ does not represent some generic mass, but all humanity in its entire particularity, uniqueness and facets. On the cross, in Christ, this substantiated unity of human diversity is the bridge between the Cross and Pentecost, when the Holy Spirit is poured out on all flesh.[230] A critical confrontation with the feminist criticism of the overemphasis of the self-sacrifice of Christ can strengthen the christological foundation in Stephenson's argumentation.

One question which Stephenson does not attempt to answer in her monograph, yet itself because of Russell's understanding of the church,[231] relates to being a sign for the world: When pneumatology is of such central significance, what about the women who exhibit no explicit connection to an experience of the Holy Spirit in their lives?[232] In other words: What responsibility does the Pentecostal church have toward women (or generally toward the social needs of people) outside the church?[233]

229. See also Solivan's statements on *Transformation* below.
230. See also Macchia, *Jesus the Holy Spirit Baptizer*, 256–61.
231. Stephenson, *Dismantling the Dualisms*, 160.

232. As distinct from "general" social injustice, with feminism it is however the case that the church (at least the Western church) lags behind social development. Thus, the church has work ahead of what the secular world has already achieved.

233. One non-Pentecostal interpretation which could be helpful with the clarification of this question is Ragaz's concept stating that when the church closes their ears to Him, God might well also speak prophetically through secular societal movements. In this connection, Macchia speaks of "Analogies of the Kingdom" (see Macchia,

Samuel Solivan: An Approach with Latin American Roots

Samuel Solivan's parents emigrated from Puerto Rico to East Harlem, NY, where he grew up with his five brothers. At the age of fourteen, Samuel received the call to full-time ministry. After his graduation from high school, he was conscripted into the Air Force, from which he was then discharged on medical grounds. He attended the Central Bible College in Springfield, MO, where he graduated in 1970 with a Bachelor of Arts degree. In 1973, Samuel was encouraged by the Reformed Church in America to further his studies and was invited to attend the Western Theological Seminary, Missouri. Solivan identified himself as "an Arminian, a Latino, and a Pentecostal," and conformed to everybody else in the usual profile of a Western Theological Seminary—a student. Solivan found his training formative: "There's been no other community that was so powerful in transforming and equipping me. Western Theological Seminary is the institution that has most marked my life." He graduated in 1979 and, one year later, he began a Research Degree for a Master in Sacred Theology at the Union Theological Seminary in New York City. After several years' service as a missionary in Venezuela, Solivan returned to the Union Theological Seminary to study for a PhD. During this time, he served as a pastor at the Bethel Reformed Church in New Jersey and later at the Old First Reformed Church in Brooklyn. Dr. Solivan changed to the Pentecostal denomination of the Assemblies of God and relocated to Boston, where he taught Christian Theology at the Andover Newton Theological School and at the Harvard Medical School. In 1999, Solivan relocated once again, this time to Puerto Rico, where he served as Vice President of Religious Affairs at the InterAmerican University.[234] With his book *The Spirit, Pathos and Liberation. Toward an Hispanic Pentecostal Theology,* Solivan wanted to make a theological contribution to the socio-ethical worldview of the Pentecostal Movement. He did this by formulating a Hispanic Pentecostal Theology. The focus of the following section is directed toward this very formulation.

"Analogies of the Kingdom," 9). Moltmann also comes to a similar interpretation in Moltmann, *Crucified God,* 33–34. What significance this concept may beear for the involvement of the Pentecostal church with society, we shall consider in the following central chapter on Moltmann.

234. WTS, "2017 Distinguished Alumnus."

Context

Solivan opens his book with a sophisticated analysis of the term Hispanics. In North America, all Spanish-speaking people are labeled with this collective term. However, stereotypes are also associated with the term Hispanic, and such a sweeping generalization is in no way justified in respect of the reality of the Hispanics because the community of the North American Hispanics is, as Solivan says, a multi-cultural and multi-language community. Solivan examines this diversity in depth and identifies two factors which essentially define the identity of the Hispanics: Factor (a) is the *cultural background*, factor (b) is the *migration/immigration background*.

- The *cultural factor* relates to the language and cultural diversity of the so-called Hispanics. Solivan claims that the approximately 22 million[235] North American Hispanics (statistic from 1998) originate from four groups: "(1) Mexican Americans or Chicanos; (2) Puerto-Ricans (or New Ricans); (3) Cubans; and (4) other Latin Americans."[236] Within these four groups, the Mexican Americans comprise the greatest majority, with 59.8 percent. In second place, with 13.8 percent, are the Puerto Ricans.[237] The third-largest group is formed by the Cuba-originated Hispanics, with 5.5 percent. The remaining 20.9 percent originates from the Dominican Republic, Central and Latin America. This means that Hispanics have a whole range of mother tongues, such as Spanish, Portuguese, Quechua, Guajiro, etc. Many Hispanics are bilingual (at least 79 percent also speak English in addition to their mother tongue), and ethnic differences are also discernable. Hispanics can have black or white skin color, they can have Mulato or Indian ancestry or they can carry a mixture of all these elements within them. As a concrete example for the diversity described above, the Cubans who migrated in 1959 can be cited, the majority of whom belonged to the middle class and had white skin color. In contrast to these are the Hispanics who immigrated from Mexico, the majority of whom belonged to the poorest level of society and often had colored skin.

235. Solivan, *Spirit, Pathos and Liberation*, 17. Solivan points out that this information is not very reliable. It is assumed that the number of North American Hispanics overall could be about thiry million. The vagueness of the information arises from the estimated number of the so-called unregistered immigrants.

236. Solivan, *Spirit, Pathos and Liberation*, 17.

237. This includes Puerto-Ricans living in Puerto Rico who have US American citizenship on the basis of the Jones Act of 1917 in Solivan, *Spirit, Pathos and Liberation*, 17.

- In relation to the m*igration/immigration factor*, it must be noted that there are Hispanics whose forefathers already lived in North America before the emergence of the USA (e.g., the inhabitants of New Mexico) or Hispanics whose homeland has been annexed by the USA (e.g., Puerto Rico). Furthermore, there are Hispanics who have immigrated into the USA from the Caribbean, South America and Latin America.[238] The self-perception of these two categories has similarities but can also differ considerably. Thus, for example Hispanics originating from New Mexico consider themselves as migrants, Puerto Rica-originating Hispanics as expatriates, whilst both, as US-American citizens, have the expectation to be treated as such. Immigrants, as a rule, do not share the expectation of expatriates but rather anticipate being treated as foreigners and having to build their entire lives from scratch.[239] This difference is seemingly unrecognized by Americans originating from Europe. Thus Solivan observes:

> Unlike many new immigrants who expect to start at the bottom and to be treated as foreigners, Puerto Ricans and Mexican Americans do not have the same expectation—although they are treated as though they should. We have to ask why this is so. History seems to point to a racial and ethnic bias that favors Northern Europeans over people of color. The history of American race relations, both past and present, supports such a conclusion.[240]

Despite all the differences, the similarities of the North American Hispanics have created a kind of joint destiny. So the common linguistic and cultural heritage, arising from the earlier Spanish colonial power, unites them. However, there are yet further factors that have an impact: The blood of the white conquistadores has been mixed with the blood of African slaves and Caribbean Indians, and thus its carriers have been made *Mestizos*. In addition, widespread poverty is an experience which unites Hispanics (even though Hispanics have established themselves in all social classes over the years).

---

238. In addition, there is the subcategory of the Secundos and other Americans whose parents, grandparents or even earlier ancestors migrated or immigrated to America, who themselves were born in the USA. For more on the complexity and significance of these factors, see Solivan, *Spirit, Pathos and Liberation*, 18. The phenomenon described therein was first identified by the sociologists and anthropologists, Dr. John Useem and Dr. Ruth Hill Useem using the term Third Culture Persons. See also Pollok et al., *Third Culture Kids*.

239. Solivan, *Spirit, Pathos and Liberation*, 17.

240. Solivan, *Spirit, Pathos and Liberation*, 17.

Solivan identifies four factors which influence and unify the great majority of Hispanics in their life experience: "Language, our common experience of suffering, our common Christian heritage and the fact that a large majority of Hispanics are bilingual—provide a linkage between us for the purpose of mutual struggle and liberation."[241] Hispanics who are able to identify with the above-stated experience would not fail to integrate this experience into their theology. On the basis of the four factors mentioned, it is a theology of survival, in the truest sense of the word: "Hispanic theology is a survival theology that challenges 'what is' with 'what is to come,' a faith experience that dares to sing the songs of Zion even in a foreign land."[242] This experience theology begins with—as its name implies—the experience of faith. Solivan points out the fact that the living conditions of Hispanics is often so adverse that they involve an urgency that makes it impossible to wait for a critical reflection of practice.

> What is meant here is that survival faith, as survival theology, must not and cannot wait for critical, rational constructs in order to begin. History has taught the poor that the objective tools of rational discourse have often become the instrumentation of oppressive forces that keep them hungry and ignorant.... There is a place for critical reflection and discourse, but the question is where and when it comes on the journey. As Gustavo Gutiérrez and others have pointed out, theology is of a second order of things; being, loving, is the first order.[243]

However, Hispanic Theology is not shaped by the present experience alone. Hispanic Theology is a syncretism of collective experience, colonial-Catholic roots[244] and conservative Protestant mission theology,[245] which also includes Pentecostal influences.[246] Generally, the Pentecostal Movement exerts great power of attraction to the Hispanic community. Solivan attributes this to elements which are typical for the Pentecostal Movement:

> Pentecostals are autonomous; they are indigenous and self-governing. Hispanic Pentecostal women play a far greater role in

---

241. Solivan, *Spirit, Pathos and Liberation*, 21.
242. Solivan, *Spirit, Pathos and Liberation*, 26.
243. Solivan, *Spirit, Pathos and Liberation*, 26.
244. Solivan, *Spirit, Pathos and Liberation*, 28.
245. Solivan, *Spirit, Pathos and Liberation*, 29.
246. Solivan, *Spirit, Pathos and Liberation*, 30.

the life and ministry of the church than do their Anglo/American counterparts. Pentecostal pneumatology determines who in the congregation will be the leaders: they are those whose gifts of the Holy Spirit in their lives are brought as witness to the congregation. In this context, questions of gender play a lesser role than in other Protestant traditions. This is not to say that male dominance is absent, but a cursory observation of the Pentecostal pulpit will readily support the thesis that there are more Pentecostal women in the ordained ministry than in other Protestant denominations.[247]

Besides autonomy and leadership concepts, the Pentecostal church service also exerts great appeal:

> In Pentecostal worship, exuberance, music and passion in religious expression are important factors in attracting the poor. Pentecostal worship is an 'event.' It is an occasion for the poor and suffering masses to gather together in their common pain and faith to share with one another, and God, their needs and hopes.... In worship, Pentecostals know afresh what was meant when Paul said that in Christ there is neither male nor female, slave nor free, Jew nor gentile, rich nor poor (Gal 3:28). Pentecostal worship and community are the historical manifestations of that hope. It is a community where the dispossessed become leaders, where the voiceless are empowered by the Holy Spirit to speak not only for themselves but also for God. The non-persons, the invisible ones, become visible; the non-person is accepted as a full person, respected and loved. The Pentecostal church continues to be the testing ground for the Holy Spirit's transformative work of *orthopathos*.[248]

Orthopathos

Here we shall concern ourselves with one of Solivan's theological key terms, namely *orthopathos*. For Solivan, the meaning of *orthopathos* arises from the background of failed *orthodoxy*. What is meant by this? Although Wesleyan, non-Wesleyan-Protestant and Roman Catholic orthodoxy have enriched Solivan's understanding of God, Christ and the Holy Spirit, these sources have left a bitter aftertaste. Because in his understanding,

---

247. Solivan, *Spirit, Pathos and Liberation*, 31.
248. Solivan, *Spirit, Pathos and Liberation*, 31.

orthodoxy has failed to represent the whole counsel of God.[249] The Integrity of Catholic, as well as Protestant orthodoxy has suffered as a result of the partnership with their dominant population groups. Orthodoxy had its own aspirations undermined when it became an instrument of the powerful. For Solivan, orthodox Christianity has lost its integrity and its authority to speak to American minorities as a result of its alliance with the socio-economical structures which favor the present status quo.[250] The inability of American Protestant orthodoxy to integrate the poor demands a new/different approach to North American Christianity.

However, not only orthodoxy has failed, but also orthopraxis. Latin American and Black Liberation Theology propagated an orthopraxis which focused on the poor and their needs. Both wings of Liberation Theology emphasize the history and the destiny of oppressed people. Through it, much of the concern of God for the oppressed and marginalized could again be recognized. However:

> It appears that many who espouse a liberating orthopraxis lack an existential link to the poor. They speak in the name of the poor but usually know of them only by historical reverence or past acquaintance. The power and authenticity present in the early voices of liberation theologians have been diluted by the pressures of academic advancement, the shallowness of bandwagon marketing and the passion-impaired temperament of the American academic culture. Even if this were not the case, there still remains a need for an orthopathic perspective that can enrich and inform both orthodoxy and orthopraxis, helping to make them more sensitive and open to the memory and insight of those who suffer.[251]

Orthopathos, according to Solivan, overcomes the division of the cognitive (orthodoxy) and action (orthopraxis). He is convinced that theological reflection and practice can only be made intact again when orthopathos is brought in as a dialogue partner. Solivan understands *ortho* not in the usual sense of "correct" or "right" but more in the sense of "liberating." He even uses *pathos* in a broader sense, which includes pain, suffering, oppression, exclusion and poverty.[252] He sees this understanding of orthopathos as founded in God, who reveals Himself in the Old

249. Solivan, *Spirit, Pathos and Liberation*, 35.
250. Solivan, *Spirit, Pathos and Liberation*, 36.
251. Solivan, *Spirit, Pathos and Liberation*, 36.
252. Solivan, *Spirit, Pathos and Liberation*, 148.

and New Testaments as the God who is moved by people, who is in solidarity with them and who, in Christ, has overcome the self-destructive tendencies of humanity.[253] Pathos deriving from God *must* have a concrete impact on theology and interpersonal relationships:

> The compassionate God of the Exodus is present today sitting with those who weep along the gutters of East Harlem and the South Bronx. God is the one who is present in the cardboard boxes of the homeless. This same God is not the perfect, untouched prime mover or first cause envisioned by Aristotle and Aquinas, but God is the prime mover and first cause, albeit touched and moved by our brokenness.... Oppressed persons (for example, the crack addict) are characterized as in a pathetic situation, a condition of self-alienation. This condition should be the starting point for our consideration of a liberating theology and pastoral praxis. If we take the oppressed seriously, we should draw close to their condition to be informed, affected and perhaps transformed by God in response to it. We must draw near and see, hear, feel and experience the overwhelming reality of this pathetic condition. To take the poor seriously is to be engaged in their condition deeply enough to respect the experience of their pathos as a legitimate source for theological reflection and pastoral engagement—what Metz has called the subversive memory of suffering.[254]

Christ and the Holy Spirit play a central role in orthopathos: "Jesus Christ, the incarnated Logos, is the fullest expression of orthopathos, and the Holy Spirit is the comforter charged by God and the Son to empower orthopathic transformation in our lives as we accept the gift of Christ as Lord."[255] This orthopathos will now, as already stated above, amalgamate orthodoxy and orthopraxis, by bringing "empathic concern for the suffering into the act of doing theology."[256] Orthopathos is always seeking opportunities whereby human suffering can be turned into a resource of liberation. Special attention is directed specifically toward suffering which has been generated by oppressive class, racist and sexist systems.[257]

---

253. Solivan, *Spirit, Pathos and Liberation*, 54.

254. Solivan, *Spirit, Pathos and Liberation*, 59–60. See Metz, *Faith in History and Society*, 58, 97–113.

255. Solivan, *Spirit, Pathos and Liberation*, 60.

256. Solivan, *Spirit, Pathos and Liberation*, 60.

257. Solivan, *Spirit, Pathos and Liberation*, 61.

Ortho pertains to the circumstances of the oppressed.[258] In understanding and addressing their pathos, those affected are empowered to overcome their circumstances. This begins before overcoming their external circumstances, through awakening and establishing self-worth and honor in the people who are suffering.[259] The work of the Holy Spirit takes a central role in this process:

> This orthopathic consciousness is informed by several sources: the Scriptures, Christian tradition, socio-economic *concientización* (awareness), family relations, and the personal experiences of sufferers. The work of the Holy Spirit brings all these together. It is the Holy Spirit who is the transformer of the sufferer, and the sufferer's circumstance, into liberating *orthopathos*. The best examples of orthopathic transformation are found in Romans 8:2. and John 1:14 (the incarnation of the Logos); that is, moving us from flesh (sarx) to glory (dóxa), or in other words from apathy to liberation, is the orthopathic work of the Holy Spirit. The Holy Spirit works in the world (the socio-political) and in us (illuminating the Scriptures discerned through the tradition). This same Spirit produces faith as knowledge, both cognitive and affective. Imparting courage is the work of the Spirit, for instance, in the radical conversion of former addicts who hear the Word and/or are overcome by love in an encouraging community.[260]

Starting Points for Orthopathos

For Solivan, the starting points for orthopathos are, on one hand, the biblical Scriptures, and on the other hand, the suffering of the Hispanic community. It is precisely the suffering within the biblical Scriptures that provides the Hispanic community with their unsurpassed authority:

---

258. A theology of orthopathos begins in the particularity of the American Hispanic experience of poverty with the Exile as their focus point. From this particularity, universal themes have been addressed. In dialogue with other streams of Liberation Theology, however, even the limitation of poverty shows itself as a starting point: "Black theologians have critiqued it from the vantage point of race, that is blackness, feminist from the aspect of gender, and Asian theologians from the aspect of ethnicity. These have not denied the importance of the category of the poor, but have pointed to its limitations" (Solivan, *Spirit, Pathos and Liberation*, 96–99). Regarding this point, Solivan comes to the conclusion that the category of suffering is a very effective and inclusive starting point for dealing with the themes of justice and compassion.

259. Solivan, *Spirit, Pathos and Liberation*, 62.
260. Solivan, *Spirit, Pathos and Liberation*, 62.

"When one is a member of a minority, and the entire establishment is trying to convince one that one is wrong, it is necessary, for sheer psychological and political survival, to find an authority that goes beyond the hostile environment."[261] Although they live in a Western industrial nation, some of their living areas, such as, for example, the South Bronx, are in many respects reminiscent of desolate post-war Europe. Residential buildings are often without heating, warm water, electricity or sanitation facilities. The lack of prospects arising from such an environment often expresses itself in criminality and drug abuse. The church is the place where the people search for answers to their prayers.[262] In this environment, the Hispanic church is called to be the church of the oppressed, who read the biblical texts and recognize parallels between the Scripture and their own life circumstances. "There we see the plight of an oppressed community, the wandering in a wilderness of unfamiliar laws, customs, social and economic structures, the presence of foreign priests who speak of a god who seems different from their God. But mirroring is not the only gift from Scripture; solutions are given, too."[263] God is never indifferent to human suffering. He will transform our mourning into dancing (Ps 30:11). God's concern for the suffering, the afflicted, the widow, the orphan, the poor, the stranger is a core theme of the Old Testament:[264] "The fact that God is touched, moved and concerned with us is the very foundation of our hope."[265] Thereby the fellowship of God with people maintains a central aspect.[266] However, "to see, hear and know that suffering exists and to be moved by it is not enough. Even solidarity is apathetic if it does not strengthen one toward transformation. Sympathy and empathy must move from the initial stages of solidarity to transformation."[267] God understands suffering and the concrete needs of the Israelites. He called and empowered Moses to liberate the Israelites in His name. He decided to lead the oppressed out of their pathos condition into Shalom, from captivity into freedom. However, the Exodus story also shows that God works within the boundaries of human pathos. In this sense, God's

---

261. Justo L. González quoted in Solivan, *Spirit, Pathos and Liberation*, 70.
262. Solivan, *Spirit, Pathos and Liberation*, 71.
263. Solivan, *Spirit, Pathos and Liberation*, 71.
264. Solivan, *Spirit, Pathos and Liberation*, 74.
265. Solivan, *Spirit, Pathos and Liberation*, 76.
266. Solivan, *Spirit, Pathos and Liberation*, 75.
267. Solivan, *Spirit, Pathos and Liberation*, 76.

answer to the distress of the Israelites is not an instant solution which is affected by a miraculous intervention, but rather a

> long-term engagement with us in community and mutual caring. . . . It is this relational character within which an orthopathic transformation is possible. Outside loving, trusting relationships, there are few solutions to suffering. Mutual caring in community as modelled in the Old Testament covenant continues to be an indispensable aspect of *orthopathos* essential for empowering the move from pathos to *orthopathos*, from apathy to liberation.[268]

John 1:14 refers back to the Exodus events and leads us to the further point where God identifies Himself so much with us human beings that He Himself became a human being, in Jesus.[269] It is in this incarnation of Christ that the promise of God's care for the oppressed and suffering finds its zenith. The incarnation of God in Christ is understood as the expression of God's covenant with humanity. This covenant is "far more than just solidarity, it is more than mere sympathy—it is transformation."[270] God, in Christ, has not merely identified with the suffering of human beings, but rather with human beings per se. In His incarnation, God makes Himself vulnerable and weak. And yet, ultimately, this weakness reveals itself as strength: It is the suffering of Christ and His death through which death itself is overcome. Hope in (or despite all) weakness is the central expression of orthopathos. God's identification with us human beings through the incarnation of Christ is fundamental. A Christian anthropology can be derived and constructed only when it originates in Christology. The transformation affected through the incarnation will be the foundation and example for the changes affected through us. Comprehending who Christ the human being is has become fundamental to recognizing who we are. In the incarnation of Christ, God has revealed what it means to be truly human.[271]

---

268. Solivan, *Spirit, Pathos and Liberation*, 76–77.
269. Solivan, *Spirit, Pathos and Liberation*, 80.
270. Solivan, *Spirit, Pathos and Liberation*, 73.
271. Solivan, *Spirit, Pathos and Liberation*, 81.

Theological Principles of Orthopathos

From the above-mentioned starting points, Solivan derives three theological principles of orthopathos:

The principle of identification: For several reasons, the aspect of identification is key to passing from pathos to liberation: The isolation in which many suffering people find themselves is broken. The incarnation reintroduces people to the context of the suffering ones: God Himself, in Jesus, has declared to us humans that He stands alongside us in our suffering. He does this not only in solidarity as a compassionate onlooker, but also as the One who transforms suffering into liberation. Thus, Christ's identification with us not only overcomes our isolation but also serves to motivate us from being in solidarity to liberation.[272] With the principle of identification, the opportunity for community is created, through relationships. Fellowship with others places suffering people into a broader, larger context. This provides new opportunities for support and also a new context for the critical consideration of suffering. In this process, the Holy Spirit once more plays a central role:

> A pneumatological perspective also takes on an interlocutory role between the poles of particularity and universality. The Holy Spirit is active in both. It is the person and the work of the Spirit that keep us from reducing all of suffering to a private distress. The Spirit draws the suffering not only to God but to one another. The absence of a pneumatology leaves one alone amid the suffering. One is left to overcome on one's own terms and abilities. The absence of a liberating spirit results in the pessimism and despair of Dostojevsky's Ivan in *The Brothers Karamazov* who, in the face of suffering, could only rebel against God.[273]

The suffering persons gain a new perspective from which they can deal with their situations. Furthermore, identification also demythologizes the individuality of suffering. Often, suffering people settle in their pathos because they have the feeling that nobody else can understand their suffering. This settling repeatedly leads to self-justification of one's own victim role. Christ's identification with suffering people declares to the world that suffering no longer remains unchallenged and that its cause has been judged. God understands, He has partaken of our suffering and, in Jesus, gives healing. To know that we are not alone, to know

---

272. Solivan, *Spirit, Pathos and Liberation*, 81–82.
273. Solivan, *Spirit, Pathos and Liberation*, 102.

that God cares and publicly stands alongside the oppressed permeates the promise of liberation with faith—not just as hope but far more as certainty. The certainty that the present circumstances will not continue forever and that suffering does not have the last word expresses God's promise that Shalom, i.e., justice with peace, will come, and is already breaking into the present.[274]

The Principle of Location: In the prologue of his gospel, John establishes that the Word did not merely become flesh but that He dwelt amongst us and thereby became present amongst human beings. Already since the beginning of creation, God has repeatedly sought fellowship with His creatures. John, the evangelist, writes that, in Christ, God's fellowship with us human beings has found its culmination. Jesus is the new point of intersection, God's place of encounter with His creatures. The fact that God became a poor Galilean and not a Prince of Jerusalem is merely an example of God's restorative love.[275] God's choice of position amongst human beings has implications for our praxis of liberation. Just as God, through Christ, sought fellowship with us human beings, so should we also seek out the places where isolated, lonely people are suffering. We are required to break into the cycle of isolation and to bring love, faith and hope into these situations. Identifying with the suffering requires time but also a repositioning of ourselves. Liberation must be built. We must learn to dwell among the suffering, just as the prophets did (e.g., Ezek 3:14–15). Without presence, which creates fellowship and solidarity, through seeking out the suffering people in the place where they are and thus breaking into their isolation and restoring their self-worth, orthopathos is inconceivable. The orthopathic process cannot develop without fellowship between us and the others.[276]

The Principle of Transformation: Although identification and location are important, the significance of *transformation* is, and always will be, unsurpassed for orthopathos. Fellowship with suffering people does not automatically lead to changing their pathos. This fellowship may well prove to be comforting, helpful and sometimes, for a limited time, even liberating. However, it will not lead to a fundamental change in the situation nor empower the people affected with a reinterpretation of their suffering. Identification and location are important in order to address their concrete needs, but it is primarily transformation, the concrete

---

274. Solivan, *Spirit, Pathos and Liberation*, 82.
275. Solivan, *Spirit, Pathos and Liberation*, 83.
276. Solivan, *Spirit, Pathos and Liberation*, 84.

manifestation of Shalom, grace and compassion which heals and makes whole. Solivan writes:

> John's prologue tells us that as a result of Jesus' identification and location, He and others witnessed the glory (δόξα) of God, characterized as full of "grace and truth." . . . The manifestation of God's glory in the incarnation of Jesus announces and anticipates the reign of truth grounded in grace already present among the disciples and the Jewish people in the person of Jesus.[277]

The gospel of John points out that the glory of the incarnated Christ has fundamental transforming consequences for suffering and marginalized people. So, for example, grace and compassion are evident as an expression of δόξα in the story of the adulterous woman (John 8:3–11) or in the case of blind Bartimaeus (John 9:1–12). In these and other accounts of miracles and healings, it is evident that Jesus reacted to specific need. His work went far beyond the aspects of solidarity and presence to the concrete transformation of the circumstances.

The three theological principles described above illustrate what is possible when the transforming love of God breaks into a life. However, the effecting power in them is the presence and strength of the Holy Spirit. Only through the Holy Spirit is it possible to penetrate the reality of our struggle and to overcome our alienation with grace. Orthopathos is the existential bridge between orthodoxy and orthopraxis and identifies the nature of sin in all its manifestations—be it personal, systematic or structural—as the root of evil.[278] Identification and location address the systematic aspects of suffering, but only the power of the Holy Spirit leads to orthopathos:

> Hopeful struggle (to the faithless, an oxymoron) is the charisma of the Spirit of God that binds to God the sufferers who trust and hope. This is why the poor must sing: we believe the promise that God does care and that love will overcome. Hopeful struggle is a sign of orthopathos: do disallow despair in suffering because God's pathos holds the future.[279]

---

277. Solivan, *Spirit, Pathos and Liberation*, 85.
278. Solivan, *Spirit, Pathos and Liberation*, 86.
279. Solivan, *Spirit, Pathos and Liberation*, 74.

Powerlessness

The powerlessness of the suffering poor is evident. But even in a society which is driven by power, powerlessness is the power of the poor. Paul refers to this paradox in his letter to the Corinthians (2 Cor 12:9–10; 13:4) and also in the Book of Hebrews (Heb 11:34). Orthopathos manifests itself amongst the powerless, and, in this respect, pathos can also be defined as a form of powerlessness. Powerlessness is often understood as an apathetic state. However, it is also a powerful instrument to confront power, as has already been proven, for example in Jesus but also in nonviolent movements such as those of Gandhi and Martin Luther King Jr. The correct use of weakness for the liberation of suffering people is one aspect of orthopathos.[280] In this connection, it is important not to glorify weakness, powerlessness or suffering under any circumstances, since this would be destructive. Nevertheless, to consciously understand that weakness is strength is a starting point. "Orthopathic powerlessness is a sober and liberating appropriation of power by the powerless in their freedom to risk."[281] If we believe that God is on the side of the weak and oppressed, then we can and must, according to Solivan, trust His method of resolution. This is far more difficult than trusting one's own capabilities of exerting influence. Yet, it is this very trust that awakens hope.[282] Orthopathos, despite powerlessness, is full of hope because it does not orientate itself toward the present situation but toward the promises of God. However,

> This trust in the promises of God—at times almost blind and often uncritical—falls prey to a hope that is not Christian. For example, among Pentecostals and Charismatics there are those who preach a gospel of prosperity. They "hope" soon to become financially wealthy based on the promises found in Scripture and their willingness to engage in some ritual act of giving to others. Christian hope, as noted by Segundo Galiléa, differs from this type. Christian hope, he states, "is the security to obtain, posses, and enjoy 'what we cannot see.' If we saw it with the senses, or with human logic, or with scientific and natural projections, then we would no longer hope. We would project into the future, with reasonable farsightedness, the consequence of present causes."[283]

---

280. Solivan, *Spirit, Pathos and Liberation*, 87.
281. Solivan, *Spirit, Pathos and Liberation*, 86.
282. Solivan, *Spirit, Pathos and Liberation*, 89.
283. Segundo Galiléa quoted in Solivan, *Spirit, Pathos and Liberation*, 90.

In this connection, Solivan appreciates Moltmann's *Theology of Hope* and, at the same time, expresses criticism of it since he misses the value of the present experience for the strengthening of faith in it. In contrast to Moltmann, the orthopathic approach believes that promises already fulfilled in the past are significant for faith and hope. Because: "The truth of the promise fulfilled yesterday and today is the base upon which the future of hope is grounded."[284] Hope is justified in faith which is motivated by the promise of God. This hope is acted out by trusting in God's truth and grace. In order to overcome our destructive pathos, the Holy Spirit, the creator of faith, has been given to us, He who generates hope, a hope which dares to wait trustingly and to endure until God's reign is realized amongst us.

According to Solivan, *godly care, kenotic empathy, the strength of weakness* and *hope* are four biblical images (amongst many others) which make apparent the transforming power of orthopathos and the work of the Holy Spirit in the life of the suffering.[285]

The Holy Spirit

The theme of suffering, according to Solivan, is hardly ever brought into association with the Holy Spirit. But this is not the case in Hispanic theology. Against the background of Hispanic reality, the association of suffering and the Holy Spirit is central: "The possibility of moving from a pathetic situation to a liberating life requires the active participation of the Holy Spirit."[286] This begins in the first instance with the interpretation of the Bible:

> If Pentecostals are to move from practice to orthopraxis they must trust the orthopathic leading of the Holy Spirit. This will often place them in tension with the received biblical tradition and interpretation of conservative Christianity. Only the orthopathic leading and activity of the Holy Spirt can empower Pentecostals to risk questioning and reinterpreting the Scriptures in light of their own experience and insights.[287]

---

284. Solivan, *Spirit, Pathos and Liberation*, 91. See also Solivan's comment on Moltmann (91n45). Moltmann writes: "Hope's statements of promise, however, must stand in contradiction to the reality which can at present be experienced. They do not result from experience but are the condition for the possibility of new experiences" (Moltmann, *Theology of Hope*, 18).

285. Solivan, *Spirit, Pathos and Liberation*, 92.

286. Solivan, *Spirit, Pathos and Liberation*, 102.

287. Solivan, *Spirit, Pathos and Liberation*, 145.

When reading the holy Scripture, the Holy Spirit helps contextualise biblical truths, He will retain biblical texts which have previously been reduced to a literary form and at the same time help take into account literary idiosyncrasies.[288] The Holy Spirit helps build the bridge between biblical truth and contemporary culture. The Holy Spirit helps the community understand that the Bible demands to be read in its vocative voice.[289] because the Scripture will not primarily be interpreted, but rather, far more, it will interpret and guide us.[290] And not least, the Holy Spirit also helps us to read the Bible politically—Solivan calls this way of reading "Spanish reading."

> This "Spanish reading" is made possible by the Holy Spirit. Discerning the sign of the times happens through a transformative pneumatology. It is the Holy Spirit who comes to hearten the poor and the suffering, and this pneumatological consciousness links us with Christ's own source of power and to the tradition of the early church. It is that gift of God to us that equips us to do battle and win over the forces of evil and injustice. It is this same Holy Spirit who gives us wisdom for engaging the principalities and powers that daily seek to overwhelm us. It is a pneumatology that does not distinguish between the Spirit that empowered the apostles and the Spirit who comes to us.[291]

Such a pneumatology recognizes the Holy Spirit as the comforter even today.[292] Even today, the Holy Spirit wants to transform suffering people and their circumstances,[293] overcomes alienation through grace[294] and awakens hope.[295] For Solivan, the work of the Holy Spirit is, in the first place, the prerequisite for hope, love and faith.[296] However, the Holy Spirit is also at work when seemingly no changes are apparent:

> Even though our communities remain destroyed, and we are forced to live our lives in inhuman living conditions, we can still attest to the transforming work of the Holy Spirit in peoples'

---

288. Solivan, *Spirit, Pathos and Liberation*, 96.
289. Solivan, *Spirit, Pathos and Liberation*, 108, 132.
290. Solivan, *Spirit, Pathos and Liberation*, 96.
291. Solivan, *Spirit, Pathos and Liberation*, 131.
292. Solivan, *Spirit, Pathos and Liberation*, 60.
293. Solivan, *Spirit, Pathos and Liberation*, 62.
294. Solivan, *Spirit, Pathos and Liberation*, 86.
295. Solivan, *Spirit, Pathos and Liberation*, 91.
296. Solivan, *Spirit, Pathos and Liberation*, 103.

lives, empowering them to overcome their suffering, misery and despair. Those who were once no people are a new people; those who had no voice are given a voice; those who were nobodies are now somebodies. This is what the Spirit does in the lives of those who open themselves to His presence and power. This is what we call *orthopathos*. In spite of the environmental and the socio-economic realities of one's immediate context, the Spirit brings change. The Spirit empowers those who believe to overcome their situation of pathos.[297]

Furthermore, for Solivan, the Holy Spirit is a Spirit who maintains the diversity of the different cultures and works through them. In this respect, he speaks of particularity. As an example, he uses the Acts of the Apostles 2 as the paradigm for a multilingual church:

> Yet God in his infinite wisdom and purposefulness intentionally chose to engage the global character of this audience by attending to its particularity rather than its common denominator, which, for the most part, would have been determined by their common dependent relationship with Rome. This would have been reflected in their having to speak Greek or Aramaic. The fact that the Holy Spirit empowered the disciples to speak to the crowd in their own dialects and languages is evident in the reaction of some who were confounded because they heard each in their own *dialect* (διαλέκῳ): "Behold are not all these who are speaking Galileans? How do we hear them each in our own *dialect* in which we are born?" Others exclaimed, "We hear them speaking in our own *languages* (γλώσσις)" (Acts 2:5–11). The mission of the church and the nature of the reign of God would fundamentally require respect for and take into account the cultural pluralism of the nations. Contrary to the status quo of the Romans' sense of cultural superiority over and against the other nations, the church would have to posit a counter model to that of the socio-political arrogance of the Roman empire and even of Judaism. This model is alluded to by St. Paul when writing to the Galatians: "There cannot be Jew nor Greek; there cannot be slave nor freeman; there cannot be male nor female; for you are all one in Christ" (Gal 3:28; Col 3:11).[298]

---

297. Solivan, *Spirit, Pathos and Liberation*, 111.
298. Solivan, *Spirit, Pathos and Liberation*, 114–15.

Solivan points out that we are challenged to give ear to the work of the Holy Spirit in other cultural contexts. However, this will have consequences:

> This requires that the individual in his or her particularity be taken seriously; and what is more serious than to start with the person's cultural-linguistic identity as in Acts 2? This is especially true in the context of dong theology. Speech, language and the written word are the principal mediums of theological discourse. Given this, how can we justify imposing on our dialogical partner the prohibition of employing their most important means of critical engagement, the use of their language and cultural matrix?

> The paradigm of Acts 2, the Holy Spirit empowering the people to hear and to understand and the church to speak and to be understood, serves as an example of how essential the culture and language of the unreached is for reaching them. This willingness to move beyond one's own cultural-linguistic limitations to reach the neighbour is an expression of (divine) love.[299]

As then, even today the Holy Spirit speaks to the whole of creation, and He does so in the most diverse ways, in the most varied of languages and cultures. Thereby, the Holy Spirit also creates a foundation for the overcoming of prejudice against the "others." This means nothing less than that, through the Holy Spirit, a universality is given amid all particularities; namely, a unity in diversity. Solivan also explains this unity with the Holy Spirit:

> The cultural glossolalia modelled on the day of Pentecost called people to place their own cultural particularities within the liberating circle of the global village. Pentecostals speak of the affirmation of all people and cultures, each having their place and contributions. Cultures of linguistic arrogance, or the imposition of one language over another, undermines the nature of our oneness by making it language based. If the presence of the Spirit of Christ is not in and among us no amount of cultural imposition or socio-political control will be enough to make us one people.[300]

---

299. Solivan, *Spirit, Pathos and Liberation*, 117.
300. Solivan, *Spirit, Pathos and Liberation*, 118.

This means that even our own particularity, through the Holy Spirit, can be part of His concert which He performs in His fullness throughout the entire Body.[301]

It is also worth noting that Solivan, similarly to Ragaz, does not reduce the work of the Holy Spirit to an inner-church function: "Needless to say, there are occasions that witness to the presence of *orthopathos* outside of the Christian community."[302] However, whilst Ragaz merely releases the Holy Spirit from the church, Solivan has also developed concrete criteria and boundaries for the work of the Holy Spirit outside the church, providing orientation through the approach of orthopathos:

> Yet a closer examination of them in light of the biblical claims would seem to indicate the absence of some crucial aspects which are necessary if a complete orthopathic liberation is to occur. Among these are the inner peace of God known in Christ and made available by the Holy Spirit, and acts of repentance and reconciliation with God and neighbour that manifest an eschatological dimension of the blessed hope. The absence of this eschatological dimension diminishes the very character of hope. Hope, love and faith in the orthopathic liberation process are not psychogenic, rather, they are the work of the Holy Spirit, the Spirit of Christ reconciling us to God, to ourselves and to our neighbours.[303]

Critical Appraisal

In Spring 1996, Samuel Solivan commented critically on the Memphis Miracle in *Pneuma* 18.1.[304] Two years after publishing his article, he introduced his approach of orthopathos and thereby made an important contribution to sensitizing the general public to the realities of everyday life for Hispanic people. Because his approach is an approach of liberation, it is not surprising that the theology of orthopathos shows conspicuous

---

301. Solivan, *Spirit, Pathos and Liberation*, 142, 143.
302. Solivan, *Spirit, Pathos and Liberation*, 109–10.
303. Solivan, *Spirit, Pathos and Liberation*, 110.
304. Solivan, "From Azusa to Memphis," 113–40. Solivan's criticism does not simply validate reconciliation and forgiveness between Black and White in the abstract, but he welcomes and affirms it explicitly and states that reconciliation must go much further: "What is needed is respect for *all* people and not just between Blacks and Whites. A mutuality of respect between Blacks and Whites alone is at best hypocritical and at worst a denial of the dignity of all people" (Solivan, "From Azusa to Memphis," 130).

parallels to other liberation theologies. What is new is that Solivan developed the familiar approaches further. He appropriated Gutierréz's term *poverty* as the starting point and then further developed it by using the umbrella term *suffering*. He rightfully points out that the term *poverty* hardly does justice to the multi-layered distress of the marginalized. The new breadth of his starting point provides new challenges for liberation. Solivan takes this challenge, amongst other things, by thematizing the social isolation of suffering people[305] and then pointing out that it is not enough to be a "church *for* the poor." Rather, the approach of orthopathos requires that the church must be located amongst the poor in order to become a "church *of* the poor."

Moreover, Solivan further develops Juan Luis Segundo's *Liberation of Theology*, a continuation of Gutiérrez's Theology of Liberation. Segundo introduces the hermeneutic circle, in which the praxis inspired by the holy Scripture is incorporated as a corrective of orthodoxy. Segundo's goal is to overcome the ideologization of orthodoxy using the hermeneutic circle. However, Solivan demonstrates the limitations of praxis as a corrective and introduces the orthopraxis and orthodoxy of orthopathos as the corrective, complementary and connecting element. This leads to fundamental renewal, as liberation is theologically conceived and practiced. For example, hitherto, orthopraxis could be practised without any further influence "from outside." Orthopathos also understands praxis not as something that can be done from outside but rather as something positioned within living proximity to the suffering that must be developed and practiced. Only in this way can a transforming process happen which, through the collective experience of the Holy Spirit, will liberate suffering people from their isolating self-occupation. It is this collective experience which opens them to a greater reality that is bigger than themselves and thereby liberates them from isolation.

With a strong emphasis on pneumatology, Solivan has developed liberation theology quite fundamentally: Whilst, according to Gutiérrez,

---

305. Dorothee Sölle tackles the aspect of isolation in even greater detail than Solivan. She writes: "As in the way we experience physical pain, perhaps toothache, all the other organs can become unimportant, without feeling, one is merely that tooth, so it is especially with continual life-threatening suffering, as for example in starvation camps. Everything else retires as insignificant, the person concentrates on his suffering, and as with lust, nothing counts any more, except the one thing. Extreme suffering privatizes the person totally, it destroys his capacity for communication. Through the night of pain—in insanity, in the incurable disease—nothing can be said. People who vegetate in this cannot be reached by others, even when one cannot abandon one's attempt to reach them" (Sölle, *Leiden*, 89).

the Holy Spirit obtains His significance primarily in accordance with liberation, according to Solivan, without the work of the Holy Spirit, actual liberation is plainly inconceivable.[306] In a similar way to Cone, Solivan also sees the presence and the work of the Holy Spirit in the still oppressed community of today. However, where, according to Cone, the Holy Spirit empowers to withstand and endure, according to Solivan, the Holy Spirit goes further: He leads to change. Orthopathos desires the transformation of pathos. Equally, Solivan further develops Cone's "Eyes to see and heart to feel." Again, it is the approach of orthopathos which gives orientation: "To see, hear and know that suffering exists and to be moved by it is not enough. Even solidarity is apathetic if it does not strengthen one toward transformation. Sympathy and empathy must move from the initial stages of solidarity to transformation."[307] The Holy Spirit will transform; however He will not allow Himself to be reduced to this mode of working. Solivan points out that God's Spirit works differently, in and through the Hispanic diversity. The diversity of languages and cultures in place are to be affirmed as God-intended in order not to miss the staggering variety and range of the works of God's Spirit. At the same time, it is the Holy Spirit who brings and holds together the body of Christ in its entire spectrum, so that the diversity of the church is not torn apart. It is the Holy Spirit who creates unity in diversity.

I would like to add two critical thoughts to these recognized works. First, as raised earlier when reviewing the works of Cone and Gutiérrez, also in the case of Solivan, we note a one-sided liberation of the oppressed, where liberation of the oppressor is not a theme. However, as Moltmann already wrote in 1978, even the oppressors need liberation. Not only suffering people are in need of liberation but also those who are responsible for the suffering of others. God also desires to liberate them by saving them from their sin.[308] In the same vein, Dorothee Sölle points out that not only distressed people suffer in their isolation, but also the oppressors are subjugated to isolation. They also isolate themselves and must be liberated from a life which rotates around the avoidance of sorrow (thereby rotating around oneself).[309] The Holy Spirit also wishes to

---

306. See also Lovett, "Black Holiness-Pentecostal," 162.

307. Solivan, *Spirit, Pathos and Liberation*, 76.

308. See Moltmann, *Experiences in Theology*, 241; "Probleme und Chancen," 527–38.

309. "Because walls have been erected between the suffering subject and reality, one finds out about the suffering of others only indirectly, one sees starving children on the

give them (and not only suffering people) the experience of fellowship, which brings them together in community with the marginalized and thus liberates from their isolation.

Precisely because the Holy Spirit represents such a central role in Solivan's approach of orthopathos, it is all the more astonishing that his approach to liberation does not include a reconciliation that includes the oppressor, the privileged.[310]

Secondly, I would like to respond to Solivan's criticism of Moltmann. Solivan suggests Moltmann is too one-sidedly fixated on the revelation of the Holy Spirit[311] and thereby depreciates the significance of experience.[312] Solivan bases his judgment on the publication by Christopher Morse, who in *The Logic of Promise*[313] makes precisely this allegation of Moltmann. Back in 1979, the criticism expressed by Morse may perhaps have been justifiable for those times; however, would like to point out that as early as in 1980, in *The Trinity and the Kingdom of God*, Moltmann dedicated an entire section to the experience of God, where he addressed and dealt with its significance as well as its limitations.[314] Later, in *Experiences in Theology*, Moltmann even went as far as to say: "First comes the experience, then the theology; first the passion, then the action."[315] Only in the experience that man has with God and in the memory of these experiences does the revealed future receive its credibility: "The

---

screen, and this relationship with the sufferings of others is characteristic for our entire perception. . . . The person who seeks this kind of freedom from suffering goes into quarantine, to a germ-free place, where dirt and bacteria do not touch him, where he is alone with himself, even when this 'with himself' includes the small family. Wishing to remain free of suffering, regression into apathy can be a form of fear of contact, one does not wish to be touched, infected, stained, involved, one keeps himself as far away as possible, worries about his own affairs, privatizes himself until he is stupefied" (Sölle, *Leiden*, 53–54).

310. See also the critical appraisal on Cone.

311. See also Solivan's comment on Moltmann in *Spirit, Pathos and Liberation*, 91n45. Moltmann writes: "Hope's statements of promise, however, must stand in contradiction to the reality which can at present be experienced. They do not result from experience, but are the condition for the possibility of new experiences" (Moltmann, *Theology of Hope*, 18).

312. Solivan, *Spirit, Pathos and Liberation*, 91.

313. See Solivan, *Spirit, Phatos and Liberation*, 91n44, 46.

314. Moltmann, *Source of Life*, 2–4. Further statements on the significance of the experience with God have been published, for example, in Moltmann, *Kirche in der Kraft*, 38; *Geist des Lebens*, 32–90, which may well constitute the most significant argument on this matter.

315. Moltmann, *Experiences in Theology*, 44.

story of godly promises is retold in the form of the remembered hopes of the people. This is remembrance in which one can live, and which therefore is particularly vital for life."[316] To me, it seems problematic that Solivan, with the publication of his book in 1998, supported an opinion expressed about Moltmann which was published eleven years earlier without verifying it. All the more, since Moltmann in the meantime had published further books and articles. Had Solivan checked Morse's statement against the primary sources, then he would have found an advocate of his own concerns in Moltmann.[317]

Finally, it must be said of Solivan that the approach of orthopathos has at least shaped academic Pentecostal theology in inestimable ways. This is true even though, besides the literature already mentioned, he has hardly published any academic publications. The few works that he has published are therefore all the more significant, in particular for Hispanic Pentecostal theology.

Amos Yong: An Approach with Asian Roots

Amos Yong, the son of Chinese Malaysians, was born on July 26, 1965, in Malaysia. At the age of ten, he and his family moved to the US, where his parents worked as missionaries amongst Chinese migrants in California.[318] Yong studied at Bethany College in Santa Cruz[319] (AoG) from 1983 and was ordained at the end of his studies. In 1993 and 1995, he graduated with a master's degree from the *Western Evangelical Seminary* and then *Portland State University. In* 1999, Yong earned a PhD from Boston University in the field of Religion and Theology.[320]

The focus of Amos Yong's research is not principally in the social justice/social ethics. Nevertheless, as a theologian, he is of interest for the present dialogue especially because of his monograph *In the Days of Caesar. Pentecostalism and Political Theology*, published in 2010. As the title suggests, the book addresses the two (often understood as mutually exclusive) topics of Pentecostalism and politics.[321] In his monograph, Yong

---

316. Moltmann, *Experiences in Theology*, 33.

317. Even though Moltmann takes up the aspect of pathos, it should be noted that phatos is pneumatologically developed more thoroughly by Solivan.

318. Yong, *Spirit Poured Out on All Flesh*, 17–32.

319. Yong, *Spirit Poured Out on All Flesh*, 9.

320. Lee, "Alum Profile."

321. Yong, *Days of Caesar*, xvii.

uses the term Pentecostalism to refer to all churches and movements that define themselves as Pentecostal or charismatic—even though in *In the Days of Caesar* he places the emphasis on classical Pentecostalism.[322] Yong fundamentally references the terms politics and political theology to life in the public sphere. By the public sphere he understands the place in which "various dimensions of religion, culture, society, economics, and government converge and interface."[323] Yong thus defines the two terms more broadly than usual.[324]

Yong's intentions in this book are threefold: (a) to correct Pentecostal stereotypes regarding politics and theology, (b) to provoke fellow Pentecostals to reflect theologically on their spirituality in relation to politics, and (c) to provide a distinctive Pentecostal reflection on the topic of theology and politics in order to make a constructive contribution to broader Christendom.[325]

In the first part of his book, Yong presents the various approaches of the global Pentecostal Movement with regard to its practice in the public sphere, followed by a historical overview of his understanding of political theology. The first part concludes with an introduction and rationale of the methodology applied in the second part of the book. The following analysis will deal only briefly with the first part of Yong's monograph but more extensively with the second, constructive part, in which he expands upon his Pentecostal contribution to the dialogue on socially relevant practice. Because of Yong's broad approach and the variety of topics he addresses, this chapter is the most comprehensive among the intra-Pentecostal voices.

---

322. "I will, however, tend to privilege what sociologists call classical Pentecostalism—churches and groups derived from Azusa Street revival in Los Angeles during the first decade of the twentieth century—as being at least somewhat representative to non-classical aspects of modern Pentecostalism" (Yong, *Days of Caesar*, xviii).

323. Yong, *Days of Caesar*, xix.

324. Mostly, the term politics is associated with the formal aspects of public accountability in the local, national, or international sphere. See also Yong, *Days of Caesar*, xix, 3.

325. Yong, *Days of Caesar*, xix.

Evaluation and Methodology of Pentecostal Political Theology

Yong opens his book with an evaluation of Pentecostal politics. Taking into account the fact that Pentecostal epicenters have shifted to the global South, Yong uses data collected mostly in Asia, Africa, and Latin America.[326]

Yong believes that three groups can be identified within the worldwide Pentecostal churches with regard to their approach to politics:

- The first group, which in his opinion represents the vast majority, are Pentecostals who would describe themselves as apolitical. Yong lists various reasons for this passive political attitude. On the one hand, he points to theological motives, which he attributes to a dispensationalist worldview[327] and biblical literalism, which (to the detriment of politics) invest their energy in evangelism and world mission. Political engagement is seen by this group as a waste of time and as unbiblical.[328] Another important factor in this apolitical attitude is that dispensationalism and biblical literalism are often prevalent among the socially and culturally disenfranchised. In these circles, the struggle for daily survival is a reality that barely allows them the "luxury" of being politically active. Often, poverty automatically means exclusion from the political sphere because it is usually accompanied by language barriers, lack of property and, especially for people with a migrant background, lack of political rights or citizenship.[329] Often, this is aggravated by a charismatic worldview whereby sin is understood as the cause of God's wrath, which has negative consequences for political and economic life.

- Yong describes the second group as political Pentecostals. As an example of politically active Pentecostals, Yong cites the Latin American Union of Evangelicals in Politics, founded in 1991, which has successfully put forward candidates in elections several times. The candidates often engage in the fight against corruption, support conservative family values (e.g., the fight against abortion), defend freedom of faith (in particular in favor of preaching the Gospel) and

---

326. Yong, *Days of Caesar*, 3.

327. For explanations of dispensationalism, see the section "Pentecostal Hope" below, 202.

328. Yong, *Days of Caesar*, 5.

329. Yong, *Days of Caesar*, 6.

fight against the spread of poverty.[330] Another example of politically active Pentecostals is Pentecostal nationalism in Zambia. Under the government of President Chiluba (1991–2002), the country was Christianized for ten years.[331] In Nigeria, on the other hand, the political involvement of Pentecostals is strongly influenced by the fear of Islamization. Pentecostal spirituality finds concrete expression, for example, in the "'warfare prayer' to overthrow the principalities and powers 'behind' the nation's political structures," which means the demonization of Islam, the fight against Sharia law, as well as the targeted mission to the (Muslim) pagans.[332]

- Yong calls the third group apolitical-political Pentecostals. With this somewhat unmanageable term, Yong describes a Pentecostal spirituality that is not consciously politicized but is nevertheless political in its spirituality. This can happen in different ways. Among other examples, Yong mentions the call to hold prayer nights in favor of Christian presidential candidates in Nigeria.[333] Furthermore, he sees the values and culture of Pentecostal communities shaped by spirituality as political because they are often opposed to the values practiced in society: "For example, in his ethnographic study of Pentecostalism in Argentina, Daniel Míguez shows how Pentecostal churches provide companionship and solidarity in the form of 'family,' or 'sisterhood,' that is an alternative to existing neighborhood patronage networks and clientelism."[334] These lived-our values are noticed by society and thus offer an alternative to the usual practice.

In a detailed subsection, Yong presents a historical outline.[335] of political theology, in line with the contemporary relationship or approaches to Pentecostal political theology described above, in which he summarizes biblical, historical and current approaches. Yong concludes that we already see in the Bible, and even more so in church history, that there were the most diverse practices and understandings of the political. However, his conclusion does not lead him to assume that one Christian practice is automatically as good as any other. On the contrary,

330. Yong, *Days of Caesar*, 8.
331. Yong, *Days of Caesar*, 9.
332. Yong, *Days of Caesar*, 10.
333. Yong, *Days of Caesar*, 12.
334. Yong, *Days of Caesar*, 13.
335. Yong, *Days of Caesar*, 40–82.

"Rather, Christian theological faithfulness and political engagement is a context-specific affair, albeit one guided by the discerning application of both theological and political norms."[336] Furthermore, he observes that the domain of the political in history and the present is very broad and comprehensive. Thus, he sees the political as linked to economics, socio-economic lifestyle, social doctrine, gender and role issues, class issues, ethnicity, etc. Finally, Yong notes that the different approaches in the history of Christianity do not provide a unified and conclusive answer about the relationship between politics and theology, as all previous concepts are in tension with each other, some even contradicting each other.[337]

In the third main chapter, Yong addresses the methodological question of how a normative theology of the political can be developed which, as a starting point, begins with a Pentecostal-global pneumatology.[338] For Yong, in order to actually satisfy the claim of being Pentecostal-global, this must include the following criteria: Holy Scripture has a normative role to play, whilst being interpreted with an experience-oriented hermeneutic.[339] Secondly, the plurality inherent in the global Pentecostal Movement is to be reflected.[340]

To accomplish this, Yong chooses The Fivefold Gospel as an interpretive structure. He justifies this as follows: "The fivefold gospel has recently been proposed by some Pentecostal theologians as representing 'the theological heart' of the movement.[341] It consist, in sum, of the good news of Jesus as savior, sanctifier, Spirit-baptizer, healer, and coming king."[342] Yong goes on to justify the interpretive structure he has chosen with the following reference:

> With regard to pneumatological and methodological pluralism, the fivefold framework presents a pluriform and polyphonic Christology, pneumatology, and by extension soteriology. There is not just one view of Jesus as the anointed one of God, nor only one view of what Jesus has been anointed to accomplish. Hence the pluralism of Pentecostalism on the ground—i.e., as it exists in the global south and around the world, and as I have

---

336. Yong, *Days of Caesar*, 82.
337. Yong, *Days of Caesar*, 83.
338. Yong, *Days of Caesar*, 86.
339. Yong, *Days of Caesar*, 89–90, 92.
340. Yong, *Days of Caesar*, 90.
341. See also, for example, Thomas, "Pentecostal Theology."
342. Yong, *Days of Caesar*, 95.

documented already in the first chapter with regard to Pentecostalism as it interfaces with the public sphere, it can be said to reflect, even if only instinctively rather than intentionally, the pluralism inherent in the fivefold theological construct.... The result is that Pentecostal theology informed and structured by the fivefold formulation will itself be sensitive to the pluralism of the Pentecostal experience on the one hand, while also being open to providing a distinctively Pentecostal and pneumatological accent on the pluralism that exists in the theological academy on the other hand.[343]

Pentecostal Salvation as Deliverance from the Powers

a) Pentecostal Beliefs and Practices

Yong defines the core Pentecostal soteriology as follows:

> For Pentecostals, fundamentally, salvation is to be found in Jesus and in his name, "for there is no other name under heaven given among mortals by which we must be saved" (Acts 4:12).... But the life, death on a cross, resurrection, and ascension to heaven of Jesus Christ have made possible reconciliation between God and humankind. By repenting from their sin and placing faith in the person and work of Christ, human beings are regenerated by the power of the Holy Spirit, adopted as sons and daughters of God, and justified, sanctified, and, eschatologically, glorified. This, in gist, is what it means to confess Jesus as savior.[344]

This definition links Pentecostals with a wide spectrum of other Protestant churches. For Pentecostals, however, salvation through Christ involves far more than redemption from sins: For them, salvation in Christ also includes deliverance from disease, poverty and other socio-economic evils. Especially in the Pentecostal churches of the global South, deliverance from demonic powers, which are often interpreted as the cause of all kinds of ills such as political corruption, AIDS, unemployment, etc., is seen as an important component:[345] "Jesus as savior is understood not only as healer but also as deliverer, and, in some cases, as exorcist, and Pentecostal services thus include moments in the liturgy devoted to

---

343. Yong, *Days of Caesar*, 97.
344. Yong, *Days of Caesar*, 122–23.
345. Yong, *Days of Caesar*, 123.

prayer for the sick as well as to rituals of deliverance and exorcism."[346] Against this background, it becomes clear that the global Pentecostal Movement has a holistic understanding of salvation which anticipates the liberating work of Christ in everyday life.

Pentecostal soteriology encompasses the conviction that the cause of experienced hardships is spiritual.[347] Paul's statement in Ephesians, that "our struggle is not against 'beings of' flesh and blood, but against the powers and authorities of darkness that rule over the earth, against the rulers of spirits in the invisible world who are behind all evil" (Eph 6:12, New Geneva Translation) is interpreted to mean that "economic challenges, business failures, unemployment, poverty, and even famine, etc., are works of the devil and his demons, all whom have been sent 'to steal and kill and destroy' (John 10:10)."[348] Only the spiritual struggle against the powers behind these hardships can, according to this understanding, ultimately overcome the social problems: "The key to economic success therefore resides in the churches' properly engaging in spiritual warfare prayer (oftentimes involving fasting, laying on of hands, exorcisms, Spirit-filled worship, etc.) against the cosmic powers that beset believers and their communities."[349]

Yong rightly points out that Pentecostal cosmology certainly provides a theoretical explanation for the seemingly incomprehensible economic correlations. If social advancement proves impossible despite all efforts, then supernatural explanations for those affected seem quite plausible: "Witchcraft provides a theory about how the supernatural invisible realm impacts the material realms of human fortunes, and how dependence on such powers enables the achievement of both economic wealth and political power."[350] Nevertheless, Pentecostals will insist that cooperation with demonic powers is ultimately doomed to failure. Earnest trust in God and the Holy Spirit will, they are convinced, despite temporary setbacks, ultimately overcome poverty and even create enough abundance for material blessings to reach others.[351] It is striking how close Pentecostal cosmology is to the worldviews of the traditional

---

346. Yong, *Days of Caesar*, 123.
347. Yong, *Days of Caesar*, 126.
348. Yong, *Days of Caesar*, 126.
349. Yong, *Days of Caesar*, 126.
350. Yong, *Days of Caesar*, 128.
351. Yong, *Days of Caesar*, 128.

religions of the global South. This is also the reason for Yong's critical question to the Pentecostal church:

> In short, can Pentecostal Christianity be said to have challenged such indigenous beliefs and practices, or is the result, in the end, simply another variation on a similar theme? And beyond this question of the potentially prophetic dimension of Pentecostalism is the alethic question regarding the truth of the matter: Do Pentecostal and indigenous cosmologies rightly portray the way things are regarding the principalities and powers?[352]

Yong also points to the problem of territorial warfare, which in its practice demonizes "opponents" of all kinds. Thus, Pentecostal cosmology assumes that spiritual powers rule over nations and territories in the biblical worldview. Derived from 1 Corinthians 8:4–6; 10:19–21, Pentecostals assume that these are powers of a demonic, ungodly nature. Also significant is Daniel 10:12–13 and 10:20–21, which inspires the Pentecostal worldview of territorial powers—with tangible implications for Pentecostal political practice:

> As a result, notions of spiritual warfare against territorial spirits have emerged across the spectrum of global Pentecostalism. By this is meant the concerted and focused activity of congregational and para-church agencies that identifies the "spiritual strongholds," over specific geographic territories, cultural regions, or national governments or institutions, engages and/or resists the corporate sins and activities perpetuated by such spirits, and mobilizes sustained warfare prayer devoted to neutralizing, binding, and rendering impotent such spiritual realities. . . . When successful, entire people groups and even nations are believed to be delivered from the powers of darkness and converted to Christ, and this will result in a divine visitation of forgiveness, healing, and blessing.[353]

The problematic thing about the practice of territorial warfare is that often a "demonization" of the "opponents" takes place. Yong cites examples from Brazil in which socialist candidates are called "candidates of the devil."[354] Another problematic practice of demonization can be observed in the multi-religious environment: "Given the dualistic framework of the Pentecostal cosmology, Jesus' words, 'Whoever is not with me is

---

352. Yong, *Days of Caesar*, 129.
353. Yong, *Days of Caesar*, 130–31.
354. Yong, *Days of Caesar*, 313.

against me' (Luke 11:23), lend themselves to the conclusion that the non-Christian option receives its mandate, empowerment, and agenda from the prince of darkness himself."[355] As an actual example, Yong points to the situation in Nigeria, where the population is divided fairly equally between Muslims and Christians, and both groups aggressively demonize each other in their struggle for land rights, economic control and political power.[356] Yong describes the most evil form of demonization of "opponents" as that which is misused as justification and legitimization for political oppression and military activities. As a grim example, Yong cites Rios Montt, president of Guatemala from 1982 to 1983. Montt, who joined a neo-Pentecostal church, was accused of human rights violations against Indians. The pastor of Montt's church justified the president's actions with the words: "The army doesn't massacre the Indians. It massacres demons, the Indians are demon possessed; they are communists."[357] Yong rightly condemns these excesses of Pentecostal practice and is critical of such destructive forms of spiritual warfare: "Pentecostals must rethink some of their traditional theological notions, especially the tendency to demonize their political opponents, if they are going to engage the political and public sphere in a more responsible way in their second century of existence."[358] And further:

> In short, the politics of Pentecostal deliverance has been shown to be too easily hijacked by uncritical nationalistic aspirations. Pentecostal spirituality and piety, buttressed by a complex cosmology of spirits, principalities and powers, has been applied dualistically in naïve ways, resulting not only in "politically incorrect" practices, but in theologically heretical ideas and practically dangerous political agendas. Can such Pentecostal notions about salvation, deliverance, and powers be redeemed for a viable political theology today?[359]

Yong answers the preceding question with a yes and an exclamation mark. However, according to his approach, this can only be done in dialogue with other traditions that are also concerned about the demonic powers and authorities.

---

355. Yong, *Days of Caesar*, 132.
356. Yong, *Days of Caesar*, 132.
357. Yong, *Days of Caesar*, 132–33.
358. Yong, *Days of Caesar*, 133.
359. Yong, *Days of Caesar*, 134.

b) Non-Pentecostal Approaches in Dealing with Powers and Authorities

Here, Yong deals primarily with the positions of Tillich, Berkhof, Yoder, Ellul, and Wink, with Tillich being discussed in the greatest detail because of his influence on the other theologians. According to Yong, Tillich understands the demonic as the inverse side of salvation history.[360] Whilst salvation history connects (God and the Kingdom of God proclaimed as absolute and final), the demonic disrupts, fragments and polarizes history.[361] In this respect, for Tillich, the demonic is an inevitable aspect of theological history: "History, Tillich noted, should be seen as 'a battlefield of the divine and the demonic,'[362] and as a 'continuous fight . . . between divine and demonic structures.'"[363] From the perspective of the 1930s, Tillich now sets out to identify manifestations of the demonic and believes he can recognize two of these manifestations in the economic and political arena. Economically, Tillich sees the demonic in the capitalist production system:

> It was "the autonomy of the capitalistic economic system, with all its contradictions, and the mass disintegration and destruction of meaning in all spheres of historical existence which it produces"; more precisely: "The economic sphere of historical existence, which has become autonomous, has brought all the other spheres of human historical life into subjection to itself and has deprived them of independent meaning; thus it has set in motion a great process of mass disintegration, the movement of which is subject to destructive laws."[364] Further, the effect of capitalism on society in general, and on individuals that comprise society, "take the typical form of 'possession,' that is, of being 'possessed'; its character is demonic."[365] Capitalism, which presumed the competition of individuals and corporations against one another, produced a split consciousness: competition was necessary for the economic system, although it engendered and relied upon attempts to overcome the other—such is a characteristic feature of demonic systems.[366]

---

360. Yong, *Days of Caesar*, 136.
361. Yong, *Days of Caesar*, 136.
362. Tillich, "Kingdom of God and History," 117, cited in Yong, *Days of Caesar*, 137.
363. Tillich, *Protestant Era*, xvii, cited in Yong, *Days of Caesar*, 137.
364. Tillich, "Kingdom of God and History," 131, cited in Yong, *Days of Caesar*, 137.
365. Tillich, *Political Expectation*, 50, in Yong, *Days of Caesar*, 137.
366. Yong, *Days of Caesar*, 136.

Instead of the "demonic" capitalist system, Tillich, like Ragaz, Barth, and other theologians of the 1930s, propagated a religious socialism oriented toward the Kingdom of God.[367]

In the political sphere, Tillich perceives the demonic in a nationalism that polarizes the particular nations, as well as in the authoritarianism of a government. Especially in the authoritarianism of Russian Bolshevism, Tillich sees this manifested through its dictatorial exercise of power and "unrestricted exercise of power [that] drives men into presumption toward God and to destruction of the human values which belong to the Kingdom of God: formal justice, truthfulness and freedom."[368] Accordingly, Tillich interprets in Hobbes's *Leviathan*

> a "demonic symbol, [signifying] the all-consuming might of the state."[369] The demonic manifestation of nationalism, on the other hand, involves the mistaken identification of finite nations as constituting "the supreme good to all who belong to it."[370] In the ancient world, "primitive Christianity challenged the Roman state as a demonic power, having the ambiguity of the demonic to be creative and destructive at the same time, establishing order and compelling men to the worship of itself."[371] Other examples given later included the Germanic, British, Russian, and even American empires, each of which was a materialisation, however ambiguous, of the demonic in its "self-elevating claim to ultimacy."[372]

In all these remarks, for Tillich, the demonic is primarily a religious category: "Hence, economic and political expressions of the demonic were fundamentally religious in character, which meant that even religious claims could become demonic."[373] By not succumbing to the seductions of greed and "elevating oneself above others" and trusting in the power of the Holy Spirit, Christ overcame the demonic and thus exposed all the false and demonic absolutes of history.[374]

---

367. Yong refers here to Tillich's essays "Religious Socialism," "Basic Principles of Religious Socialism," and "Christianity and Marxism," *Political Expectations* as a whole, and chapter 11 in *The Protestant Era*.

368. Tillich, "Kingdom of God and History," 135, in Yong, *Days of Caesar*, 138.

369. Tillich, *Political Expectation*, 100, in Yong, *Days of Caesar*, 137.

370. Tillich, "Kingdom of God and History," 133, in Yong, *Days of Caesar*, 138.

371. Tillich, *Protestant Era*, 168, in Yong, *Days of Caesar*, 137.

372. Tillich, *Systematic Theology*, 3:344, in Yong, *Days of Caesar*, 138.

373. Yong, *Days of Caesar*, 138.

374. Yong, *Days of Caesar*, 138.

In his further discussion of the powers and authorities, Yong deals with the thoughts of Berkhof, Yoder, Ellul, and Wink, which are also definitely oriented toward the baselines of Tillich in their approaches. In addition to Tillich's approach, Hendrikus Berkhof introduces to the discussion a stance which assumes the redeemability of the powers.[375] John Howard Yoder introduces the position of non-violent resistance to the powers.[376] Jacques Ellul sees the powers and authorities as more than mere structures. In his creative period, he vacillates back and forth between a personal and a structural understanding (evil as a dynamic) of powers and forces.[377] Ellul rejects the idea that powers are creatures of God who will ultimately conform to God's will. For him, the redeemability of the powers is inconceivable because Jesus' victory was accomplished by not engaging with them.[378] Walter Wink's contribution lies in the interpretation of the authorities as powers which

> constituted, through their violent mechanisms, a "domination system," that perpetuates a fallen and anti-God world order. Developing Berkhof's idea of the redeemability of the powers and embracing Yoder's advocacy of a path of non-violent resistance against the powers, Wink believes that the present world-order can be redeemed and transformed into a "dominant-free," system, and that this happens through the spiritual practices of loving and forgiving our enemies, praying for God's intervention, and doing the works of righteousness that bring about the healing of a divided world.[379]

In Wink's account, the biblical powers and authorities refer to a whole spectrum of realities: they can manifest themselves as man-made institutions, as cosmic elements or as personified structures (e.g., laws) or events (e.g., death).[380]

---

375. Yong, *Days of Caesar*, 139–40.

376. Yong, *Days of Caesar*, 140.

377. Yong, *Days of Caesar*, 141.

378. Thus Ellul writes: "The principalities and powers were themselves stripped of power because they encountered the one who did not compete with them but let himself be stripped. They did not meet a victor. They met a prisoner who gave himself up to them. The powers were thus stripped of the one thing they have, namely the power to vanquish. They had nothing here to vanquish" (Ellul, *Ethics of Freedom*, 159, in Yong, *Days of Caesar*, 142). Yong, *Days of Caesar*, 142n78, points out the compatibility of Ellul's approach with Yoder's non-violent approach.

379. Yong, *Days of Caesar*, 143–44.

380. Yong, *Days of Caesar*, 144.

In view of the ecumenical discussion on powers and authorities, Yong asks whether the considerations from Berkhof to Wink may be valid for us as legitimate interpretations of the biblical material. Specifically, this raises two fundamental questions: What do the powers and authorities mentioned in the Bible refer to, and can they be restored?[381] Based on the Pauline use of the terminology (which corresponds with the usage in the Lukan works), Yong interprets the biblical term *exousia* (authorities or powers) as both spiritual and socio-political in nature.[382] Regarding the restorability of the powers and authorities, Yong takes his bearings from the Letter to the Colossians: "For in Him all things were created, in heaven and on earth, the visible and the invisible, whether thrones or dominions, whether powers or authorities. The whole universe was created through Him and for Him. He was before all things, and in Him all things hold together" (Col 1:16–17). Yong tends to believe that powers and authorities can be restored. He comes to this conclusion on the basis of various Pauline statements, such as: "For God was pleased to have all His fullness dwell in Him, and through Him to reconcile all things to Himself, whether on earth or in heaven, by making peace through His blood shed on the cross" (Col 1:19–20).

c) Continuation:

Yong sees his continuation as a contribution to the discussion on the interface between the powers and politics.[383] Firstly, he examines how the early church responds to various forms of oppression in the context of Acts, namely: How does the church respond to oppression by the state, how does it respond to oppression by a pagan environment, and how does it respond to the deities of the nations? Yong answers these questions using specific situations in the Acts of the Apostles as examples, but without claiming his answers to be exhaustive.

Yong sees the church's response to oppression by the state in Acts 4:24 as the worship of God by the church. In worshiping God, the church remembers that every government, every authority is subordinate to God and, therefore, in situations of state resentment, the church turns to God

---

381. Yong, *Days of Caesar*, 145.
382. Yong, *Days of Caesar*, 148.
383. Yong, *Days of Caesar*, 151.

with prayer, worship and praise.[384] In this respect, Yong sees the worship of God as a form of political engagement to counter the powers of the world in the power of the Holy Spirit.[385] In addition to state oppression, several times Acts also records confrontations with the pagan, Greek/Roman environment. In these confrontations (examples cited in Acts 16:19; 19:19–27), Yong sees three levels of encounter with pagan and occult phenomena: signs and wonders, which lead to a transformation of the political order (e.g., in Paphos); public exorcisms organized as an ecclesiastical purification rite (e.g., in Ephesus) and ritual exorcisms (e.g., in Philippi and Ephesus), which in different ways have an impact on regional political economies.[386] The third category of confrontation with powers and authorities that Yong examines is that of the church with the deities of the nations. For example, in Lystra, there is a confrontation between Paul and the Greek deities Zeus and Hermes (Acts 14:8–18), the deities of Athens (17:16–34) and Artemis of Ephesus (19:27–37). In these confrontations, Yong thinks he can see, by the reactions of the early church, that they advocate a clear position of their own, but they act in a way that is both discriminating and calm and without unnecessary provocation.[387] From these observations Yong draws the following conclusions:

> Part of the unfolding of the Lukan narrative details the liberating and redeeming power of the Holy Spirit who enabled Jesus to go about "doing good and healing all who were oppressed by the devil" (Acts 10:38). More precisely, part of the encounter between the Holy Spirit and other spirits involved exorcism and the "cleansing" of the public square. This leads to my second point: that exorcism understood as a public rite of purification may be a liturgical practice that can be beneficially adapted so that the church's worship includes not only prayer and praise but also deliverance as a mode of public engagement. If this is so, then spiritual warfare may be retrieved and reimagined as a viable form of political praxis so that the church can effectively exist amidst the principalities of the cosmos and the powers of the polis—in short, so that the church can be a viable and alternative cosmopolis.[388]

---

384. Yong, *Days of Caesar*, 152.
385. Yong, *Days of Caesar*, 152.
386. Yong, *Days of Caesar*, 153.
387. Yong, *Days of Caesar*, 154.
388. Yong, *Days of Caesar*, 155.

Based on these insights, Yong formulates the following goal: "I want to retrieve and reappropriate Pentecostal political praxis for the purposes of articulating a liturgical politics of worship."[389] Habits, character and behavior are shaped by the joint prayer, songs and Scripture readings, and thereby also ethically and politically. This shaping does not happen 'only' through the act of remembering, but also in the order expressly promised by God. The discrepancy between the promise and the current social order can be experienced in the liturgy and the call to action. Yong identifies worship, prayer and exorcism as formative liturgical elements.[390] For Yong, worship in the Pentecostal church is primarily to be understood as a collective act of the community.

> Pentecostal worship, consisting of prayer, singing (including "singing in the Holy Spirit"), praise, the testimony, interactive preaching, tarrying at the altar, and the operation of the charismatic gifts of the Holy Spirit, etc., carves out political space and enables a new political identity to emerge over social space and social time among Pentecostal communities. In the global south, especially, observe how Pentecostal liturgical practices dominate their weekly rhythms . . . and their concomitant seasons of fasting shape the Pentecostal expectation of divine provision in a hostile polis; and how the intensity of Pentecostal praise and worship is a public expression of an alternative community consisting of brothers and sisters in Christ through the Holy Spirit. With these practices, Pentecostals are not only engaging with God, but also with the spiritual realm of the principalities and powers—taking authority over the turmoil in their personal lives, the devastations of their economies, and the challenges in the public domain (many Pentecostals live in regions of the world where they are persecuted for their faith).[391]

With regard to prayer, Yong is not so much concerned with prayers articulated explicitly as political (e.g., intercession for the state government), but more fundamentally with the form and function of prayer. The question therefore arises as to what prayer expresses, in and of itself. For Yong, it consists of two sides: On the one hand, prayer expresses that one's own agenda, plans and ideas are subordinate to God's will, therefore it expresses dependence on God. On the other hand, "prayer recognizes

---

389. Yong, *Days of Caesar*, 155.
390. Yong, *Days of Caesar*, 156.
391. Yong, *Days of Caesar*, 156.

that our opponents are, scandalously, not only other human beings and institutions, but the principalities and powers, and that therefore the most effective weapons, even in the domains of the social, economic, and political, are spiritual (Eph 6:10–18)."[392] Prayers are thus also speech acts which seize the public space as a place from which the church will not allow itself to be displaced, and it helps shape it.

According to Yong, a liturgical practice of exorcisms is hardly ever practiced. However, he is also of the opinion that liturgical traditions which do not regularly practice exorcisms are not shaping the congregation sufficiently in terms of their political practice. One way to do this is to practice a political theology that celebrates and confesses Christ's victory over all powers and authorities. This will "enable focus on the demonic, not for its own sake but for the sake of constituting the church as an alternative cosmopolis amidst the many fallen principalities, to engage in non-violent witness directed toward the redemption of the powers."[393]

Pentecostal Holiness: A Sanctified Theology of Culture

a) Pentecostal Beliefs and Practices

As a second aspect of the Fivefold Gospel, Pentecostals usually refer to Jesus' work of sanctification.[394] Yong sees at least four sanctification theology approaches in the classical Pentecostal tradition, which are briefly outlined here. The first, more or less systematically articulated approach, was penned by William H. Durham and arose as a reaction to the Wesleyan doctrine of the "second work of grace." He sees the doctrine of the "second blessing" as the cause of the subdued fervor within various "holiness churches": In Durham's opinion, this above-mentioned two-phase doctrine provides an excuse for those who have not yet had the second experience to invest less serious effort into their pursuit of sanctification. Durham therefore emphasizes the full salvation of the believer at conversion, which has been completed with Christ's death on the cross:

> The holiness of Christ was imputed to the believer once and for all, thus regenerating the soul and enabling a holy life (while rendering superfluous the need for a subsequent experience of

---

392. Yong, *Days of Caesar*, 157.
393. Yong, *Days of Caesar*, 165.
394. Yong, *Days of Caesar*, 166.

sanctification). To be sure, the baptism of the Holy Spirit made possible the further maturation of the believer, but this was not a second work of sanctification.[395]

Durham's "finished work" soteriology laid the groundwork for two further approaches. The Oneness tradition, which emerged in the years after Durham's death, takes the "finished work" approach further by declaring that not only was sanctification imputed at conversion, but it also regards the baptism in the Holy Spirit as imputed. The Oneness movement sees no biblical basis for the separation of conversion and Spirit baptism. They even see Peter's answer in Acts 2:38 as confirming the opposite: "Repent and be baptized every one of you in the name of Jesus Christ! Then God will forgive your sins, and you will receive his gift, the Holy Spirit." Thus Yong writes:

> According to this view, conversion is initiated by repentance, involves in one package the regeneration of water baptism (in Jesus' name rather than according to the trinitarian formula), and culminates in the reception (baptism) of the Holy Spirit (evidenced with the sign of speaking in tongues as the classical Pentecostal argument usually goes). Sanctification is thus part and parcel of salvation, properly considered, which means also that holiness is both the immediately expected fruit and the ongoing lifelong expression of the regenerating work of the Holy Spirit.[396]

Yong sees the so-called Keswick Movement as a typical representative of a third approach which, whilst inclined toward Durham's approach, rejected the Oneness doctrine. The Keswick representatives, like Durham, also reject the idea of a second sanctification experience but support the opinion that the work of the Holy Spirit takes place in three distinct phases:

> Initial sanctification occurred at conversation, understood largely by the believer; ongoing sanctification occurred over the course of the remainder of the believer's life, culminating at either death (glorification) or the eschaton (parousia); and the baptism of the Holy Spirit, which was subsequent to conversion but denoted a purified life, empowered to bear witness to the gospel.[397]

---

395. Yong, *Days of Caesar*, 169.
396. Yong, *Days of Caesar*, 169.
397. Yong, *Days of Caesar*, 170.

The fourth approach is that of the Pentecostals who have their roots in the Holiness Movement and were forced to rethink their previous position because of Durham's criticism. One of the most renowned representatives in this context is Joseph H. King. Yong summarizes King's position in three points:

> First, whereas Keswickian-influenced denominations like the AOG delineated between initial sanctification (occurring at conversion) and ongoing sanctification (culminating in glorification), Pentecostal holiness churches talked about initial and full sanctification, with the difference that the latter—full sanctification and full salvation—was understood to occur in a distinct experience subsequent to conversion in this life whereby the sin nature would be fully suppressed or eradicated (Pentecostal holiness groups disagree about this specific issue). Second, whereas most Pentecostal groups (except the Oneness organizations) followed Durham in identifying the baptism with the Holy Spirit as a separate experience of empowerment to witness, Pentecostal holiness retained the Wesleyan doctrine of instantaneous and entire sanctification as a second work of grace and added to that the distinctively Pentecostal doctrine of Spirit-baptism for spiritual consecration and empowerment to witness as a third work of grace. Third, if the emphasis on holiness diminished over time in Pentecostal churches that did not understand sanctification as a subsequent work of the Holy Spirit, then the Pentecostal holiness movement as a whole was able to retain a much more vigorous commitment to personal holiness as a way of life, given its affirmation of the possibility of full Christian perfection.[398]

In the four Pentecostal approaches to sanctification described above, there are two biases: The Keswick bias, which understands purity as empowerment for mission and evangelism through the Holy Spirit (in short: "consecration for") and the bias stemming from the Holiness Movement, which understands sanctification as cleansing from the impurities of the fallen world (i.e., "setting apart from").

Yong draws the following conclusions regarding the interface between the understanding of sanctification and culture:

> In short, holiness Pentecostals have been of two hearts and minds about culture: a sectarian side that claims to reject the world, and a mission-driven side that seeks to reform and

---

398. Yong, *Days of Caesar*, 172–73.

transform society. This unique combination, however, has produced a sanctified church that has perennially been in quest of sanctified politics and a viable theology of culture. Perhaps one way forward might be the exploration of sanctified aesthetics, or theology of the arts, broadly conceived.[399]

Yong now traces the tension between consecration for and separation from in the subject of sanctification, in dialogue with three non-Pentecostal voices.

b) Extra-Pentecostal Approaches

Yong chooses John Howard Yoder, Stanley Hauerwas and representatives of the New Monasticism Movement as ecumenical dialogue partners. These are all dialogue partners whose orientation Yong describes as "post-Constantinian theologies." What he understands by this term is clarified by Yoder, the first dialogue partner.

Yoder, in his book The Politics of Jesus, is critical of the dominant church model which began to prevail in the fourth century, and which he calls the state church. He even speaks of a "Constantinian bondage" of the church, which, through its affiliation with the state, in many respects ceased to be free to live out its God-given vocation as the salt and light of the world. In concrete terms, Yong takes up four of Yoder's aspects in which this very bondage became tangible:

> Politically, the church was co-opted by the state so that even when the church was in control, its modus operandi was dictated by political exigencies rather than by the gospel. Socially, the church was relocated to the center of society rather than being capable of speaking prophetically from the margins. Ethically, the church's way of life was accommodated to the mores and value system(s) of the dominant culture rather than living out the distinctive ways of Jesus. And finally, theologically, the church's self-understanding was increasingly measured by the logic of the public square rather than by its own sources and practices. The result was a collapse of the distinction between the church and the world.[400]

---

399. Yong, *Days of Caesar*, 181.
400. Yong, *Days of Caesar*, 183.

Yoder sees the church of believers (member's church), or the church that is independent of the state, as an alternative to the popular- or state-church model. Yoder defines this alternative church model as a community of people who, of their own free will, feel they belong to Christ, essentially through a conversion experience, and who share with one another the desire to model their lives on the example of Christ.[401] In *The Politics of Jesus*, Yoder describes how this approach, as an alternative society, does not mean withdrawing from the world in a sectarian way, but as a way to be taken seriously as a political force in the world without becoming part of realpolitik. Yoder formulates a model of political theology, which Yong designates as diaspora, or exile, politics. In view of this, the designation is appropriate because Yoder, in his explanation, draws parallels between the church that is independent of the state and the Babylonian exile of the Israelites. Yoder believes that the Jews in exile acknowledged the surrounding pagan culture as their habitat. Thus, they spoke the predominant language, moved within the culture that was foreign to them with natural ease but stayed true to their original culture and the values conveyed by the Torah (such as practicing aniconic monotheism, honoring father and mother, work ethic, circumcision, etc.). It is precisely this loyalty to their original culture which, without isolating them from the world, set them apart from the rest of society and thereby placed them in a unique position because the exiles influence the public space of Babylonian society from the periphery. They are not bound by its realpolitik and thus have possibilities which are not available to the Babylonians.[402] Yoder sees a continuation of this "exile politics" in the life and work of Christ:

> The way of Christ did not lead to political quietism but rather to political radicalism, precisely in and through the church's living out of the Jubilee economics of sharing and liberation, the nonviolent politics of forgiveness and reconciliation, and the prophetic mysticism of peace and justice. The Way of Jesus was thus neither political, as conventionally construed, nor sectarian, as sociologically defined in terms of a withdrawal from the world; rather, the church was most politically radical when it did not ape the ways of the world but instead lived out of its innermost convictions as "an alternative social group."[403]

401. Yong, *Days of Caesar*, 183.
402. Yong, *Days of Caesar*, 184.
403. Yong, *Days of Caesar*, 183.

Applied to the context of today, it is therefore important for Yoder that "Christian communities needed to firmly resist 'being in charge' so as not to compromise their distinctive witness."[404] At the same time, this distinctiveness does not mean retreating from the public sphere, but rather active participation, consecrated and marked by otherness. Specifically:

> Thus for Yoder, the distinctive Christian practices like binding/ loosing in prayer, breaking bread and sharing together, baptism (understood as the formation/creation of a new community), the relativizing of the priestly hierarchy, and the empowerment of all the people of God—all of these can be translated into non-religious terms. The multiplicity of gifts is a model for the empowerment of the humble and for the end of hierarchy in social process. Dialogue under the Holy Spirit is the ground floor of the notion of democracy.[405]

In this respect, for Yoder, separation from and consecration for are inseparably bound together so that the church can fulfil its calling to be salt and light in this world.

Yong brings Hauerwas into the discussion as a second dialogue partner. Hauerwas was, as he says of himself, strongly influenced by Yoder.[406] Yong focuses his discussion on the two works in which Hauerwas (together with William H. Willimon) discusses and develops[407] Yoder's exile policy. Hauerwas sees the members of the church as "resident aliens" in this world, who within their "colony" maintain and affirm[408] their original and "distinctive language and lifestyle." It is the otherness inherent in the DNA of the church which sets it apart from the rest of society and places it on its margins. It is precisely this otherness that accounts for its effectiveness:

> The church in this framework does not have a social strategy, but is a social strategy, with its primary political task and responsibility being "to worship Christ in all things," and to "be odd."[409] Yet resident aliens are not sectarians—if such is defined

404. Yong, *Days of Caesar*, 186.
405. Yong, *Days of Caesar*, 186.
406. Yong, *Days of Caesar*, 186.
407. See Hauerwas and Willimon, *Resident Aliens*; *Where Resident Aliens Live*.
408. Hauerwas and Willimon, *Resident Aliens*, 12, in Yong, *Days of Caesar*, 187.
409. Hauerwas and Willimon, *Resident Aliens*, 45; *Where Resident Aliens Live*, 61–66, in Yong, *Days of Caesar*, 187.

sociologically as that form of religious life that evolves later into a fully-fledged church type—but specially trained to embody their stories and engage the world. Such engagement, however, occurs not on the world's terms, but as defined by exemplary saints.[410]

Yoder and Hauerwas correspond in their desire to free the church from its Constantinian bondage. At the same time, there is a discernible essential difference between the two: Where Yoder is of the opinion that a pluralistic society is fundamentally receptive to the voices of minorities, Hauerwas maintains that a discourse between the church and society is not possible at all.

For Yong, Hauerwas places the focus of his approach unequivocally on the individual who exemplifies holiness. For the continuing discourse, Yong now seeks a dialogue partner who works with congregational expressions of separation and consecration.[411]

At this point, Yong introduces the New Monastics Movement to the discussion. Basically, the New Monastics see themselves as part of the tradition of monastic movements that emerged in the fourth century. The movement, the majority of whose members have an evangelical background, is characterized by the integration of a simplistic lifestyle, and engagement in social transformation.[412] Various influences are discernible in the practice of the New Monastics: Ascetic elements from the Orthodox and Catholic traditions are integrated and help overcome the fundamentalist and conservative elements of their evangelical spirituality. Besides the monastic tradition, the approaches of Yoder and Hauerwas are also clearly perceptible.[413] Yoder's distinctive of the church, for example, is propagated in the form of a clear separation between church and state. There is no creed at the center of his understanding of spirituality, but the following of a Christ "of the heart, of the feet and of the hands, a real-life figure who can be emulated in his interactions with sinners and the world, not just worshipped."[414] Also Hauerwas maintains that the key to mission does not consist in a socially transforming strategy but rather in the embodiment of Christ. The early movement's understanding of sanctification was also shaped accordingly:

410. Yong, *Days of Caesar*, 187.
411. Yong, *Days of Caesar*, 190.
412. Yong, *Days of Caesar*, 192.
413. Both theologians are also repeatedly cited by representatives of the New Monastics. See, for example, Claiborne, *Irresistible Revolution*.
414. Yong, *Days of Caesar*, 193.

For the New Monasticism, then, holiness is less a set of rules to be followed than a set of marks to be improvised. Contemplation is less about rigorously focusing the mind than it is on cultivating a posture and life of prayer. Sanctification is considered in terms not only of purification but of bearing witness to the peculiarity of Jesus' way of being in the world. In a sense, the New Monastics are "ordinary radicals," as they like to call themselves: ordinary when compared to previous generations of monastics, perfectionists, and even holiness Christians, but radical when compared to both contemporary Christendom and the wider culture of our time.[415]

c) Continuation

Yong considers a pneumatological approach as fundamental for a Pentecostal political theology which relates to sanctification. He cites three reasons for this:

> First, it provides a transcendent and theological legitimation of Jesus' normativity so that we can recognize both his cultural embeddedness as a first-century Mediterranean Jew and his announcing and bringing about the kingdom under the power of the Holy Spirit. Second, the gift of the Holy Spirit preserves the diversity of tongues (languages) in a way that undermines any attempt to reconstruct or re-establish Christendom; rather, the many tongues signify the many centers that those on the margins need to heed and respect, rather than replace. But finally, in eschatological perspective, the Holy Spirit nevertheless inspires the many tongues to give glory to God, each in their own distinctive language; in this way, the Pentecost narrative signifies not only the preservation of the many tongues but also anticipates the final redemption of the many languages and cultures of the world.[416]

For Yong, it is clear that not all social/cultural elements are equally receptive to God's sanctifying work. The question therefore arises: "What aspects of culture are both constitutive of the wholeness (holiness) that fulfils human aspiration (the criterion of harmony) and open to reflect the

---

415. Yong, *Days of Caesar*, 194.
416. Yong, *Days of Caesar*, 201.

splendour of divine holinesss."[417] In other words, how can God's presence and activities be recognized within culture, and accordingly, how can it be decided which practice of sanctification—separation or consecration—is appropriate? Yong, in conformity with Cheryl Sanders,[418] chooses the sanctified aesthetic as the criterion of delineation. But what does he mean by this, and how should it be carried out? Yong explains his approach by referring to the working of the Holy Spirit, who purified and renewed the many languages, through the Pentecost event. The same Spirit works and releases the different gifts through the many members of the Body (1 Cor 12). Against this background, the worship of God happens through a diversity of agents and participants, as well as through a broad spectrum of expressions and rituals, be it in the form of liturgies spontaneously in improvisation: "In short, the worship of the sanctified church is beautiful because the Holy Spirit orchestrates a harmonization out of the many ritual moments, embodied movements, genres of activities, functional roles, and media instruments that interrelate when the saints are gathered together in Jesus' name."[419] Within Pentecostal spirituality, a multiplicity of elements come into effect. Yong names specific African elements which can be attributed to different cultural groups. Yet, "rather than being a mere or bland syncretism of gospel and culture, these adaptations of African aesthetics may be seen instead as examples of what Walter Hollenweger calls 'theologically responsible syncretism,' which looks for signs of the Holy Spirit's redemption of the many tongues and cultures of the world."[420] However, a sanctified aesthetic is more than the harmonious participation of different cultures. For Yong, this also implies the formation of a community which enables its members to set aside their worldly social identities and instead develop a culture which sets itself prophetically against the secular culture where it stands in conflict with the Kingdom of God.[421] By embodying the sanctified aesthetic in the community of saints, and thereby allowing it to be visible to society, it challenges it: "In short, a sanctified aesthetics redeems culture in part by challenging its unholy elements insofar as these are resistant and not conformable to the harmony and beauty of the trinitarian God."[422] For Yong, the spiritual creation of

417. Yong, *Days of Caesar*, 206.
418. See also Sanders, *Saints in Exile*.
419. Yong, *Days of Caesar*, 207.
420. Yong, *Days of Caesar*, 207.
421. Yong, *Days of Caesar*, 208.
422. Yong, *Days of Caesar*, 208.

beauty is an eschatological event "that sanctifies, transfigures, fulfills, and perfects things, even in their fallenness, in order to renew the world in the glorious beauty of the triune God."[423] The beauty of the salvific future, which God has prepared for His creation, will be made visible through His Body, the church. This making visible of the sanctified aesthetic is by no means limited to the church:

> Because of the gift of the Holy Spirit at Pentecost and the accompanying tongues and gifts, not only Christian art but human creation in general can be potentially sacred and revelatory of the beauty and holiness of God. Not only art, but music, sculpture, architecture, poetry and drama can be redemptive in mediating the present and eschatological salvation of God.[424]

Pentecostal Power: Prophetic Politics of Civil Society

The third aspect of the Fivefold Gospel is "Jesus, the Holy Spirit baptizer." Within the Pentecostal Movement, the baptism in the Holy Spirit is understood by the majority as empowerment for mission. It is no coincidence that Yong sees the baptism in the Holy Spirit in particular as pointing the way forward in his discussion of the "politico-prophetic theology of mission and socio-cultural evangelization."[425]

a) Pentecostal Beliefs and Practices

Yong introduces the reader to the origins of the Pentecostal doctrine of Jesus as the Holy Spirit baptizer through one of the founding fathers, Charles Fox Parham, who links Spirit baptism to four biblical motifs:

> First, the prophetic reference to God's "abundant rain, the early and the latter rain" (Joel 2:23), was read within a premillennialist hermeneutical framework and thought to foreshadow the "last days," outpouring of the Spirit (Acts 2:17). Second, this "promise of the Father" (Acts 1:4) would counter the distressing skepticism of the end times (cf. 2 Tim 3:1; 2 Peter 3:3) with the power of the Holy Spirit, who would embolden believers to bear witness to the gospel to the ends of the world (Acts 1:8).

---

423. Yong, *Days of Caesar*, 209.
424. Yong, *Days of Caesar*, 209.
425. Yong, *Days of Caesar*, 211.

Third, the Spirit's empowerment would be for the purpose of world evangelization just before the parousia: "This good news of the kingdom will be proclaimed throughout the world, as a testimony to all the nations; and then the end will come" (Matt 24:14). Finally, according to the Acts narrative, the indisputable sign of the baptism of the Spirt was the gift of speaking in other tongues or languages—the apostles knew "that the gift of the Holy Spirit had been poured out even on the Gentiles, for they heard them speaking in tongues and extolling God" (Acts 10:45–46; cf. 19:1–6).[426]

The Pentecostal Movement understood the outpouring of the Holy Spirit as a sign of the imminent return of Christ. The imminent expectation, coupled with the baptism in the Holy Spirit, which was also understood as empowerment, gave the evangelization of the world a high priority and urgency. Even though the experience of the missionaries was that the languages wrought by the Holy Spirit were usually manifest as glossolalia and not xenolalia,[427] the motivation for the missionaries was nevertheless great enough to continue with their ministry. Already in the early beginnings of Pentecostal mission, Pentecostal Melvin Hodges[428] conceived the idea of the so-called indigenous church, which made it a principle that mission on the ground should primarily be driven by indigenous people and not by missionaries. Hodges further propagated the conviction that all believers should be led into the experience of the Holy Spirit so that the church could develop into a self-supporting, self-governing and self-missioning active community. In this mission model, missionaries would merely have an advisory function.[429] This concept helped the Pentecostal church to break away from the previous colonial missionary paradigm and to follow new missionary methods, which Yong considered to be the main reason for its missionary success.[430] A further step in the development of Pentecostal mission theology was taken by

---

426. Yong, *Days of Caesar*, 213–14.

427. *Glossolalia*: speaking in tongues. *Xenolalia*: the ability to speak identifiable human language without having learned it. Hollenweger, *Charismatisch-pfingstliches Christentum*, 33.

428. Melvin Hodges was strongly influenced by the Anglican Roland Allen, whose approach of the indigenous principle (in short, a church that is self-supporting, self-governing, and self-missionary) he then developed further. See Yong, *Days of Caesar*, 224.

429. Yong, *Days of Caesar*, 215.

430. Yong, *Days of Caesar*, 215.

Paul Pomerville,[431] who supplemented elements of Hodge's approach with further pneumatological considerations. His trinitarian-pneumatological missiology contains the following three central elements: the recognition of the diversity of the global Pentecostal-charismatic movement, the connection between the work of the Holy Spirit and the breaking-in of God's kingdom, and the development of God's kingdom in relation to the trinitarian revelation of God.[432]

As examples of how differently the Pentecostal Movement lives out its missionary mandate, Yong cites the South Korean Pentecostal church, represented by the church of Yonggi Cho,[433] and M. G. "Pat" Robertson,[434] who works in the USA. Whilst Cho seeks to evangelize and socially reform the public sphere more through the ecclesiological approach, Robertson practices a "confrontational interaction with the political" approach, as Yong calls it, which engages in a kind of "political evangelism" through a news network and ministries.[435] Despite the different methodologies, Yong asks whether Cho and Robertson are not "both living out the Pentecostal theology Spirit-baptism as endowing believers with the daring needed to bear witness to the gospel in a fallen world, but are doing so in different contexts."[436] The resulting question for Yong is which of the two methodologies can be regarded as more legitimate from a theological point of view.

b) Extra-Pentecostal Approaches

As non-Pentecostal dialogue partners, Yong chooses representatives of Radical Orthodoxy as counterparts. Radical Orthodoxy, a self-designation of the movement, can essentially be traced back to John Milbank.[437] Where conservative Pentecostals and Evangelicals identify secularized humanism as the main problem of Western post-Christian society, radical Orthodox believers consider secularized liberalism to be the central

---

431. See Pomerville, *Third Force in Missions*.
432. Yong, *Days of Caesar*, 216.
433. Yong, *Days of Caesar*, 216–20.
434. Yong, *Days of Caesar*, 221–25.
435. Yong, *Days of Caesar*, 221.
436. Yong, *Days of Caesar*, 225.
437. See Milbank, *Radical Orthodoxy*.

problem to combat.[438] According to Milbank, since the Enlightenment, society has adopted secular rationalism as a narrative, whose nihilism, wickedness, desire for power, hedonism and materialism, also assert claims on theology.[439] On the basis of the values mentioned above, Milbank declares secular rationalism to be "post-Christian paganism," even "anti-Christianity,"[440] which must be resisted. Theology therefore has the task of disengaging itself from appropriation by secular rationalism, not by developing an apologetic on the basis of secularism, but by bringing the Christian narrative back to the center as the only standard.[441] As a result, Milbank considers this claim to be legitimate because the Christian narrative is not only for the church but has universal validity.[442] In the practice of the church, the Christian narrative becomes tangible, and similar to Yoder's view, a contrast society emerges in its midst. Although Milbank, in accord with Augustine, speaks rather of a "counter-city," in which a counter-history, a counter-ethics and a counter-ontology are created, in contrast to secular society.[443] Specifically: "By nurturing the central practices of charity, the forgiveness of sins, and reconciliation, then, the church becomes a redemptive community, a 'city of God,' that contrasts with the practices of earthly cities."[444]

Another voice of radical orthodoxy which Yong introduces is that of D. Steven Long, who takes the view that theology is the "queen of all sciences" and should influence every other science—especially economics.[445] Whilst Milbank primarily criticizes the legitimacy of the social sciences as the basis of "human social understanding," with Long, the focus is criticism of the market, which "misdirects human desires and thereby offers a false sense of satisfaction, a false salvation, and a false catholicity."[446] This must be changed by putting economics in its place through theology: "In other words, the desires distorted by market economics need to be reordered toward that which will finally be satisfying, and the false goods offered by the market need to be critiqued

438. Yong, *Days of Caesar*, 226.
439. Yong, *Days of Caesar*, 227.
440. Yong, *Days of Caesar*, 227.
441. Yong, *Days of Caesar*, 228.
442. Yong, *Days of Caesar*, 229.
443. Yong, *Days of Caesar*, 228.
444. Yong, *Days of Caesar*, 229.
445. Yong, *Days of Caesar*, 239.
446. Yong, *Days of Caesar*, 231.

by theological notions of what is transcendentally good, true, and beautiful."[447] However, this is only possible to the extent that the community of believers manages to create an alternative economic model which "exposes the pretensions of the market."[448]

As the third and last representative of radical orthodoxy, Yong introduces Graham Ward. According to Yong, he differs from Milbank in that he is less polemical and more dialogical in relation to secular culture.[449] Whilst Milbank strives to put the secular in its place, Ward sees opportunities to reclaim the secular as a sign of the restorative power of the church:[450]

> Ward prefers to use the language of the economics of redemption. So if the Gospel narratives are invitations to participation in the soteriological work of Christ, and if the church is the historical and material community that mediates the saving love of God, the wider culture is a field upon which the economy of salvation is played out. In this wider field, human cultural productions—literature, the arts, media, etc.—both reflect human participation in the divine creativity and provide analogies anticipating the redemptive works of God . . . In short, insofar as the goodness, symbols, and beauty of culture and its forms participate in the transcendental good, true, and beautiful, to that same degree they anticipate the final reclamation of human cities and their sanctification and transformation as cities of God.[451]

c) Continuation

Yong's aim now is to bring the Pentecostal doctrine of the baptism of the Holy Spirit and aspects of radical orthodoxy into dialogue with each other in order to develop a continuative political-theological position. Yong begins this task by formulating a prophetic theology of civil society, and for this he focusses on the events described in Acts.[452] Yong observes three expressions of what he calls prophetic politics: First, the early Christians gave their loyalty, above all else, to God. Their commitment

---

447. Yong, *Days of Caesar*, 231.
448. Yong, *Days of Caesar*, 231.
449. Yong, *Days of Caesar*, 237.
450. Yong, *Days of Caesar*, 238.
451. Yong, *Days of Caesar*, 237.
452. Yong, *Days of Caesar*, 238.

to the state was subordinate to this first commitment.[453] Second, the state was urged to maintain law and order.[454] Third, the early Christians explicitly bore witness to their faith in the public sphere. This included witnessing to political leaders.[455] But Yong also detects a more subversive prophetic-political working of the Holy Spirit: within the church, the opportunity arose to experience intercultural friendships and active equality.[456] Furthermore, people in the house churches were equipped to live their life according to the example of Jesus.[457] And finally, within the Christian community, a doctrine was disseminated which changed the believers' way of life and also had political and economic consequences on society.[458] From these observations, Yong concludes that the Spirit-given empowerment for witnessing expresses itself in a variety of ways in different contexts and situations.

For Yong, in contrast to the understanding of radical orthodoxy, the sanctification of society does not take place through the eradication of the secular in society, but (as in his remarks on the powers and authorities) through its redemption. For, in his view, the secularization of society is not to be understood as an anti-Christian development, but as something that "had its own creational integrity and even autonomy."[459] Accordingly, for Yong, the redemption of society does not take place in a return to the pre-Enlightenment condition of society, in which theology is once again declared the queen of all sciences. Rather, it consists of the church introducing a theology into society which "provides a discursive, critical, and prophetic perspective on any national or political ideology in the light of the gospel."[460]

With regard to the dialogue with Radical Orthodoxy, Yong concludes that, whilst criticism of European and American secularism is justified, the same criticism cannot carry the same weight in the underdeveloped areas of the majority world: "In other words, we need a multiplicity of prophetic discourses—some socially engaged, others more dialogical, and still others more unapologetically kerygmatic and

---

453. Yong, *Days of Caesar*, 239.
454. Yong, *Days of Caesar*, 241.
455. Yong, *Days of Caesar*, 242.
456. Yong, *Days of Caesar*, 242.
457. Yong, *Days of Caesar*, 243.
458. Yong, *Days of Caesar*, 243.
459. Yong, *Days of Caesar*, 253.
460. Yong, *Days of Caesar*, 254.

even prophetic, etc.—in order to respond to the diverse political contexts within which we find ourselves."[461] Yet, this challenge does not only exist at a global level but is also present at the local level: Civil society is formed by the most varied participants, each with their own economic and sociocultural realities of life. This diversity poses a real challenge for prophetic politics: Namely, that the church "challenges the domination of the state through empowering the many voices in the civic sphere but at the same time also avoids becoming just one more ideology within the cacophony of voices that constitute civil society."[462] In order to meet this challenge, Yong defines two levels on which the church can live out its prophetic politics: On the first level, the church is a place/forum where prophets are nurtured and built up, who then develop the competence to speak, debate and engage in issues that (primarily) concern the church.[463] On a second level, the church also engages with the world outside the church. This, as we have seen, can happen in different ways:

> If Robertson's grassroots Christian Coalition movement is a more explicit form of prophetic engagement with the world, Cho's home cell groups are a more implicit, but precisely for that reason, more potentially subversive mode of prophetic interface. Here also the Radical Orthodoxy's notion of the church existing as and amidst a complex public space is also helpful for considering the many ways the church interacts with the orders, guilds, networks, and organizations that constitute the civil and public square. . . . But a prophetic politics of civil society not only trains disciples of Christ for the prophetic task and empowers the church to exist as a leaven in the civic sphere, but also emboldens confrontation with the principalities and powers when necessary.[464]

The central question for Yong is therefore not whether but how the missionary mandate of Jesus, to make disciples of all nations (Matt 28:20), will be implemented.[465]

---

461. Yong, *Days of Caesar*, 263.
462. Yong, *Days of Caesar*, 249.
463. Yong, *Days of Caesar*, 250.
464. Yong, *Days of Caesar*, 250–51.
465. Yong, *Days of Caesar*, 250.

Pentecostal Health and Wealth: A Theology of Economics

As the fourth aspect of the Fivefold Gospel, Yong deals with the aspect of "Jesus, the healer," onto which the question of the health and wealth gospel has virtually imposed itself. In this chapter, Yong principally wishes to address the question of a theology of economy, whereby he also begins this chapter with an insight into Pentecostal theology and practice.

a) Pentecostal Beliefs and Practices

Right at the beginning, Yong raises the pertinent question: "How do we get from Jesus as healer to Jesus as wealth-provider, and what does this shift mean for Pentecostalism and political economy?"[466] In fact, the connections are anything but obvious at first glance, but they make sense because of Yong's explanations of the development of the Pentecostal maxim Jesus as healer into the health and wealth gospel. Already in the early beginnings of the Pentecostal church, as a legacy of the Holiness Movement, the belief in miraculous healings was established. It is striking that originally, primarily Christocentric and soteriological aspects were the rationale for God's supernatural healing: "Pentecostals embraced Jesus' healing ministry as intimately connected with his saving work, and concluded from biblical texts such as Isaiah 53:4, and its citation in 1 Peter 2:24 that bodily healing was included in the atonement."[467] Yong even goes so far as to say that the beliefs of Pentecostals in the early days of the movement implied that "experiencing the wholeness of the body was what it meant to receive the full salvation wrought by Christ."[468]

In the mid-twentieth century, in the move of the Latter Rain Revivals, the sanctification practice of the Pentecostals experienced a resurgence. This occurred in a variety of ways: In connection with the prophecy of Joel, Pentecostals related the promise of the Early Rain to the events of the Azusa Street Revival. The Latter Rain, with reference to Joel 2:23, was indicative of the spiritual revival of the present generation of the brethren in faith. This revival was anticipated in conjunction with the preaching of the gospel, closely associated with signs and wonders. Accordingly, these expectations were also preached by the Latter Rain evangelists in their annunciations. For many of these evangelists, healings were "not

---

466. Yong, *Days of Caesar*, 258.
467. Yong, *Days of Caesar*, 259.
468. Yong, *Days of Caesar*, 260.

only christological and soteriological but also an eschatological sign: it provided a foretaste of the wholeness of the coming kingdom."[469]

The following wave of renewal, the Charismatic Renewal, showed a significant difference to the preceding awakenings: Whilst the Pentecostal churches had previously reached primarily the poorer sections of the population,[470] the Charismatic Renewal appealed to the majority of members from established churches and thus reached a middle-class and bourgeois section of the population. This "new" clientele had different, new needs, which led to an expansion of the understanding of salvation:

> Thus the nature of Jesus as healer expanded in the charismatic movement beyond that of bodily healing to include psychosomatic healing and the healing of the emotions. These "middle-class afflictions," (as I call them) highlighted the importance of having a multifaceted theology of healing—i.e., healing as a result of receiving the forgiveness of sins, healing of the body, deliverance/exorcism, and healing of the inner person, memories, (often suppressed), or hurt emotions.[471]

The Charismatic Renewal initiated a rethinking amongst Pentecostals of their own healing practice, which led its development toward a more holistic understanding: "Human wholeness, in other words included, but was not reducible to physical well-being."[472]

In the 1950s and 1960s, various evangelists such as Kenneth Hagin, Kenneth Copeland, Oral Roberts and others, merged the above-mentioned aspects of healing and integrated them into their preaching and practice. Those evangelists then also emphasized the responsibility of believers "to claim his or her healing and material blessings by faith, in the name of Jesus, based on the promises of the Bible."[473] In reference to biblical verses such as 3 John 2; John 10:10; and many other texts that mention the connection of faith and the fulfillment of blessings and healings, the theology known to us today as Word and Faith was formed. "In these circles, bodily healing was but one dimension of the abundance promised to believers, and the salvation of God formerly realized in the

---

469. Yong, *Days of Caesar*, 261.
470. At least up to and including the 1960s. See Yong, *Days of Caesar*, 261.
471. Yong, *Days of Caesar*, 261.
472. Yong, *Days of Caesar*, 261.
473. Yong, *Days of Caesar*, 262.

present only in the healing of the body was now seen to be realized across the various domains of human social, economic, and material life."[474]

Yong points out that there are entirely justifiable criticisms of the theology and practice described above, which is commonly described as the prosperity gospel. Unfortunately, scandals keep coming to light, in which preachers of this very prosperity gospel have enriched themselves at the expense of credulous brothers and sisters in faith. A spirituality with an understanding of healing which also includes economic aspects does not necessarily need to have the characteristics of an anti-gospel, as Yong illustrates using a critical analysis of the practice and works of the Afro-American Thomas Dexter Jakes, the Redeemed Christian church of God in Nigeria, and the Ghanaian Pentecostal Mensa Otabil.[475]

b) Extra-Pentecostal Approach

Yong chooses the tradition of Catholic social teaching as an ecumenical dialogue partner.[476] He justifies this choice by saying that Catholic social teaching deals substantially with issues that are relevant to current economic questions, that the Catholic church has been deeply touched by the Catholic Charismatic Renewal Movement[477] and that there has been a dialogue between the Pentecostal Movement and the Catholic church for decades.[478]

There are three aspects of Catholic social teaching that Yong considers important: First, the encyclicals emphasize the dignity of the human person, which they justify with natural law and biblical revelation.[479] Secondly, the encyclicals emphasize the central role of the church, whereby it participates in the healing and restoration of the world. Indeed, this restorative and healing action is fully understood as part of the church's

---

474. Yong, *Days of Caesar*, 263.

475. For a more detailed account of the three practical examples, see Yong, *Days of Caesar*, 265–74.

476. The Catholic Social Teaching is a collection of papal encyclicals which, beginning with *Rerum Novarum*, includes all subsequent encyclicals dealing with economic issues (Yong, *Days of Caesar*, 277). See also Leo XIII, *Rerum Novarum*.

477. The extent to which the influence of the Charismatic Renewal actually had an impact on the publications of the Congregation for the Doctrine of the Faith is not further described by Yong. He merely refers to secondary literature.

478. Yong, *Days of Caesar*, 275.

479. Yong, *Days of Caesar*, 279.

calling.[480] Thirdly, the church protects the rights of individuals, values their initiative and encourages them in their creativity. It thus protects the claim to private property and encourages the acquisition of such property. At the same time, the encyclicals point out that this very private property should be used for the benefit of the common good.[481] These three values lead Yong to assess Catholic social teaching as "a theological tradition focused on wholeness and redemption—the Hebraic notion of Shalom, in its broader sense—rather than merely a set of guidelines for social life or political economy."[482] The very fact that Catholic Social Teaching is not a textbook for socioeconomics leads to different applications in practice. For example, in response to the economic challenges arising during the Reagan administration, a 1986 pastoral letter from the United States Catholic Bishops proposes an approach described by Yong as "structural, interventions, and top-down approaches to modern economic challenges that can be more readily guided by the church's magisterium."[483] In contrast, there is a practice in North American culture, developed under the philosopher and theologian Michael Novak, which strongly emphasizes individual "responsibility, initiative, and creativity."[484] Whilst the United States Catholic Bishops placed the emphasis of Catholic Social Teaching on the church's mission to heal and restore, and put this into a practice which, with guided interventions, acts upon the market (through redistribution), Novak places his emphasis on the dignity of people and from this develops the emphasis on the personal responsibility of individuals.[485] Yong sees these different interpretations as an indication that both approaches, intervention at the structural level and initiative at the private level, are only continuative in combination with each other. Yong explains this interplay with the notions of subsidiarity and solidarity, which can also be found as such within Catholic Social Teaching.[486] Subsidiarity is based on a hierarchical structure of society. Within this society there is simultaneously relative autonomy within various hierarchical levels (e.g., family, private property, companies, etc.), each of which is protected by the higher level, but at the same time, limited by it. Whilst the power of

---

480. Yong, *Days of Caesar*, 279.
481. Yong, *Days of Caesar*, 279.
482. Yong, *Days of Caesar*, 279.
483. Yong, *Days of Caesar*, 281.
484. Yong, *Days of Caesar*, 285.
485. Yong, *Days of Caesar*, 285.
486. Yong, *Days of Caesar*, 289.

the state/authority is therefore limited, equally, it is also inherently acknowledged. The same also applies to individuals, whose autonomy is recognized, but at the same time, they are part of the greater whole.[487] The relationship between individuals and authority is determined by solidarity, which "crosses multiple divides that keep human beings apart from, and antagonistic toward, others. Solidarity is the call to love our fellow human beings . . . regardless of their race, ethnicity, nationality, class, or capacity, in order to work toward the common good at both local and global levels."[488] It is this interplay of subsidiarity and solidarity that portrays an ideal social economy. However, Yong rightly points out that "the issues of self-interest, greed, competition and corruption that drive much of the neoliberal global market."[489] are addressed neither by the bishops nor by Novak. In order for the principle of solidarity to take effect, Yong, following D. Steven Long,[490] rightly poses the question of "how the desires of private individuals can be morally and spiritually formed in a free market economy."[491] For Yong, the answer is obvious: "If the market economy is to be redeemed, then the church has to provide an alternative telos—another set of desires—that can contribute to the healing of the world."[492]

c) Continuation

Based on the insights gained above, Yong sets himself the goal of articulating a political theology of Shalom, which combines healing and wholeness with economic justice. As in the previous subject areas, Yong turns to the Lukan double work as a first step. What Yong presents in relation to Jesus' healings is that Luke gives his readers more than just a picture of individually experienced miracles. When Jesus heals, the gospel is always proclaimed, faith is awakened and the Word of God is spread.[493] Physical healings not only have an effect at an individual level, on the body, mind and soul, but also always result in the reintegration of the healed

487. Yong, *Days of Caesar*, 289–92.
488. Yong, *Days of Caesar*, 292.
489. Yong, *Days of Caesar*, 293–94.
490. See the criticism already mentioned by Yong in the sub-section "Pentecostal Health and Wealth," 195–97.
491. Yong, *Days of Caesar*, 294.
492. Yong, *Days of Caesar*, 294.
493. Yong, *Days of Caesar*, 296.

person into society, and thus an all-encompassing effect on the life of the person concerned emerges.[494] In practicing the sharing of possessions in the Jerusalem community, as described in the Acts of the Apostles, another dimension of comprehensive salvation is demonstrated: The needs of the underprivileged are met within the community through sharing. Those who have share with those who do not have. As a motive behind this "biblical communism."[495] Yong sees not so much an intention to create an alternative economy but rather to create an alternative way of life "with economic features emerging out of the fellowship of those gathered in the name of Jesus."[496] Yong sees all these elements, along the lines of Luke 4:18–19, with the Jubilee Year as the guiding principle behind the multiple facets of salvation, which also becomes tangible in the followers of Jesus in the Acts of the Apostles.[497] Although the people of the early church were subject to the Roman economic system, they lived an alternative way of life within their sphere of influence (i.e., among themselves but also toward outsiders), which followed the principle of the Jubilee Year and thus also signalled the heavenly economy.[498]

Yong sees the informal economy[499] as a possible sector in which the church can engage and practice Jubilee Year values, which is not feasible in the regular market.[500] In the largely unregulated informal economy, there are many negative aspects that surpass the formal economy in destructiveness (e.g., lack of regulations regarding worker protection, etc.). At the same time, a look at the informal economy also shows opportunities and potential for the church:

494. Yong, *Days of Caesar*, 297.
495. Yong, *Days of Caesar*, 299.
496. Yong, *Days of Caesar*, 298.
497. Yong, *Days of Caesar*, 300.
498. Yong, *Days of Caesar*, 303.

499. Yong defines the informal economy as follows: "By definition, the informal economy exists outside the regulated (and legislated) economy. An extremely heteronomous domain, the informal economy includes street vendors, rickshaw/cart pullers, shared transportation, recyclers, petty traders/hawkers, small item producers, (very) small business owners (often at street corners rather than in their own rented or owned building), [etc.] . . . Of course, informal economic activity is prevalent both in regions (and nations) working to enter the global economy and during periods of economic crisis and recession in developed nations. But there is also enough of a continuum between the formal and informal economies—rather than a strict demarcation between them—that even in industrialized environments, upwards of one-fourth of all economic activity occurs in the informal sector" (Yong, *Days of Caesar*, 304).

500. Yong, *Days of Caesar*, 304.

> Rather than being dominated by the economy of exchange and its supply-and-demand transactions, the church is guided by an pneumatological economy of grace that highlights charity (giving without anticipation of return), forgiveness (not only of sins but also of debts), and solidaristic fellowship (nurtured through interpersonal relations, common meals, and daily interactions).[501]

Yong sees an informal economy based on local relationships, and thus on local needs, as a real alternative to the dictates of the formal economy. As much potential as the informal economy may hold, it is important to remember that any system is only as good as the people who move within it.[502] This again raises the question of how to change human desires. How can it be avoided that, as in the formal economy, also in the community of believers only one's own individual salvation is sought? How can corrupted desires reorder themselves?[503] To this end, Yong points to God and his action as it is revealed, for example in the Eucharist. In the celebration of the Eucharist, the heart is "directed toward the transcendental and theological domain."[504] God, His nature and activity are revealed very tangibly in this meal and the people are invited to participate in it. In this respect, the symbolism embedded in the celebration is intended to be more than a religious symbol, rather, an inspiration for imitation in all areas of life, including economic matters:

> The eucharistic rite thus instantiates an economy of sharing rather than one of greed; inculcates a reverence for creation's provisions rather than exploitation of the environment; calls attention to an economy of debt remission rather than dept collection; and rejects the politics of power in favor of the politics of egalitarianism.[505]

However, Yong quite categorically also sees the potential in the everyday community of the church "to shape human hearts in a distinctively trinitarian and kingdom-oriented direction."[506] This takes place when the individual "is subordinated to being in solidarity with the community; competition is replaced by bearing one another's burdens; and

---

501. Yong, *Days of Caesar*, 307.
502. For Yong's further thoughts on this, see Yong, *Days of Caesar*, 314.
503. Yong, *Days of Caesar*, 313.
504. Yong, *Days of Caesar*, 313.
505. Yong, *Days of Caesar*, 313.
506. Yong, *Days of Caesar*, 313.

profits are understood instead as communal sharing, achievements, and investments."[507]

Pentecostal Hope: A Political Theology of History and the Eschaton

The fifth and final aspect of the Fivefold Gospel is "Jesus, the soon-coming King," in which Yong explores the theme of eschatology.

a) Pentecostal Beliefs and Practices

Yong focuses on the dispensationalist[508] view of the "end times," a widespread eschatological model within the global (especially Anglo-American) Pentecostal church.[509] Dispensationalism is an eschatological pattern of interpretation which is oriented (with varying nuances) toward the following cornerstones:

- That God relates to the world in chronologically successive dispensations (periods of time), each with different covenantal or governmental features (here, there is often disagreement about exactly how many dispensations the Bible reveals or discusses)

- That the present age of the church is an interlude between two dispensations featuring the centrality of Israel, and that Israel (comprised of the Jews) and the church (constituted primarily of gentiles) are related but quite distinct expressions of the elect people of God

- That the transition to the next dispensation will be marked by the removal of the church (according to 1 Thess 4:17), which event will inaugurate a seven-year period of worldwide woe and suffering known as the Great Tribulation (from the various reverences to seven years in the book of Revelation)

---

507. Yong, *Days of Caesar*, 313.

508. Dispensationalism was developed by John Nelson Darby in the nineteenth century. The end-time model divides the history of salvation, as a rule, into seven dispensations (households/orders of salvation), which replace each other and where each follows new laws/orders that supersede those of the preceding dispensation. Dispensationalism became widespread, in particular, through the Scofield Study Bible, whose explanations are based on the dispensationalist model of interpretation and hermeneutics (Yong, *Days of Caesar*, 318). For further discussion, see Stadelmann, "Dispensationalism."

509. Yong, *Days of Caesar*, 320.

- That at the end of the Tribulation period, Christ will return (with the church) to judge the world and establish his thousand-year reign (according to Rev 20:4) on the earth.[510]

According to the dispensationalist understanding, the final battle between Satan and Christ will take place at the end of the thousand-year kingdom, in which Satan will be defeated, followed by the final judgment and the subsequent new creation. Israel plays a central role in the dispensationalist end-times timetable: The great tribulation is preceded by the restoration of the State of Israel, which is accompanied by an intensification of the political situation in the Middle East, the establishment of a global governmental system and the rebuilding of the temple in Jerusalem. Because of this prominent role of Israel, adherents of dispensationalism tend to categorize Israel's enemies as enemies of God: "Israel's enemies are uncritically understood to also be God's enemies and this means that Palestinians, Arabs, and others allied with Palestinian and Arab interests are at best absent from consideration and at worst framed in negative theological light."[511]

Yong is critical of the dispensationalism that is widespread in the Pentecostal church. He criticizes, firstly, that this end-time model promotes an escapist attitude oriented toward the hereafter, and secondly, he criticizes the minimal emphasis on God's saving work in the present—the ultimate focus is on the rapture, the great tribulation and the thousand-year kingdom.[512] It is therefore not surprising that ecological issues, in particular, are hardly discussed in Pentecostal circles.[513] For Yong, these aspects described are in contradiction to a Pentecostal practice which, as already explained above, fundamentally cultivates a comprehensive understanding of salvation that anticipates God's liberating work at every level of human existence.[514] Yong therefore concludes: "Pentecostals have been misguided by the dispensationalist framework, as such a system either assumes fundamental theological presuppositions or leads to certain theological conclusions that are counterintuitive to Pentecostal spirituality."[515] As a constructive response to the pessimistic approach

---

510. Yong, *Days of Caesar*, 319–20.
511. Yong, *Days of Caesar*, 321.
512. Yong, *Days of Caesar*, 224.
513. Yong, *Days of Caesar*, 329.
514. Yong, *Days of Caesar*, 326.
515. Yong, *Days of Caesar*, 325. See also Althouse, *Spirit of the Last Days*, 23–25.

of dispensationalism, Yong argues for a positive, pneumatologically oriented apocalypticism:

> What we need is to replace the futuristic apocalypticism of dispensationalism with another eschatological sensibility more congenial to Pentecostal and charismatic piety. If dispensationalistic apocalypticism emphasizes the future devastation, disaster, and doom that will overtake the earth, the etymology of "apocalyptic" also includes the sense of a revelatory unveiling of what was previously hidden. I urge shifting away from a futuristic apocalypticism of destruction toward the pneumatological apocalypticism of the earliest followers of the Messiah, preserved by Luke, in which the last days' "portents in the heaven above and signs on the earth below" (Acts 2:19) are not signs of the final desolation but rather nature's reactions to the outpouring of the Holy Spirit on all flesh.[516]

b) Extra-Pentecostal Approaches

In search of eschatological designs that incorporate the criteria outlined above, Yong analyzes approaches by Daniel Boyarin (who contributes a Jewish political theology),[517] Daniel Bell (a Methodist theologian and representative of radical orthodoxy),[518] and Peter Scott (an Anglican theologian with a creation theological contribution).[519]

In his engagement with Boyarin, Yong challenges the dispensationalist understanding of Israel's eschatological role and redefines its meaning. Yong begins by giving a Lukan interpretation of the term "end times": First, that the end times began with the restoration of Israel, with the life, death and resurrection of Christ, and was continued by the disciples of Jesus. Second, that the restoration of Israel involves the fulfillment of the promise of being a blessing to the peoples of the earth. The fulfillment of this promise begins through the outpouring of the Holy Spirit on the Gentile nations and their salvation. Thus, besides the Jews, gentile Christians are now also part of God's people. And thirdly, that "this universal salvation . . . does not revoke the distinctiveness of Israel's role and place in God's providential history and even in the eschatological consummation,

516. Yong, *Days of Caesar*, 330.
517. See Boyarin, *Radical Jew*.
518. See Bell, *Liberation Theology*.
519. See Scott, *Political Theology of Nature*.

since the one salvation does not annul but preserves the many tongues of the human cultural-linguistic experience."[520] Yong's Lukan interpretation of the end times and the associated role of Israel corresponds with Boyarin's approach, which deals with Jewish self-understanding and identity against the background of Pauline theology.[521] Yong sees the implications of this new interpretation of Israel's role in the end times as follows:

> In sum, an ecclesiological eschatology will affirm a pneumatological and apocalyptic politics that sees the Holy Spirit's Pentecostal outpouring as a harbinger of the future but impending salvation of God that will finally make ready the many-ness of the world for the Parousia and usher in the full and final harmonious rule of the kingdom.[522]

By basing the beginning of the end times on the outpouring of the Holy Spirit at Pentecost, the futuristic emphasis of dispensationalism is softened in some ways, or as Yong puts it: "The 'not yet' of the salvation history of the gentiles includes a paradoxical 'already' with regard to the Holy Spirit's liberative activity in times and places of the world."[523] The assumption that God's end-time restorative activity began in Christ and has been taking place through his Spirit for two thousand years, greatly enhances the significance of the present, in contrast to dispensationalism. However, with the emphasis on the "already," as Yong rightly points out, there is also the danger of an over-realized eschatology at the expense of the "not yet."[524] To prevent this, there is a need for "a charismatic and pneumatological apocalypticism that affirms the Holy Spirit's past, present, and future breaking into, and redemption of history's times and places."[525] In developing such an eschatology, Yong draws on elements from Daniel Bell, who is strongly oriented toward liberation theological approaches and emphasizes the associated importance of forgiveness. Yong takes these elements and combines them with Pentecostal pneumatology, and formulates the following approach:

> The outpouring of the Holy Spirit—upon Jews, proselytes, those far away at the ends of the earth, and "everyone whom the Lord

---

520. Yong, *Days of Caesar*, 333.
521. Yong, *Days of Caesar*, 334, 336.
522. Yong, *Days of Caesar*, 337.
523. Yong, *Days of Caesar*, 338.
524. Yong, *Days of Caesar*, 338.
525. Yong, *Days of Caesar*, 338.

> our God calls" (Acts 2:39)—means that the people of God are enabled to refuse to cease suffering and to forgive because they follow in the footsteps of the suffering Servant who did not withhold forgiveness from his persecutors. The good news that he declared by the Holy Spirit's power regarding freedom from oppression was also enacted in his forgiving sinners, including those who sinned against him. . . . Hence this miracle of the Day of Pentecost is what allows for the redemption of history in a mode that avoids both the Scylla of a dispensationalist futurism or the Charybdis of a liberationist-Marxist-socialist utopianism. The outpouring of the Holy Spirit upon those from every nation under heaven produces the apocalyptic affection of the Holy Spirit that binds people, even enemies, together and makes forgiveness possible. It is this good news of forgiveness of sins that facilitates reconciliation of all in enmity and strife, fosters solidarity across peoples, tribes, and nations, and brings about the harmony of many otherwise opposing voices for the Glory of God. The result is not the end but the redemption of history; not an escape from the world's (coming) tribulations but an empowerment perseverance in view of its eschatological transformation; not a temporary human accomplishment in the present but the opportunity to participate in the apocalyptic (revelatory) in-breaking of the Holy Spirit from the (heretofore hidden) divine future.[526]

For Yong, the outpouring of "the Holy Spirit on all flesh" includes not only the salvation of the Jews and gentiles but also the redemption of the cosmos.[527] For Yong, the pneumatological-trinitarian oriented theology of creation, as developed by Peter Scott, points the way. Scott's trinitarian framework is envisioned as follows:

> (1) An incarnational theology that provides for a cosmic and holistic view of God in relationship to the world; (2) a pneumatology of fellowship that emphasizes the sociality and solidarity of humanity within its wider environment; and (3) a Trinitarian eschatology that understands human nature ultimately as neither natural (i.e., dependent wholly on nature) nor unnatural (independent of nature) but rather interlaced with the God of the crucified and resurrected Jesus Christ.[528]

---

526. Yong, *Days of Caesar*, 341–42.
527. Yong, *Days of Caesar*, 341.
528. Yong, *Days of Caesar*, 345.

Yong's interest in Scott's theology of creation is focused, in particular, on his pneumatological statements. For Scott, the ecological problem (man's destruction of creation) is primarily a theological problem—not a scientific one. "Thus a theological revisioning is required in order to overcome the alienation not only between God and the world but also between humanity and its cosmic environment."[529] Since the same Spirit who brooded over chaos before creation is also the one who sustains and will renew and complete creation, he also has a central role in changing human practice.[530] Scott therefore concludes:

> The Holy Spirit's actions are eschatological actions, and as such they "renew the varied and variable social relations between humanity and nature and enable their fuller openness" to God's future. In other words, the world considered as the fellowship of all flesh and as a democracy of the commons invites the revaluation of all things as having particular and unique contributions to make toward a Shalomic environment of the coming kingdom.[531]

This leads Yong to pursue an eschatological Pneumatology, which "emphasizes the apocalyptic revelation of the Holy Spirit rather than demolition of the world. The outpouring of the Holy Spirit in these last days is thus, at least in part, a response to the groanings of creation and its creatures, even at the very ends of the earth."[532]

c) Continuation

In contrast to the previous four continuations, Yong incorporates all the insights gained in the book into his last paragraph. In doing so, Yong is guided by the question of "what difference does it make to be an eschatological people of the Holy Spirit in respect of theology and Christian praxis in the public square."[533]

Yong opens his approach by stating that the end of time has broken into the world with and in Jesus Christ. This starting point does not remove the tension between the "already" and the "not yet," but "invites

---

529. Yong, *Days of Caesar*, 346.
530. Yong, *Days of Caesar*, 347.
531. Yong, *Days of Caesar*, 346.
532. Yong, *Days of Caesar*, 347.
533. Yong, *Days of Caesar*, 347.

a living out of an eschatological faith in a way that links the gospel's 'eschatological claims with one's present manner of life.'"[534] Yong exemplifies what holistic restoration entails with the healing of the paralytic at the Beautiful Gate (Acts 3:1–21). The incident involves four levels of salvation: "That of the healing of the body, that of the restoration of Israel, that of the renewal of the Jubilee economy, and that of the redemption of the world and all things."[535] This includes, ultimately, the renewal of the powers and authorities.[536] But: "Such a universal restoration does not, however, result in any simplistic doctrine of universalism. Rather these eschatological contentions are best considered subjunctively with their fulfillment hinging upon the response of free creatures."[537] Yong vehemently argues that an eschatological doctrine that merely reduces itself to believing what will happen sometime in the future, falls short. His opinion is that eschatology is also intended to be an orientation for Christian practice in the present.

> This means doing the things that Jesus did, not out of ordinary human effort but, as he did, in the power of the Spirit, in order to proclaim and herald the coming kingdom. The Christian hope, with other words, is not merely about a future restoration, but about the present gift of the Spirit who draws us into the history of Jesus wherein we meet the God who is to come.[538]

What does this actually mean in concrete terms? Yong sums it up as follows: At Pentecost, God consecrated a new eschatological people of God, comprising both Jews and gentiles. This new people of God embodies an alternative polis, whose practice is based on values such as generosity, sharing and mutuality. "The church's liturgical imagination enables its eschatological performance in the public square as a people of prayer, praise, worship, sacraments, and even exorcism—all of which combine to bear witness to the powers of the way of the cross in anticipation of cosmic restoration and rehabilitation to come." A sanctified pneumatological imagination empowers the church in its calling and commissioning for world mission, by testifying to the restorative possibilities which are available "to human culture and civic and social life." And last but not least:

534. Yong, *Days of Caesar*, 348.
535. Yong, *Days of Caesar*, 349.
536. Yong, *Days of Caesar*, 351.
537. Yong, *Days of Caesar*, 351.
538. Yong, *Days of Caesar*, 352–53.

The church's charismatic imagination seeks to participate in the gracious hospitality of God so that the many gifts of the Holy Spirit can unleash an economy of Shalom that yearns and works for the reconciliation of all, seeks a just, common, and environmentally sustainable way of life, and anticipates the renewal of the ends of the earth, all of creation, perhaps even the cosmos itself.[539]

This also ultimately changes the view of history and the cosmos as a whole: "History and cosmos now become the site and even field of the Holy Spirit's eschatological activity, and those upon whom the Holy Spirit has been given now cry out for the kingdom and emphatically live out a political theology of suffering and hope."[540]

Critical Appraisal

Yong has succeeded in presenting a distinctively Pentecostal outline of political theology. I find it fascinating that his outline is linked to the framework of the Fivefold Gospel and that it is offered from the perspective of the North American Pentecostal church. At the same time, this framework is, at least partially, contradictory to Yong's intention to develop a global Pentecostal-political theology.[541] The Fivefold Gospel, which certainly belongs to a Wesleyan-North American Pentecostal tradition, is not nearly as widespread in the worldwide Pentecostal church as Yong postulates.[542] Yong to some extent compensates for this one-sidedness by including Pentecostal voices from the global South and the Asian region. What is remarkable is the breadth of subjects, theologies, traditions and concepts that Yong introduces. He is undoubtedly well-informed in the most varied range of subjects. This breadth inspires, stimulates discourse and challenges the readers to question their own positions from new perspectives. At the same time, I wonder why Jesus' self-understanding is not given greater prominence, especially against the background of the Fivefold Gospel. Jesus' significance can hardly be reduced to his functions as healer, savior, etc. The question arises, for example, as to how he interacted with the people he healed. In Mark 10:51, for example, we observe how Jesus, even in the face of the blind man's obvious need, asks

539. Yong, *Days of Caesar*, 354.
540. Yong, *Days of Caesar*, 358.
541. Yong, *Days of Caesar*, xviii.
542. In this connection, see Alexander, "Wolfgang Vondey's Pentecostal Theology," 4; Cartledge, "Pentecostal Theology," 185–86.

him what he wants. He listened to the voice of the blind man, not simply imposing "his" solution. By asking the blind man what he wants, Jesus conveys dignity to him by not reducing him to his disability. This could mean, especially within the framework of a theology of health and wealth (and beyond), that the dialogue and interaction with the victims, those affected, is part of such a theology. Is it not precisely their voice which matters when discussing what is actually experienced and considered as unjust and, far more importantly, what would be just in the face of their experience of injustice? It is interesting that Yong makes this very approach, the conversation with the "afflicted," the central approach in his book *Theology and Down Syndrome* by showing what a theology with and for people with Down syndrome could look like.

Similar arguments apply to Jesus as the soon-coming King. The fact that he is coming again as king is significant. However, no less significant, it seems to me, is how Jesus understands and lives out his dominion. In chapter 3.2, Yong discusses the impact of Jesus' reign on the Jewish-Roman establishment. At the same time, it is surprising that Jesus as prince and bringer of peace (Isa 9:5–6; Acts 10:36) is hardly mentioned as a topic (in chapter 4.2, Yong criticizes violence in the context of spiritual warfare, but does not fundamentally address the issue of non-violence as a characteristic of Jesus' rule). This is all the more surprising because, (a) peace is a central characteristic of God's coming kingdom, which is crucial right from the beginning in Luke's Gospel (e.g., Luke 2:14); (b) in the first decades, pacifism was an obvious expression of Pentecostal spirituality (whereby we had a Pentecostal voice which provided a substantial contribution); and (c) Christians (and thus also Pentecostals) have been and still are victims of violence in the majority world (whereby the voices of those affected can provide another important contribution).[543] The question of the non-violent reign of Jesus is relevant also because this is an issue that concerns the worldwide Pentecostal church: those who suffer from violence are confronted with the question of how they intend to react to it, but also those Pentecostals who live in industrial nations and use their political, military and economic power in a variety of ways that are often also experienced as violent by the majority world.

In the chapter "Pentecostal Salvation as Deliverance from the Powers," Yong chooses exclusively non-Pentecostal dialogue partners who basically come from the position of the redeemability of the powers. I

---

543. See the continuously updated "World Persecution Index" on Open Doors (https://www.opendoors.de/christenverfolgung/weltverfolgungsindex).

think that at least one counter-position (e.g., Karl Barth), would have made the discourse more fruitful. In my opinion, the discourse with Barth would have been more auspicious for several reasons: First, Barth does not assume the redeemability of the powers but sees the possibility of overcoming them without violence. This overcoming is birthed in prayer and continued by action, from which Barth expects direct ethical and political consequences.[544] Second, his approach to sin and the demonic, discussed in the Kirchlichen Dogmatik, is developed in the light of Christ's work of reconciliation. This approach is, according to Krötke, "unprecedented in the history of the Christian doctrine of sin," and with its unique christological reference, is full of potential for the dialogue with Pentecostal spirituality.[545] Third, in his demonology, Barth refers to Christoph Blumhardt's experience with the healing of Gottliebin Dittus. This is significant in as much as Blumhardt constitutes an important influence for the beginnings of the German-speaking Pentecostal church.[546] The mutual point of connection in Blumhardt offers a welcome starting point for the discourse between Barth and the Pentecostal church.

In connection with Jesus as sanctifier, Yong reflects on the church and how it can position itself within society so as not to lose its status of sanctification. I agree with Yong that there are many arguments in favor of the approach of positioning the church on the margins of society so that it does not come under the pressure of realpolitik. I am also convinced that the church should raise its voice prophetically and lives as a contrasting society in the midst of civil society. Whether it actually raises this prophetic voice from the periphery of society or perceives its role as a contrasting society is a completely different question. This becomes clear in the example of the German churches under Nazi rule in the Third Reich: The only noteworthy resistance within religious circles against Nazi ideology came from the Confessing church, a group from the state church, i.e., a church which was in so-called Constantinian bondage, whilst the so-called free churches, for example, the Pentecostal churches,

---

544. See also Barth, *Jesus Christus*, 647; *Christliche Leben*, 208, 470.

545. Krötke Wolf, "Sünde und Nichtiges," in Beintker, *Barth Handbuch*, 342.

546. For example, Johann Widmer, one of the three founding fathers of the Pentecostal association BewegungPlus, does not refer to Pentecostal theologians in respect of his healing and deliverance ministry but exclusively to Blumhardt. See also Wenk, "Pfingstliche Pneumatologie," 276.

implemented the directives on racial segregation in their services[547] lock, stock, and barrel.

The constructive dialogue with the ecumenical voices that Yong introduces into the dialogue is refreshing. It is of interest that Yong builds substantially on these non-Pentecostal voices in his elaborations, especially when it comes to questions of social ethics. I am of the opinion that there would also have been voices from the Pentecostal tradition which could have made a more substantial contribution (see the above example of non-violence).

Yong points out two important aspects which are significant for the present work: First, it is clear from Yong's statements that there is an inherent pneumatological deficit in Pentecostal theology and practice: The Pentecostal Movement represents a one-sided supernatural pneumatology which regards salvation, healing, etc. as exclusively "from above" and spiritual, even when this pertains to natural matters such as, for example, physical healing, deliverance from demonic oppression, answered prayer in respect of economic issues. However, Yong challenges Pentecostals to recognize the working of the Holy Spirit not only in but also through natural means.[548] The Spirit works not only through miraculous means but also through worldly and material processes to bring about God's Shalom.[549] The multidimensional way in which the Holy Spirit works leads us on to the second aspect that Yong suggests: that also justice in the Holy Spirit is multi-layered, namely ecclesiastical, cultural, economic,

---

547. I quote from section 7 of the statutes adopted by the Mülheimer Verband German Pentecostal Church (1938): "In the racial legislation we see a divinely intended and biblically justifiable endeavour to purify and keep the people pure from alien-racial mixture. The removal of the Jews from the community of our people, as well as from the other peoples, is for us a process according to divine providence and divine will" (Junghardt and Vetter, *Ruhrfeuer*) To be fair, it must be said that all Free church associations adopted and implemented the racial laws more or less without protest. Within the Free churches there were only exceptions who resisted the Nazi system. See Uhlmann, *Kirchengeschichte*.

548. Yong, *Days of Caesar*, 209.

549. Yong, *Days of Caesar*, 297–303. Thus Hollenweger also challenges Pentecostals to consider more closely the Hebrew Ruach in the Old Testament, which is the Holy Spirit of Life that can be sensed in all areas of life, even the "non-sacred" (see Hollenweger, "Creator Spiritus"). Also of interest is Hollenweger's claim that the division between 'natural' and 'supernatural' is fundamentally problematic biblical-theologically, because the concept of the supernatural does not exist at all in Hebrew, and the term hyperphysikos (supernatural) does not appear anywhere in the New Testament (Hollenweger, *Charismatisch-pfingstliches Christentum*, 252).

political and ecological.⁵⁵⁰ These observations are significant for the following chapter, because they have also been thematized by Moltmann.

In his book, Yong provides many stimulating and well-argued ideas about what a Pentecostal politic could look like. Deriving these ideas eschatologically and pneumatologically opens up interesting perspectives for the practice of the Pentecostal church and beyond. Against the background of the numerous positive and negative examples of Pentecostal practice, however, it also becomes clear that an eschatological dynamic of itself is no guarantee of social ethics faithful to the Gospel. The same also applies to the baptism in the Holy Spirit, which did not bring a great breakthrough in social ethics. The sobering question arises: How is it that although believers are being filled with the Holy Spirit, racism, individualism, capitalism, chauvinism, sexism and ecological indifference continue to spread unashamedly, even in Pentecostal-charismatic churches? I hope to find answers to this question from the dialogue between the Pentecostal voices and Jürgen Moltmann in the following chapter.

Insights from the Inner-Pentecostal Discourse

With reference to section 1.6.3, which partly clarifies the methodological approach of this thesis, I would like to summarize the main findings of chapter 3 in a concise evaluation. This will be done in two steps, following the third and fourth heuristic principles.

Range of Socio-Ethical Topics

The dialogue partners selected for this work were determined, on the one hand, on the basis of general acceptance within the Pentecostal academic discourse, and on the other hand, on the basis of the third heuristic principle, which states that Pentecostal theologians selected for the dialogue must represent as great a variation as possible. Therefore, this variation was created by selecting dialogue partners from as diverse cultural contexts as possible, with different research emphases within the topic area of social justice.⁵⁵¹ In a first step, I present the range of social ethical topics that the above dialogue partners address.

---

550. Yong, *Days of Caesar*, 208, 346.
551. See also the introduction to the section "The Methodology of the Dialogue," 4–6.

In Solivan's work, we find liberation from oppressive class systems as the primary concern. At the same time, he also addresses liberation from the oppressive racist and sexist systems, and from suffering in general. Wenk focuses on the liberation of people for community. In so doing, discrimination by gender, status, and ethnicity are specifically thematized and, more broadly, solidarity with oppressed lives is addressed. Stephenson focuses on the liberation of women from structural oppression, specifically mentioning liberation from sexism and patriarchism. Yong points to the importance of the church's independence from the state in order to have the freedom to work for the increase of God's kingdom. To this end, he specifically mentions overcoming poverty through economic justice and a commitment to ecology. These are the socio-ethical fields which the four Pentecostal theologians deal with.

Commonalities Among the Different Socio-Ethical Issues

In a second step, we orient ourselves toward the fourth heuristic rule, the analysis of commonalities: The rationale for the analysis of commonalities is "that with the maximum structural variation of perspectives on the object, only those aspects of the data of variation shall remain constant which were examined by the respective subjective perspectives, that is to say, they can be regarded as 'closer to the object' than the different images of the object which Rule 3 has dictated we collect."[552] In other words: What factors do Solivan, Wenk, Stephenson, and Yong share with regard to their social ethics despite all their differences?

The Analysis reveals that all four authors regard encounter as an important factor by which injustice or inequalities are uncovered, which can point to a potential complement and set social ethical processes in motion.

> For Solivan, the encounter with suffering people, which is based on the principle of localization, is a christologically founded fundamental principle of liberation and is imperative for identification with the needy.[553] In the encounter with the suffering, the personal, systematic and structural root of suffering is addressed through identification and localization.[554] For Wenk, the

---

552. Kleining, *Entdeckende Sozialforschung*, 242.
553. Solivan, *Spirit, Pathos and Liberation*, 83.
554. Solivan, *Spirit, Pathos and Liberation*, 86.

encounter between community and the marginalized triggers the process of self-definition for the new people of God. In this process, the parties involved depend on each other to recognize and implement God's intentions.[555] The encounters of the different groups permanently challenge the new people of God to review life and practice.[556] Stephenson takes up the theme of encounter by pointing to the importance of women and of their voices being heard and recognized as equal in the community, since otherwise it is not a community of equals.[557] Yong sees the community of believers as a place where the unequal (needy and privileged) meet, and thereby are given the opportunity to counterbalance inequality.[558] The encounters within the community of believers have the potential to shape hearts with a trinitarian and Kingdom orientation.[559]

My decision to subsume the aspect described above under the term "encounter" was accompanied by an extended struggle. *Experience, concern, involvement,* and *participation* were other terms that I initially saw as possible titles—they all showed partial aspects of what I was trying to capture, but none of these terms could fully express what I was looking for. The term *encounter* cannot do this either. Despite knowing that various theologians (for example, Barth and Brunner) use *encounter* differently than I do here, I decided to use this term anyway. The reason for this is that ultimately *encounter* always precedes *experience, concern, involvement* and *participation*. Theophanies can be cited as biblical examples, such as the revelation of God in the burning bush (Exod 3:1–10), God's appearance before his people on Mount Sinai (Exod 19:16–20) or the Pentecost miracle (Acts 2:1–4). In all these examples, God reveals Himself in an encounter with people, which is followed by concern, involvement and participation. In this sense, the term *encounter*, as I use it in this work, is to be understood as a *starting point* of Pentecostal social ethics created by God.[560]

555. Wenk, *Community-Forming Power*, 314.
556. Wenk, *Community-Forming Power*, 286.
557. Stephenson, *Dismantling the Dualisms*, 180.
558. Yong, *Days of Caesar*, 299.
559. Yong, *Days of Caesar*, 313.
560. We find a similar wrangling over the terms *participation* and *encounter* in Wolfgang Vondey's article "The Full Gospel: A Liturgical Hermeneutics of Pentecost." He writes: "The foundational connection to the day of Pentecost shapes the pneumatological and christological imagination always from Pentecost to Pentecost, that is, in a contemporary encounter with the Holy Spirit of Christ seen as a participation in the

This already touches on a further aspect that connects the four authors: "unity in particularity." This means that the encounter only becomes fruitful when the parties encountering one another not only become aware of their differences but also recognize the various voices as worth hearing and significant. Thus, unity in particularity is anything but a form of "pious" collectivism; rather, it affirms the diversity and sees this as an important characteristic of the community.

Solivan points out the importance of the particularity of Hispanic reality by showing not only that a variety of Hispanic realities exists, but that some of them differ massively.[561] At the same time, through the work of the Holy Spirit, identification with the others, despite all the differences, is not only possible but imperative for God's kingdom to break out.[562] In his approach, Wenk refers to the various groups that differ in culture, language, moral norms, etc., yet are brought together by God's Spirit to form a messianic exodus community.[563] This process is only successfully completed when the dialogue between the parties involved reaches an adequate conclusion, that is to say, when the marginalized become part of the new Exodus community.[564] Stephenson sees the reconciliation of unequals, e.g., Jews and Gentiles, as the foundation of the soteriological work of God's Spirit in Acts 2, thereby creating a community of equal parties.[565] Yong several times refers to Pentecost and the experience of the many languages which are worked by the one Spirit, and thereby endorses multiplicity which, in all its diversity, actually has the same restoration and redemption as its goal.[566] The fact that this diversity at the same time

---

original event" (Vondey, *Handbook Pentecostal Spirituality*, 173). It is about becoming part of what happened at Pentecost, about participating in this event. This event always presupposes an encounter—with God, the encounter between created and Creator; and with humans, the encounter among the created. This encounter becomes the starting point for everything that follows. Something that also speaks in favor of the term *encounter* is that it also guarantees a certain "unavailability" of the other person. Similarly, the term *encounter* is also used by Keith Warrington. He considers the encounter with God to be a prior experience that shapes the understanding of self, mission and Scriptures, as well as interaction with fellow humans. Warrington, *Pentecostal Theology*, 20.

561. Solivan, *Spirit, Pathos and Liberation*, 17.
562. Solivan, *Spirit, Pathos and Liberation*, 102, 117.
563. Wenk, *Community-Forming Power*, 31.
564. Wenk, *Community-Forming Power*, 286.
565. Stephenson, *Dismantling the Dualisms*, 112–13
566. Yong, *Days of Caesar*, 201.

underlies an equality which has practical ramifications, is likewise seen by Yong as having been established at the Pentecost event.[567]

This brings us to a further observation: It is noticeable that with all four voices, pneumatology as an individual spiritual experience is hardly of importance. Rather, the focus is on a collective spiritual experience, which is interpreted in terms of the community.

Thus, for Wenk, God's Spirit is the agent that integrates people into the community and allows them to participate in the worldly dimension of salvation.[568] The specific works of the Holy Spirit should be indicative of their ethical and moral significance and implications for the further history of the community.[569] Solivan refers to the Holy Spirit, which not only affirms the cultural particularity within the people of God, but moreover holds them together as one people despite their diversity.[570] Through the soteriological dimension of God's works through the Holy Spirit, Stephenson sees the conversion and initiation of peoples and genders as equal participants in the new people of God.[571] Yong emphasizes the importance of miraculous healings as a means of reintegration into the community.[572] He also sees the Holy Spirit's empowerment for mission, which in turn brings the focus onto the community, its transformation and its growth.[573]

Furthermore, Yong, Stephenson and Wenk show similarities in their approach to eschatology. They all point to the importance of the eschaton for the present day.

Yong points to the importance of the eschatological promises as pointing the way to understanding the present, in order to develop a more holistic concept of salvation which opens up new options for the people of God.[574] For Wenk, it is the eschatological horizon that provides orientation as to what injustice is, and how it can be overcome. Furthermore, it is also this eschatological horizon which points the way to how the newly won freedom in Christ can be lived, and what must be done in order not to

---

567. Yong, *Days of Caesar*, 354.
568. Wenk, *Community-Forming Power*, 288.
569. Wenk, "Reconciliation and Renunciation," 32.
570. Solivan, *Spirit, Pathos and Liberation*, 118.
571. Stephenson, *Dismantling the Dualisms*, 119.
572. Yong, *Days of Caesar*, 297.
573. Yong, *Days of Caesar*, 211–13.
574. Youg, *Days of Caesar*, 352–53.

lose it.[575] Stephenson refers to eschatology as something that is intended to descend upon the church in the present day and to become visible.[576]

In the remainder of this paper, I shall refer to this eschatological approach as collaborative eschatology.[577] It is difficult to analyse Solivan's eschatology on the basis of his orthopathos approach. In contrast to the other three theologians, for him, eschatology does not play a critical role. Solivan only mentions it in a brief passage, where he describes it as a blessed hope which is given to the contemporary church as a pivotal element for reconciliation with God and fellow human beings.[578] Nevertheless, on the basis of this brief reference, it can be said that, even for Solivan, the future eschatological hope is intended to influence present action, and therefore for him also it is more than a consolation for the hereafter.

A collaborative eschatology presupposes a hope which counts on God's healing and, above all else, accomplishing eschatological intervention—otherwise the collaboration has no purpose. It is this hope which allows the church to participate in the quest for justice, even when all the signs of the present ridicule this hope.

Wenk sees trust as the foundation of freedom, love as the living space of freedom. Love in turn releases hope, which forms the "horizon" of freedom. For: "Freedom is . . . always hopeful."[579] In Solivan's approach, hope generally plays an important role.[580] However, it also finds a connection to eschatology directly in the critical debate on "now and not yet."[581] For Stephenson and Yong, hope is implicit: Stephenson takes up the idea of hope in her evaluation of Letty Russell's approach, where she speaks of the "memories of the future."[582] For Yong, as for Solivan, hope appears in connection with the tension of the "now and not yet."[583]

---

575. Wenk, *Erneuerung durch Begegnung*, 116.

576. Stephenson, *Dismantling the Dualisms*, 181.

577. The term was coined by John Dominic Crossan. See Stewart, *Resurrection of Jesus*, 178.

578. Solivan, *Spirit, Pathos and Liberation*, 110.

579. Wenk, *Erneuerung durch Begegnung*, 105.

580. See also Solivan, *Spirit, Pathos and Liberation*, 82, 90–92, 103–10.

581. Solivan, *Spirit, Pathos and Liberation*, 91.

582. Stephenson, *Dismantling the Dualisms*, 181.

583. Yong, *Days of Caesar*, 252–54.

Main Features of a Pentecostal Social Ethic

A Pentecostal social ethic which is oriented to Solivan, Wenk, Stephenson, and Yong can be described as follows, based on the insights gathered in chapter 3:

- *Encounter*: Regardless of whether it concerns liberation from oppressive class systems, liberation from oppressive racist and sexist systems, or from suffering in general, liberation from discrimination by gender, status, ethnicity, or, more fundamentally, solidarity with lives under oppression, overcoming poverty through economic justice, or commitment to ecology, encounter is the starting point in the formation of a Pentecostal social ethic.

- *Unity in particularity*: The encounter then becomes fruitful when the parties encountering one another are not only aware of their differences, but also acknowledge the different voices as worth listening to, and significant for the community. The community affirms difference and sees this as a characteristic of itself.

- *Pneumatology*: The work of the Holy Spirit does not have its meaning primarily as an individual spiritual experience but is interpreted in terms of the common life of the community.

- *Collaborative eschatology*: The future, promised Kingdom of God, with its values and norms, guides the ethos of the church. The community of believers is called to live in the here and now according to the principles of the coming Kingdom of God and to embody them in the present.

- *Hope*: A collaborative eschatology presupposes the hope that God will consummate the Kingdom which dawned in Christ. It is this hope which enables the church to participate in the Kingdom of God again and again, despite all opposition, disappointments and failures.

So much for the commonalities within the approaches of Solivan, Wenk, Stephenson and Yong. The social ethical themes and commonalities specified and compiled here will guide the dialogue with Moltmann in the following chapter.

3

Social Justice According to Jürgen Moltmann

As already mentioned, Moltmann sees himself as a partner in dialogue with Pentecostal theology, which, conversely, also applies to numerous Pentecostals who have sought dialogue with him and his theological work.[1] This chapter focuses on Moltmann's social ethics and the role pneumatology plays in this.

Introductory Thoughts

Jürgen Moltmann, born on April 8, 1926, in Hamburg, experienced the horrors of war in his youth. In 1939, first his father and then, in 1943, he himself were drafted into the Wehrmacht. In 1945, Moltmann was taken prisoner by the British. During his three years of imprisonment in Kilmarnock, Scotland, he began studying Protestant theology, which he later continued in 1948 at the University of Göttingen. Under Otto Weber, Moltmann wrote a dissertation on Christoph Pezel. In 1952, he married Elisabeth Wendel and became a pastor in Bremen-Wasserhorst, as well as a student minister. In 1957, Moltmann completed his habilitation and accepted a professorship at the Church University of Wuppertal. In 1963, he moved to the University of Bonn. From 1967 until his retirement in

---

1. See, for example, *Journal of Pentecostal Theology* 2:4 (1994).

1994, he worked as a professor of systematic theology at the Eberhard Karls University in Tübingen.[2] Moltmann attracted international attention in 1964, when he further developed Ernst Bloch's *The Principle of Hope* into the *Theology of Hope*.

In my discussion of Moltmann, I concentrate on his work *The Spirit of Life: A Universal Affirmation*. Other sources are consulted where they complement *The Spirit of Life*. As a starting point, I chose Moltmann's missiology,[3] which, as we shall see, is directly related to the topic of social justice. In this context, it should be mentioned that Moltmann wrote *Ethics of Hope*, which, however, does not explore social ethics as such. However, his work is permeated by socio-ethical thoughts and implications. Therefore, Moltmann's socio-ethical approach cannot be described per se but must be derived from the focal points of his theological thinking.

Mission, Hope, and Identity

At first glance, it may seem jarring to open the discussion about Moltmann's theology with the question of missiology and not, for example, with the question of pneumatology. My reason for doing this is that Moltmann himself placed the question of mission at the beginning of his first pneumatological draft, *The Church in the Power of the Holy Spirit*. If we want to theologically grasp the significance of Moltmann's pneumatology for social ethics, we must also follow his arguments about the understanding of mission.

The central idea that Moltmann places before all missiological considerations is that the church does not "have" a mission, "but the very reverse: that the mission of Christ creates its own church. Mission does not come from the church; it is from mission and in the light of mission that the church has to be understood."[4] Moltmann places the question "What

---

2. All biographical data is taken from Moltmann, *Broad Place*.

3. A comprehensive analysis of Moltmann's understanding of mission can be found in Wrogemann's dissertation on Mission and Religion in the twentieth century (Wrogemann, *Mission und Religion*).

4. Moltmann, *Power of the Spirit*, 10. Klaus Bockmühl comes to similar conclusions. In 1974, he wrote: "Questions around decisions of recent mission theology), that the church is constituted by the missionary mandate, since it is essentially a confessional fellowship. . . . Mission [is] not just one activity of the church among others but the touchstone for all activities" (Bockmühl, *Was heisst heute Mission*, 41, 46, my translation). The church does not just do mission, but "mission drives the church" (40, my translation). See also Bosh, *Transforming Mision*, 372.

can I hope for?" before the questions of the goal and of human activity within the framework of the mission, because "mission is the hope of faith in action."[5] This hope is not just any old hope for an ideal, but rather, it is focused on the gospel: "The hope of the Christian faith is founded and opened wide by the promise of the gospel. Mission therefore happens out of calling and out of the promise of the risen Jesus and in the power of obedience and in the patient impatience of hope."[6] Jesus' promise is nothing less than the Kingdom of God and thus an eschatological hope. Believers are invited, within the framework of following Jesus, to make themselves the helpers of this very kingdom. This is not "only" about reconciliation, but about nothing less than the restoration of the entire creation:

"Christ's resurrection does not say: *restitutio in integrum* through reconciliation. It says: reconciliation in order hat the world may be transformed and newly created. It says: justification of sinners so that there may be a just world for all created beings."[7] The life, work and death of Christ are normative for the understanding and content of this restorative work:

> The word *mission*—meaning sending and being sent—encompasses the whole of Jesus' work and the whole of the diverse work of his charismatic community. . . . Therefore all proclamation is mission, but not all mission is proclamation. Healing, teaching, baptising, delivering, making peace and advocating for justice are other essential tasks of mission.[8]

But suffering, death and resurrection are also part of the life of Jesus Christ because "the messianic mission of Jesus is only fulfilled in his death and is put into full force through his resurrection. Through his history it becomes the church's gospel for the world. Through his death and resurrection the church participates in his mission, becoming the messianic church of the coming kingdom and man's liberation."[9] The church which orients itself to Christ and knows itself to be called and sent by him has a part in God's mission, the *Missio Dei*:

---

5. Moltmann, "Das Ziel der Mission," 1, my translation.
6. Moltmann, "Das Ziel der Mission," 1.
7. Moltmann, "Pluralistische Theologie," 189.
8. Moltmann, "Probleme und Chancen," 409, my translation.
9. Moltmann, *Power of the Spirit*, 83.

> To grasp the missionary church theologically in a world-wide context means understanding it in the context of the *missio dei*. Mission comprehends the whole of the church, not only parts of it, let alone the members it has sent out. To proclaim the gospel of the dawning kingdom is the first and most important element in the mission of Jesus, the mission of the Holy Spirit, and the mission of the church; but it is not the only one. Mission embraces all activities that serve to liberate man from his slavery in the presence of the coming God, slavery which extends from economic necessity to Godforsakenness. Evangelization is mission, but mission is not merely evangelization. In the missionary church the widow who soes charitable works belongs to the same mission as the bishop who leads the church, or the preacher of the gospel. The church's endowment with the spirit of liberty and the powers of liberation knows distinctions, but not divisions.[10]

It is clear that Moltmann distances himself from a separation between the sacred and the trivial. So he says, agreeing with Gutiérrez, "There is only one history, which has Christ as its goal,"[11] and concludes, "if this is true, then the economic, political and cultural liberations of men and women from exploitation, repression and alienation belong just as much to the work of redemption as the forgiveness of sins and hope for eternal life."[12] All members of the church are included in this mission and empowered by the Spirit of God: "The all-embracing messianic mission of the whole church corresponds to Christ's messianic mission and to the charismatic sending of the Spirit 'which shall be poured on all flesh.'"[13] Moltmann understands this mission in the power of the Holy Spirit as a joint discovery of where and how the church has its place in the history of God.[14]

As mentioned above, in this voyage of discovery, *all* are involved through the power of the Holy Spirit: "The whole congregation has 'spiritual' and charismatic gifts, not merely its 'spiritual' pastors. The whole congregation and every individual in it belong with all their powers and potentialities to the mission of God's kingdom."[15] According to

10. Moltmann, *Power of the Spirit*, 10–11.
11. Moltmann, *Spirit of Life*, 124.
12. Moltmann, *Spirit of Life*, 124.
13. Moltmann, *Power of the Spirit*, 11.
14. Moltmann, *Power of the Spirit*, 11.
15. Moltmann, *Power of the Spirit*, 10.

Moltmann, the church was born of the cross: "The birth of the church out of the cross of Christ leads the church to take its stand beneath the cross, if it remains consistent, in opposition to the systems of life governed by *nomos* and *ananke* and assailed by these systems of life, their laws and their gods."[16] In this sense, mission is also participation in the "salvific opposition of God to the existing world."[17]

According to Moltmann, participation in God's opposition affects the identity of the followers of Jesus. How? According to Moltmann, God reveals himself in the opposite, i.e., in the godless: "In concrete terms, God is revealed in the cross of Christ who was abandoned by God. His grace is revealed in sinners. His righteousness is revealed in the unrighteous and in those without rights, and his gracious election in the damned."[18] Those who identify with Christ inevitably cannot help but to do as Christ did:

> Christian identification with the crucified Christ means solidarity with the sufferings of the poor and the misery both of the oppressed and the oppressors. On the other hand, if this solidarity is seriously accepted, selflessly and without reserve, it is in itself an identification with the one who was crucified and "became poor, so that by his poverty you might become rich."[19]

A church that appeals to Christ, or in other words, identifies with Christ, cannot help but show solidarity with the oppressed and marginalized: "But for the crucified Christ, the principle of fellowship is fellowship with those who are different, and solidarity with those who have become alien and have been made different."[20] Moltmann goes even further in his understanding of the church:

> Its principle of justification is not similarity, but the justification of the other (Hegel), the creative making righteous of the unrighteous and the attribution of rights to those who are without rights. Consequently, the church of the crucified Christ cannot be assimilated to what is different and alien to it. Nor can it shut itself away from what is alien in a social ghetto, but for the sake of its identity in the crucified Christ, must reveal him and itself away, by following him, in what is different and alien.

---

16. Moltmann, *Power of the Spirit*, 89. See also Moltmann, *Spirit of Life*, 86.

17. This is how Wrogemann describes Moltmann's approach in Wrogemann, *Mission und Religion*, 205, my translation.

18. Moltmann, *Crucified God*, 27.

19. Moltmann, *Crucified God*, 25.

20. Moltmann, *Crucified God*, 28.

Otherwise, it does justice neither to the one to whom it appeals nor to those to whom he revealed himself. Only in the practical form of fellowship with others can it bear witness to the crucified Christ and live out in life the justification of the godless in which it believes, and from which it derives its own life.[21]

Christian identity "comes to a head only in the context of non-identity, self-emptying for the sake of others and solidarity with others. It cannot be established in isolation, but only revealed in contact with others."[22] What does that mean? Moltmann comes to the following conclusion: "Thus the place where the question of identity can meaningful be asked is the situation of the crisis of identity, brought about by meaningful self-emptying and solidarity."[23]

The Spirit of God and Moltmann's Social Ethics

After we have considered what Moltmann means by the term *mission*, the question arises as to what he feels when he uses the term *Spirit*, because this is fundamental for Moltmann's understanding of mission, as well as for his social ethics. To do this, we begin with Moltmann's critique of the term *Spirit* as it is used in Western parlance.

The *ruach* of God as the Materializing Spirit of God

Moltmann points out that there is a key difference in the meaning of the word *Spirit* between Western languages and Hebrew:

> If we wish to understand the Old Testament word *ruach*, we must forget the word "spirit," which belongs to Western culture. The Greek word πνεῦμα, the Latin spiritus, and the Germanic Geist/ghost were always conceived as antitheses to matter and body. They mean something immaterial. Whether we are talking Greek, Latin, German or English, by the Spirit of God we then mean something disembodied, supersensory and supernatural. But if we talk in Hebrew about Yahweh's ruach, we are saying: God is a tempest, a storm, a force in body and soul, humanity and nature. The Western cleavage between spirit and body, spirituality and sensuousness is so deeply rooted in our languages

21. Moltmann, *Crucified God*, 28.
22. Moltmann, *Crucified God*, 17.
23. Moltmann, *Crucified God*, 18.

that we must have recourse to other translations if we want to arrive at a more or less adequate rendering of the word *ruach*.[24]

The literal meaning of *ruach* is so multi-layered that it seems impossible for Moltmann to find a simple paradigm that would summarize the issues addressed in a single term.[25] He therefore uses the Old Testament concept of Spirit in several contexts: (a) *Ruach* "is the confronting event of God's efficacious presence," and vice versa "we have to understand the happenings of God's presence as *ruach*." "In the creative power of life, God is present. Every efficacious presence of God is determined by the *ruach* and, as Calvin said, has to be interpreted pneumatologically."[26] (b) In addition to the theological personal notation for *ruach* as the presence of God, there is also the dimension of power: "The *ruach* as Yahweh's *ruach* is of course transcendent in origin; but it is equally true to say that as the power of life in all the living it is immanently efficacious. The creative power of God is the transcendent side of the *ruach*."[27] (c) In addition to the *ruach* as an occurrence of the personal presence of God and the *ruach* as an immanent life force, Moltmann also sees the *ruach* as a space in which one experiences "as the space of freedom in which the living being can unfold. That is the experience of the Spirit: 'Thou has set my feet in a broad place' (Ps 31:8)."[28]

On the basis of the contexts mentioned above, Moltmann develops the seemingly contradictory description of the "immanent transcendence," of the Spirit.[29] Such an understanding of the Spirit is of fundamental importance, as then every

> experience that happens to us or that we have, can possess a transcendent, inward side. The *experience of God's Spirit* is not limited to the human subject's experience of the self. It is also a constitutive element in the experience of the "Thou," in the experience of sociality, and in the experience of nature. "God's spirit fills the world and he who holds all things together knows every sound" (Wis 1:7). It is therefore possible to experience God *in, with and beneath* each everyday experience of the world,

---

24. Moltmann, *Spirit of Life*, 40. Interestingly, despite his criticism, Moltmann retains the use of the word in "Spirit" in *The Spirit of Life*.
25. Moltmann, *Spirit of Life*, 40.
26. Moltmann, *Spirit of Life*, 42.
27. Moltmann, *Spirit of Life*, 42.
28. Moltmann, *Spirit of Life*, 43.
29. Moltmann, *Spirit of Life*, 31–34.

if God is in all things, and if all things are in God, so that God himself "experiences" all things in his own way.[30]

To be able to experience God in all things presupposes—if we follow Moltmann's logic—an immanent transcendence of all things. It is based on the theological understanding that the Spirit of God is the power of creation and the source of life: "If we can call what for us is nature, 'God's creation,' we have already invoked its immanent transcendence."[31] The result is that we "have then recognized the Creator's right to what he has created. And in so doing we have also acknowledged the rights of our fellow creatures themselves, rights which exist quite apart from their value for us."[32] This leads to the fact that we "carry experiences of the world into the experience of God."[33] For "'reverence for life' is absorbed into reverence for God, and the veneration of nature becomes part of the adoration of God. We sense that in everything God is waiting for us."[34] One experiences that one is part of a greater whole:

> To experience the fellowship of the Spirit inevitably carries Christianity beyond itself into the greater fellowship of all God's creatures. *For the community of creation*, in which all created things exist with one another, for one another and in one another, is also *the fellowship of the Holy Spirit*. Both experiences of the Spirit bring the church today into solidarity with the cosmos, which is so mortally threatened.[35]

Because one can recognize oneself as part of the cosmos through fellowship with the Spirit, for Moltmann, the Christian experience of the Spirit does not separate us from the world, but rather leads to a new understanding, to a new hope for and a new solidarity with the world. Humankind is not redeemed *from* but *with* the world.[36] At the same time, humans are independent beings, despite their connection with the world. Precisely this independence, according to Moltmann, is called into question if the Spirit can only be experienced through the official acts and

---

30. Moltmann, *Spirit of Life*, 34–35.
31. Moltmann, *Spirit of Life*, 35–36.
32. Moltmann, *Spirit of Life*, 36.
33. Moltmann, *Spirit of Life*, 36.
34. Moltmann, *Spirit of Life*, 36.
35. Moltmann, *Spirit of Life*, 10.
36. Moltmann, *Spirit of Life*, 89.

proclamation of the church.[37] According to Moltmann, the church does not have a monopoly on the work of the Spirit:

> The Holy Spirit is not tied to the church. The Spirit is not concerned about the church as such. He is concerned with the church, as he is with Israel, for the sake of the kingdom of God, the rebirth of life and the new creation of all things.
>
> The relation of the church to the Holy Spirit is the relation of *epiklesis*, continual invocation of the Spirit, and unconditional opening for the experiences of the Spirit who confers fellowship and makes life truly living.[38]

Another aspect that Moltmann emphasizes in connection with the Old Testament term *ruach* is the female side of God's spirit. Here, Moltmann uses the theologies of Makarios, Zinzendorf, Wesley and Francke, which advocated for a female understanding of the Spirit. Moltmann particularly emphasizes Zinzendorf's image of the Trinity as a family. Knowing that this is only "an image of the unrepresentable God,"[39] for him there is a corrective to a patriarchal image of God the Father, who has the Spirit at one hand and Christ at the other hand:

> For there God is a solidarity, ruling and determining subject, whereas here the Tri-unity is a wonderful community. There the reflection of the triune God is a hierarchical church. Here the reflection of the triune God is a community of women and men without privileges, a community of free and equal people, sisters and brothers. For the building of this new congregational structure, the motherly ministry of the Holy Spirit, and the Try-unity as a community, are important.[40]

For Moltmann, the biblical discourse about the Holy Spirit, through which believers are born and whom the Holy Spirit comforts like a mother, bears traits of *ruach Yahweh*, which in Hebrew is declined in the feminine. For him, this female-maternal association is a corrective to the male idea of the Trinity, which, as mentioned above, also has an impact on the understanding of the church: "When the Trinity forms a fellowship, it corresponds to the true human fellowship of men and

---

37. Moltmann, *Spirit of Life*, 2.
38. Moltmann, *Spirit of Life*, 230.
39. Moltmann, *Spirit of Life*, 160.
40. Moltmann, *Source of Life*, 37. See also Moltmann, *Spirit of Life*, 171–74.

women. A certain de-patriarchalisation of the image of God also results in a de-patriarchalisation and de-hierarchisation of the church."[41]

The Shekinah of God as the Presence of God in the World

As a further central element of pneumatology, Moltmann describes the Old Testament concept of the *Shekinah*, which for him is "the descent and indwelling of God in space and time, at a particular place and a particular era of earthly beings and in their history."[42] It is "not a divine attribute. It is the presence of God himself."[43] The *Shekinah* is "not God in his essential omnipresence. It is his special, willed and promised presence in the world. The Shekinah is God himself, present at a particular place and at a particular time."[44] She is the dwelling of God with Her people and is there at the destruction of the temple and "accompanies the people into exile."[45] The *Shekinah* is "present in the synagogues, among the judges, with the wretched, the sick, and so forth."[46] It is the *Shekinah* that shows the relevance of the "presence of God's Spirit in the desolation of the beings he has created."[47] Three aspects of the *Shekinah* are of particular importance to Moltmann:

1. The doctrine of the Shekinah makes the personal character of the Spirit clear. The Spirit is the efficacious presence of God himself. The Spirit is the presence of God in person. The Spirit is more than one of God's attributes, and more than a gift of God to what he has created. The Spirit is *God's empathy*, his feeling identification with what he loves.

2. The concept of the Shekinah also draws attention to *the sensibility of God the Spirit*. The Spirit indwells. The Spirit suffers with the suffering. The Spirit is grieved and quenched. The Spirit rejoices when we rejoice. When it descends and takes up its habitation and indwelling in wandering and suffering created beings, the Spirit thrusts forward with intense

---

41. Moltmann, *Spirit of Life*, 160.
42. Moltmann, *Spirit of Life*, 47.
43. Moltmann, *Spirit of Life*, 48.
44. Moltmann, *Spirit of Life*, 48.
45. Moltmann, *Spirit of Life*, 48.
46. Moltmann, *Spirit of Life*, 48.
47. Moltmann, *Spirit of Life*, 47.

longing for union with God, and sighs to be at rest in the new, perfected creation.

3. The idea of the Shekinah points towards *the kenosis of the Spirit*. In his Shekinah, God renounces his impassibility and becomes able to suffer because he is willing to love. The theophany of the Spirit is not anthropomorphism, but is made possible through his indwelling in created being.[48]

Moltmann also sees these aspects of the Old Testament *Shekinah* idea in the New Testament idiom of the *descent* of the Spirit and the Spirit's *rest* on Christ:

> What is meant is the self-restriction and self-humiliation of the eternal Spirit, and his feeling identification with Jesus' person and the history of his life and suffering—just as, according to the rabbinic idea, God's Spirit has committed itself to the history of Israel's life and sufferings.[49]

According to Moltmann, when the Spirit of God leads Jesus, Jesus accompanies Him on His way: "And if the Spirit accompanies him, then it is drawn into his sufferings, and becomes his companion in suffering. The path the Son takes in his passion is then at the same time the path taken by the Spirit, whose strength will be proved in Jesus' weakness."[50] But even if the Spirit is bound to the destiny of Jesus through the *Shekinah*, the Spirit does this "without becoming identical with him."[51] In this event, the Spirit becomes the *Spirit of Jesus Christ* and, thus also the *Spirit of Passion* and the "*Spirit of Christ crucified*." In this context, Moltmann refers to the Epistle to the Hebrews, which connects the Passion of Christ with the work of the Spirit:

> Christ "through the eternal Spirit offered himself without blemish to God" (Heb 9:14). The value of the sacrifice does not depend solely on the one surrendered. It has to do with the mode of the surrender too. And in this happening Christ is determined through the eternal Spirit. The Spirit is not something he possesses. It is the power that makes him ready to surrender his life, and which itself sustains this surrender.[52]

---

48. Moltmann, *Spirit of Life*, 51.
49. Moltmann, *Spirit of Life*, 61.
50. Moltmann, *Spirit of Life*, 62.
51. Moltmann, *Spirit of Life*, 62.
52. Moltmann, *Spirit of Life*, 63.

In these formulations, pneumatology is linked to Christology.[53] It is characteristic of this connection that the Spirit in Christ does not lead to triumphalism but sets one free to serve in the kingdom of God:

> John 3:34 describes this unique endowment with the Spirit as "without measure." It marks the beginning of the kingdom of God and the new creation of all things. The Spirit makes Jesus "the kingdom of God in person," for in the power of the Spirit he drives out demons and heals the sick; in the power of the Spirit he receives sinners, and brings the kingdom of God to the poor.[54]

It is this power of the Spirit that lets Jesus accept sinners. It is this power that allows Jesus to bring the Kingdom of God to the poor: "This energizing power of God is given him not for himself but for others: for the sick, the poor, sinners, the dying."[55] For Moltmann, the cross and the Spirit are inseparable: "According to the testimonies of the first Christians, it was the Easter jubilation over Christ's resurrection that released the stream of charismata in the congregations. The pentecostal movement begins at Easter."[56] This connection of pneumatology to Christology is significant for discipleship (and thus also for the church). It means nothing other than that *living in the Holy Spirit* is always *following Jesus*.[57] This discipleship

> leads to conflict with the powers and the powerful of "this world," and to the bearing of the cross. Separation from the powers and compulsions of "this world" necessarily conduces to solidarity with the victims of these powers and compulsions, and to intervention on their behalf. The indescribable joy over the Easter rebirth of life therefore shows itself in resistance to this world of death and in the determined refusal to accustom ourselves inwardly to death.
>
> Peace with God the Creator inevitably and inescapably means not making peace with the systematic destruction of creation by this society of ours. For the person who experiences the

---

53. Moltmann, *Spirit of Life*, 17. In *The Source of Life*, Moltmann even writes: "A true theology of the cross is Pentecost theology, and Christian Pentecost theology is a theology of the cross."

54. Moltmann, *Spirit of Life*, 61.

55. Moltmann, *Spirit of Life*, 61.

56. Moltmann, *Spirit of Life*, 188.

57. Moltmann, *Spirit of Life*, 153. See also Moltmann, *Way of Jesus Christ*, 92; WCC, *Community of Women and Men*, 52.

peace of God "in the heart" begins to hope for peace on earth, and therefore begins to resist peacelessness, armaments and war in the world of human beings, and exploitation and devastation in the world of nature. People who experience the justification of those without rights under Christ's cross begin to hope for the new creation of justice for everyone and everything, so they begin to resist the wrong that is done to the weak. In *faith* we experience the peace of God, in *hope* we look ahead to a peaceful world, and in *resistance* to violence we confess God's peace. In faith we receive the consolation of the Spirit in suffering, but in hope we look to the future of a new creation in which there will be no more mourning and no more pain and no more crying; and in the struggle against the unnecessary suffering of other creatures, we witness to life.[58]

The Spirit that Creates, Judges, and Recreates

In the introduction to his book *The Spirit of Life*, Moltmann points out that in Protestant as well as Catholic theology, the Holy Spirit is understood as the spirit of salvation. It is a spirituality based on *filioque*, which understands the Holy Spirit only as the Spirit of Christ. According to Moltmann, this understanding causes a piety that seeks salvation in the afterlife but does not expect this for life on earth.[59] Moltmann counters that the Holy Spirit is not only the *Spirit of Christ* (and thus actually the redeeming Spirit) but at the same time also the *Spirit of the Father* (who is *ruach Yahweh*), i.e., the Spirit of creation.[60] Moltmann classifies a theology that sees the Holy Spirit merely as a redeemer who rescues the soul from this valley of tears and this frail physical shell "into the heaven of blessed spirits" not as Christian but as gnostic.[61] In accordance with the creed of the early church, he counters such theology with the "resurrection of the flesh." He concludes: "But if redemption is the resurrection of the body and the new creation of all things, then the redeeming Spirit of Christ cannot be any Spirit other than Yahweh's creative *ruach*."[62] For Moltmann, it is always the Spirit that brings the work of the Father and

---

58. Moltmann, *Spirit of Life*, 154–55, my translation.
59. Moltmann, *Spirit of Life*, 8–9.
60. Moltmann, *Spirit of Life*, 8.
61. Moltmann, *Spirit of Life*, 9.
62. Moltmann, *Spirit of Life*, 9.

the Son to their goal: "This means that we have to understand every created reality in terms of energy, grasping it as the realized potentiality of the divine Spirit."[63] Based on Psalm 104:29–30 and Proverbs 8:22–31, he understands the *ruach Yahweh* as the spirit who creates creation and simultaneously maintains it.[64] An interesting aspect that Moltmann points out is the *Spirit as judge*. As the Spirit of justice, He sides with the victims, in which he becomes present and palpable "in *the pain of people without rights* over their deprivations."[65] At the same time, he declared himself "in *the guilty conscience* of the people who commit violence," which can also manifest itself in internal "uncertainty, fear of one's own self and aggression towards oneself and other people."[66] To those who remain in the wrong, the Spirit denies its peace:

> *In negative terms*, this divine justice is shown in world history by *the instability of unjust conditions*, which have to be kept on an even keel by more and more violence, more and more police, more and more military control. Peace is a fruit of justice. This is true of social peace in a society too, and it is no less true of peace between nations. All that grows on the foundation of injustice is organized peacelessness. So unjust systems have feet of clay. They have no lasting development. The hidden presence in world history of the divine justice in God's Spirit "destabilizes," so to speak, human systems of injustice, and sees to it that they cannot last.[67]

However, the Spirit also reveals itself as the *Spirit of justification*: the Spirit of God is "*the presence of Christ* among and in the victims of violence: Christ is their brother—they are his family and the community of his people.... The Spirit is Christ's solidarity with them."[68] In the case of the perpetrators, the Spirit of God is "*the atoning power* of Christ's substitution among and in the perpetrators. Christ is 'the God of sinners.' The Spirit is Christ's atoning power for them and in them."[69] It is this Spirit that pours out divine love to keep the 'self-destructive human

---

63. Moltmann, *God in Creation*, 23.
64. For more information, see Moltmann, *God in Creation*, 9–13.
65. Moltmann, *Spirit of Life*, 142.
66. Moltmann, *Spirit of Life*, 142.
67. Moltmann, *Spirit of Life*, 143.
68. Moltmann, *Spirit of Life*, 143.
69. Moltmann, *Spirit of Life*, 143.

fellowships' alive in order to be healed. True fellowship is only possible through the power of the Spirit:

> The Holy Spirit is the righteousness and justice of God which creates justice, justifies and rectifies. In the Spirit, lasting community with God, with other people and with nature become possible. That is why we can in this sense also call the Holy Spirit *the justification of life*. In the Spirit life again becomes worth loving. In the Spirit, human beings again become capable of loving life. In the Spirit life's intricate interactions again become fruitful. The rectifying Holy Spirit is God's "yes" in justice to the life of each and all of us, and the life of each with all of us.[70]

With the concept of justification, perpetrators and victims are addressed in different ways. In his discussion of sin, Moltmann does not limit himself to a personalized concept of sin. He also addresses the destruction of the environment, bringing up the topic of structural sin.[71] On the one hand, these structures are made by people; on the other hand, these structures also determine people.[72] What is ominous about these structures is that people experience themselves as victims and perpetrators at the same time.[73] However, Moltmann leaves open the question of what justification actually means for people who find themselves in this "vicious circles."[74]

In addition to the Spirit of creation and the Spirit of justification, Moltmann sees a third force in pneumatology, namely *the Spirit that creates something new*. He writes about the work of the Spirit in Christ:

> The indwelling of the Spirit brings the divine energies of life in Jesus to rapturous and overflowing fullness. John 3:34 describes this unique endowment with the Spirit as "without measure." It marks the beginning of the kingdom of God and the new creation of all things. The Spirit makes Jesus "the kingdom of God in person," for *in the power of the Spirit* he drives out demons and heals the sick; in the power of the Spirit he receives sinners, and brings the kingdom of God to the poor. This energizing

---

70. Moltmann, *Spirit of Life*, 143.
71. Moltmann, *Spirit of Life*, 139.
72. Moltmann, *Spirit of Life*, 140.
73. Müller-Fahrenholz, *Kingdom and the Power*, 161.
74. Moltmann, *Spirit of Life*, 139.

power of God is given him not for himself but for others: for the sick, the poor, sinners, the dying."[75]

It is remarkable that the overflowing power of the Spirit is not aimed at the bearer of the Spirit, but at fellow human beings, the co-creation.[76] Moltmann names the experience of the Spirit based on Rom 8:23; 2 Cor 1:22; 5:5; Eph 1:14 as "beginning (ἀπαρχή)," and "advance pledge or foretaste (ἀρραβών) of the coming kingdom of glory."[77] Interestingly, Moltmann does not refer to the charismatic powers of the Spirit as supernatural, but (referring to Heb 6:5) as "the powers of the age to come."[78] The Spirit that creates anew "does not draw the soul away from the body, nor does it make the soul hasten towards heaven, leaving this earth behind. It places the whole earthly and bodily person in the daybreak colours of the new earth."[79]

In summary, Moltmann says of creation, justification, and new creation by the Spirit: "As God's Spirit, the Spirit 'opens doors' which were shut before. That is, it throws open new chances and possibilities for the gospel. This is the Spirit of the One who created the world and guides its history by bearing and enduring its contradictions."[80]

The Spirit of Freedom

In order to understand Moltmann's contribution to social ethics, it is also important to examine his understanding of freedom. This, in turn, is strongly influenced by pneumatology. However, let us start from the beginning: In discussing the term *freedom*, Moltmann mentions Ernst Bloch's thesis: "Where the great lord of the world reigns, there is no room for liberty, not even for the liberty of the children of God."[81] Such a freedom and understanding of authority only allows the choice between "God *or* freedom."[82] Moltmann rejects this understanding because it misses the biblical understanding of freedom and authority. Moltmann contrasts

75. Moltmann, *Spirit of Life*, 61.
76. Moltmann, *Spirit of Life*, 61.
77. Moltmann, *Spirit of Life*, 74.
78. Moltmann, *Spirit of Life*, 74.
79. Moltmann, *Spirit of Life*, 95.
80. Moltmann, *Spirit of Life*, 103.
81. Moltmann, *Spirit of Life*, 104.
82. Moltmann, *Spirit of Life*, 107.

Bloch's revolutionary concept of freedom and conservative understanding of authority with the biblical testimony of human experiences of liberation with God. Exodus and resurrection play a central role here:

> For Israel, the experience of God and experiences of liberation are two aspects of the same thing. According to the first commandment (Exod 20:2), God reveals himself to the people as "the Lord" by leading them out of slavery into the promised land of liberty. Israel experienced God's "lordship" as her liberation, and in the experience of her liberation had this unique experience of God. Through faith in Jesus the messiah, Christians have very much the same experience: "Now the Lord is the Spirit, and where the Spirit of the Lord is, there is freedom" (2 Cor 3:17). In the Spirit, Christ is manifested as "the Lord," and in the Spirit people experience what it is to be free. According to the experiences of Israel and according to the experiences of Christian faith, the experience of God and the experience of freedom are so deeply fused that they belong indissolubly together and become almost synonymous.[83]

Moltmann admits that this connection, "to identify the Lord with liberation and his lordship with liberty is difficult for us today because of our own painful experiences."[84] According to Moltmann, this has to do with the fact that the term *Lord* is often associated with the *domination* of one over the other and thus also with the oppression of the other. The only way to understand who "God the Lord," really is consists in listening to the stories of God in which people have experienced God as Lord.[85] As already mentioned, this happens in the Exodus story, to which Latin American liberation theology also refers. Therefore, it should not come as a surprise that Moltmann describes Latin American liberation theology as "the first convincing outline to combine belief in God with the will to be free, as the biblical traditions enjoin."[86] He sees the connection of the historical concept of God with the eschatological concept of the kingdom of God as an important characteristic. It is this combination that gives liberation theology its dynamism: "The God of history is on the way to his kingdom. Believing God means hoping for his kingdom. If this is so, the dynamic of the future becomes constitutive for experience of

---

83. Moltmann, *Spirit of Life*, 99.
84. Moltmann, *Spirit of Life*, 100.
85. Moltmann, *Spirit of Life*, 100.
86. Moltmann, *Spirit of Life*, 109.

God in the present."[87] It is this unified historical perspective of God and the kingdom of God that also suggests a unified perspective of liberation and redemption:

> The unified perspective stretching towards liberation and redemption is the logical consequence of this unified historical perspective that stretches towards God and the kingdom of God. Liberation theology does not accept two different histories, a world history and a salvation history, for salvation history has to do with the salvation of this whole created world. Consequently nature and grace belong together. Redemption embraces every human being and the whole human being; and we must add that it embraces humanity and the earth, for the Redeemer is the Creator of all things. To look at Christ is to see that redemption takes in all the dimensions of being and brings the whole of existence to its perfecting. So it follows that "there is only one history, which has Christ as its goal." If this is true, then the economic, political and cultural liberations of men and women from exploitation, repression and alienation belong just as much to the work of redemption as the forgiveness of sins and hope for eternal life.[88]

For Moltmann, the hope of salvation and the experience of liberation are inseparable in practice. At the same time, he is aware that not all expectations can be turned into experiences, but new experiences can be made with these expectations.[89] Separating liberation and redemption, according to Moltmann, "equals separating what is joined in God's Spirit."[90] It is precisely his belief in "the resurrection of the dead and the life of the world to come," that prompts him to declare. "[I] resist the forces of death and annihilation here and now, and must love life here on earth so much that I try with everything I have to free it from exploitation, oppression and alienation."[91] The same is true for him in reverse: "because I love life, and stand up for its justice, and fight for its freedom wherever it is threatened, I hope that one day death will be swallowed up in the victory of life, and that then 'there will be no mourning nor crying nor pain any more' (Rev 21:4f)."[92]

87. Moltmann, *Spirit of Life*, 111.
88. Moltmann, *Spirit of Life*, 111–12.
89. Moltmann, *Spirit of Life*, 112.
90. Moltmann, *Spirit of Life*, 112.
91. Moltmann, *Spirit of Life*, 112.
92. Moltmann, *Spirit of Life*, 112.

How is this very experience of salvation and liberation continued further? If we orient ourselves towards the biblical events, then we find:

> The *Exodus* leads to the *covenant*. This means that liberation theology will turn into federal theology simply of its own accord, and the liberating politics of the people in which liberation theology is embedded will turn into democratic politics. It is only in a covenant of free men and women that liberation, once experienced, can be preserved, and it is only in such a covenant that the dangers of new oppression can be averted.[93]

How exactly is this to happen? Moltmann defines three levels in this regard: The first level is the *freedom experienced as a subject*. Humankind is embraced as a subject by God because "the truth that makes me free is the truth to which I myself assent."[94] It is given in Christ and therefore does not lie "in insight into a cosmic necessity or a necessity of world history, nor in the autonomous right of disposal over oneself and one's property."[95] The believer experiences it much more so in "being possessed by the divine energy of life, and participation in that energy."[96] For Moltmann, from this belief follows that "unexplored creative powers of God are thrown open in men and women." For him, faith is, therefore, nothing less than "becoming creative with God, and in his Spirit. Faith leads to a creative life which is life-giving through love, in places where death rules and people resign themselves, and surrender to it."[97] The subjective level of freedom can neither be decreed nor taken away, but this subjective freedom alone is not enough: It does not correspond to the full freedom that can be found in God.

With this, Moltmann introduces the second level of freedom, *freedom as fellowship*. Moltmann clearly distances himself from an understanding of *freedom as domination*, as freedom was understood in the early days of liberation theology.[98] *Domination* does not create a fellowship of freedom for all.[99] Moltmann rightly refers to the fact that a society in which everyone is free does not mean that it is also one of solidarity:

---

93. Moltmann, *Spirit of Life*, 113.
94. Moltmann, *Spirit of Life*, 114.
95. Moltmann, *Spirit of Life*, 115.
96. Moltmann, *Spirit of Life*, 115.
97. Moltmann, *Spirit of Life*, 115.
98. For Moltmann's critique of *freedom as domination* see the section in Gutiérrez, Apriciation and criticism, 51–54.
99. Moltmann, *Spirit of Life*, 117.

"Carried to its logical conclusion, this is a society of free and equal but solitary individuals. No one disposes over anyone else, everyone disposes over himself."[100] Such a fellowship is not a fellowship created by the *God of love*: "Freedom as domination destroys life. As domination, freedom is not freedom in its true sense. The truth of human freedom is to be found in the love that longs for life. This leads to unhindered, open community in solidarity."[101] Love as a component of freedom is compelling: "It is only in love that human freedom enters its free world."[102] How is this love expressed as the truth of freedom? Moltmann explains this as follows: "I become truly free if I open my life for other people and share it with them, and if other people open their lives for me, and share them with me. Then the other person is no longer the limitation of my freedom, but its extension."[103] In this sense, *freedom as fellowship* is a "counter-movement to the history of class conflict and the struggle for power, in which freedom could only be interpreted as domination."[104]

Faith in Christ leads beyond freedom as fellowship. Moltmann describes the Christian faith essentially as a hope of resurrection.[105] The hope of resurrection founded in Christ is directed toward the future and opens up the third level of freedom, *freedom as the future*.[106] Moltmann understands the freedom of the Christian life as "participation in God's creative acts."[107] This action of God is future-oriented. In contrast to the past, which has no scope for creativity, the future is open and, with God, full of possibilities:

> Up to now we have seen freedom either as domination, in the relationship between subject and object, or as sociality, in the relationships between equal determining subjects. Now we discover freedom in the relationship of determining subjects to the project they share. Without this dimension freedom has not been fully understood. In the relationship to a shared project,

100. Moltmann, *Spirit of Life*, 118.
101. Moltmann, *Spirit of Life*, 119.
102. Moltmann, *Spirit of Life*, 118.
103. Moltmann, *Spirit of Life*, 118.
104. Mark Wallace has radically extended this thesis: "To follow the Holy Spirit's revolutionary prompting is to risk a liminal existence vulnerable to attack by mainstream members of society who bitterly resist the mixing of opposites and the crossing of cultural boundaries" (Wallace, *Fragments of the Holy Spirit*, 6).
105. Moltmann, *Spirit of Life*, 119.
106. Moltmann, *Spirit of Life*, 119.
107. Moltmann, *Spirit of Life*, 119.

freedom is a creative movement. Anyone who transcends the present in the direction of the future in thought, word and act is free. Freedom has to be understood as the free space for creative freedom.[108]

It is this future dimension that transforms a "freedom from" into a "freedom to."[109] In the encounter with the liberating God, humankind experiences freedom as an experience of God: "What Israel experienced in its liberation from Egypt as God's revelation as 'Lord,' is experienced by believers in their fellowship with Christ. In this they experience the freedom of the Holy Spirit.... The liberating God of Israel is active in Jews and Gentiles in the 'Spirit.'"[110] For Moltmann, this spiritual experience is tied to Christ. Moltmann sees this reference explicitly in Paul's second letter to the Corinthians (3:17): "Where the Holy Spirit of the Lord is, there is freedom." This connection is significant:

> In practical terms this means that discipleship of Jesus and the liberating Spirit act together, in order to lead people into true freedom. Pentecostal and charismatic experiences of the Holy Spirit become spiritualistically insubstantial and illusory without the personal and political discipleship of Jesus. Personal and political discipleship of Jesus becomes legalistic and arid without the spirituality which "drinks from its own wells," to quote Gutiérrez.[111]

The dominion of God is expressed in the liberation of creation. God's dominion is, therefore, experienced by humans as freedom and has "nothing to do with slavery, either outward or inward."[112] The three dimensions of freedom mentioned above "are explored through faith, through love, and through hope. In them we correspond in our relationships to the liberating, the social, the coming God."[113]

---

108. Moltmann, *Spirit of Life*, 119.

109. Moltmann, *Spirit of Life*, 120.

110. Moltmann, *Spirit of Life*, 120, my translation. I rather use for this quote my own translation, since the official translation, printed by Fortress Press, replaced "Spirit" with "Christ," which is not true to the German original.

111. Moltmann, *Spirit of Life*, 121.

112. Moltmann, *Spirit of Life*, 121, my translation.

113. Moltmann, *Spirit of Life*, 122.

Sanctification

After considering the links between social ethics and pneumatology, we now turn to the subject of sanctification. As we shall see, there are key elements to Moltmann's social ethics in his exploration of the topic of sanctification.

For Moltmann, social justice is inevitably linked to the concept of *salvation*. This is clearly expressed in the four social dimensions that Moltmann assigns to the salvation of God and which he formulated as early as the World Mission Conference in Bangkok (1972–1973):

1. Salvation takes effect in the struggle for economic justice and against the exploitation of human beings by human beings;
2. Salvation takes effect in the struggle for human dignity against political oppression by other human beings;
3. Salvation takes effect in the struggle for solidarity against the alienation of human beings;
4. Salvation takes effect in the struggle for hope against despair in individual life. Without social justice there is no political liberty; without political liberty cultural alienations cannot be overcome; without cultural identity there is no personal hope—and vice versa.

> These four dimensions are interconnected, but different situations call for different priorities. There are varying gifts and tasks, but there is one Spirit and one salvation.[114]

How does Moltmann connect the social dimensions of salvation with sanctification? Sanctification is usually linked to human action in relation to moral rather than social demands.[115] Interestingly, Moltmann does not link sanctification to human action but to the action of God: "The word 'sanctification' is then used for a divine act through which God chooses something for himself and makes it his own, thus letting it participate in his nature. In this way the Creator 'sanctifies' the sabbath and makes it the feast of creation."[116] As further examples, God names the election of the people of Israel the temple, the holy city and the holy land, which he sanctifies thereby. So: "What belongs to God is holy, like

---

114. Moltmann, *Ethics of Hope*, 37.
115. Moltmann, *Spirit of Life*, 174–75.
116. Moltmann, *Spirit of Life*, 174.

God himself. It follows from this that sanctification is an act of God in us and for us, like justification and calling. The people whom God justifies he also sanctifies (Rom 8:30)."[117] It is this choosing by God that makes "unsanctified, sinful men and women . . . pronounced holy, and made holy, by God out of grace for Christ's sake. . . . 'The communion of saints' in the Apostles' Creed is not an assembly of people who are saints in the moral sense. It is simply the community of pardoned sinners, reconciled enemies, believers."[118] In this sense, humankind also finds its justification in God's salvific work. This justification includes both victims and perpetrators.[119]

Moltmann places the concept of *justification* very close to the concept of *rebirth*:

> If we call this event justification, we are describing it as the operation of Christ. If we call it regeneration, we are describing the operation of the Holy Spirit. We need both viewpoints if we are to understand the event completely. If the discipleship of Jesus has also to be understood as life in the Holy Spirit, then being-in-Christ and life-from-the-Spirit mean the same thing, but seen from different sides.[120]

The interlinking of justification and rebirth means nothing less than that God's promise in sanctification is interlinked with God's demand of discipleship: "Sanctification as gift leads to sanctification as charge. For whatever God declares to be holy ought to be kept holy by human beings: the sabbath, the people, created beings. God's community with us is the foundation and motive for our community with God."[121] However, this demand has nothing to do with performance:

> So to sanctify life does not mean manipulating it religiously and morally. It means being freed and justified, loved and affirmed, and more and more alive. Life in God's Spirit is a life entrusted to the guidance and drive of the Holy Spirit, a life that lets the Holy Spirit come.[122]

---

117. Moltmann, *Spirit of Life*, 174.
118. Moltmann, *Spirit of Life*, 174.
119. Moltmann, *Spirit of Life*, 129–38.
120. Moltmann, *Spirit of Life*, 153.
121. Moltmann, *Spirit of Life*, 147.
122. Moltmann, *Spirit of Life*, 176.

Sanctification is based on acceptance by God and finds expression in gratitude for life: "If whatever God has made and loves is holy, then life is holy in itself, and to live life with love and joy means sanctifying it. We do not first sanctify it through what we make of our lives. We already sanctify it through our very existence."[123] At the same time, sanctification has an effect that has a clear direction: "The 'Holy' Spirit is the Holy Spirit who sanctifies life, and he sanctifies it with the Creator's passion for the life of what he has created, and with the Creator's wrath against all the forces that want to destroy it."[124] It is God Himself who gives immeasurable value to life in all its dimensions, and it is the reverence for the preciousness of this life that opens up new possibilities: "Reverence for one's own life and life from the Holy Spirit of life lead beyond moral self-control, and throw open a new spontaneity of faith."[125]

Moltmann uses Methodist John Wesley's understanding of sanctification to illustrate that the life-negating and life-destroying forces can have different forms and different contents at different times and that sanctification as an expression of discipleship must also emphasize different points.[126] He concludes:

> The *vita christiana* is always related to its time and context. If the Christian life sees itself as a witness to Christ and God's Spirit, then it cannot be a religious reflection of the given ethics of a particular society; nor can it be related to these ethics in a merely negative sense either. As a witness to salvation, the Christian testimony must be related to the sicknesses of the given *society in a healing way*.[127]

Sanctification cannot avoid naming everything that threatens and wants to destroy life.[128] The question arises: "For what sicknesses of our time will the Christian life prove to be healing?"[129] The following are two examples that Moltmann describes as diseases of our time: In the Sheffield Report, which deals with the fellowship of women and men in the church, there is a long dialogue between Jürgen Moltmann and his wife

---

123. Moltmann, *Spirit of Life*, 176.
124. Moltmann, *Spirit of Life*, 178.
125. Moltmann, *Spirit of Life*, 173.
126. Moltmann, *Spirit of Life*, 173.
127. Moltmann, *Spirit of Life*, 171.
128. Moltmann, *Spirit of Life*, 163.
129. Moltmann, *Spirit of Life*, 171.

Elisabeth Moltmann-Wendel about patriarchal structures within the church.[130] Another example is the issue of environmental destruction, which Moltmann addresses directly in connection with sanctification.[131]

"The God who creates justice for those who suffer violence, the God who exalts the humiliated and executed Christ—that is the God of hope for the new world of righteousness and justice and peace."[132] The salvation of this God is all-embracing. Moltmann says:

> The soul in the body, the person in the community, the community in the sequence of generations, the generations of human beings in the shared house of the earth. If we perceive human life as existing in these interrelated sectors, we begin to live less ruthlessly and more sensitively. Then life *at the expense* of others is no longer possible. Life *together with* others is enjoined on us. . . . "Sanctification today" does not merely include a healthful life. It also means accepting human life's natural frailty and mortality.[133]

With that, returning to Moltmann's quote which, in the introduction to this section, explores the four social dimensions of salvation: An ethics that orients itself to this very God can consequently be "neither a conformist responsibility in the world nor a separatist flight from the world. It is guidance for changing the world."[134]

---

130. Moltmann and Moltmann-Wendel, "Menschlich werden," 37–53.

131. Moltmann, *Spirit of Life*, 172. Moltmann writes there: "You shall love God and this earth and all your fellow creatures with all your heart, and with all your soul, and with all your might! Anyone who loves 'the living God' loves the life of all living things. Reverence for life always begins with respect for weaker life, vulnerable life. In the world of human beings this means the poor, the sick, and the defenceless. The same is true for the world of nature. The weaker plant and animal species are the first creatures to be threatened by extinction. Reverence for life must apply to them first of all, since they require protection.

Today sanctification means defending God's creation against human aggression, exploitation and destruction. This has a personal dimension: what am I doing about my consumerism and my refuse? Am I part of the throw-away society or am I resisting it in creation's name? It has a social dimension too: how can Christians, in joint discussion and shared worship, arrive at a reverent life-style? And there is also a political dimension: what laws for?" (Moltmann, *Spirit of Life*, 172).

132. Moltmann, *Ethics of Hope*, 40.

133. Moltmann, *Spirit of Life*, 173.

134. Moltmann, *Ethics of Hope*, 40.

Unity in Diversity, Diversity in Unity

The aspect of *fellowship* is already apparent in Moltmann's examination of the topic of sanctification. But how does Moltmann think of *fellowship* and where are these considerations of importance in the context of social ethics?

For Moltmann, fellowship is not only a theological entity, but also a social construct: The life of the church is part of social ethics, and because the church is part of God's mission, Moltmann's understanding of mission is, in turn, fundamental to his social ethics. The topic is touched on for the first time in *The Crucified God* and recurs repeatedly in his works right up to *Ethics of Hope*. Moltmann deals with the following questions in this context: Who belongs to the church? How do people belong to the fellowship of believers? What is the relationship of believers to God, to each other and to the world? The answer that Moltmann formulates to the above questions is, in its most concise form: *unity in diversity and diversity in unity*.[135]

Moltmann's first discussion about the fellowship of believers is not pneumatologically but rather epistemologically or christologically based. In his work *The Crucified God*, he deals with the platonic thesis "like is known only by like," which bases *knowing* in *recognition* (this is the analogical recognition principle).[136] However, the analogical recognition principle is one-sided and does not apply, for example, in the relationship between man and God—God could then only be recognized by God: "If like is known only by like, then the Son of God would have had to remain in heaven, because he would be unrecognizable by anything earthly."[137] The analogy must therefore be expanded to include the dialectic principle of recognition. This principle, which can be traced back to Hippocrates, assumes that recognition is only in the opposite: applied to Christian theology, this means: "God is only revealed as 'God' in His opposite: godlessness and abandonment by God. In concrete terms, God is revealed in the cross of Christ, who was abandoned by God. His grace is revealed in sinners. His righteousness is revealed in the unrighteous and in those without rights, and his gracious election in the damned."[138] For the church, this means:

---

135. Moltmann, *Spirit of Life*, 180–81.
136. Moltmann, *Crucified God*, 26.
137. Moltmann, *Crucified God*, 27.
138. Moltmann, *Crucified God*, 27.

> The theology of the cross must begin with contradiction and cannot be built upon premature correspondences.... If a being is revealed only in its opposite, then the church which is the church of the crucified Christ cannot consist of an assembly of like persons who mutually affirm each other, but must be constituted of unlike persons.... Its principle of justification is not similarity, but the justification of the other (Hegel), the creative making righteous of the unrighteous and attribution of rights to those who are without rights....
>
> Nor can it [the church] shut itself away from what is alien in a social ghetto, but for the sake of its identity in the crucified Christ, must reveal him and itself, by following him, in what is different and alien. Otherwise, it does justice neither to the one to whom it appeals nor to those to whom he revealed himself.[139]

In *The Spirit of Life*, Moltmann makes it clear that this approach has a pneumatological dimension, even if it is not explicitly mentioned, where he shows that *the Spirit of God* is also the *Spirit of Passion* and the *Spirit of Christ Crucified*.[140]

An interesting justification for *unity in diversity* can be found in *Church in the Power of the Spirit*. There, Moltmann advocates for the thesis that, first and foremost, the church must reflect the dominion of Christ in itself. Here, too, it becomes clear how fundamental ecclesiology (and thus also missiology) is to understanding Moltmann's social ethics: The church of Jesus has to represent the lordship or dominion of Jesus and not the prevailing conditions of society—otherwise it is a church, but not Jesus' church:

> It cannot be a racial church that allows segregation and racial discrimination within its own fellowship. It cannot be a class church that sanctions class division and class struggle from above within its own fellowship. It cannot be a male church that tolerates patriarchal structures of rule within itself. It cannot be a national church that affirms national arrogance through its own borders and ideas. Corresponding to the liberating lordship of Christ, for the church: "There is neither Jew nor Gentile, neither slave nor free, nor is there male and female, for you are all one in Christ Jesus." (Gal 3:28; see also Rom 10:12; 1:12–13). In the church of Christ, the religious, economic and gendered

---

139. Moltmann, *Crucified God*, 28. For expansion on this, see Moltmann, *Experiences in Theology*, 169; *Spirit of Life*, 18–28.

140. Moltmann, *Spirit of Life*, 62. See "The Shekinah of God as the Presence of God in the World" in chapter 3, 229–32.

privileges that apply in the wider environment are suspended. But if they have been suspended and are no longer valid, then another power prevails here, the power of the Holy Spirit.[141]

Moltmann emphasizes that the church is not "holy dominion," but rather the "fellowship of believers who follow the one Lord and have been laid hold by the same Spirit."[142] It is "in principle the community of equals," who are "equipped with equal rights and equal dignity." Why? Moltmann's reasoning is: "All have the gift of the Spirit."[143]

Moltmann's probably most comprehensive and many-faceted explanation of *unity* and *diversity* can be found in *Spirit of Life*. A first pneumatological reference can be found in the examination of the concept of *ruach*[144] and its relationship to God the Father and God the Son. With regard to *ruach*, which represents female attributes in the Trinity, Moltmann formulates specific socio-ethical demands on the fellowship of believers: "If the Trinity is a community, then what corresponds to it is the true human community of men and women. A certain de-patriarchalization of the picture of God results in a de-patriarchalization and de-hierarchalization of the church too."[145]

For Moltmann, another starting point for *unity in diversity* is charisms. For Moltmann, every life, in its particular uniqueness, has the potential to be a gift. This life is "always specific, never general. Life is everywhere different, never the same. It is female or male, Yong or old, handicapped or non-handicapped, Jewish or Gentile, white or black, and so forth."[146]

Moltmann understands this specific life, in relation to 1 Cor 7:20–21, as a charism:

> When a person is called, whatever he is and brings with him becomes a charisma through his calling, since it is accepted by the Spirit and put at the service of the kingdom of God. So a Christian Jew should remain a Jew, and live according to the Torah. A Christian Gentile brings his Gentile existence into the community. Being a woman is a charisma and must not be surrendered in favour of patriarchal and male ways of thinking and

141. Moltmann, *Power of the Spirit*, 106.
142. Moltmann, *Power of the Spirit*, 106.
143. Moltmann, *Power of the Spirit*, 106.
144. See section "The *ruah* of God as the Materializing Spirit of God.
145. Moltmann, *Spirit of Life*, 160.
146. Moltmann, *Spirit of Life*, 180.

behaving. And in social conflicts too, being a Christian begins at the point where the man or woman is reached. . . . According to Ernst Käsemann, what he wants to say is that the lordship of Christ thrusts deeply into the secularity of the world. It is not merely special religious phenomena which become a "charismatic experience" for the believer.[147]

For Moltmann, the diversity of charisms is imperative for the health of the church. Only in their "free fullness," do they liberate and thus serve life.[148] With reference to 1 Cor 12:4, Moltmann emphasizes that it is the one Spirit that is working in the many gifts. At the same time, he critically remarks: "Today we have to stress the very opposite: there is one Spirit but there are many gifts. There is one God, who creates everything, but there are as many powers and energies as there are created beings. Love should unite the different gifts . . . but freedom must release these different gifts, is what we have to say today."[149] For Moltmann, this explicitly includes *all* life: "So the weak, the foolish and the people with disabilities also have their special charisma in the community of Christ's people. Why? All will be made like in form to the crucified Christ, because the crucified Christ has assumed not only true humanity but the whole misery of men and women too, so that he can heal it."[150] For Moltmann, every human life is "life assumed by God in Christ, and in him already partakes here and now in God's eternal life," which, in turn, means "whatever has been assumed by the Son of God who became human and was crucified, is then already whole, good and beautiful in God's sight."[151] This beauty has nothing to do with a romantic or idealized concept of people with disabilities but rather with the revelation of God in suffering, in need and limitation:

---

147. Moltmann, *Spirit of Life*, 182. In his explanations, Moltmann follows, as he says himself (181), Käsemann, "Amt und Gemeinde."

148. Moltmann, *Spirit of Life*, 182.

149. If the "free fullness of their diversity" applies for the benefit of the charisms, the question of using the charisms for the benefit of diversity also conversely arises. Moltmann questions this critically: "Where are the charismata of the 'charismatics' in the everyday world, in the peace movement, in the movements for liberation, in the ecology movement? If charismata are not given us so that we can flee from this world into a world of religious dreams, but if they are intended to witness to the liberating lordship of Christ in this world's conflicts, then the charismatic movement must not become a non-political religion, let alone a de-politicized one" (Moltmann, *Spirit of Life*, 186).

150. Moltmann, *Spirit of Life*, 192.

151. Moltmann, *Spirit of Life*, 192.

> In the pains, slights and disablements, and in "the sufferings of the Spirit," God's suffering power is revealed. So there is no good diaconal, or charitable, service given by the non-handicapped to the handicapped unless they have previously perceived and accepted the diaconal ministry of the handicapped to the non-handicapped. Congregations without any disabled members are disabled and disabling congregations.[152]

This has wide-ranging consequences for the church, its social structure and, therefore, also for social ethics: "If . . . we start from the early Christian experience of Pentecost, we have to develop a pneumatological concept of the church: there is one Spirit and many gifts. Everyone concerned, whether man or woman, is endowed and committed through his or her calling, wherever he or she is, and whatever he or she is."[153] Not only must the church be rethought in this regard, but also what God does outside of it:

> Because the Spirit is poured out "on all flesh," merely ecclesiastical flesh cannot be meant. Cultural experiences and movements too are shot through by the Spirit. Whatever accords with the fulfillment of the Joel promise in church and culture is the operation of the Spirit. Whatever contradicts it is spiritless and deadly.[154]

Eschatological Hope, Ethics, and Spirit

In the areas considered so far, whether mission, hope or pneumatology, the concept of eschatology has repeatedly arisen. In the following section, how eschatology is relevant to Moltmann's social ethics is considered.

For Moltmann, the source and goal of any hopeful (socio-ethical) action is the eschatological promise of the coming kingdom of God. That this hope must necessarily be of an eschatological nature is because only hope directed toward the future of God is able to break through present boundaries:

> In our traditions, past hopes and experiences are always preserved. That has its value, but it is only limited value. No tradition should determine the future. At best, it can pave the way for

---

152. Moltmann, *Spirit of Life*, 193.
153. Moltmann, *Spirit of Life*, 240.
154. Moltmann, *Spirit of Life*, 240–41.

the future. The Spirit itself is always creating something new and is full of surprises. He is not bound by tradition but takes from them what points the way to the future. Christianity is more than a tradition, it is a hope.[155]

The eschatological kingdom of God shows the ultimate historical possibilities and threats based on the promise of the resurrection and the cross of Christ.[156] In this respect, for Moltmann, *Christian eschatology* is always "future of Christ," and its language is one of promise.[157] For example, the promise of the resurrection of the dead leads "at once to love for the true life of the whole imperilled and impaired creation," the "promise of divine righteousness in the event of justification of the godless leads immediately to the hunger for divine right in the godless world," with the "struggle for public, bodily obedience."[158] The promised but not yet realized future stands in contradiction to the given reality. This is where Christian ethics comes in, standing in opposition to the given reality in the light of Christ's resurrection. In summary, one can say that the eschatological promises of the coming kingdom of God are the pivot and source of all Christian behavior for Moltmann:

> Because the kingdom of God is the future of all history, it transcends the historical future and all anticipations within history. But in this very way, the kingdom will become the power of hope in history and the source of these anticipations with which we prepare the way for the coming of God.[159]

The Holy Spirit plays a key role in this. It is the experience of the Spirit that first awakens the longing for the coming, eschatological kingdom: "The experience of the Spirit is the reason for the eschatological longing for the completion of salvation, the redemption of the body and the new creation of all things. Impelled by the Spirit, Christians cry 'Maranatha, come, Lord Jesus!' (Rev 22:20)."[160] It is precisely this experience of the Spirit that does not lead to a longing for the hereafter but rather awakens the longing for the incursion of God's future into the present, and this incursion, in turn, is fundamental to the understanding of social ethics:

155. Parfey, *Gemeinschaft von Frauen und Männern*, 47, my translation.
156. Moltmann, *Theology of Hope*, 224–45.
157. Moltmann, *Theology of Hope*, 225.
158. Moltmann, *Theology of Hope*, 225.
159. Moltmann, *Ethics of Hope*, 36–37.
160. Moltmann, *Spirit of Life*, 73.

> It is the experience of the Holy Spirit which makes Christians in every society restless and homeless, and on the search for the kingdom of God (Heb 13:14), for it is this experience of God which makes them controvert and contravene a godless world of violence and death. The Spirit makes them rich in experience and rich in hope, but poor and lonely in a world gone wrong. The cry for the coming of the Holy Spirit takes up out of the depths the cries of the dumb, and brings them before God.[161]

According to Moltmann, even the cry for the assistance of the Spirit is the work of the Spirit, because: "The sighs of fettered creation are taken up by the sighs of the Spirit who dwells in it, and are brought before God. The cry for God is itself divine."[162] However, the eschatological work of the Spirit not only brings about a longing and participation in its groaning. His work also demands to be visible and concrete in the present. Moltmann illustrates this using the Book of Joel. The prophet Joel promises an end-time outpouring of the Spirit (3:1–5), which is quoted in Acts 2:17–21:

> The eschatological hope for experience of the Spirit is shared by women and men equally. Men and women will "prophesy" and proclaim the gospel. According to the prophecy in Joel 2, through the shared experience of the Spirit the privileges of men compared with women, of the old compared with the Yong, and of masters compared with "men-servants and maidservants" will be abolished. In the kingdom of the Spirit, everyone will experience his and her own endowment and all will experience the new fellowship together.[163]

Moltmann relates biblical testimony to the current longing for a new form of fellowship between the sexes and says: "The 'new community of women and men' which is being sought in many churches today is a question of experience of the Spirit."[164] At the same time, he is of the opinion that the eschatological promise is not fulfilled.

> The experience of the Spirit in the present is the beginning (ἀπαρχή) and advance pledge or foretaste (ἀρραβών) of the coming kingdom of glory (Rom 8:23; 2 Cor 1:22; 5:5; Eph 1:14). In

---

161. Moltmann, *Spirit of Life*, 73–74.
162. Moltmann, *Spirit of Life*, 76.
163. Moltmann, *Spirit of Life*, 239.
164. Moltmann, *Spirit of Life*, 239.

this the new creation of all things is already experienced—experienced now, for all, representatively and in anticipation.[165]

With all his emphasis on the work of God's Spirit, Moltmann tries to avoid a separation of the *natural* and *supernatural*, since this is neither helpful nor does it further progress understanding. At the same time, it is important to distinguish between the reality and constraints of this "world" and God's works and interventions. Moltmann achieves this by understanding all works of the Spirit as part of eschatological reality: "In the experience of the Spirit, the Spirit's charismatic energies will interpenetrate body and soul. These energies are not 'supernatural' gifts. They are 'the powers of the age to come' (Heb 6:5)."[166] Against this background, Moltmann also claims that the concept of the church, and thus also its mission and ethics, must be developed pneumatologically, with the starting point being the early Christian Pentecostal experience.[167] Only in this way can the previous limits be overcome and the light of the future kingdom of God shine in the church of the present: "The pneumatological concept of the church discerns that church and culture are interwoven in the interplay of the 'spiritual'—which means life-giving—impulses conferred on 'all flesh.'"[168] Using the example of man and woman, Moltmann explains this as follows:

> In this case the eschatological experience of the Spirit takes in both Christianity and the feminist movement, and brings them into a mutually fruitful relationship. Feminist theology mediates between the two in as much as a powerful trend in it uncovers the often suppressed traditions in Christian history which have to do with the liberation of women, and works for the psycho-social liberation of women in church and society. Christianity learns from the feminist movement that the patriarchal disparagement and suppression of women's charismata are sins against the Spirit. The feminist movement can learn from Christianity, and from other movements, that it is not merely a question of the human rights of women; it is a matter of the rebirth of all the living. And through both Christianity and the feminist movement, men will be liberated from the dominating role which isolates them from life and alienates them from themselves,

---

165. Moltmann, *Spirit of Life*, 74.
166. Moltmann, *Spirit of Life*, 74.
167. Moltmann, *Spirit of Life*, 239.
168. Moltmann, *Spirit of Life*, 241.

freed for their true humanity, their own charismata, and for a community with women on all levels in society and the church, a community which will further life.[169]

169. Moltmann, *Spirit of Life*, 241.

4

Social Ethics in Dialogue
Convergences and Divergences between Moltmann and the Pentecostal Voices

AFTER EXPLAINING MOLTMANN'S *PNEUMATOLOGY* in correlation with *social ethics*, the cornerstones of Pentecostal social ethics (pneumatology, encounter, unity in particularity and particularity in unity, collaborative eschatology and hope) are set in dialogue with Moltmann. Aspects from the beginnings of Pentecostalism and the non-Pentecostal voices are also considered. In the following sections we will see where there are fundamental differences between Moltmann and the Pentecostal position, and how these complement or further one another.

Collaborative Pneumatology

Pentecostals have already taken a critical stance on Moltmann's pneumatology laid out in *The Spirit of Life* within the framework of *JPT* 4 (1994) 5–58. Likewise, in that dialogue, Moltmann also gave a response in *JPT* 4 (1994) 59–70 to the Pentecostal assessments.[1] That dialogue is considered here only to a very limited extent; the focus in the following discussion is on the socio-ethical implications of pneumatology.

---

1. A continuation of the same dialogue is the answer to Moltmann's response by Macchia, "Spirit and the Life."

What the Pentecostal voices, and also Moltmann, have in common is that the work of the Holy Spirit does not primarily have its significance in the individual experience of the Holy Spirit. Rather, the work of the Holy Spirit is interpreted with regard to living together in fellowship. If we look at the various accents of the Pentecostal voices, we find that there are definitely parallels in Moltmann's pneumatology: For Wenk, God's Spirit is the agent that integrates people into the community and allows them to participate in the worldly dimension of salvation.[2] The specific works of the Holy Spirit should be indicative of its ethical and moral significance and its implications for the further history of the community.[3] Moltmann offers a comparable approach to liberation: The liberating experience of faith brought about by turning toward Christ becomes the basis for dealing with fellow humans.[4] The individual experience of God in dealing with one's neighbor finds expression in caring solidarity toward fellow humans and thus shapes the fellowship.[5]

Stephenson finds the aspect of pneumatology described above in the soteriological works of God's Spirit. Stephenson points to the conversion and initiation of peoples and generations wrought by the Holy Spirit. The works of the Holy Spirit on the gentiles are interpreted as God's claim that these gentiles also belong to God's people. The spiritual experiences of the individuals point the way for the social ethics of the new people of God.[6] Moltmann attaches the soteriological dimension of the Holy Spirit by showing that justification is not an event that can be separated from rebirth, but that justification is to be understood *as* rebirth.[7]

Yong emphasizes the importance of the Holy Spirit's empowerment for mission, which, in turn, brings the focus onto the community and its transformation and growth.[8] Moltmann also takes up this aspect in connection with mission. He emphasizes "the gift of the church community with the Holy Spirit of freedom and liberation," which, despite the different gifts, knows no separation of the fellowship.[9]

---

2. Wenk, *Community-Forming Power*, 288.
3. Moltmann, *Spirit of Life*, 32.
4. Moltmann, *Spirit of Life*, 99–100.
5. Moltmann, *Spirit of Life*, 126.
6. Stephenson, *Dismantling the Dualisms*, 110.
7. Moltmann, *Spirit of Life*, 149.
8. Yong, *Days of Caesar*, 211–52.
9. Moltmann, *Spirit of Life*, 11.

Solivan refers to the Holy Spirit, which not only affirms the cultural particularity within the people of God but, moreover, holds them together as one people despite their diversity.[10] His argument, like Moltmann's, places the emphasis on the Holy Spirit-given gifts of believers, with emphasis on Acts 2 and the gift of tongues. God's Spirit empowers the followers of Jesus to speak the languages and dialects of the different peoples present in Jerusalem.[11] Thereby, the Holy Spirit also creates a foundation for the overcoming of prejudice against the "others."[12] However, overcoming prejudices does not go far enough for Solivan. For him, the fullness of the Holy Spirit only finds expression in the variety of different cultures.[13] Moltmann also sees the empowerment of the Spirit of God as a work that unites His people in their diversity. Moltmann does not attach this to speaking in tongues or extraordinary works of the Holy Spirit, but points out that through the Spirit of God *everything* that constitutes the believer becomes a charism.[14] This not only includes the cultural background of the believers, but also their gender, biography, etc. Moltmann rightly emphasizes that differences between people go beyond culture, race, gender, class, etc. For Moltmann, where the barriers of privilege of the environment are overridden in the church, that is where the power of the Holy Spirit prevails.[15] It is a "fellowship of equals," who are "endowed with equal rights and equal dignity," because "all have the gift of the Holy Spirit."[16]

It is noticeable that Moltmann strongly ties the work of the Holy Spirit to Christ with regard to social ethics, without the Holy Spirit being subordinated to Christ. A strength of this approach is a "grounding" of Moltmann's pneumatology, which, based on Christ's life and suffering, stands against any form of triumphalism and appreciates the work of the Holy Spirit in the creaturely. Moltmann's approach rightly questions the Pentecostal understanding of charisms, which all too often reduces the works of the Holy Spirit to spectacular miracle works, and thereby

10. Solivan, *Spirit, Pathos and Liberation*, 118.
11. Solivan, *Spirit, Pathos and Liberation*, 117.
12. Solivan, *Spirit, Pathos and Liberation*, 118.
13. Solivan, *Spirit, Pathos and Liberation*, 142–43.
14. Approaches to overcoming the traditional Pentecostal distinction between the natural and the supernatural can also be found in Pentecostal journals, such as Yong, "Spirit at Work in the World."
15. Moltmann, *Power of the Spirit*, 106.
16. Moltmann, *Power of the Spirit*, 106.

overlooks the creaturely effects of the Holy Spirit.[17] What is striking about the Pentecostal voices is that, in relation to social ethics, they heavily emphasize the Pentecost of Acts 2. It is no exaggeration to say that Acts 2 is *the* pneumatological focal point of Pentecostal theology—and thus also of Pentecostal social ethics. As a result, the eruptive incursion of God as the starting point for pneumatological/eschatological social ethics is more consciously accentuated in the Pentecostal voices than is the case with Moltmann.[18] In this regard, Pentecostal spirituality and theology has always had a certain proximity to forms of apocalypticism, i.e., the incursion of God into this story.[19] Interestingly, the four Pentecostal voices then "land" in a place similar to Moltmann's: they also have a "grounding" or concretization and materialization of God's salvation in this world.[20] This makes perfect sense—social ethics is ultimately about responsible behaviour toward and with each other in the here and now. It is also notable that both parties, despite the emphasis on the immanent dimension, do not dismiss the transcendent dimension of God's work.[21] The impression arises, at least with regard to social ethics, that Moltmann and the Pentecostals are approaching these things in very different ways, but they are actually closer together than it appears at first glance.

Moltmann and the Pentecostal voices agree that, to put it simply, God's Spirit creates space in which people are invited to participate in the work of the Holy Spirit. With reference to collaborative eschatology,[22] this pneumatological approach might be called *collaborative pneumatology*. The starting point for collaborative pneumatology is the Holy Spirit, and the works also happen primarily through the Holy Spirit. At the same time, people share responsibility: it is in the people's hands to decide whether to engage in and participate in the works of the Holy Spirit. The context of

17. Wenk also pointed this out in Wenk, "Spiritual Gifts."

18. Wariboko writes that in the Pentecostal understanding grace is viewed as "disruptive," something that "breaks into the order of things" allowing "freedom to appear, to flourish as such." But the Pentecostal principle also describes a force that is immanent to life, as a "movement toward openness to future possibilities." In short, the Pentecostal principle points to that which is both transcendent and immanent: "Grace expresses the hidden potentials of a situation, existence, or life, as well as transcends them" (Wariboko, *Pentecostal Principle*, 2).

19. Land, *Pentecostal Spirituality*, 58–121.

20. See Volf, "Materiality of Salvation."

21. See in particular Moltmann, *Resurrected to Eternal Life*.

22. See the terminology used by N. T. Wright and J. D. Crossan around *collaborative eschatology*.

collaborative pneumatology is the fellowship of believers—the fullness of the Holy Spirit is found only within the body of Christ.

As already mentioned, Acts 2 plays a role in the theology and tradition of the Pentecostal Movement that can hardly be overestimated. It has also already been mentioned that Acts 2 is a true focal point of pneumatology. Focal points inherently combine many aspects in a very condensed manner. The strength of these concentrations is that they have the potential to develop powerful dynamics. It is also noticeable that Pentecostal theology has been increasingly discovering the broad scope of the topics that are touched on in Acts 2. It has also already been mentioned that Acts 2 plays a subordinate role for Moltmann. This aspect of Moltmann's pneumatology has been repeatedly criticised by Pentecostal theologians. This criticism is not repeated here—it is up to the members of other church traditions to judge how Pentecostal theology, with Acts 2 as its starting point, can support the further development of their own theology—just as it is the task of the Pentecostal church to allow itself to be challenged and complemented by the other church traditions. Moltmann's pneumatological breadth and holistic approach is impressive. With this breadth, Moltmann can help the Pentecostals see aspects in Acts 2 that have previously been undiscovered by them, and to let them bear fruit. It is precisely this that makes it clear how important the dialogue between the different theological voices is.[23] In turn, Pentecostal pneumatology, with its starting point in Acts 2, contributes the experience of God's eruptive presence to the development of an ecumenically broad pneumatology.

Another important pneumatological focal point for social ethics can be found in Romans 8, as Wenk has pointed out.[24] The implications to be drawn require further development, and it is to be hoped that the various theological traditions can also be brought into a fruitful dialogue in this process.

---

23. Wariboko makes a similar point when he says, that the "number and diversity of tongues point to the irreducibly pluralistic nature of the power of the new. No one individual, entity, or institution is capable of incarnating it alone. No human being can be self-sufficient in holding the force of creativity, in storing the wind in his or her bosom." Pentecost is "a reflection of the irreducible pluralistic nature of existence, serendipitous nature of creativity, and restlessness of becoming" (Wariboko, *Pentecostal Principle*, 20).

24. See section "Romans 8:18–30 as a Basis for Social Ethics" above, 102–5.

Encounter[25]

For Moltmann, the aspect of encounter does not appear as an independent category, but it is, nonetheless, an important and recurring element of his theology. The encounter between a person and God is of central importance: "Experience comes first and then the theology; first the passion, then the action."[26] Only in the encounter the associated experience that a person has with God, and in the memory of these experiences, does the revealed future gain its credibility: "The story of the divine promise is told and passed on in the form of the remembered hopes of the people. This is remembrance in which one can live, and which is essential for living."[27] It is also in the experience of God that, according to Moltmann, the experience of liberation is located:

> For Israel, the experience of God and experiences of liberation are two aspects of the same thing. According to the first commandment (Exod 20:2), God reveals himself to the people as "the Lord" by leading them out of slavery into the promised land of liberty. Israel experienced God's "lordship" as her liberation, and in the experience of her liberation had this unique experience of God.[28]

This experience also applies in the New Testament context:

> Through faith in Jesus the messiah, Christians have very much the same experience: "Now the Lord is the Spirit, and where the Spirit of the Lord is, there is freedom" (2 Cor 3:17). In the Spirit, Christ is manifested as "the Lord," and in the Spirit people experience what it is to be free. According to the experiences of Israel and according to the experiences of Christian faith, the experience of God and the experience of freedom are so deeply fused that they belong indissolubly together and become almost synonymous.[29]

---

25. For a discussion on the use of the term encounter, see the section in chapter 2, "Commonalities Among the Different Socio-Ethical Issues," 214–219.

26. Moltmann, *Experiences in Theology*, 24. Of course, the importance of the human-human encounter for Moltmann should not be underestimated (e.g., Moltmann, *Spirit of Life*, 236–48). The human-human encounter is also a topic of discussion for all Pentecostal voices and there are no fundamental differences here for Moltmann. Therefore, this aspect will not be examined in more detail in the context of the dialogue.

27. Moltmann, *Experiences in Theology*, 33.

28. Moltmann, *Spirit of Life*, 111.

29. Moltmann, *Spirit of Life*, 111.

This inseparable connection between the encounter with God and the experience of liberation is the basic tenor of the encounter as an important contribution by Moltmann to pneumatologically based social ethics. If the God of the Bible is the God of liberation, then the requirement on the church of Jesus and its social ethics can be no other than that this liberation experience should also be accessible for all people who encounter this very church. In other words, the encounter with God, as an experience of liberation, is fundamental for all further encounters, whether as individuals or as a church in the collective.

Similarly to Moltmann, the God-human encounter is also of central importance for Solivan. He explicitly refers to the incarnation of Christ[30] and emphasizes the identification of God with suffering. In the encounter with God, in which he himself becomes a poor Galilean and has thus identified himself with the oppressed, Solivan points out the role-modelling in God's actions: Injustice is only tackled when there is identification with the sufferer. This identification, in turn, only happens in fellowship with those affected, in the sense of not being a "church *for* the poor," but becoming a "church *of* the poor."[31] Moltmann gives the impression that he understands the encounter between God and people more broadly and fundamentally than Solivan does. Solivan primarily links the experience of liberation with Jesus' role-modelling for the behavior of the fellowship of believers, whereas Moltmann fundamentally understands the experience of God and the experience of freedom as inseparable experiences that are constitutive for the people of God: the liberating experience of God creates identity.[32] Those who identify with Christ cannot help but to do as Christ did: "Christian identification with the crucified Christ means solidarity with the sufferings of the poor and the misery both of the oppressed and the oppressor."[33] In other words, for Moltmann, the liberating encounter with God does not primarily lead to "correct" behavior, but to a new identity, from which new behavior is only secondarily born. The new identity in Christ allows the follower of Christ to naturally turn to "others" and to show solidarity with them.[34] In this sense, Christian identity can only be revealed in the encounter with the "other."

30. Solivan, *Spirit, Pathos and Liberation*, 83.
31. Solivan, *Spirit, Pathos and Liberation*, 84.
32. Moltmann, *Crucified God*, 25.
33. Moltmann, *Crucified God*, 25.
34. Moltmann, *Crucified God*, 28.

The idea that Christian identity can only be revealed in an encounter in solidarity with others is foreign to the Pentecostal voices in terms of this exclusiveness. However, Wenk comes close to Moltmann with his approach: For him, the identity of the fellowship of believers is formed by God's Spirit in the encounter with others and strangers.[35] Thus, for Wenk too, the encounter with the other, with the stranger, is central, not for revelation, but for the formation of the identity of the people of God.

The encounter with the other and the stranger as a starting point for a changed approach or reorientation of behavior can be found both in Moltmann and in the Pentecostal voices. Moltmann takes up this aspect in connection with the eschatological experience of the Holy Spirit, which occurs in the interaction between church and culture.[36] For Solivan, the human-human encounter becomes the starting point for solidarity-based action, where those who are not affected share in the suffering of those affected on a personal, systematic and structural level.[37] This experience makes them fellow victims and allows them to take action against the abuses. For Wenk, the encounter between the fellowship and the marginalized triggers the process of self-definition for the new people of God. In this process, the parties involved depend on each other to recognize and implement God's intentions.[38] The encounters between the different groups constantly challenge the new people of God to examine life and practice.[39] Yong sees the community of believers as a place where the unequal (needy and privileged) meet and are thereby given the opportunity to counterbalance inequality.[40] The encounters within the fellowship of believers have the potential to shape hearts with a Trinitarian and Kingdom orientation.[41] For Stephenson, the inclusion of women as equal partners is essential for the design of church structures and the understanding of service, as otherwise the church does not do justice to its God-founded identity as a community of equals.[42]

It is striking that, for some dialogue partners, Christian identity repeatedly plays a significant role in the area of encounters, whether it is

35. Moltmann, *Experiences in Theology*, 281.
36. Moltmann, *Spirit of Life*, 239–40.
37. Solivan, *Spirit, Pathos and Liberation*, 86.
38. Wenk, *Community-Forming Power*, 314.
39. Wenk, *Community-Forming Power*, 286.
40. Yong, *Days of Caesar*, 299.
41. Yong, *Days of Caesar*, 313.
42. Stephenson, *Dismantling the Dualisms*, 189.

in the form of the question of what the "identity markers" of Christian identity actually are (Stephenson and Wenk), or is identity the starting point that leads to encounters in the first place (Wenk), or is it identity that essentially defines how encounters are formed at all (Yong). The legitimate question arises as to whether pneumatologically based social ethics should not begin with the question of *identity* rather than *encounter*. As mentioned above, Moltmann argues that "Christian identification with the crucified Christ means solidarity with the sufferings of the poor and the misery both of the oppressed and the oppressor."[43] This means nothing other than that those who have their identity in Christ cannot help but act like Christ, which in turn makes identity the decisive starting point for pneumatologically based social ethics: the liberating experience of God creates a new identity in Christ which, in turn, results in behavior that corresponds to the identity. If this is the case, then the question arises as to which experiences or aspects are important for Pentecostal identity. Hollenweger has compellingly shown that this question can be answered in various ways.[44] If we look for an answer within the framework of the Pentecostal origins, several elements spring to mind: on the one hand, there is the liberating spiritual experience that released an integrating dynamic in a segregated society.[45] The interpretation of spiritual experiences against the background of the Acts 2 and Joel 3 narrative is of such identity-forming importance that it gives its name to the emerging movement.[46] Furthermore, the importance of mission for the self-understanding of the Pentecostal Movement can hardly be overestimated.[47] Equally important to Pentecostal spirituality and its self-understanding are its roots in the Holiness Movement.[48] What other elements will be considered fundamental to Pentecostal identity will certainly be the subject of further debate.

43. Moltmann, *Crucified God*, 29.
44. See Hollenweger, *Pentecostalism*, 33–36.
45. See section "History and Context," 57–63.
46. See section "History and Context," 57–63. Further, the importance of Acts 2 and Joel 3 is highlighted by the fact that the two narratives are also fundamental to the approaches of Stephenson, Wenk, Solivan, and Yong.
47. As we have seen with Moltmann, clarification of the understanding of mission has direct implications for social ethics, 221–25. The same applies to Wenk, who uses the Missio Dei to show that a holistic understanding of mission has a decisive influence on the self-image/identity of the church and its actions. Wenk, *Erneuerung durch Begegnung*, 58.
48. See section "History and Context," 57–63.

Unity in Particularity and Particularity in Unity

Unity in particularity and *particularity in unity* are central themes of Moltmann's theology. In the research, four different justifications that Moltmann uses to argue for unity in particularity were identified: in *The Crucified God*, there is an epistemological approach,[49] and in *Church in the Power of the Spirit* a christological argumentation.[50] In both approaches, a pneumatological factor implicitly resonates. As justified and significant as both approaches are, the focus will be on the explicit pneumatological reasoning behind *unity in particularity* and *particularity in unity*. There are two lines of reasoning, and both approaches can be found in *The Spirit of Life*.

- First, there is a line of pneumatological reasoning in relation to the attributes of the *ruach*: in addition to the male attributes of God, with the *ruach*, female attributes are also revealed as part of the Trinity. There is a certain correspondence to the equality of female and male attributes in the fellowship of believers: a de-patriarchalization of the image of God also results in a de-patriarchalization and de-hierarchization of the church.[51]

- Second, Moltmann bases his reasoning on the Pauline doctrine of charisms. In doing so, he argues (and Stephenson and Wenk follow a similar argument)[52] that the outpouring of the Holy Spirit is not only an empowerment of believers, but also has an inherent soteriological dimension.[53]

Where the Pentecostal tradition usually associates charisms with extraordinary works of the Holy Spirit (speaking in tongues, prophecy, miraculous healing, etc.), Moltmann takes a broader approach: for him, humankind itself, with everything profane that it brings with it, is, through the calling of Christ accepted by the Holy Spirit and placed at the service of the kingdom of God.[54] In concrete terms, this means that all life accepted in Christ by the Holy Spirit is empowered in all its facets to

49. Moltmann, *Crucified God*, 26–27.
50. Moltmann, *Power of the Spirit*, 200.
51. Moltmann, *Spirit of Life*, 160.
52. See Stephenson, *Dismantling the Dualisms*, 112; Wenk, *Erneuerung durch Begegnung*, 59.
53. Moltmann, *Spirit of Life*, 143.
54. Moltmann, *Spirit of Life*, 181–82.

be of equal value and to serve the community, whether man or woman, disabled, suffering, a stranger, etc.⁵⁵ As different as people are, everything they are and bring with them becomes a charism, and thus significant for the fellowship of believers: "If . . . we start from the early Christian experience of Pentecost, we have to develop a pneumatological concept of the church: there is one Spirit and many gifts. Everyone concerned, whether man or woman, is endowed and committed through his or her calling, wherever he or she is, and whatever he or she is."⁵⁶ What Moltmann and all Pentecostal voices have in common is that they understand everyone to be full members of the new people of God. It is not enough for them to be merely tolerated or allowed to work in it.⁵⁷ As important as the *encounter* is as a starting point for pneumatological social ethics, an encounter only becomes fruitful when the other party is perceived as equal, through whom God's Spirit potentially wants to speak to us. The same applies even more so to the church: the people of God established by Pentecost are only God's people when everyone participates as equals, their voices are heard and their contributions help shape the culture and values of the new Exodus community.⁵⁸

Again, the question arises as to whether the clarification of the identity as a people of God founded by Pentecost, the *encounter* and the *unity in particularity* and *particularity in unity* precede or must be part of pneumatologically based social ethics. After all, how can I engage with the other person without fear of overadaptation if I do not know who I am and what constitutes my identity as part of the new Exodus community? How can one heed the legitimate challenge inherent in Lisa Stephenson's statement, "The way forward for Pentecostals is to own their identity and allow pneumatology to shape their theology and praxis."⁵⁹ if one does not develop and integrate the dimension of pneumatology as part of one's

---

55. Moltmann, *Spirit of Life*, 194.

56. Moltmann, *Spirit of Life*, 240.

57. See Moltmann, *Spirit of Life*, 193; Solivan "From Azusa to Memphis," 130; Wenk, *Erneuerung durch Begegnung*, 10–11; Stephenson, *Dismantling the Dualisms*, 89–90; Yong, *Days of Caesar*, 201.

58. Or as Wariboko puts it, Pentecost is "a reflection of the irreducible pluralistic nature of existence, serendipitous nature of creativity, and restlessness of becoming" (Wariboko, *Pentecostal Principle*, 20). So "Pentecostal" pluralism symbolized at Pentecost reaches for freedom. Wariboko notes that pluralism in the light of Pentecost is not relativism. It is the encounter of ever-new commitments in the Holy Spirit of life (30). It gives rise to "a community of creative possibilities" (31).

59. Stephenson, *Dismantling the Dualisms*, 194.

identity? The fact that, for the Pentecostal voices, Acts 2 plays a central role, becomes clear in chapter 3 in the intra-Pentecostal dialogue. Moltmann also refers to Acts 2, although, in comparison to the Pentecostal theologians, this plays a subordinate role for him: there are just two statements that refer to the events of the New Testament Pentecost: Moltmann relates one to the promise of Joel 3:1–5 that is fulfilled in Acts 2 and thus equalises the privileges of men with respect to women.[60] The other statement deals with speaking in tongues in Acts 2, in which Moltmann shows that the worship experience of churchgoers does not have to be limited to listening, but can also include the participation of the many.[61] Even if Acts 2 plays a subordinate role in Moltmann, pneumatology plays an important role in his theology for the formation of identity for followers of Christ. A dialogue between the identity grounded in Pentecostal experience, based on Acts 2, and the identity pneumatologically established by Moltmann would be clarifying and furthering for both parties.[62]

Collaborative Eschatology

A dialogue on eschatology between Jürgen Moltmann and Pentecostal theologians was conducted by Peter Althouse in 2003.[63] In the dialogue conducted here, the focus is on the importance of eschatology for social ethics. Here, too, parallels can be discovered between Moltmann and the Pentecostal theologians. Yong points out that the eschatological doctrines "are not merely beliefs about what will happen in the future but are also orientations for Christian practice in the present."[64] For Wenk, it is the eschatological horizon that provides orientation as to what injustice is and how it can be overcome.[65] Stephenson refers to eschatology as something that is intended to descend upon the church in the present day, and to become visible.[66] In Moltmann, we find a combination of the

---

60. Moltmann, *Spirit of Life*, 239.
61. Moltmann, *Spirit of Life*, 184–87. Moltmann also only addresses the Pentecost of Acts 2 in connection with the authorization for mission (278), the Holy Spirit that gives the charisms at Pentecost and reveals the vision of God's new creation (211) and the word that touches the heart through the Holy Spirit (103).
62. See, for example, Wenk, "Kingdom of Peace," 16–39.
63. Althouse, *Spirit of the Last Days*.
64. Yong, *Days of Caesar*, 352.
65. Wenk, *Erneuerung durch Begegnung*, 116.
66. Stephenson, *Dismantling the Dualisms*, 181.

different approaches found in the Pentecostals. For him, too, eschatology provides orientation for the present: eschatology is "Christ for his redeeming future"[67] that intends to shape the present. For example, the promise of the resurrection of the dead leads "at once to love for the true life of the whole imperiled and impaired creation."[68] However, the emphasis of Moltmann's eschatology is less on orientation than on change.[69] This change happens through the Holy Spirit in an interaction between church and culture, and has the potential, precisely because it is developed pneumatologically, to overcome the limits of what was previously possible.[70] In this, both church and culture are to be changed.[71]

As already mentioned, eschatology barely plays a role in Solivan's orthopathic approach. Solivan only mentions it in a brief passage, where he describes it as a *blessed hope* that is given to the contemporary church as a pivotal element for reconciliation with God and fellow human beings.[72] Since the following section focuses on the topic of hope, we will delve deeper into Solivan's approach there.

Moltmann's thoughts, recorded in the Sheffield Report, are considered significant for the further development of pneumatologically based eschatology:

> In our traditions, past hopes and experiences are always preserved. That has its value, but it is only limited value. No tradition should determine the future. At best, it can pave the way for the future. The Spirit itself is always creating something new and

---

67. Moltmann, *Power of the Spirit*, 224.

68. Moltmann, *Power of the Spirit*, 205.

69. Wariboko does grant Christ universal significance in defining the Pentecostal principle. He refers to Christ as the one who was, is, and is to come (Rev 1:8) and then summarizes Moltmann to the effect that Christ is viewed as dynamically embodying that which was continually new, that which "asks for, creates, and sustains the alternative possibilities, the unexpected path" (Wariboko, *Pentecostal Principle*, 6).

70. Moltmann, *Spirit of Life*, 240.

71. Moltmann, *Spirit of Life*, 241. Wariboko says appropriately that the baptism in the Holy Spirit through the living Christ "is not once and for all but continual." It leads to the never-ending disruption and fulfillment of life caused by grace. It is not confined to Pentecostals, nor even to the church. It is "an empowerment toward creative transformation, generally in terms of human being in the world" (Wariboko, *Pentecostal Principle*, 3). The Pentecostal principle involves all of life and not just Christian or Pentecostal life. It does not point reductively to a miraculous intrusion of God into the ordinary but rather of the "'miraculous' nature of the ordinary." In this light, Pentecostalism as a particular movement is merely one fragmentary embodiment among others of the universal Pentecostal principle (4).

72. Solivan, *Spirit, Pathos and Liberation*, 110.

is full of surprises. He is not bound by tradition, but takes from them that which points the way to the future.[73]

The question arises as to where tradition prevents the Holy Spirit from shaping the present and the future. This question must also be asked. As Moltmann mentioned in the quote—tradition is not bad per se: it can prepare the way for the future and yes, the Holy Spirit uses it where it serves the coming kingdom of God. As suggested by Moltmann, there is also an interplay in Pentecostal theology, a lively dialogue with culture and other theological traditions—and there is still a lot to learn from these encounters on both sides. At the same time, it is important to note that there is often a discrepancy between academic Pentecostal theology and the actual community practice in the local churches. This becomes clear in the discussion about the role of women in the church community, to give just one example.[74] It is obvious that the power of tradition is real, even in the short history of Pentecostalism, and should not be underestimated.

The question arises as to how the renewal that God's Spirit is creating can also be anticipated in everyday church life. In *Pentecostal Salvation as Deliverance from the Powers*,[75] Yong describes worship as a place where habits, character and behavior are shaped ethically and politically through common prayers, songs and Scripture readings. This shaping does not happen "only" through the act of remembering, but also in the order expressly promised by God.[76] concrete example of such a practice with the non-Pentecostal voices has already been detailed in this work: James Cone describes how the seventh day of the week, Sunday, acquires an eschatological importance in the African American context: Not only a change in the day of the week takes place, but far more, on this day the congregation experiences a rupture in time—the future, eschatological Kingdom of God becomes present through the power of the Holy Spirit in the here and now of the church service. The all-changing power of the Holy Spirit is manifested in the worship service, which does not bring about the cosmic eschaton, but transforms the identity of the people and thus also the entire assembled fellowship. This finds expression in

---

73. Moltmann and Moltmann-Wendel, "Menschlich werden," 47 (my translation).

74. In this context, I remember the impressive plenary presentation by Cheryl Bridges Johns, part of the SPS Conference on March 7, 2014, in Springfield, MO, which painfully described the discrepancy detailed above.

75. See section "Pentecostal Salvation as Deliverance from the Powers," 169–72.

76. Yong, *Days of Caesar*, 156.

the songs, emotions and worship structures and the encounters of the faithful.[77] In many respects, these observations also apply to the worship services of the early Pentecostal church.[78]

It can well be imagined that a consciously eschatological orientation of the worship services, which helps the fellowship to anticipate and visualise the future kingdom of God, also has a socio-ethical effect. In this context, Moltmann's view that all work of the Holy Spirit is to be understood as being part of eschatological reality could be of interest to the Pentecostal church: "In the experience of the Holy Spirit, the Holy Spirit's charismatic energies will interpenetrate body and soul. These energies are not 'supernatural' gifts. They are 'the powers of the age to come' (Heb 6:5)."[79] Even though in this statement Moltmann is primarily making a declaration of war on the term supernatural, the idea that charismatic powers are the powers of the coming age is extremely interesting. This is not least because the focus leads away from the individual interpretation of the charisms toward a collaborative pneumatology which, in turn, interprets the charismatic experience in terms of its importance for the collective.

Eschatological Hope

Collaborative eschatology presupposes hope—because without hope, collaboration makes little sense. With regard to the voices considered in this work, the impression is that it is not possible to determine unequivocally whether, in practice, hope precedes eschatology or eschatology precedes hope—both seem possible. It seems certain that there is an interaction between the two concepts. In this respect, it is more appropriate to speak of *eschatological hope*. As described above, it is not about the superficial realization of salvation, but about hope that counts on the coming of God's eschaton. Greater clarity lies in determining the relationship between experience and hope. Moltmann writes: "Experience comes First and then the theology; first the passion, then the action."[80] Only in the experiences that a person has with God, and in the remembrance of these experiences, is the manifest future of their credibility maintained:

---

77. Cone, "Sanctification and Liberation," 175–92.

78. See section "History and Context," 57–63.

79. Moltmann, *Spirit of Life*, 74. This is also the case in Moltmann, "Liberation in the Light of Hope."

80. Moltmann, *Experiences in Theology*, 24.

Solivan's *Orthopathic Hope* places just as much value on experience in relation to hope.[81] There are also parallels in Stephenson: they can be seen in her analysis of Letty Russell's approach, where she speaks of the "memories of the future."[82]

A hope grounded in experience is inevitably confronted with the tension of *now and not yet*. Yong addresses this tension,[83] as does Solivan.[84] Because of the tension of *now and not yet* that is frequently seen among the Pentecostals, the question arises as to whether Moltmann does not also address this aspect. In the research, the answer was found in an essay from 1974 in which Moltmann coined the phrase *hope against hope*, which does not use the phrase *now and not yet*, but does touch on the idea:

> Many enthusiastic liberation movements have been ruined by their superficial optimism. Without that "hope against hope," which is born out of the readiness for suffering and cross, resistance and confidence do not gain any firm ground. Franz Kafka expressed this soberly and yet hopefully in his depiction of the "world without men." "It is no refutation of the expectation of an ultimate liberation if on the next day the prison remains still unchanged or actually becomes tighter, or even if it is expressly declared dismantled. All this can rather be the necessary presupposition for the ultimate liberation." The visage of Job has characterised the Exodus people of Israel for centuries. It remains the orientation point for all liberation movements which in the depths of their hope come upon the messianic kingdom of "man." The freedom of the resurrection which was revealed through the forsaken, oppressed and crucified Son of man remains the sign of hope for the hopeless.[85]

According to Moltmann, any Theology of Hope that has not integrated suffering will fail when it comes to the idea of *not yet*. In contrast, in any Theology of Hope that has integrated suffering, suffering can become a resource through the power of the Holy Spirit.[86] Regarding this, in the context of orthopathos, Solivan speaks of suffering as

---

81. Solivan, *Spirit, Pathos and Liberation*, 90–92. For Solivan's criticism of Moltmann, see chapter 2, section "Powerlessness," 155–56.
82. Stephenson, *Dismantling the Dualisms*, 181.
83. Yong, *Days of Caesar*, 352–54.
84. Solivan, *Spirit, Pathos and Liberation*, 91.
85. Moltmann, "Liberation in the Light," 417.
86. Moltmann, *Spirit of Life*, 193.

a resource that serves as a starting point for theological reflection and pastoral engagement.[87] It seems obvious: if hope is to be sustainable, then it cannot avoid dealing with disappointment, setbacks and suffering. Solivan beautifully shows that these negative experiences are more than just the 'other side of the coin' and can even become an inspiration and source of new pathways. The same applies to James Cone, who masterfully shows the connections between everyday suffering and worship in the African American experience. In the intra-Pentecostal context, alongside Solivan's discussion in *The Spirit, Pathos and Liberation*, there are also thoughts on a theology of suffering in Yong's 2007 book *Theology and Down Syndrome*. A monograph on this topic was published in 2019 by Pamela F. Engelbert under the title *Who is Present in Absence? A Pentecostal Theological Praxis of Suffering and Healing*. In contrast to accounts of experience and testimonies, Pentecostal theological debates on the subject of suffering are rare. A Pentecostal theology of suffering with reference to questions of social ethics is a task that still lies ahead of Pentecostal academics and could make a significant contribution to the further development of Pentecostal social ethics.

However, the tension of *now and not yet* raises another question, which Moltmann originally formulated in relation to mission, but which also arises with regard to eschatological hope: *What* can I hope for?[88] For Moltmann, the answer lies in the future of God[89]—in this context, he also refers to the future kingdom of God.[90] Only there is it possible for there to be something new that can go beyond what has gone before.[91] It is "founded and opened wide by the promise of the gospel."[92] It is a hope that counts on God's healing and, above all, accomplishing eschatological intervention. It is this that allows the church to participate in the quest for justice, even when all the signs of the present ridicule this hope. Wenk takes a similar direction. He puts hope in the following context: for him, trust is the basis of freedom, and love is the habitat of freedom. Love,

---

87. Solivan, *Spirit, Pathos and Liberation*, 60–61.

88. Moltmann, "Ziel der Mission," 1.

89. That this hope for Moltmann, as for the Pentecostal voices, is neither a comfort for the hereafter nor a dispersion of the hereafter in the present has been shown already above.

90. E.g., Moltmann, *Ethics of Hope*, 36.

91. Moltmann, *Spirit of Life*, 103.

92. Moltmann, "Ziel der Mission," 1, my translation.

in turn, releases hope, which forms the "horizon" of freedom, because "freedom is . . . always hopeful."[93]

Yong[94] and Solivan[95] describe the *prosperity gospel* as at least somewhat problematic, in which the dimension of the *not yet* is almost entirely resolved. *Prosperity theology* is widespread in Pentecostal charismatic circles and takes the position that material abundance is promised through Christ in the here and now. In their criticism, Yong and Solivan show that the Pentecostal charismatic practice of the *prosperity gospel* awakens at least some hopes that do not coincide with God's promised salvation.[96] Moltmann does not comment on the *prosperity gospel*, which is not surprising, given that it is a predominantly non-denominational phenomenon. However, Moltmann's reflections on dealing with property and responsibility relating to economic power[97] can provide valuable insight on dealing with poverty and property in a healthy and hopeful manner. An in-depth dialogue between Pentecostal theologians and Moltmann, in which the questions of what we as the body of Christ can hope for, what can be expected in the tension of *now and not yet*, and what the specific responsibility/role of the church is in this context are likely to be of great interest for pneumatologically based social ethics (and beyond).

Another issue Pentecostals associate with hope is that of *spiritual warfare*. Of the Pentecostal theologies examined in this work, only Amos Yong addresses this aspect of Pentecostal spirituality.[98] Even if the other Pentecostal voices do not address *spiritual warfare*, it is, nevertheless, an important element of Pentecostal charismatic practice.[99] The fact that only one in four Pentecostal voices takes on the topic of *spiritual warfare* is highly symptomatic—academic theology usually gives this topic a wide berth, and if it is dealt with at all, then mostly with considerable reservation. It is, therefore, not surprising that Moltmann also does not offer any thoughts on the subject of *spiritual warfare*. Nonetheless, there are common touchpoints, namely in the elder *J. C. Blumhardt*.[100] The begin-

93. Wenk, *Erneuerung durch Begegnung*, 105.
94. Yong, *Days of Caesar*, 257–73.
95. Solivan, *Spirit, Pathos and Liberation*, 90.
96. Yong, *Days of Caesar*, 263–68.
97. Moltmann, *Ethics of Hope*, 165–66.
98. See section "Pentecostal Salvation as Deliverance from the Powers," 169–72.
99. For example, see Quaas, "Befreiungsdienst und interkulturelle Seelsorge," 315.
100. See Kydd, "Healing in the Christian Church (1805–80)," 700–701; Macchia, *Spirituality and Social Liberation*.

ning of the revival that took place around Blumhardt marked the spiritual struggle for the liberation of Gottliebin Dittus. Karl Barth points out that it is the spiritual struggle for the liberation of Gottliebin Dittus that marks the beginning of the revival in Möttlingen, in which the Blumhardt story[101] and thus also *religious socialism* began. Although Moltmann describes Blumhardt as an important influence on his theology of the kingdom of God,[102] he does not say a word about the events in Möttlingen. This is different from the Pentecostals from the German-speaking area: for them, it is precisely Blumhardt's testimony about his struggle to free Gottliebin that they discuss (such as in Johann Widmer's writings.[103]

Why should the topic of *spiritual warfare* (and also Blumhardt in this context) be of interest for the present dialogue? There are three reasons. First, representatives of the reformed church (to which Moltmann also belongs) point out that there is definitely a need for a "Lutheran" *spiritual warfare* at the church base. Claudia Währisch-Oblau[104] wrote in the July–September 2011 issue of the *Ökumenische Rundschau* [Ecumenical Review]: "I believe there is a need to develop a protestant theology and practice of spiritual warfare. Here, one can fall back on Luther and Blumhardt as well as on the Desert Fathers."[105] The second reason to address *spiritual warfare* in the context of social justice is that it directly relates to empowering the powerless. Quoting Währisch-Oblau again:

> A theology and practice of spiritual warfare turns poor, powerless and marginalized groups into agents who can influence their own lives and that of those around them. Many protestant churches in Africa, Asia and Latin America have long since adopted practices of deliverance ministry and spiritual warfare because they take the needs of their members seriously. However, in doing so, they often uncritically adopt

---

101. Bart, *Versöhnung*, 194.

102. E.g., Moltmann, *Broad Place*, 97.

103. Johann Widmer was one of the three founding fathers of the Swiss *BewegungPlus* Pentecostal denomination. See Rossel, *Erinnerungen an die Zukunft*, 24–26. Specifically, Widmer refers to Blumhardt in his three-volume work *Im Kampf gegen Satans Reich* [Fighting Satan's Kingdom], which he published from 1948 to 1952. See Widmer, *Im Kampf gegen Satans Reich*, 1:7, 16; 3:44–51.

104. Rev. Claudia Währisch-Oblau holds a doctorate in theology (Heidelberg, University). She is a member of the United Evangelical Mission leadership team and is the departmental head of Evangelization.

105. Währisch-Oblau, "Spiritual Warfare," 314 (my translation).

charismatic and neo-Pentecostal theologies that urgently need to be questioned.[106]

The German psychiatrist and psychotherapist Martin Grabe provides the third important reason. In the *Magazin für Psychotherapie und Seelsorge* [Magazine for Psychotherapy and Pastoral Care], in an article on exorcisms in psychotherapy, Grabe describes the importance of externalizing evil. He rightly points out that if people reconcile themselves with all the adversities of life or if they try to integrate all the adverse things they have experienced in their life, they can seldom achieve salvation. There are things that may not or cannot be integrated because they are destructive and evil. It is necessary to reject these destructive elements or externalize them so that they can no longer continue their destructive effects.[107] This is also valid in the context of social ethics: it is, therefore, impossible to expect that victims will reconcile themselves with the reality of racism, sexism, violence, etc., and integrate the experiences they have had into their lives. Spiritual warfare offers victims the opportunity to articulate and externalize the harm they have experienced. This makes *spiritual warfare* an instrument that, as already quoted, turns "poor, powerless and marginalized groups into agents who can influence their own lives and that of those around them."[108] The practice of *spiritual warfare* awakens hope in victims by externalizing the evil experienced and proclaiming Jesus' victory over all dark forces—even over those that are still up to mischief. Incidentally, Karl Barth sees this hope as *the* central aspect, as *the* central spiritual truth in Blumhardt's struggle to free Gottliebin Dittus.[109]

---

106. Währisch-Oblau, "Spiritual Warfare," 314, my translation.

107. Grabe shows how this can be done by means of a therapy session in which schema therapy, developed by Jeffrey Yong, is used. This can be found in Grabe, "Dämonen Austreiben wie Jesus?," 14–19.

108. Währisch-Oblau, "Spiritual Warfare," 314.

109. Bart, *Versöhnung*, 194–96.

5

Findings in the Context of the Broader Theological Discussion

THE FOLLOWING SECTION SUMMARIZES the main results of the dialogue between the four Pentecostal voices and Jürgen Moltmann in the form of theses for a Pentecostal social ethics. Secondly, the main features of social justice are described from a pneumatological/eschatological perspective. Finally, the contribution of the work is located within the broader academic discourse.

Theses

Based on the findings above, the following aspects are considered to be central to Pentecostal social ethics:

a. A Pentecostal social ethics as examined in the voices above "emphasizes encounter with God, represented and presented by the church."[1] Because God is holy and His holiness consists in the fact

---

1. This is exactly what Rabbi Jonathan Sacks formulated from a Jewish perspective: "God asks one individual—eventually a family, a tribe, a collection of tribes, a nation—to serve as an exemplary role-model, to be as it were a living case-study in what it is to live closely and continuously in the presence of God" (Sacks, *To Heal a Fractured World*, 65).

that he heals the sick and unsanctified,[2] Pentecostal social ethics is sanctifying and healing at the same time: "Unless the holy leads us outward toward the good, and the good leads us back for renewal, the holy, the creative energies of faith run dry."[3] This Pentecostal social ethics is not primarily concerned with what people do, but rather, it is about the nature of God Himself coming into effect (His healing holiness), and the "liberation of humankind . . . [and] the nature of being human itself,"[4] as it is lived in the light of the encounter with the healing, holy God.

b. This, in turn, means that for all four Pentecostal scholars social ethics primarily begins in identity, and not in action. Social identity (and also personal identity) is always defined in relation to the "other," usually by ascribing special values and characteristics to the in-group in comparison with the other out-groups.[5] This identity is the starting point for personal and social behavior. Nationalism, racism and sexism are very strongly defined by means of demarcation from other outside groups. Julia Ebner has shown in her research that the starting point for the actions of extreme and violent groups is precisely the self-identity of the in-group through strong differentiation from and devaluation of others.[6] This action, based on an identity through differentiation is opposed to Pentecostal social ethics, which roots its identity in the narrative of Acts 2 and, therefore, leads to different, inclusive behavior that comprises reconciled and liberated togetherness. This text offers Pentecostals an identity beyond all ethnic, gender, social and political categories and, with its pneumatological and eschatological orientation, has the messianic kingdom of peace firmly in mind. As in the early church or the Azusa Street revival, the identity of the believer is defined by the "other," but others are recognized and confirmed in their otherness; identity is not created through demarcation and degradation, but through inclusion. One's own particularity is not dispelled by this, but the particularity of the others is simultaneously affirmed and confirmed

---

2. Moltmann, *Spirit of Life*, 171, 175.
3. Sacks, *Fractured World*, 9.
4. Drewermann, *Wendepunkte*, 27, my translation.
5. For an overview of Social Identity Theory (SIT), see Taifel, *Social Identity and Intergroup Relations*; Bettencourt, "Status, Differences and Ingroup Bias"; Brewer, "Psychology of Prejudice."
6. Ebner, *Wut*, 198.

because a new identity of inclusion arises through the Holy Spirit. This inclusion is defined by the Holy Spirit and thus justifies the behavior of the fellowship.[7] However, in both the exclusion and inclusion cases, the identity of a group is essentially grounded in the existence of the other. The key difference lies in the way in which the other is dealt with: through exclusion or embrace. Seen in this way, a pneumatologically based understanding of social justice paradoxically distinguishes itself from "the world" precisely by its inclusion, and understands sanctification, another central Pentecostal concept, as a radical form of mutual acceptance and affirmation by the Holy Spirit: a Spirit-wrought and therefore "sacred identity" is inherently inclusive, and that is what makes it truly exclusive, different and unique. Pentecostal identity continues to develop as the starting point for Pentecostal social ethics from the understanding of the work of the Holy Spirit in the past, its work in the present and its eschatological/anticipatory work in the future. In each case, the experience of the Holy Spirit is more than an individual experience: It is about the identity-creating spiritual experience of God's new people. In this context, the stories and testimonies that the fellowship tells about God (and His Spirit), Himself and the others are also crucial for the formation of identity.[8]

c. For all four Pentecostal theologians, social ethics seeks the presence of the Holy Spirit in all encounters: The Holy Spirit is in all of creation, and especially in creation that is suffering and threatened.

---

7. The principle of fellowship with Christ crucified is "fellowship with others and solidarity with those who have become strangers and have been made other" (Moltmann, *Crucified God*, 33, my translation). Moltmann goes even further in his understanding of the church: "Their legal basis is not equality, but the justification of the other (Hegel), the creative enactment of the unjust and the granting of rights to those without them. Consequently, the church of Christ crucified cannot assimilate itself to the other, its alien. Nor can it shut itself off from the alien in its social ghetto, but for the sake of its identity in Christ crucified, it must reveal Him and itself in His following in the other and the alien. In the practical form of its fellowship with others, only it can bear witness to Christ crucified and practice that justification of the ungodly that it believes and from which it lives" (33, my translation). Christian identity "only becomes mature in the area of non-identity, alienation to the other and solidarity with others. . . . One cannot attach it to oneself, one can only reveal it to others" (22, my translation). What does that mean? Moltmann comes to the following conclusion: "So the place where meaningful questions about identity are asked is the situation of the identity crisis, which one gets into through relevant alienation and solidarity" (22, my translation).

8. Wenk, *Erneuerung durch Begegnung*, 195. See also Plüss, *Therapeutic and Prophetic Narratives in Worship*.

Inasmuch as Pentecostal social ethics assumes that all of life is a charism, it also contributes significantly to ecological ethics, recognizing the presence of God in all life. Pentecostal social ethics is concrete in that it always arises from the encounter with and concern about suffering and injustice. It is neither abstract theory nor detached analysis, but it is the presence of the Holy Spirit in interpersonal relationships and in the relationship with creation; it takes place in the encounter. As a result, Pentecostal social ethics is neither an ethics of relativism nor an ethics of objectivism; it is an ethics of relationalism, in which the 'truth of God' is realized in concrete encounters.[9]

d. The people of God established by Pentecost is characterized by the fact that everyone participates as equals. Since all aspects of life become charisms through God's Spirit, the form, structure, spirituality and values of the fellowship are shaped by the diversity of the people who belong to it.

e. Pentecostal social ethics also recognizes the liberating work of God in this creation in the charisms of the Holy Spirit; the Holy Spirit takes all life into its mission to liberate and redeem creation. This collaborative pneumatology gives everyone a dignity and voice that is important for all others to hear. At the same time, Pentecostal social ethics will give a voice through the Holy Spirit to all life that does not have a voice in this world, whether the voice of threatened creation or degraded human beings.

f. Pentecostal social ethics is fundamentally based on the eschatological prayer of Jesus: "Deliver us from evil," and sees its contribution in overcoming evil in this world. The focus is, therefore, not on the question of knowledge of good and evil, but rather on eschatological redemption. The Spirit of God liberates us from the limits of what was previously possible by letting the eschatological future break through to the present so that new things can arise. In this sense, closeness to suffering leads to the imminent expectation of God. This imminent expectation is beyond an apocalyptic timetable, and instead, expects or seeks closeness to God. This imminent expectation also has an "apocalyptic dimension," because it expects the

---

9. This corresponds to what Michael Berra said in relation to Emil Brunner's theology in general: It is a theology beyond objectivism and subjectivism, a theology of relation (Berra, *Theology of Relationship*, 45). For an overview of different forms of objectivism and subjectivism, see Schäfer, "Objektivität Moralischer Werte."

concrete incursion of God in space and time and makes this the starting point of its participatory pneumatology and eschatology: It is only because God's Spirit was poured out that the Spirit-filled church can participate in His mission.

g. A Pentecostal social ethic primarily asks about the presence of the Holy Spirit in the midst of experienced suffering and injustice: the Holy Spirit as the presence of God in the midst of godforsakenness. Because Pentecostal social ethics primarily starts from the encounter with suffering and injustice, and asks questions regarding the presence of the Holy Spirit in this, it is not primarily "sensitive to sin" but "sensitive to suffering."[10]

h. This Pentecostal social ethics prevents Pentecostal eschatology from becoming either triumphant or speculative because its longing for the Kingdom of God (anticipation) grows from encountering the suffering and injustice of this world. Socio-ethical behavior is always anticipatory; it proceeds from the accomplished messianic kingdom of peace but is always aware of its provisional nature in this world. Responsibility in this world and hope in the hereafter are not played off against each other but are made proleptically tangible through the Holy Spirit in the here and now.

It is notable that the theses formulated against the background of the dialogue between Moltmann and Pentecostal theologians show striking parallels to the beginnings of the Pentecostal Movement. So it can already be seen how, during the revival in the Azusa Street Mission, for example, the identity of the kingdom of God,[11] unity in diversity (worshipping together as equals despite gender, racial, and social differences),[12] diversity in unity (the diverse influences that shaped the spirituality of worship),[13] and social ethics sensitive to suffering (attending to the marginalized in society)[14] are cornerstones of Pentecostal spirituality and practice.

---

10. The two categories "sensitive to sin" and "sensitive to suffering" were created by Johann Baptist Metz with regard to the life and suffering of Christ. Since Christianity as a religion refers back to its founder Christ, he views the term "sensitivity to suffering" in particular as a central touchstone as to whether Christianity actually corresponds to Christ. See Metz, *Armut im Geiste*, 63–78.

11. See, for example, Booth-Clibborn, "Should a Christian Fight?," 6–7.

12. See, for example, Seymour, *Azusa Street Papers*, 172; Bartlemann, *Azusa Street*, 51.

13. See Robeck, *Azusa Street*, 23, 57, 177.

14. See, for example, Robeck, *Azusa Street*, 14.

Social Justice: A Pneumatological/Eschatological Perspective

The aim of the research detailed in this work is to outline a pneumatologically justified Pentecostal social justice, as well as its form and significance in practice: specifically, to reveal how Pentecostal theologians justify social justice pneumatologically, what it looks like and what practice it leads to, and how the Pentecostal position differs from, supplements or covers the approach of Jürgen Moltmann.

The first question has not yet been answered because none of the dialogue partners defined what constitutes a Pentecostal pneumatologically based *social justice* or what it includes. Rather, the dialogue partners address partial aspects of *social justice* by taking up *socio-ethical* questions, namely in relation to liberation (in terms of ethnicity and gender), inclusion, political ethics, etc.

Therefore, how social justice can be understood from a Pentecostal pneumatological perspective will be defined below. This will be confined to key points that offer orientation for the further development of Pentecostal *social justice/social ethics*. The following applies in this regard: *social justice* is, per se, *ethical* and *social*, because the topic of justice is always an aspect of ethics, and a Pentecostal pneumatological ethics is always also social because the Holy Spirit is always fellowship-forming (2 Cor 13:13). All the theologians researched agree implicitly and explicitly on this, even if, as mentioned above, they have only examined individual aspects of social justice; and because Pentecostal theology is always theology that is practiced and prayed,[15] in a Pentecostal context, *social justice* is *social ethics* put into practice. In the foreground is not simply a Pentecostal pneumatological definition of social justice, but Pentecostal social ethics in practice; it is the combination of orthodoxy, orthopraxis and orthopathos that characterizes Pentecostal spirituality in general[16] and Pentecostal social ethics in particular. As already mentioned, the dialogue partners addressed aspects of social justice in the face of experienced injustice (for example, liberation, inclusion, etc.). These partial aspects certainly paint a picture against the background of which one could interpret what a Pentecostal understanding of a pneumatological social justice could be, but this picture is still somewhat blurred. Therefore, in this last section, with reference to my dialogue partners, an understanding of Pentecostal *social justice* will be presented.

15. Land, *Pentecostal Spirituality*.
16. Solivan, *Spirit, Pathos and Liberation*, 35–181.

Before we start thinking about an explicitly Pentecostal definition *social justice*, it is important to clarify what differentiates *Christian* social justice from *secular* social justice. In this regard, the article "Weltverantwortung," (World responsibility) by Siegfried is referred to.[17] Grossmann justifies the *Christian* in *Christian world responsibility* in the knowledge that every responsibility is based on the responsibility toward God. From this "basic responsibility," he derives any further responsibility toward people or things.[18] The fact that responsibility before God is always also responsibility for our fellow humans and creation is made clear in prehistory, in the dialogue between God and Cain: Because man is addressed by God, he is responsible, before God and for his fellow men (Gen 4:9–10). Following this line of argument, *Christian social justice* is defined in Christ or God Himself—otherwise it is not Christian;[19] it is the correct response (perceived responsibility) of humankind to God in regard to relationships with fellow humans and with creation. Because the understanding of Christian social justice is based on Christ, it is not based on any moral maxims, but is revealed in the following of Christ. Or in the words of Karl Rahner: "Following Christ is not the observance of moral maxims that may have been realized in Jesus, but which are also fundamentally valid and can be recognized independently of Him. Rather, it is the consummating cascade into His life and, thus, into the inner divine life given to us."[20] What this means in concrete terms for *social justice* should be defined for the two terms *social* and *justice* individually.

The term *social* is generally used synonymously with the terms *interpersonal* or intersubjective. In this sense, social means "in relationship." In connection with *justice*, the term *social* is about relationships that are lived in an appropriate balance. The relationship becomes Christian when, as explained above, it is defined in relation to God and understood as the correct answer to God's question to us.[21] Probably the most

17. Grossman, *Weltverantwortung*, 2147–49.
18. Grossmann, *Weltverantwortung*, 2147.
19. Moltmann follows the same line of argument in clarifying the question of what makes a Christian church Christian in Moltmann, *Church in the Power of the Spirit*, 11.
20. Rahner, *Betrachtungen*, 121, my translation.
21. See also Ilse Müllner on the books of the prophets: "The prophecy is about the Torah-appropriate behaviour of the Israelites, who are presented in a network of relationships. They are connected to each other, the other peoples, the country and their God. Justice is the barometer in all of these relationships. Justice is strongly and repeatedly emphasized in social relationships. If these relationships are not just, then the relationship with God is dead. For example, the book of Hosea combines its criticism of

compact and, at the same time, most prominent reference to this correct answer can be found in the gospels in the context of the double commandment to love. The double commandment is the central commandment of Christian spirituality and the focal point of Christian ethics,[22] it is *the* answer to God, which is found precisely in interpersonal relationships. That is why Jesus could say: "All the Law and the Prophets hang on these two commandments" (Matt 22:40). The starting point is the encounter with God, in which a person experiences being addressed and asked, and answers with love and loyalty to God. However, this answer to God is performed in love and loyalty to one's neighbor: The right response to God is found in righteous and responsible human relationships (Matt 25:31–46). Love of one's neighbor is born and nourished from the relationship with God.[23] The guiding principle for the right relationship with one's neighbor is, firstly, God's behavior toward people (Lev 11:44; Matt 18:23–35; Luke 6:36), and secondly, how one would like to be treated by them (Luke 6:31). This is why the stories of God's works of salvation and judgment in this world are always fundamental to the ethics of God's people. The liberation of Israel from Egypt is always a central theme in the prophetic criticism of the rich upper class of God's people.[24]

On the concept of *justice*: God reveals Himself as the only just One (Ps 71:19); he is in a righteous, i.e., just, relationship to Himself (inner-Trinitarian) and to His creation.[25] In this respect, *justice* can only be understood theologically in relation to and originating from God. For example, Ingolf U. Dalferth assumes that there must be a third party in order to do justice to equality and inequality:

> Everyone is different from everyone else, but all are equal in that they are different from the third party, by being who they are. When talking about equality, it must be specified who should be equal with whom and with regard to what. If you don't specify in

---

sacrifice with the demand for knowledge of God and solidarity, both concepts that are also used to mark the field of just relationships (Hos 6:6)" (Müller, "Gnädig ist Gott," 81, my translation).

22. Honecker, *Theologische Ethik*, 41.

23. Pöhlmann, *Abriss der Dogmatik*, 14; Warnach, *Agape*, 83.

24. See, e.g., Deut 15:15; Isa 58:6; 61:1–2; Prov 21:13, etc.

25. Karl Rahner used the incarnation to show how God's inner-Trinitarian behavior is related to his relationship to creation: "There is still incarnation. Because what was accepted back then is accepted anew every day. In this acceptance of the non-divine as the innermost property and the innermost reality of God Himself, we, too, are accepted, taken into the life of God" (Rahner, *Einübungen*, 97, my translation).

what regard people are equal, equality becomes an empty word. On the other hand, if they are said to be equal with respect to the same third party, their inequality among themselves is not denied or played down, but is included in their equality with respect to the third party.[26]

He goes on to say: "The third party must, therefore, be considered and treated in collective life in such a way that it cannot become the prey of a few."[27] The Spirit and the eschaton are that third party to relation to which all humans are equal and the differences between them are dispelled. This is because God's Spirit is poured out over all flesh. Acts 2 takes on a key role in this respect, as this event is narrated, showing how particularity is affirmed, because in the eschatological people of God, everyone is equally related to the third party, the Holy Spirit. Therefore, the equality of all human beings is only possible in relation to God (the Holy Spirit). This means that *social justice* can only be experienced within the framework of God's dominion. This dominion is the accomplished Kingdom of God.[28] What does this justice involve? The Hebrew term *tzedakah* provides us with a guide in answering this question. An important part of *tzedakah* is the dimension of *justitia*, i.e., that of just action and judgement, but this aspect *cannot* suffice when considering a world of many imbalances. *Tzedakah* takes this reality into account, because in addition to legal (*justitia*) it also includes distributive justice (*caritas*): the dimension of welfare, mercy, and goodness. While the Latin language (and contemporary languages) understand *justitia* and *caritas* as two different things, they belong together in *tzedakah*: Justice includes both just action and judgment, as well as the just distribution of God's goods and blessings;[29] mercy is not simply an expression of personal piety or even virtue, but justice in practice.

With a Christian interpretation of the two terms *social* and *justice*, we can now go further to the specifically pneumatological and Pentecostal interpretation of the term *social justice*.

Social justice is understood as something eschatological: It is everywhere where God's dominion has broken into this creation and become a reality. As an eschatological entity, it has a present, proleptic dimension as well as a future, accomplished one. In the accomplished Kingdom of

26. Dalfert, *Krise*, 222, my translation.

27. Dalfert, *Krise*, 235, my translation.

28. Or, to paraphrase Leonhard Ragaz, "the Kingdom of God is where God reigns" (Ragaz, "Zur Weltlage," 344).

29. See also Sacks, *Fractured World*, 30–42.

God, God's will occurs without limit, and then all relationships correspond to God's justice and all relationships are healthy. Then there will be *social justice*. From this, it becomes clear that a Pentecostal pneumatological understanding of social justice always has a soteriological dimension: The work of the Holy Spirit aims for the accomplishment of salvation, and thus for a salutary coexistence of the whole of creation. This salvation or the accomplishment of God's dominion is, in turn, wrought by God's Spirit.[30] God's Spirit works as the Creator, Revealer, Preserver and Perfecter of the Kingdom of God, and wherever the makes God's rule visible and tangible in the here and now, social justice prevails. Therefore, social justice is not simply a part or the epitome of Christian social ethics, but part of soteriology, eschatology and thus also missiology.

In this sense, *social justice* must be understood as part of God's dominion, as something Spirit-wrought and eschatological. Because it is always part of the ethos of the spirit-wrought fellowship in the here and now, it is also already a proleptic participation in the anticipated kingdom of God. It is ethics and the experience of salvation at the same time, and because this salvation is not yet complete, it is part of the *Missio Spiritu* and the mission of the church community.

Hence, because *social justice* has an eschatological, soteriological and missiological dimension (proleptic and anticipatory), the question of *social ethics*, therefore, always arises for the church in the face of the concrete present need and injustice: the unjust relationships within and around the church. In the misery of the present, *social ethics* poses the question of how *social justice* (just and salutary relationships) is concretely, and the future salvation of God proleptically, experienced in the here and now. Or in other words, social ethics poses the question of how God's future salvation reveals itself concretely in the misery currently experienced.

This social ethics is pneumatological because the same Spirit brings about the future, accomplished kingdom as well as the present Kingdom of God that has dawned until the whole cosmos is baptized in the Holy Spirit.[31] Notably, present and future are both part of the one history of

---

30. Pannenberg wrote: "Through the work of the Son, the kingdom of the Father, His monarchy, comes into effect in creation, and it is brought to completion by the work of the Holy Spirit, which glorifies the Son as the Father's agent and therein the Father Himself" (Pannenberg, *Systematische Theologie*, 352, my translation). Pointing in the same direction is Ragaz's discussion of the Apostles' Creed, in which he says of God that when He meets us in the form of the Holy Spirit, He creatively continues and accomplishes the Kingdom of God (Ragaz, *Glaubensbekenntnis*, 9).

31. Macchia, *Baptized in the Spirit*, 86; Swoboda, *Tongues and Trees*, 193–237.

God: "There is only one history, with Christ as the object."[32] Thus, the Spirit that accomplishes the kingdom of God is also the Spirit that enables the incursion of the Kingdom of God into the present, little by little.

The gospels and the Acts of the Apostles tell us how God establishes his dominion; they illustrate the right relationship of humans to their fellow creation by describing how God relates to His creation. From a Pentecostal-pneumatological perspective, two aspects stand out in terms of how God relates to His creation: First, they tell the story of how God is about to include and integrate all people into His kingdom; inclusion, or the fellowship-building power of the Holy Spirit, is thus a central aspect of a pneumatological understanding of social justice. Second, they tell the story in such a way that this inclusion occurs as God shares His glory and power with all, especially the marginalized. He lets them all share in His own power, by first renouncing His own power and glory and becoming a man endowed with the Holy Spirit. This theme is particularly central in the Lukan double work that is so central to Pentecostal theology.[33] Through God becoming man, the Spirit-wrought (Luke 1:35) and Spirit-filled Jesus (4:16) enables all people to share in the power and glory of God, which, in turn, is fundamental to peace on earth (2:14); peace can only come about where power, especially the power of God, is shared equally by everyone and where everyone has equal access to power.

In the second volume of Luke's double work, God continues to share His power and glory, pouring out His Spirit upon the community of His disciples and thus entering into His creation (Acts 2) so that, by partaking in God's power, they are able to renounce any claims to ethnic, gender, political or religious pre-eminence and the benefits associated with these. This Spirit-filled fellowship "not only has power," but participates in the power of God through the Holy Spirit. In their participation in the power of God, they, in turn, share it with everyone else, because the Spirit-filled fellowship knows that inclusion and integration in God's kingdom of peace can only be accomplished if all those included can participate in the power and glory of God in the same way as they do. Therefore they speak each other's languages (Acts 2) and are willing to give up their own privileges for the sake of right relationships, to change and thus let all people participate proleptically in the kingdom of the peace of God that

---

32. Gutiérrez, *Theology of Liberation*, 140, my translation.
33. Archer, *Gospel Revisited*, 43.

has come through the Holy Spirit.³⁴ A pneumatological-Pentecostal *social ethics*, therefore, pays less attention to miracle works in and of themselves, but instead aims to understand what God's Spirit wants to say to the fellowship of believers *through* the signs and wonders. The acceptance of people who are different from one's own group into one's own community, people who then also participate in the power and glory of God, will always also change their ethos, life and theological perspective. In other words, because of the self-emptying of God through the presence of the Holy Spirit in the fellowship, all share in the power and glory of God, albeit often in "their own language." Because all share equally in the power and glory of God (the distributive dimension of justice), the relationships correspond to God's justice. This righteousness is, however, only truly achieved when it includes the whole of creation because the salvation of God always encompasses the entire cosmos (Col 1:20). However, since it is the power and glory of God that all should partake of (and not just power and glory per se), any form of power and glory other than that of God is a form of abuse.³⁵

The *signs and wonders* wrought by the Holy Spirit remind people that their present social existence, which is bound up with sin and death, will one day be transcended in a new creation and liberated into an existence shaped by the sanctity and freedom of self-giving love. For example, all forms of healing indicate that the flesh is not forever bound to destruction through sin and death. Freedom is possible. It is not for nothing that *signs and wonders* are explicitly mentioned in connection with God's

---

34. Pöhlmann agrees. He says Christ's "work of redemption is never carried out with violence. Christ crucified, who exercises His power in powerlessness, is a rejection of any spirituality of violence. Unjust structures are not broken with violence, but are overcome from within—through the Spirit of God, who is the Spirit of love (Gal 5:22)" (Pöhlmann, *Heiliger Geist*, 85, my translation). A self-sacrifice exploited by oppressors must be liberated through the self-sacrifice of Christ. Thus, Christ offered His life in resistance *against* the expectations and demands of the powers of this world. He resisted the Jewish nationalistic hopes; indeed, even the expectations of His disciples. He ultimately sacrificed His life for them all, but in resistance to their exploitative expectations. Christ's understanding of self-sacrifice is a self-sacrifice in the name of resistance *and* of restoration. In this sense Jesus' self-sacrifice is a criticism of the establishment and of societal expectations. So all people are called upon to sacrifice in resistance to exploitative expectations for the Kingdom of God. In this sense, Jesus, in His self-giving, represents the resistance but also the hope of all humanity, in all its diversity and multiplicity.

35. Anthea Butler's criticism of white evangelical racism consists precisely in the fact that there were attempts to integrate black people in the 1970s, who were allowed to sing in the crusades, etc., but were not given a share of power. See Butler, *White Evangelical Racism*.

liberating actions in both the Old and New Testaments.³⁶ It is important to emphasize that in the biblical testimony, the liberating work of God is not limited to the interpersonal dimension but also finds expression at an institutional level. So we see, for example, in Acts 10 how Jews and gentiles are granted equal access to the Holy Spirit and righteous fellowship, but it is only in Acts 15 that the Council of Jerusalem converts the experience of chapter 10 into an apostolic decree and thereby "institutionalizes" it and makes it permanent. Institutional measures and structures must follow the signs and wonders so that the current breakthroughs can unfold in a sustainable way in a just koinonia over the long term. This is also evident in the Exodus: the experience of God's liberating action through signs and wonders, which was reflected in the liberation of the Israelites from Egyptian slavery, was institutionalized in the law given at Mount Sinai so that freedom would not be lost again; a fellowship shaped by the Exodus was created with rules and laws that were intended to preserve the justice and freedom achieved through the Exodus.

It is not uncommon for the liberating action of God, especially when it is ecclesiologically institutionalized by the church, to provoke resistance from the establishment. It is precisely there, in the resistance of the establishment, that the social relevance of God's liberating actions toward the poor, disadvantaged and marginalized is expressed. It is not the task of the church to seek conflict with the powerful of this world for conflict's sake—conflicts come to the church of their own accord, namely, where the church proclaims the liberating message of God's kingdom and works to support the oppressed and marginalized. The liberation of the oppressed is always a threat to the status quo of the powerful and privileged, who benefit from imbalances and concentrations of power. This means that God's liberating actions always have a political dimension.³⁷

This does not mean, however, that Pentecostal (pneumatological) social justice is primarily, or even exclusively, ecclesiological. At least in a democracy, the church has the opportunity and, thus, also

---

36. Wenk, *Community-Forming Power*, 250.

37. The revival in Azusa Street impressively illustrates this connection. The prime concern of the worship services, in which all participants took part, regardless of their cultural background, language, gender, education or skin color, was not seen by the participants as a political revolution against the prevailing social structures but as an implementation of their experiences of God (Robeck, *Azusa Street*, 99–107). Nevertheless, they were perceived as a threat by the religious and social establishment, which triggered corresponding reprisals on the part of the political authorities (e.g., Anderson and Hollenweger, *Pentecostals*, 94).

the responsibility, to politically assert its loyalty to the marginalized and oppressed outside of the koinonia. In this way, it can contribute to overcoming structural injustice on a societal level. Where necessary, the church has repeatedly raised its prophetic voice and offered non-violent resistance in other political forms of government: The church is the sign and instrument of God's liberating justice in this world. At the same time, secular social justice is, at best, an implicit testimony to the justice of God made explicit (and fulfilled) only in the koinonia of the church.[38]

A Pentecostal Approach to Social Ethics and Social Justice in the Context of the Broader Academic Discourse

The aim of this section is to locate the findings of this thesis in the broader theological discourse on social ethics.

The present work differs from classical works on social ethics, such as Emil Brunner's *The Commandment and the Orders* (1932) in that it does not contain any concrete socio-ethical fields of action (e.g., work, family, etc.), although this work is also very much concerned with the question of a just order within the community. However, this thesis does not list norms but rather points to principles that can guide Pentecostal social ethics.

By elaborating on the narrative of Acts 2 as the fundamental leitmotif of Pentecostal social ethics, this work has a strong proximity to narrative ethics,[39] in which it is assumed that human behavior is not primarily influenced cognitively but rather affectively. By including the affective dimension as the basis of human behavior, this work also differs from the approach of the protestant philosopher John Rawls in *A Theory of Justice*. Although Rawls's understanding of justice has many positive points of contact with a pneumatological-eschatological understanding of justice, his approach remains somewhat hypothetical and cognitive. He also focuses on the individual (more strongly than the Pentecostal discourse does).[40] But for him, too, a person's identity plays a fundamental role in her/his understanding of a just society. In contrast to Rawls,

---

38. On this point, I differ from the position expressed in Warrington, "Social Transformation." In contrast, I can certainly identify with Wolfgang Vondey's approach in Vondey, *Pentecostalism*, 89–110.

39. On narrative ethics, see, e.g., Joisten, *Narrative Ethik*; Mieth and Mieth, "Vorbild oder Modell?"; Chun, *Ethics and Biblical Narrative*; Wenham, *Story as Torah*.

40. See Sandel, "Procedural Republic."

however, Pentecostal social ethics (including that of Brunner in 1932) assumes that the encounter does not take place under a "veil of ignorance," but that justice is realized precisely in the knowledge of the person being encountered, i.e., the "you": "The personal or impersonal nature of the I is determined by whether its counterpart, the you, is recognized as personal or not."[41] However, the you can only be regarded as personal if it is recognized in its very specific historical and social context: those affected (e.g., the oppressed and the oppressors) find a new, shared life of justice in the specific encounter. The starting point for their social interaction, therefore, is not a veil of ignorance, but rather the concrete experience of those affected, which they bring to their encounter. The leitmotif is not a state of ignorance about one's own role in the "drama of life" but rather the pneumatological-eschatological vision of the future kingdom of God, which becomes fundamental for action in the here and now. Moreover, Pentecostal social ethics, following Brunner, emphasizes that identity always emerges in the concrete encounter: "Individuality and community are not mutually exclusive, but rather they are one and the same."[42]

Insofar as Pentecostal social ethics allows its current actions to be guided by the eschaton, it can best be classified under the approaches of Hans Urs von Balthasar, N. T. Wright, and Samuel Wells, who describe ethics as a "drama of improvisation."[43] This approach to ethics as improvization has a certain proximity to narrative ethics but goes beyond it in that not only the identity-forming narrative[44] but also the hoped-for end gives direction to our actions as Christians in this world.[45] However, Pentecostal social ethics emphasizes the presence of the Holy Spirit more fully than do Balthasar (Roman Catholic) and Wright and Wells (Anglican). Not only are memory (identity-forming narrative) and hope (eschaton) fundamental, but also the present, or obedience to the work of the Holy Spirit in the present—similar to the ethics of Deuteronomy, where the call to obedience in the present flows from memory (liberation) and hope (the promised land).[46] At the same time, the work of the Holy Spirit

---

41. Brunner, *Wahrheit als Begegnung*, 287, my translation.

42. Brunner, *Wahrheit als Begegnung*, 285, my translation.

43. Balthasar, *Prologomena*; Wright, "How Can the Bible Be Authoritative?"; Wells, Samuel, *Improvisation*.

44. For Pentecostals, Acts 2.

45. From the perspective of New Testament ethics, see Hays, *Moral Vision of the New Testament*.

46. See Brueggemann, *Deep Memory*.

in Pentecostal social ethics is always connected to the specific fellowship of believers; the Holy Spirit works in and through the fellowship.[47]

Similar to the New Testament ethics in Hays's *The Moral Vision of the New Testament*, the current work shows the vision that guides Pentecostals and how this affects the affective dimension of human behavior (narrative ethics).[48] Hays assumes that the vision, the ethos, is fundamental to practical ethics. Although Pentecostal social ethics is less about morality and more about social interaction, this study emphasizes the importance of the Pentecostal ethos for social ethics, as does Hays in his work on New Testament ethics. Nevertheless, a Pentecostal social ethics goes beyond the pure ethics of conviction (Kant) by showing what shapes conviction (ethos): the identity-forming narrative of Acts 2 and the hope of the eschaton. Pentecostal social ethics thus aims to be faithful to its origin and its hope.

Another significant voice in the discussion on social ethics is the theologian and philosopher Nicholas Wolterstorff. His concept of justice is also of interest for the positioning of the current work. He argues in his book *Justice: Rights and Wrongs* that justice is the recognition of rights and dignity. These rights and dignity are based on the value of the legal entity: the simple fact that every person is human. However, the value from which rights arise is only inherent in humans because it was bestowed by God. Wolterstorff derives this knowledge from the Old and New Testaments.[49] In this work, however, it is assumed that the central question of biblical ethics is not primarily that of the generally valid rights of all people but rather that of the just relationship between people (and creation).[50] So the question is not *what are your and my rights as the basis of ethics?* but *what does a just relationship between you and me look like in this particular situation?* But what is the point of reference to define a just relationship? Dalferth argues that a just relationship between an I and a you needs a third party from which the I and the you equally differ. Without that there is no equality between human beings.[51] Dalfert further writes: "In each case, the reference to the respective third party constitutes the parity that is important in the corresponding grouping and which cannot be negated, denied or lost without dropping out of this."[52]

47. See Thomas, "Reading the Bible"; Yong, *Spirit-Word-Community*.
48. See Hays, *Moral Vision*, 187–206, 469–71.
49. See chapters 3 and 5 in Wolterstorff, *Justice*.
50. This is similar to Theissen, *Erleben und Verhalten*, 403–19, esp. 408–9.
51. Dalfert, *Krise*, 227–88.
52. Dalfert, *Krise*, 323, my translation.

In other words, compared to this third party, we are all creatures and "not God," not creators. Nobody has created themselves. Therefore, it is vital for Dalferth that: "The third party must, therefore, be considered and treated in collective life in such a way that it cannot become the prey of a few."[53] No individual, no group and no tradition can claim God for itself alone. This aspect, in turn, is very close to the Pentecostal principle that the Spirit of God was poured out on all flesh.[54] Despite their differences, Wolterstorff and Dalfert have one essential element in common; both approaches are based on an "Anselmian" methodology. Neither begins with an attempt to prove the existence of God but rather both fundamentally presuppose this and, accordingly, establish the equality of all people in relation to a third party (God), compared to whom all others are equal.[55] In this sense, Wolterstorff agrees with Dalferth (and, therefore, also with my approach). Fundamental rights do not exist without God or the third party; in other words, the idea of fundamental rights can only develop in an environment in which a counterpart is recognized, i.e., God, in relation to whom all individuals are equally different.

Another significant voice is the Anglican theologian Oliver O'Donovan, whose approach in *Resurrection and Moral Order: An Outline for Evangelical Ethics* demonstrates interesting parallels to Pentecostal social ethics. Like the Pentecostal approach, O'Donovan holds that "Christian ethics must grow from the gospel of Jesus Christ."[56] This means that protestant ethics is not an independent theological topos but rather an aspect of soteriology, which deals with the new life in Christ.[57] Parallels to Pentecostal social ethics can also be seen in O'Donovan's understanding of a tripartite division of human redemption: the past moment (in God's redemptive action in Christ), the present moment (in

53. Dalfert, *Krise*, 235, my translation.

54. See Vondey, *Scandal of Pentecost*.

55. Dalfert writes: "People are not God's neighbors because they see themselves that way, but they can see themselves that way because they are that way. Their existence precedes every constitutive act of human beings. If you are only there because God makes himself your neighbor, then that is true even if you ignore it: only those who are there can build a world for themselves, and only those for whom God becomes their neighbor are there. That is why one cannot offend one's fellow human beings and fellow creatures without also offending the Creator, who is closer to them than anyone else or even to themselves. And that is still the case, even if you do not know or want to know anything about it" (Dalfert, *Die Krise*, 281, my translation). See also Wolterstorff, *Rights and Wrongs*, xi.

56. O'Donovan, *Resurection*, 11.

57. O'Donovan, *Resurection*, 12, 224.

which God's Spirit enables humans to participate in the new creation) and the future moment (in which redemption will be accomplished). Perhaps the most striking difference to Pentecostal social ethics lies in O'Donovan's interpretation of eschatology. For O'Donovan, the eschaton, the future Kingdom of God, is primarily the test (judgment) and criterion to assess which moral behavior will endure and have a future. In other words: What moral action will endure in the eschatological judgment? Pentecostal social ethics also takes this aspect up, but its eschatology goes beyond the question of what actions will endure and have a future, but rather it asks how the eschaton determines our actions now today. For example, the element of eschatological *hope* is a driving force that should not be underestimated to stand up for justice against all current circumstances.[58] Furthermore, comparable to Moltmann's approach,[59] Pentecostal social ethics is always an ethics of hope, which makes claim to the eschatological promise, "Behold, I am making all things new" (Rev 21:5). This opens up Pentecostal social ethics to change, as it is prepared to leave behind that which exists and is known. It allows itself to be called by the accomplished Kingdom of God and to take new paths where what is known does not correspond to what is to come. In this sense, O'Donovan connects the Pentecostal approach with the fact that both, in their own way, make the eschatological future fruitful for the present, and that Pentecostal social ethics is also guided by the "vision" of the eschaton and not just by the idea of judgment.

One aspect of Roman Catholic social ethics has already been addressed in the discussion of Gustavo Gutiérrez's liberation theology. In addition to liberation theology, socio-ethical questions are dealt with in the Catholic tradition within the framework of *moral theology* and *social doctrine*, while I focus on social doctrine here.[60] The Roman Catholic

58. Solivan writes: "Hopeful struggle (to the faithless, an oxymoron) is the charisma of the Spirit of God that binds to God the sufferers who trust and hope. This is why the poor must sing: we believe in the promise that God does care and that love will overcome. Hopeful struggle is a sign of orthopathos: to disallow despair in suffering because God's pathos holds the future" (Solivan, *Spirit, Pathos and Liberation*, 74). Moltmann takes up hope against the backdrop of the mission by asking himself *what can we expect, what can we hope for?* and answers the question as follows: "The hope of the Christian faith is founded and opened wide by the promise of the gospel. Mission, therefore, happens out of calling and out of the promise of the risen Jesus and in the power of obedience and in the patient impatience of hope" (Moltmann, "Ziel der Mission," 1, my translation). Both Moltmann and Solivan show examples of how important eschatological hope can be for the actions of the church.

59. See Moltmann and Moltmann-Wendel, "Menschlich werden," 47.

60. The social doctrine of the Roman Catholic church "encompasses the church's

social doctrine has largely been presented in encyclicals, although in recent decades social documents belonging to individual churches have acquired significance for the entire church.[61] Despite a certain pluralization that has taken place in recent decades, according to Anzenbacher, there is a consensual core within Catholic social doctrine:[62] It is based on three principles. The *personality principle* is the strongest principle of Roman Catholic social doctrine and is considered indispensable.[63] The basis of the personality principle is the incarnation of Christ, which is valid for all people, regardless of their "race, origin, gender or whatever characteristics," and gives them an inviolable dignity and expresses the fact that every person has an unconditional right to life.[64] A parallel to Rawls's understanding of inalienable human rights can be seen here. The second principle of Catholic social doctrine is the *principle of solidarity*, which, building on the principle of personality, assumes that seeking and granting fellowship are fundamental to the dignity of every human being. The continuation of the solidarity principle, is the *subsidiarity principle*.[65] The principle of subsidiarity is a principle of responsibility: Everyone has personal responsibility. If one's own strengths are not sufficient, "the more complex or 'higher-ranking' parts of a society is obliged to help itself."[66] In classifying Pentecostal social ethics in comparison to Roman Catholic social doctrine, three striking differences can be seen: Roman Catholic social doctrine is a casuistic form of social ethics[67] which, similarly to that of Emil Brunner, deals with specific social fields of action, whereas the Pentecostal social ethics outlined in the current work show fundamentals that can provide guidance to the further Pentecostal social ethical discourse. The second, fundamental difference that stands out is that the Roman Catholic social doctrine recorded in the encyclicals, which claims to organize society with just principles, is defined

---

teaching on the entire area of coexistence in human society, how this should be set up and ordered and how people should behave in smaller and larger groups or as individuals in this society and its institutions" (Lienemann, *Grundinformation Theologische Ethik*, 279, my translation).

61. These include, for example, the documents of Latin American liberation theology already mentioned. See Anzenbacher, "Katholische Soziallehre," 885–88.

62. Anzenbacher, "Katholische Soziallehre," 887.

63. Lienemann, *Grundinformation Theologische Ethik*, 281.

64. Lienemann, *Grundinformation Theologische Ethik*, 281, my translation.

65. Honecker, *Einführung Theologische Ethik*, 341.

66. Lienemann, *Grundinformation Theologische Ethik*, 282, my translation.

67. See, for example, McKenna, *Concise Guide to Catholic Social Teaching*.

exclusively by the clergy, who are academically educated and exclusively male. Pentecostal social ethics, on the other hand, strives to ensure that the voices of all players are heard and influence the design process. The third and final key difference is that the Roman Catholic tradition designates *caritas (charity)* as the heart of its social teaching.[68] Pentecostal social ethics, on the other hand, combine caritas (charity) and justitia (justice); they belong inseparably together (which is comparable to the approach of Jonathan Sacks).[69]

A further significant voice is the systematic theologian and student of Moltmann, *Michael Welker*. His monograph *God's Spirit: Theology of the Holy Spirit* (1992) is not a social ethics, but consistently shows that pneumatology and social justice are inextricably linked (my translation). A deeper dialogue between Welker's pneumatology and Pentecostal social ethics would need to be conducted elsewhere, but I would like to take up one of his statements here: Welker criticizes the lack of interest in social issues in Pentecostal-charismatic spirituality.[70] However, since the publication of Welker's pneumatology, the interest of Pentecostal theologies in the topic of social ethics has grown significantly. The topic has been addressed in numerous publications, some of which were covered in chapters 2–5. However, the current work also shows that Welker's criticism of the beginnings of the Pentecostal church is not entirely correct. It is true that Pentecostal theologians have long neglected social engagement and social ethics in academic reflection. As shown in chapter 2, this does not mean that social questions and social practice were nonexistent within the Pentecostal tradition. The concern for social justice was practiced from the beginning. In order to trace social ethics in the Pentecostal tradition, one must always examine its practice in order to derive its theology. Examples of this have been shown.

It is clear that Pentecostal social ethics has a number of points of contact with a wide variety of theological socio-ethical approaches. However, a Pentecostal approach, with its roots in the biblical narrative of Acts 2 and its hopeful faithfulness to the eschaton, is a distinct voice that

---

68. Benedict XVI writes: "Charity is at the heart of the Church's social doctrine. Every responsibility and every commitment spelled out by that doctrine is derived from charity" (Benedict XVI in Schlag, *Handbook of Catholic Social Teaching*, 4).

69. Gustavo Gutiérrez's intra-Catholic criticism, which he put forward in his *Teología de la Liberación*, also points in the same direction.

70. Welker, *Gottes Geist*, 25–27.

makes a complementary contribution to the chorus of many languages in the field of social ethics.

Further Questions

The following topics are considered to be important for further discourse on Pentecostal social ethics:

- What importance or consequences does historically/theologically based[71] Pentecostal identity (the identity-establishing narrative) have for Pentecostal social ethics?[72]
- Who is counted as a dialogue partner, whose voice should be heard and taken seriously? Is this "all flesh," or are unconscious qualifying decisions made about who "belongs" and who does not?[73]
- How can identity and thus also ethical values be experienced and conveyed within the framework of the worship service without the service becoming an ethical/educational event?[74] The following question also arises: How can the grammar of ethics be learned outside of a sermon in a worship service?[75] What does the ethics of witnessing look like?[76]
- What is injustice? From this follows the question: What does a Pentecostal theology of suffering[77] look like and what is its contribution to pneumatologically based social ethics?

71. In the Hebrew Bible, history is a remembrance and prophecy of God's work. See also Brueggemann, *Creative Word*, 9. In this respect, the question of Pentecostal identity is linked to the interpretation of the beginnings and current experiences.

72. In this context, Paul Ricœur should be mentioned with his *social identity* approach, which could be useful for further development. See Ricœur, "Narrative Identity," esp. 77.

73. Stephenson, *Dismantling the Dualisms*, 89–114; Solivan, *Spirit, Pathos and Liberation*, 113–40; Cone, *Cross*, 30–64, clearly illustrated the form that these qualifying decisions could have.

74. In this context, James Cone provided a fundamental analysis of the Afro-American service in a 1977 article which shows how ethical values can be experienced in the liturgy. See Cone, "Sanctification and Liberation."

75. See Hofheinz and Eberhardt, *Tradierung von Ethik im Gottesdienst*. In particular, the essay by Bernd Wannenwetsch, "Der Politische Gottesdienst der Kirche," 169–210, which provides helpful reflection here.

76. See also Plüss, *Therapeutic and Prophetic Narratives in Worship*.

77. Several authors have already made contributions to the Pentecostal theology of suffering. In this context, see Johns and Stephenson, *Grieving, Brooding and*

- Are the aspects of Pentecostal social ethics examined here (encounter, unity in particularity, collaborative pneumatology, collaborative eschatology and hope) also found with other Pentecostal theologians? Are the same, or other, aspects addressed?
- What are the implications of Romans 8 as the focal point of Pauline pneumatology for pneumatologically based social ethics?[78]
- Social ethics always overlaps with other ethical topics. What impact does Pentecostal social ethics have on political ethics,[79] medical ethics, work and business ethics and environmental ethics?[80]
- Various contemporary social and political developments, such as increasing nationalism, fragmentation of society and war have parallels to the period when the Azusa Street revival was taking place. With its integrative spirituality, the Pentecostal revival obviously hit the nerve of its time. Which aspects of the early Pentecostal Movement are significant in the current social context for the Pentecostal churches of today, and need to be rediscovered, and possibly also reinterpreted, in order to become a healing and reconciling force in a fragmenting society?

Transforming; Mittelstadt, *Reading Luke-Acts in the Pentecostal Tradition*, 126–31; Engelbert, *Who is Present in Absence?* It is important to examine to what extent these approaches are useful for social ethics and in which areas further fundamental work is required. Interesting extra-Pentecostal contributions are provided by, e.g., Dabney, *Kenosis des Geistes*; Sölle, *Leiden*.

78. See Wenk's thoughts on Romans 8 in "Romans 8:18–30 as the Basis of Social Ethics" above 102–5.

79. Yong, *Days of Caesar*, is somewhat abstract in its approach. Specifically, questions such as: How does the church deal with structural injustice? How does the church maintain its prophetic voice, whether positioned on the fringes or at the centre of society?

80. The following two books are relevant here: Wallace, *Fragments of the Holy Spirit*; Swoboda, *Tongues and Trees*. Specifically, the question arises as to what consequences Pentecostal social ethics have for ecological ethics and vice versa.

Bibliography

Alexander, Estrelda. *Limited Liberty: The Legacy of Four Pentecostal Woman Pioneers.* Cleveland, OH: Pilgrim, 2008.
———. *The Women of Azusa Street.* Cleveland, OH: Pilgrim, 2005.
Alexander, Estrelda, and Amos Yong, eds. *Philipp's Daughters: Women in Pentecostal-Charismatic Leadership.* Eugene, OR: Pickwick, 2009.
Alexander, Kimberly Ervin. "Wolfgang Vondey's Pentecostal Theology: Living the Full Gospel: A Conversation on a Pentecostal Migrant Family Road Trip." *Journal of Pentecostal Theology* 28.1 (2019) 4.
Alexander, Kimberly Ervin, and R. Hollis Gause. *Women in Leadership: A Pentecostal Perspective.* Cleveland, OH: Center for Pentecostal Leadership and Care, 2006.
Althouse, Peter. *Spirit of the Last Days: Pentecostal Eschatology in Conversation with Jürgen Moltmann.* JPTSS 25. Sheffield: Continuum International, 2003.
Anderson, Allan H., and Walter J. Hollenweger, eds. *Pentecostals After a Century: Global Perspectives on a Movement in Transition.* JPTSS 15. Sheffield: Sheffield Academic, 1999.
Anzenbacher, Arno. "Katholische Soziallehre." In *RGG4*, 2:885–88.
Archer, Ken. *The Gospel Revisited: Toward a Pentecostal Theology of Worship and Witness.* Eugene, OR: Pickwick, 2011.
Augustine, Daniela C. *Pentecost, Hospitality, and Transfiguration: Toward a Spirit-Inspired Vision of Social Transformation.* Cleveland, TN: CPT, 2012.
———. *The Spirit and the Common Good: Shared Flourishing in the Image of God.* Grand Rapids: Eerdmans, 2019.
Balthasar, Hans Urs von. *Prologomena.* Vol. 1 of *Theo-Drama: Theological Dramatic Theory.* San Francisco: Ignatius, 1988.
Barfoot, Charles H., and Gerald T. Sheppard. "Prophetic vs. Priestly Religion: The Changing Role of Women Clergy in Classical Pentecostal Churches." *Review of Religious Research* 22 (1980) 2–17.
Barth, Karl. *Das Christliche Leben: Abt. II. Fragmente aus dem Nachlass, Vorlesungen 1959–1961.* Vol. 4/4 of *Die Kirchliche Dogmatik.* Edited by Hans-Anton Drewes and Eberhard Jüngel. 3rd ed. Zürich: EVZ, 1999.
———. *Jesus Christus der Knecht als Herr.* Vol. 4/2 of *Die Kirchliche Dogmatik.* 2nd ed. Zürich: EVZ, 1961.

---. *Die Lehre von der Versöhnung*. Vol. 4/3 of *Die Kirchliche Dogmatik*. Zollikon-Zurich: Evangelischer AG, 1959.

Bartlemann, Frank. *Azusa Street*. New Kensington, PA: Whitaker, 1982.

Beaman, Jay. *Pentecostal Pacifism: The Origin, Development, and Rejection of Pacific Belief Among the Pentecostals*. Eugene, OR: Wipf & Stock, 1989.

Beintker, Michael. *Barth Handbuch*. Tübingen: Mohr Siebeck, 2016.

Bell, Daniel M., Jr. *Liberation Theology After the End of History: The Refusal to Cease Suffering*. London: Routledge, 2001.

bell hooks. *Talking Back: Thinking Feminist, Thinking Black*. Boston: South End, 1989.

Berra, Michael. *Towards a Theology of Relationship: Emil Brunner's Truth as Encounter in Light of Relationship Science*. Eugene, OR: Pickwick, 2022.

Bettencourt, B. A. "Status, Differences and Ingroup Bias: A Meta-Analytical Examination of the Effects of Status, Stability, Status Legitimacy, and Group Permeability." *Psychological Bulletin* 127.4 (2001) 520–42.

Betz, Hans Dieter, et al., eds. *Religion in Geschichte und Gegenwart: Handwörterbuch für Theologie und Religionswissenschaft*. 4th ed. 9 vols. Tübingen: Mohr Siebeck UTB, 2008.

Blumhofer, Edith L. *The Assemblies of God: A Chapter in the Story of American Pentecostalism*. Vol. 1: *To 1941*. Springfield: Gospel Publishing House, 1989.

---. *Restoring The Faith. The Assemblies of God, Pentecostalism, and American Culture*. Urbana, IL: University of Illinois Press, 1993.

Bockmühl, Klaus. *Was Heiss heute Mission? Entscheidungsfragen der neueren Missionstheologie*. Basel: Brunnen, 2000.

Bolli, Heinz. *Schleiermacher-Auswahl: Mit einem Nachwort von Karl Barth*. München: Siebenstern Taschenbuch, 1968.

Bonnhoeffer, Dietrich. *Ethik*. Dietrich Bonnhoeffer Werke 6. Gütersloh: Gütersloher, 2006

Bosh, David J. *Transforming Mission: Paradigm Shifts in Theology of Mission*. Maryknoll, NY: Orbis, 1991.

Booth-Clibborn, Samuel. "Should a Christian Fight?" In *Early Pentecostals on Nonviolence and Social Justice: A Reader*, edited by Brian Pipkin and Jay Beaman, 6–16. Eugene, OR: Pickwick, 2016.

Boyarin, Daniel. *A Radical Jew: Paul and the Politics of Identity*. Berkley: University of California Press, 1994.

Brewer, M. B. "The Psychology of Prejudice: Ingroup Love and Outgroup Hate?" *Journal of Social Issues* 55 (1999) 429–44.

Brueggemann, Walter. *The Creative Word: Canon as a Model for Biblical Education*. Philadelphia: Fortress, 1988.

---. *Deep Memory, Exuberant Hope: Contested Truth in a Post-Christian World*. Minneapolis: Fortress, 2000.

Brunner, Emil. *Das Gebot und die Ordnungen. Entwurf einer protestantisch-theologischen Ethik*. Tübingen: Mohr Siebeck, 1932.

---. *Wahrheit als Begegnung*. 2nd ed. Zurich: Zwingli, 1963.

Buber, Martin. *Das dialogische Prinzip*. 13th ed. Gütersloh: Chr. Kaiser/Gütersloher, 2014.

Buess, Eduard, and Markus Mattmüller. *Prophetischer Sozialismus: Blumhardt—Ragaz—Barth*. Freiburg: Exodus, 1986.

Burgess, Stanley M., and Eduard M. van der Maas, eds. *The New International Dictionary of Pentecostal and Charismatic Movements*. Rev. and ext. ed. Grand Rapids: Zondervan, 2003.

Butler, Anthea. *White Evangelical Racism: The Politics of Morality in America*. Chapel Hill: University of North Carolina Press, 2021.

———. *Women in the Church of God in Christ: Making a Sanctified World*. Chapel Hill: University of North Carolina Press, 2007.

Cartledge, Marc J. "Pentecostal Theology: Living the Full Gospel." *Journal of the European Pentecostal Theological Association* 38.2 (2018) 185–86.

Chun, Min S. *Ethics and Biblical Narrative: A Literary and Discourse-Analytical Approach to the Story of Josiah*. Oxford Theology and Religion Monographs. Oxford: Oxford University Press, 2014.

Claiborne, Shane. *The Irresistible Revolution: Living as an Ordinary Radical*. Grand Rapids: Zondervan, 2006.

Claiborne, Shane, and Chris Haw. *Jesus for President: Politics for Ordinary Radicals*. Grand Rapids: Zondervan, 2008.

Cone, James H. *The Cross and the Lynching Tree*. Maryknoll, NY: Orbis, 2013.

———. "Sanctification and Liberation in the Black Religious Tradition." In *Sanctification and Liberation: Liberation Theologies in the Light of the Wesleyan Tradition*, edited by Theodore Runyan, 174–92. Nashville: Abingdon, 1977.

———. *The Spirituals and the Blues: An Interpretation*. New York: Seabury, 1972.

Congregation for the Doctrine of the Faith (CDF). "Instructio De Quibusdam Rationibus 'Theologiae Liberationis.'" *Acta Apostolica Sedis* 76 (1984) 876–909.

Cox, Harvey. "Cox on His Critics." In *The Secular City Debate*, edited by D. Callahan, 86–87. New York: Macmillan, 1966.

Dabney, D. Lyle. *Die Kenosis des Geistes: Kontinuität zwischen Schöpfung und Erlösung im Werk des Heiligen Geistes*. Neukirchen-Vluyn: Neukirchener, 1997.

Dalferth, Ingolf. "'Everybody Bids You Welcome': A Multicultural Approach to North American Pentecostalism." In *The Globalization of Pentecostalism: A Religion Made to Travel*, edited by Murray Dempster et al., 222–52. Oxford: Regnum, 1999.

———. *Die Krise der öffentlichen Vernunft. Über Demokratie, Urteilskraft und Gott*. Leipzig: Evangelische Verlagsanstalt, 2022.

Daniels, David D. "They Had a Dream." *Christian History* 58 (1998) 19–21.

———. "Transcending the Exclusionary Ecclesial Practices of Racial Hierarchies of Authority: An Early Pentecostal Trajectory. Ecclesiology and Exclusion." In *Boundaries of Being and Belonging in Postmodern Times*, edited by Dennis Doyle et al., 19–21. Maryknoll, NY: Orbis, 2012.

Dempster, Murray W., et al., eds. *Called & Empowered: Global Mission in Pentecostal Perspective*. Peabody, MA: Baker Academic, 1991.

Dempster, Murray W., et al., eds. *The Globalization of Pentecostalism: A Religion Made To Travel*. Oxford: Regum, 1999.

Dilschneider, Otto A. "Die Geistvergessenheit der Theologie." *Theologische Literaturzeitung* 86.4 (1961) 255–66.

Donald Dayton. *Theological Roots of Pentecostalism*. Grand Rapids: Baker Academic, 1987.

Drewermann, Eugen. *Wendepunkte: oder Was eigentlich besagt das Christentum?* Ostfildern: Patmos, 2014.

Ebner, Julia. *Wut. Was Islamisten und Rechtsextreme mit uns machen*. Darmstadt: Wbg. Theiss, 2018.

Ellul, Jacques. *The Ethics of Freedom*. Grand Rapids: Eerdmans, 1976.
Engelbert, Pamela F. *Who is Present in Absence? A Pentecostal Theological Praxis of Suffering and Healing*. Eugene, OR: Wipf & Stock, 2019.
Flückiger, Felix. "Ragaz Leonhard (1868–1945)." In *Evangelisches Lexikon für Theologie und Gemeinde*, edited by Helmut Burkhardt et al., 3:1645. Wuppertal: R. Brockhaus, 1994.
Frankel, Viktor. *Der Mensch vor der Frage nach dem Sinn*. 19th ed. Munich: Piper GmbH, 1985.
Frei, Daniel. *Die Pädagogik der Bekehrung. Sozialisation in chilenischen Pfingstkirchen*. Kirchen in der Weltgemwinschaft 8. Wien: Lit, 2011.
Gilkes, Cheryl Townsend. *"If It Wasn't for the Women . . .": Black Women's Experience and Womanist Culture in Church and Community*. Maryknoll, NY: Orbis: 2001
Gill, Deborah M., and Barbara Cavaness. *God's Woman Then and Now*. Springfield: Frace & Truth, 2004.
Grabe, Martin. "Dämonen Austreiben wie Jesus? Was moderne Psychotherapie mit spiritueller Wirklichkeitswahrnehmung verbindet." *Psychotherapie und Seelsorge* 3 (2016) 14–19.
Grant, Jacqueline. "The Sin of Servanthood." In *A Troubling in My Soul: Womanist Perspectives on Evil and Suffering*, edited by Emilie M. Townes, 199–218. Maryknoll, NY: Orbis, 1993.
Grez, Stanley J., and Roger E. Olson. *Twentieth-Century Theology: God and the World in a Transitional Age*. Downers Grove, IL: Intervarsity, 1992.
Grossmann, Siegfried. "Weltverantwortung, christliche." In *Evangelisches Lexikon für Theologie und Gemeinde*, edited by Helmut Burkhardt et al., 3:2147–249. Wuppertal: R. Brockhaus, 1994.
Gunkel, Hermann. *The Influence of the Holy Spirit: The Popular View of the Apostolic Age and the Teachings of the Apostle Paul*. Göttingen: Vandenhoeck & Ruprecht, 1888.
Gutiérrez, Gustavo. *Aus der eigenen Quelle trinken. Spiritualität der Befreiung*. Translated by Horst Goldstein. Munich: Chr. Kaiser, 1986.
———. "The Task and Content of Liberation Theology." In *The Cambridge Companion to Liberation Theology*, edited by Christopher Rowland, 19–38. Cambridge: Cambridge University Press, 2007.
———. *A Theology of Liberation*. Rev. ed. Maryknoll, NY: Orbis, 1973.
Hardmeier, Roland. "Das ganze Evangelium für eine heilsbedürftige Welt. Zur Missionstheologie der radikalen Evangelikalen." PhD diss., University of South Africa, 2015.
Hauerwas, Stanley, and William H. Willimon. *Resident Aliens: Life in the Christian Colony*. Nashville: Abingdon, 1989.
———. *Where Resident Aliens Live: Exercises for Christian Practice*. Nashville: Abingdon, 1996.
Haustein, Jörg, and Giovanni Maltese, eds. *Handbuch pfingstliche und charismatische Theologie*. Göttingen: Vandenhoeck & Ruprecht, 2014.
Hays, Richard B. *The Moral Vision of the New Testament: Community, Cross, New Creation: A Contemporary Introduction to New Testament Ethics*. San Francisco: Harper Collins, 1996.
Heimowski, Uwe. *Die Heilsarmee. Practical Religion—gelebter Glaube*. Schwarzenfeld: Neukirchner, 2006.

Hofheinz, Marco, and Kai-Ole Eberhardt, eds. *Die Tradierung von Ethik im Gottesdienst. Symposiumsbeitrage zu Ehren von Hans G. Ulrich*. Ethik im Theologischen Diskurs 26. Berlin: Lit, 2019.

Hollenweger, Walter J. *Charismatisch-pfingstliches Christentum. Herkunft, Situation, Ökumenische Chancen*. Göttingen: Vandenhoeck & Ruprecht, 1997.

———. "Creator Spiritus: The Challenge of Pentecostal Experience to Pentecostal Theology." *Theology* 81.679 (1978) 32–40.

———. *Enthusiastisches Christentum. Die Pfingstbewegung in Geschichte und Gegenwart*. Zurich: Zwingli, 1969.

———. *Erfahrungen der Leibhaftigket*. Interkulturelle Theologie 1. München: Kaiser, 1979

———. *Geist und Materie*. Interkulturelle Theologie 3. München: Kaiser, 1988.

———. *Pentecostalism: Origins and Developments Worldwide*. Peabody, MA: Hendrickson, 2005.

———. "Social Justice and the Pentecostal/Charismatic Movement." In *NIDPCM* 1076–79.

Honecker, Martin. *Einführung in die Theologische Ethik*. Berlin: de Gruyter, 1990.

Interdisziplinäre Arbeitskreis Pfingstbewegung (IAP). "Über uns." IAP, January 9, 2014. https://www.glopent.net/iak-pfingstbewegung/ueber-uns.

Johns, Cheryl Bridges. *Pentecostal Formation: A Pedagogy Among the Oppressed*. JPTSS 2. Eugene, OR: Wipf & Stock, 2010.

———. "Pentecostal Spirituality and the Conscientization of Women." In *All Together in One Place: Theological Papers from the Brighton Conference on World Evangelisation*, edited by Harold D. Hunter and Peter D. Hocker, 153–65. Sheffield: Sheffield Academic, 1993.

Johns, Cheryl Bridges, and Lisa P. Stephenson, eds. *Grieving, Brooding and Transforming. The Spirit, The Bible, and Gender*. Leiden: Koninklijke Brill NV, 2021.

Joisten, Karen. *Narrative Ethik. Das Gute und das Böse erzählen*. Berlin: Akademie GmbH, 2007:

Junghardt, Adelheit, and Ekkehart Vetter. *Ruhrfeuer. Erweckung in Mülheim an der Ruhr 1995. 1905–2005: Christus Gemeinde Mülheim*. Cieszyn, Poland: Drukarnia Wydawnictwa ARKA, 2004.

Käsemann, Ernst. "Amt und Gemeinde im Neuen Testament." In *Exegetische Versuche und Besinnungen*, 109–34. Vol. 1. Göttingen: Vandenhoeck & Ruprecht, 1960.

Kay, William. Review of *God in Creation* by Jürgen Moltmann. *EPTA Bulletin* 6.3 (1987) 107–9.

Kleining, Gerhard. *Lehrbuch Entdeckende Sozialforschung*. Vol. 1. Weinheim: Psychologie Union, 1995.

———. "The Qualitative-Heuristic Approach to Theory." In *Areas of Qualitative Psychology—Special Focus on Design*, edited by Leo Gürtler et al., 27–34. Tübingen: Ingeborg Huber, 2005.

Kliewer, Gerd U. *Das neue Volk der Pfingstler. Religion, Unterentwicklung und sozialer Wandel in Lateinamerika*. Studien zur interkulturellen Geschichte des Christentums 3. Frankfurt am Main: Lang, 1975.

Krusche, Werner. *Wirken des Heiligen Geistes nach Calvin*. Göttingen: Vandenhoeck & Ruprecht, 1957.

Kydd, R. A. N. "Healing in the Christian Church." In *NIDPCM* 698–711.

Land, Steven Jack. *Pentecostal Spirituality: A Passion for the Kingdom*. Cleveland, OH: CPS, 1993.
Lawless, Elaine. *Handmaidens of the Lord: Pentecostal Women Preachers and Traditional Religion*. Philadelphia: University of Philadelphia Press, 1988.
"Leaders of Latin American Renewal Meet in Colombia." *New Covenant* 3.2 (1973) 26–27.
Lee, Hye Jin. "Alum Profile: Amos Yong, PhD 1999." Center for Global Christianity & Mission, Boston University, February 7, 2013. https://www.bu.edu/cgcm/2013/02/07/alum-profile-amos-yong-ph-d-1999.
Leo XIII. *Rerum Novarum*. Encyclical given May 15, 1891, St. Peter's, Rome. https://www.vatican.va/content/leo-xiii/en/encyclicals/documents/hf_l-xiii_enc_15051891_rerum-novarum.html.
Lienemann, Wolfgan. *Grundinformation Theologische Ethik*. Göttingen: Vandenhoeck & Ruperecht, 2008.
Lovett, L. "Black Holiness-Pentecostal Implications for Ethics and Social Transformation." PhD diss., Emory University, 1979.
Macchia, Frank D. "Analogies of the Kingdom of God in Missions and Social Concern in the Message of Christoph Blumhardt." Unpublished paper, n.d.
———. *Baptized in the Spirit: A Global Pentecostal Theology*. Grand Rapids: Zondervan, 2006.
———. "The Spirit and the Life: A Further Response to Jürgen Moltmann." *Journal of Pentecostal Theology* 5 (1994) 121–27.
———. *Spirituality and Social Liberation: The Message of the Blumhardts in the Light of Wuerttemberg Pietism*. Pietist and Wesleyan Studies 4. London: Scarecrow, 1993.
———. "Theology, Pentecostal." In *NIDPCM* 1120–40.
Mattmüller, Markus. *Leonhard Ragaz und der religiöse Sozialismus. Eine Biographie*. Vol. 1. Zollikon/Zürich: EVZ, 1957.
McKenna, Kevin E. *A Concise Guide to Catholic Social Teaching*. Notre Dame, IN: Ave Maria, 2002.
Menzies, Robert. *The Development of Early Christian Pneumatology with Special Reference to Luke-Acts*. Sheffield: JSOT, 1994.
———. *Empowered for Witness: The Spirit in Luke-Acts*. Sheffield: JSOT, 1994.
Metz, Johann Baptist. *Armut im Geiste. Passion und Passionen*. Münster: Aschendorf, 2007.
———. *Faith in History and Society: Toward a Practical Fundamental Theology*. New York: Crossroad, 2007.
Mieth, Dietmar, and Irene Mieth. "Vorbild oder Modell? Geschichten und Überlegungen zur Narrativen Ethik." In *Ethisch handeln lernen*, edited by Günter Stachel et al., 106–15. Zürich: Benzinger, 1978.
Milbank, John. *Radical Orthodoxy. A New Theology*. London: Routledge, 1999.
Mittelstadt, Martin. *Reading Luke-Acts in the Pentecostal Tradition*. Cleveland, TN: CPT, 2010.
Moltmann, Jürgen. *Auferstanden in das ewige Leben. Über das Sterben und Erwachen einer lebendigen Seele*. Gütersloh: Gütersloher, 2020.
———. "Bankok 1973—eine Mission an uns!" *EvTh* 33 (1973) 209–13.
———. "The Blessing of Hope: The Theology of Hope and the Full Gospel of Life." *JPT* 13.2 (2005) 147–61.
———. "Die Befreiung der Unterdrücker." *EvTh* 38 (1978) 527–38.

———. *A Broad Place: An Autobiography*. Translated by Margareth Kohl. London: SCM, 2007.

———. *Church in the Power of the Spirit: A Contribution to Messianic Ecclesiology*. Translated by Margareth Kohl. Minneapolis: Fortress, 1993.

———. *The Crucified God: The Cross of Christ as the Foundation and Criticism of Christian Theology*. Translated by R. A. Wilson and John Bowden. Minneapolis: Fortress, 1993.

———. "Dient die 'pluralistische Theologie' dem Dialog der Weltreligionen?" *EvTh* 49 (1989) 528–36.

———. "Die Entdeckung der Anderen. Zur Theorie des kommunikativen Erkennens." *EvTh* 50 (1990) 400–414.

———. *Ethics of Hope*. Translated by Margareth Kohl. Minneapolis: Fortress, 2012.

———. *Experiences in Theology: Ways and Forms of Christian Theology*. Translated by Margareth Kohl. Minneapolis: Fortress, 2000.

———. *God in Creation: A New Theology of Creation and the Spirit of God*. Translated by Margareth Kohl. Minneapolis: Fortress, 1993.

———. "Liberation in the Light of Hope." *Ecumenical Review* 26.3 (1974) 413–29.

———. "On the Abundance of the Holy Spirit: Friendly Remarks for Baptised in the Holy Spirit by Frank D. Macchia." *JPT* 16.2 (2008) 9–13.

———. "An Open Letter to José Míguez Bonino." *Christianity and Crisis* 36.5 (1976) 57–63.

———. "Probleme und Chancen der Mission." *EvTh* 34 (1974) 409.

———. "A Response to My Pentecostal Dialogue Partners." *JPT* 4 (1994) 59–70.

———. *Resurrected to Eternal Life: On Dying and Rising*. Minneapolis: Fortress, 2020.

———. *The Source of Life—The Holy Spirit and the Theology of Life*. Translated by Margareth Kohl. Minneapolis: Fortress, 1997.

———. *The Spirit of Life: A Universal Affirmation*. Translated by Margareth Kohl. Minneapolis: Fortress, 2001.

———. *Theology of Hope: On the Ground and the Implications of a Christian Eschatology*. New York: Harper and Row, 1975.

———. *The Trinity and the Kingdom: The Doctrine of God*. Minneapolis: Fortress, 1993.

———. *The Way of Jesus Christ: Christology in Messianic Dimensions*. Translated by Margareth Kohl. San Francisco: Harper, 1990.

———. "Das Ziel der Mission." *Evangelische Missionszeitschrift* 22 (1965) 1–14.

Moltmann, Jürgen, and Elisabeth Moltmann-Wendel. "Menschlich werden in einer Neuen Gemeinschaft." In *Die Gemeinschaft von Frauen und Männern in der Kirche*, edited by Constance F. Parvey, 37–53. Neukirchen-Vluyn: Neukirchner, 1981.

Müller, Ilse. "Gnädig ist Gott und Gerecht (Ps 116,5). Bibeltheologische Perspektiven auf die Gerechtigkeit Gottes." In *Salzburger Hochschulwochen. Gerechtigkeit heute. Anspruch und Wirklichkeit*, edited by Heinrich Schmidinger, 73–106. Innsburck: Tyrolia, 2000.

Müller-Fahrenholz, Geiko. *The Kingdom and the Power: The Theology of Jürgen Moltmann*. Minneapolis: Fortress, 2001.

O'Donovan, Oliver. *Resurrection and Moral Order: An Outline for Evangelical Ethics*. Grand Rapids: Eerdmans, 1996.

Palmer, M. D. "Ethics and the Classical Pentecostal Tradition." In *NIDPCM* 605–10.

Palmer, Phebe. *The Promise of the Father: A Neglected Specialty of the Last Days.* Eugene, OR: Wipf & Stock, 2015.
Pannenberg, Wolfhart. *Systematische Theologie.* Vol. 1. Göttingen: Vandenhoeck & Ruprecht, 1988.
Parvey, Constance F., ed. *Die Gemeinschaft von Frauen und Männern in der Kirche. Der Sheffield-Report.* Neukirchen-Vluyn: Neukirchner, 1981.
Petersen, Douglas. "The Kingdom of God and the Hermeneutical Circle: Pentecostal Praxis in the Third World." In *Called & Empowered: Global Mission in Pentecostal Perspective,* edited by Murray W. Dempster et al., 44–56. Peabody, MA: Baker, 1991.
Pipkin, Brian K., and Jay Beaman, eds. *Early Pentecostals on Nonviolence and Social Justice: A Reader.* Eugene, OR: Pickwick, 2016.
Plüss, Jean Daniel. *Therapeutic and Prophetic Narratives in Worship: A Hermeneutic Study of Testimonies and Visions. Their Potential Significance for Christian Worship.* Frankfurt am Main: Peter Lang, 1988.
———. *Vom Geist bewegt, Die Geschichte der schweizerischen Pfingstmission.* Kreuzlingen: Asaph, 2015.
Pöhlmann, Horst Georg. *Abriss der Dogmatik. Ein Kompendium. 6, überarbeitete und erweiterte Auflage. Geist—Gottesgeist, Zeitgeist oder Weltgeist?* Gütersloh: Kaiser, 2002.
———. *Heiliger Geist—Gottesgeist, Zeitgeist oder Weltgeist?* Neukirchen-Vluyn: Friedrich Bahn, 1998.
Pollock, David C., et al. *Third Culture Kids: Aufwachsen in mehreren Kulturen.* Marburg: Franke, 2003.
Poloma, Margret M. *The Assemblies of God at the Crossroads: Charisma and Institutional Dilemmas.* Knoxville: University of Tennessee Press, 1989.
Pomerville, Paul A. *The Third Force in Missions: A Pentecostal Contribution to Contemporary Mission Theology.* Peabody, MA: Hendrickson, 1985.
Powers, Janet Everts. "Pentecostalism 101: Your Daughters Shall Prophecy." In *Philipps Daughters: Women in Pentecostal-Charismatic Leadership,* edited by Estrelda Alexander et al., 133–51. Eugene, OR: Pickwick, 2009.
———. "Recovering a Woman's Head with Prophetic Authority: A Pentecostal Interpretation of 1 Corinthians 11.3–16." *Journal of Pentecostal Theology* 10 (2001) 11–37.
———. "'Your Daughters Shall Prophesy': Pentecostal Hermeneutics and the Empowerment of Women." In *The Globalisation of Pentecostalism: A Religion Made to Travel,* edited by Murray Dempster et al., 313–37. Irvine: Regnum International, 1999.
Quaas, Anna D. "Befreiungsdienst und interkulturelle Seelsorge." *Ökumenische Rundschau* 60.3 (2011) 315–28.
Ragaz, Leonhard. *Die Apostel.* Vol. 6 of *Die Bibel. Eine Deutung.* Zürich: Diana, 1947.
———. *Das Evangelium und der soziale Kampf der Gegenwart.* Basel: C. F. Lendorff, 1906.
———. *Das Glaubensbekenntnis. Zur Bekenntnisfrage. Mit einer Erklärung des Apostolischen Glaubensbekenntnisses.* 2nd ed. Religiös-soziale Vereinigung der Schweiz. Zürich: Reutlimann & Co, 1942.
———. *Der Kampf um das Reich Gottes in Blumhardt, Vater und Sohn—und weiter!* Zürich/Leipzig: Rotapfel, 1922.

———. *Von Christus zu Marx—von Marz zu Christus*. 1929. Reprint, Hamburg: Furche, 1972.

———. *Weltreich, Religion und Gottesherrschaft*. Vol 2. Zurich/Leipzig: Rotapfel, 1922.

———. "Zur Weltlage: die Einigung der Christenheit: zur Stockholmer Konferenz." *Neue Wege: Beiträge zu Religion und Sozialismus* 19 (1925) 340–53.

Rahner, Karl. *Betrachtungen zum ignatianischen Exerzitienbuch*. München: Kösel, 1965.

———. *Einübungen priesterlicher Existenz*. Freiburg: Herder, 1970.

Rawls, John. *A Theory of Justice*. Cambridge: Harvard University Press, 1971.

Reiter, Johannes. "Moraltheologie, katholische." In *RGG4* 5:1495–98.

Richie, Tony L. "Approaching the Problem of Religious Truth in a Pluralistic World: A Pentecostal-Charismatic Contribution." *Journal of Ecumenical Studies* 43.3 (2008) 351–69.

Ricœur, Paul. "Narrative Identity." *Philosophy Today* 35.1 (1991) 73–81.

Robeck, Cecil M., Jr. *The Azusa Street Mission and Revival: The Birth of the Global Pentecostal Movement*. Nashville: Thomas Nelson, 2006.

———. "Pentecostals and Social Ethics." *Pneuma* 9.1 (1987) 103–7.

Roberts, Bryan R. "Protestant Groups and Coping with Urban Life in Guatemala City." *American Journal of Sociology* 73 (1968) 753–67.

Roberts, J. Deotis. *Liberation and Reconciliation: A Black Theology*. Philadelphia: Westminster, 1971.

Robins, Roger G. "A Chronology of Peace: Attitudes Toward War and Peace in the Assemblies of God: 1914–1918." *Pneuma* 6.1 (1984) 3–36.

Roebuck David, "Limiting Liberty: The Church of God and Woman Ministers, 1886–1996." PhD diss., Vanderbilt University, 1997.

Rossel, Andreas, ed. *Erinnerungen an die Zukunft. 80 Jahre in Bewegung. Das Buch zum 80. Geburtstag der BewegungPlus*. Bern: Berchtold Haller. 2007.

Rowland, Christopher, ed. *The Cambridge Companion to Liberation Theology*. Cambridge: Cambridge Universtity Press, 2007.

Runyon, Theodore, ed. *Sanctification and Liberation: Liberation Theologies in Light of the Wesleyan Tradition*. Nashville: Abingdon, 1977.

Sacks, Jonathan. *To Heal a Fractured World: The Ethics of Responsibility*. New York: Schocken, 2005.

Sandel, Michael. "The Procedural Republic and the Unbound Self." In *Communitarianism*, edited by Axel Honneth, 18–35. Frankfurt: Suhrkamp, 1993.

Sanders, Cheryl. *Saints in Exile: The Holiness-Pentecostal Experience in African American Religion and Culture*. Oxford: Oxford University Press, 1996.

Schäfer, Rainer. "Die Objektivität Moralischer Werte." *Heilderberger Graduiertenjournal für Geisteswissenschaften* 2 (2011). http://nbn-resolving.de/urn:nbn:de:bsz:16-logoi-91193.

Schlag, Martin, ed. *Handbook of Catholic Social Teaching: A Guide for Christians in the World Today*. Washington, DC: Catholic University of America Press, 2017.

Schmid-Ammann, Paul. *Die Natur im religiösen Denken von Leonhard Ragaz*. Zürich: Neuen religiös-sozialen Vereinigung, 1973.

Schmidinger, Heinrich, ed. *Salzburger Hochschulwochen. Gerechtigkeit heute. Anspruch und Wirklichkeit*. Innsbruck: Tyrolia, 2000.

Schneider, Theodor. *Zeichen der Nähe Gottes. Grundriss der Sakramenten—Theologie*. Mainz: Grünewald, 1998.

Schweizer, Eduard. *Heiliger Geist*. Berlin: Kreuz, 1978.

Scott, Peter. *A Political Theology of Nature*. Cambridge: Cambridge University Press, 2003.
Segovia, Fernando F. "Looking Back, Looking Around, Looking Ahead: An Interview with Elisabeth Schüssler Fiorenza." In *Toward a New Heaven and a New Earth: Essays in Honor of Elisabeth Schüssler Fiorenza*, edited by Fernando F. Segovia, 1–30. Maryknoll: Orbis, 2003.
Segundo, Juan Luis. *Liberation of Theology*. Eugene, OR: Wipf & Stock. 2002.
Senn, Felix. *Der Geist, die Hoffnung und die Kirche*. Zürich: TVZ, 1985
Seymour, William. *The Azusa Street Papers: William Seymour and The Apostolic Faith Mission 1906–1908*. N.p.: CreateSpace Independent Platform, 2014.
Solivan, Samuel. "From Azusa to Memphis: Where Do We Go From Here? Roundtable Discussions on the Memphis Colloquy." *Pneuma* 18.1 (1996) 113–40.
———. *The Spirit, Pathos and Liberation: Toward a Hispanic Pentecostal Theology*. Sheffield: Sheffield Academic, 1998.
Sölle, Dorothee. *Leiden*. 1st ed. Stuttgart: Kreuz, 1973.
Stachel, Günter, and Dietmar Mieth. *Ethisch handeln lernen. Zu Konzeption und Inhalt ethischer Erziehung*. Schweiz: Benzinger, 1978.
Stadelmann, Helge. "Dispensationalism." In *Evangelisches Lexikon für Theologie und Gemeinde*, edited by Helmut Burkhardt et al., 1:449. Wuppertal: R. Brockhaus, 1994.
Stähli, Martin Johann. *Reich Gottes und Revolution. Christliche Theorie und Praxis für die Armen dieser Welt. Die Theologie des Religiösen Sozialismus bei Lenohard Ragaz und die Theologie der Revolution in Lateinamerika*. Theologische Forschung 57. Hamburg/Bergstadt: Herbert Reich Evang. GmbH, 1976.
Stanley, Susie C. "Wesleyan/Holiness and Pentecostal Women Preachers: Pentecost as the Pattern for Primitivism." In *Philipp's Daughters: Woman in Pentecostal-Charismatic Leadership*, edited by Estrelda Alexander and Amos Yong, 19–37. Pickwick, 2009.
Stephenson, Lisa P. *Dismantling the Dualism for American Pentecostal Women in Ministry: A Feminist-Pneumatological Approach*. Leiden: Koninklijke Brill NV, 2012.
Stewart, Robert B., ed. *The Resurrection of Jesus: John Dominic Crossan and N. T. Wright in Dialogue*. Minneapolis: Fortress, 2006.
Stronstad, Roger. *The Charismatic Theology of St. Luke*. Peabody, MA: Hendrickson, 1984.
Swoboda, A. J. *Tongues and Trees: Toward a Pentecostal Ecological Theology*. JPTSS 40. Dorset: Deo, 2013.
Taifel, Henri, ed. *Social Identity and Intergroup Relations*. Cambridge: Cambridge University Press, 1982.
Theissen, Gerd. *Erleben und Verhalten der ersten Christen. Eine Psychologie des Urchristentums*. Gütersloh: Gütersloh, 2007.
Thomas, J. C. "Pentecostal Theology in the Twenty-First Century." *Pneuma* 20.1 (1988) 3–19.
———. "Reading the Bible from within Our Traditions: A Pentecostal Hermeneutic as Test Case." In *Between Two Horizons*, edited by J. Green and M. Turner, 108–22. Grand Rapids: Eerdmans, 2000.
———. "Women in the Church: An Experiment in Pentecostal Hermeneutics." *Evangelical Review of Theology* 20 (1996) 220–32.

Tillich, Paul. "The Kingdom of God and History." In *The Kingdom of God and History*, by H. G. Wood et al., 105–41. New York: Willet Clark & Co., 1938.
———. *Political Expectation*. Edited by James Luther Adams. New York: Harper & Row, 1971.
———. *The Protestant Era*. Translated by James Luther Adams. Abridged ed. Chicago: University of Chicago Press, 1957.
———. *Systematic Theology*. 3 vols. Chicago: Chicago University Press, 1951–1963.
Turner, M. M. B. *Power from on High: The Spirit in Israel's Restoration and Witness in Luke-Acts*. Sheffield: Sheffield Academic, 1996.
Vilafane, Eldin. *The Liberating Spirt: Toward an Hispanic American Pentecostal Social Ethic*. Grand Rapids: Erdmans, 1993.
Volf, Miroslaf. *Exclusion and Embrace: A Theological Exploration of Identity, Otherness, and Reconciliation*. Nashville: Abingdon, 1996.
———. "Materiality of Salvation: An Investigation in the Soteriologies of Liberation and Pentecostal Theologies." *Journal of Ecumenical Studies* 26.3 (1989) 447–67.
———. *Von der Ausgrenzung zur Umarmung. Versöhnendes Handeln als Ausdruck christlicher Identität*. Marburg an der Lahn: Franke, 2012.
Vondey, Wolfgang, ed. *Pentecostalism: A Guide for the Perplexed*. London: Bloomsbury T&T Clark, 2013.
———. *Routledge Handbook of Pentecostal Spirituality*. London: Routledge, 2020.
———. *The Scandal of Pentecost: A Theology of the Public Church*. London: T&T Clark, 2023.
Wacker, Grant. *Heaven Below: Early Pentecostals and the American Culture*. Cambridge: Harvard University Press, 2001.
Wagner, Peter C. *Look Out! The Pentecostals Are Coming*. 1st ed. Carol Stream: Creation, 1973.
Währisch-Oblau, Claudia. "Spiritual Warfare—Geistlicher Kampf gegen böse Mächte." *Ökumenische Rundschau* 60.3 (2011) 302–14.
Wallace, Mark I. *Fragments of the Spirit. Nature, Violence, and the Renewal of Creation*. New York: Continuum, 1996.
Ware, Frederick L. "Spiritual Egalitarianism, Ecclesial Pragmatism, and the Status of Women in Ordained Ministry." In *Philipp's Daughters: Woman in Pentecostal-Charismatic Leadership*, edited by Estrelda Alexander and Amos Yong, 215–33. Pickwick, 2009.
Wariboko, Nimi. *The Pentecostal Principle: Ethical Methodology in New Spirit*. Grand Rapids: Eerdmans, 2012.
Warnach, Viktor. *Agape. Die Liebe als Grundmotiv der neutestamentlichen Theologie*. Düsseldorf: Patmos, 1951.
Warrington, Keith. *Pentecostal Theology: A Theology of Encounter*. London: T&T Clark, 2008.
———. "Social Transformation in the Mission of Jesus and Paul: A Priority or a Bonus?" In *Movement for Change: Evangelical Perspectives on Social Transformation*, edited by David Hilborn, 38–55. Carlisle: Authentic, 2004.
Weber, Max. *The Sociology of Religion*. Translated by E. Fischoff. Boston: Beacon, 1963.
Welker, Michael. *Gottes Geist. Theologie des Heiligen Geistes*. Neukirchen-Vluyn: Neukirchner GmbH. 1992.
———. "Gottes Geist und die Verheissung sozialer Gerechtigkeit in multikultureller Vielfalt." In *Gottes Geist und Gottes Volk*, edited by Rudolf Weth, 9–29. Gütersloh: Chr. Kaiser/Gütersloher, 1994.

Wells, Samuel. *Improvisation: The Drama of Christian Ethics.* Grand Rapids: Brazos, 2004.
Wenham, Gordon J. *Story as Torah: Reading Old Testament Narrative Ethically.* Edinburgh: T&T Clark, 2004.
Wenk, Matthias. *Community-Forming Power: The Socio-Ethical Role of the Spirit in Luke-Acts.* Sheffield: Sheffield Academic, 2000.
———. *Erneuerung durch Begegnung. Wort, Geist und Gemeinschaft. Gesammelte Aufsätze.* Munich: GRIN, 2017.
———. "Das Evangelium—mehr als 'harmloser Seelenfriede.' Das Reich Gottes als Gesellschaftsverändernde Kraft." *Der Auftrag* 80 (2001) 30–33.
———. "Der Heilige Geist als Solidarität Gottes mit den Bedrängten und Ausgestossenen." In *Das Evangelium den Armen. Die Pfingstbewegung im Spannungsfeld zwischen sozialer Verantwortung und klassischem Missionsverständnis,* edited by M. Redling, 95–121. Erzhausen: FThG, 2013.
———. "The Holy Spirit as Transforming Power within a Society: Pneumatological Spirituality and Its Political/Social Relevance for Western Europe." *JPT* 11.1 (2002) 130–42.
———. "The Kingdom of Peace in Luke-Acts and What Glossolalia Has to Do With." *JPT* 31 (2022) 16–39.
———. "Pfingstliche Pneumatologie zwischen individueller Geisterfahrung und neuer sozialer Realität." *Ökumenische Rundschau* 60.3 (2011) 286–301.
———. "Pneumatologie als Solidarität Gottes mit dem bedrängten Leben: Sozialethische Überlegungen ausgehend von Römer 8,18–30." In *Das Evangelium den Armen. Die Pfingstbewegung im Spannungsfeld zwischen sozialer Verantwortung und klassischem Missionsverständnis,* edited by M. Redling, 95–124. Erzhausen: FThG, 2013.
———. "Reconciliation and Renunciation of Status as God's Final Aim for Humanity: New Testament Thoughts on the Church's Mission and Unity." *JPT* 19 (2010) 44–58.
———. "Spiritual Gifts: Manifestations of the Kingdom of God." In *The Routledge Handbook of Pentecostal Theology,* edited by Wolfgang Vondey, 301–10. London: Routledge, 2020.
———. "What Is Prophetic About Prophecies?" *JPT* 26 (2017) 178–95.
Western Theological Seminary (WTS). "2017 Distinguished Alumnus The Rev. Dr. Samuel Solivan '76." WTS, July 22, 2017. https://www.westernsem.edu/rev-dr-sam-solivan.
Widmer, Johann. *Im Kampf gegen Satans Reich.* Vol. 2. 2nd ed. N.p., 1949.
Wilson, Everett A. "Passion and Power: A Profile of Emergent Latin American Pentecostalism." In *Called & Empowered: Global Mission in Pentecostal Perspective,* edited by Murray W. Demster et al., 67–97. Peabody, MA: Baker Academic, 1991.
Wolterstorff, Nicholas. *Justice: Rights and Wrongs.* Princeton, NJ: Princeton University Press, 2008.
World Council of Churches (WCC). *The Community of Women and Men in the Church: A Report of the World Council of Churches' Conference, Sheffield, England, 1981.* Geneva: WCC, 1983.
Wright, N. T. "How Can the Bible Be Authoritative?" *Vox Evangelicae* 21 (1991) 7–32.
———. *Von Hoffnung überrascht. Was die Bibel zu Auferstehung und ewigem Leben sagt.* Translated by Rainer Behrens. Neukirchen-Vluyn: Neukirchner, 2007.

Wrogemann, Henning. *Mission und Religion in der Systematischen Theologie der Gegenwart: Das Missionsverständnis deutschsprachiger protestantischer Dogmatiker im 20. Jahrhundert.* Göttingen: Vandenhoeck & Ruprecht, 1997.

Yong, Amos. *In the Days of Caesar: Pentecostalism and Political Theology.* Grand Rapids: Eerdmans, 2010.

———. "The Spirit at Work in the World: A Pentecostal-Charismatic Perspective on the Divine Action Project." *Theology and Science* 7.2 (2009) 123–40.

———. *The Spirit Poured Out on All Flesh: Pentecostalism and the Possibility of Global Theology.* Grand Rapids, Baker Academic, 2005.

———. *Spirit-Word-Community: Theological Hermeneutics in Trinitarian Perspective.* Eugene, OR: Wipf & Stock, 2006.

———. *Theology and Down Syndrome: Reimagining Disability in Late Modernity.* Waco, TX: Baylor University Press, 2007.

www.ingramcontent.com/pod-product-compliance
Lightning Source LLC
Chambersburg PA
CBHW061428300426
44114CB00014B/1585